Making Sense of Global Health Governance

Also by Kent Buse

HEALTH POLICY IN A GLOBALIZING WORLD (with Kelley Lee and Suzanne Fustukian)

MAKING HEALTH POLICY (with Gilt Walt and Nicholas Mays)

Also by Wolfgang Hein

GLOBAL HEALTH GOVERNANCE AND THE FIGHT AGAINST HIV/AIDS (with Sonja Bartsch and Lars Kohlmorgen)

GLOBALIZATION, GLOBAL HEALTH GOVERNANCE AND NATIONAL HEALTH POLITICS IN DEVELOPING COUNTRIES: an Exploration into the Dynamics of Interfaces (with Lars Kohlmorgen)

Also by Nick Drager

GLOBAL PUBLIC GOODS FOR HEALTH: Health Economics and Public Health Perspectives (with Richard D. Smith, Robert Beaglehole and David Woodward)

INTERNATIONAL TRADE IN HEALTH SERVICES AND THE GATS: Current Issues and Debates (with Chantal Blouin and Richard Smith)

NEGOTIATING HEALTH DEVELOPMENT: a Guide for Practitioners (with E. McClintock and M. Moffitt)

TRADE AND HEALTH: Seeking Common Ground (with Chantal Blouin and Jody Heymann)

Making Sense of Global Health Governance

A Policy Perspective

Edited By

Kent Buse
Wolfgang Hein
Nick Drager

palgrave
macmillan

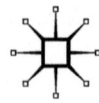

Introduction, selection and editorial matter © Kent Buse, Wolfgang Hein and Nick Drager 2009. Individual chapters © contributors 2009
Foreword © Susanne Weber-Mosdorf 2009

All rights reserved. No reproduction, copy or transmission of this publication may be made without written permission.

No portion of this publication may be reproduced, copied or transmitted save with written permission or in accordance with the provisions of the Copyright, Designs and Patents Act 1988, or under the terms of any licence permitting limited copying issued by the Copyright Licensing Agency, Saffron House, 6-10 Kirby Street, London EC1N 8TS.

Any person who does any unauthorized act in relation to this publication may be liable to criminal prosecution and civil claims for damages.

The authors have asserted their rights to be identified as the authors of this work in accordance with the Copyright, Designs and Patents Act 1988.

First published 2009 by
PALGRAVE MACMILLAN

Palgrave Macmillan in the UK is an imprint of Macmillan Publishers Limited, registered in England, company number 785998, of Houndmills, Basingstoke, Hampshire RG21 6XS.

Palgrave Macmillan in the US is a division of St Martin's Press LLC, 175 Fifth Avenue, New York, NY 10010.

Palgrave Macmillan is the global academic imprint of the above companies and has companies and representatives throughout the world.

Palgrave® and Macmillan® are registered trademarks in the United States, the United Kingdom, Europe and other countries

ISBN: 978–0–230–20992–3   hardback

This book is printed on paper suitable for recycling and made from fully managed and sustained forest sources. Logging, pulping and manufacturing processes are expected to conform to the environmental regulations of the country of origin.

A catalogue record for this book is available from the British Library.

A catalog record for this book is available from the Library of Congress.

10 9 8 7 6 5 4 3 2 1
18 17 16 15 14 13 12 11 10 09

Printed and bound in Great Britain by
CPI Antony Rowe, Chippenham and Eastbourne

To those plucky individuals, not least Sarah Jane Hawkes, striving to promote systems of governance that not only improve health outcomes, particularly among the poor, but are also paragons of legitimacy and mutual accountability – either by challenging powerful interests directly or by exploring innovative and collaborative approaches to seemingly intractable problems.

Contents

List of Figures	ix
List of Tables	x
List of Boxes	xi
Foreword by Susanne Weber-Mosdorf	xii
Acknowledgements	xiii
List of Acronyms and Abbreviations	xv
About the Contributors	xix

1. Global Health Governance: the Emerging Agenda   1
   *Kent Buse, Nick Drager, Wolfgang Hein,
   Benedikte Dal and Kelley Lee*

2. Historical Dimensions of Global Health Governance   28
   Virginia Berridge, Kelly Loughlin and Rachel Herring

3. Mapping the Global Health Architecture   47
   Gill Walt, Neil Spicer and Kent Buse

4. Conceptual Models for Global Health Governance   72
   Wolfgang Hein, Scott Burris and Clifford Shearing

5. Governance Norms in Global Health: Key Concepts   99
   Sonja Bartsch, Carmen Huckel Schneider and Lars Kohlmorgen

6. Global Health Governance and Global Public Goods   122
   Richard D. Smith

7. AIDS and Access to Medicines: Brazil, South
   Africa and Global Health Governance   137
   *Jan Peter Wogart, Gilberto Calcagnotto,
   Wolfgang Hein and Christian von Soest*

8. International Trade and Health: Loose Governance
   Arrangements across Sectors   164
   *Matthias Helble, Emily Mok, Benedikte Dal,
   Nusaraporn Kessomboon and Nick Drager*

9.	Commercial Health Governance *Kent Buse and Chris Naylor*	187
10.	Civil Society, its Organizations, and Global Health Governance *David McCoy and Margaret Hilson*	209
11.	The Role of Foundations in Global Governance for Health *John Wyn Owen, Graham Lister and Sally Stansfield*	232
12.	Global Health Partnerships: the Mosh Pit of Global Health Governance *Kent Buse and Andrew Harmer*	245
13.	Governance of Chronic Diseases *David Stuckler, Corinna Hawkes and Derek Yach*	268
14.	Fighting HIV/AIDS and the Future of Health Systems *Nina Veenstra and Alan Whiteside*	294
15.	Moving Global Health Governance Forward *Ilona Kickbusch*	320

Glossary 340
Index 346

List of Figures

4.1	The virtuous circuit of GHG	76
7.1	Timeline of decisions and conflicts around IPRs and access to medicines	142
7.2	North versus south interfacing in an emerging GHG	143
9.1	Commercial governance pathways	192
9.2	A framework for public health involvement	204
12.1	Constituency representation within 16 GHPs: 2005 and 2008 compared	258
13.1	Evolution of the global burden of disease, 2002–30	269
13.2	Input-output model of health governance	270
13.3a	Associations between country-income levels per capita and log heart disease and chronic non-communicable disease mortality rates	274
13.3b	Associations between globalization and log heart disease and chronic non-communicable disease mortality rates	275
14.1	Factors undermining the PHC approach	296
14.2	World Health Organization mortality estimates for selected countries in Africa	298
14.3	Life expectancy at birth in selected countries	298
14.4	Age profile of hospital inpatients in the medical wards of five hospitals in KwaZulu-Natal, South Africa	300
14.5	The 'AIDS transition'	301
14.6	Trends in domestic public health funding and external financing for HIV/AIDS, 2000–04	305
14.7	The widening gap between needs, commitments and disbursements for HIV/AIDS	306
14.8	Costs of HIV-related care and non-HIV-related care at clinics, a district hospital and a regional hospital in KwaZulu-Natal, South Africa	307
15.1	The action sphere of global health	325

List of Tables

1.1	The global health governance agenda: illustrative roles and responsibilities	11
2.1	Development of international organizations, 1815–1914	32
5.1	Dimensions of effectiveness	102
5.2	Dimensions of legitimacy	107
7.1	Brazil's and South Africa's fight against HIV/AIDS: similarities and differences	145
7.2	Fighting HIV/AIDS: major interfaces of Brazilian and South African NHG	154
9.1	Commercial sector actors with an interest in or impact on global health governance	189
9.2	Tactics used by industry to influence public global health governance	197
10.1	The multiple dimensions and heterogeneity of CSOs	217
12.1	Representation of key constituencies on 19 GHP boards	249
12.2	Constituency representation within 16 GHPs: 2005 and 2008 compared	258
13.1	Effect of expected changes in chronic disease mortality rates on economic growth, 2002–30	272
13.2	Five leading global health metaphors	276
13.3	Four types of policy failures: consonance, consistence, coherence and coordination	278
13.4	Pathways of private sector influences on chronic disease	283
14.1	Pros and cons of vertical and horizontal approaches to expanding care	303
14.2	The impact of HIV on health facilities in Africa	308

List of Boxes

3.1	The Global Outbreak Alert and Response Network (GOARN)	53
3.2	Treatment Action Campaign: a local network that mobilized global action	54
8.1	Diagnostic tool and companion workbook in trade and health	170
9.1	The commercial sector and the 'public' TRIPS Agreement	198
9.2	The tobacco industry and public governance	200
9.3	The ICC-UN Global Compact	202
10.1	The struggle for essential medicines, rational prescribing and affordable prices	219
10.2	The campaign to protect breastfeeding	222
10.3	The struggle to contain tobacco consumption	223
10.4	The People's Health Movement and WHO	227
12.1	Key moments in the history of GHPs	246
12.2	Seven contributions GHPs have made to global health governance	251
12.3	The functions of discourse within GHPs	252
12.4	The GFATM Country Coordinating Mechanism: a new system of rule?	255
12.5	The GFATM: a mixed response to alignment and harmonization	256
13.1	Role of economic globalization in chronic disease risks	272

Foreword

In today's increasingly interconnected and interdependent world, countries have recognized that domestic action alone can no longer assure public health security. In crafting health policies, governments are increasingly looking outwards to take into account risks and opportunities for population health that are spilling in across their borders and are, as a result, spilling over into the rest of the world. To protect the health of their populations, countries are taking steps to better manage and shape the global policy environment that affects health outcomes. The quest for better management of these risks and opportunities is leading analysts and policymakers to reassess the rules, norms, institutions and organizations that govern health policy and practice at the sub-national, national, regional and global levels.

There is an increasing recognition of the strengths, weaknesses and challenges which beset both the older and emerging systems of rules and institutional arrangements in so far as public health outcomes are concerned. It is also becoming increasingly evident that the emerging architecture, if one can call it that, is not presently adequate to respond to the emerging challenges of globalization and ensure that globalization benefits those currently left behind in the development process. There is also plenty of evidence of inadequate policy coherence, overlap and competition among global health governance initiatives, resulting in excessive transaction costs and inefficiencies. These outcomes arise as a result of the incentives and politics facing policymakers in the global system. The symptoms of this crisis of governance are illustrated by the extent to which the global community is 'off-track' to meet the health-related Millennium Development Goals and the growing burden of many infectious and non-communicable diseases. Improved understanding of what is working, what is not working and what can be changed to improve global health governance is, therefore, imperative.

This important book leads us in this direction. It takes stock of the existing understanding and practice of global health governance. The book's authors then present those with the interest and influence to shape the architecture for global health with policy-relevant and politically palatable recommendations with the overall purpose to strengthen health governance to meet our common goal – better health for all.

Susanne Weber-Mosdorf
Assistant Director-General
World Health Organization

Acknowledgements

This book is the result of a fruitful collaboration between two European groups working in the area of global health governance. One group, based in Hamburg at the German Institute of Global and Area Studies (GIGA) was conducting a project on 'Institutional Changes in Global Health Governance'. The second group of authors, mainly affiliated to the London School of Hygiene and Tropical Medicine, worked on papers commissioned by the World Health Organization between 2002 and 2006.

A workshop in Hamburg in February 2006 brought these two groups of authors together, along with a number of other scholars who had contributed to developing a deeper understanding of the character of global health governance as well as a group of practitioners in the field of global health. The workshop, entitled 'Defining and Shaping the Architecture of Global Health Governance', aimed to provide a platform for intellectual exchange, informed by practice in the field. In addition, the workshop provided an opportunity to further develop ideas and papers which would have an impact on the dynamics of global health governance itself. We are grateful to those workshop participants who shared their experience, knowledge and perspectives with us but whose work is not presented in this volume. This workshop would not have been possible without the generous financial support of the Volkswagen Foundation, the German Health Ministry and the GTZ, the main German organization for technical cooperation. We thank those institutions for their help.

The workshop was just the start of a two-year process during which chapters were developed, reviewed and revised. This work was supported by GIGA and its global health governance research team – Sonja Bartsch, Gilberto Calcagnotto, Lars Kohlmorgen, Christian von Soest and Jan Peter Wogart – as well as the Globalization, Trade and Health team of the World Health Organization, in particular Jens Gobrecht and Benedikte Dal – the latter of whom provided much required coordination among the editors. We would like to thank all of those involved in this project for engaging in the discussions on the nature and future of global health governance over the past two years. Amy Barns and Ron Labonte provided some very helpful advice in bringing additional literature to our attention.

A book like this is not only a collaborative effort of authors, but also that of many people who played a role in managing the financial, organizational and academic aspects of such a project. While the academic coordination of the editing work was with Kent Buse of the Overseas Development Institute in London, the infrastructural support was provided by GIGA. We thank the

President of the Institute, Robert Kappel, for securing that base for us. Furthermore we thank Monika Jamborek, Ingo Luplow, and Karin Putzer for carrying out the necessary administrative work, Wilma Willers and Ingrid Zieger who assisted us in many practical problems, and Enno Blanke and Tomasz Bielecki who made most of the practical work in organizing the workshop and giving us all the necessary logistic support before, during and after the conference. The views are those of the authors alone, not of the organizations for which they work.

We owe a major debt to our families for tolerating our absences while we engaged in this effort.

KENT BUSE, WOLFGANG HEIN AND NICK DRAGER

List of Acronyms and Abbreviations

AFAS	ASEAN Framework Agreement on Services
AIDS	Acquired Immune Deficiency Syndrome
AMC	Advance Market Commitment
ARISE	Associates for Research into the Science of Enjoyment
ART	Antiretroviral therapy
ARV	Antiretroviral
ASEAN	Association of South-East Asian Nations
BAT	British American Tobacco
CAFTA	Central America-Dominican Republic FTA
CCM	Country Coordinating Mechanism
CCS	Coordination Committee on Services (ASEAN)
CD	Chronic disease
CDC	Centers for Disease Control and Prevention
CEO	Chief executive officer
CHBC	Community home-based care
CHGA	Commission on HIV/AIDS and Governance in Africa
CIPIH	Commission on Intellectual Property Rights, Innovation & Public Health
CMH	Commission on Macroeconomics and Health
CODEX	FAO/WHO Codex Alimentarius Commission
COMESA	Common Market for Eastern and Southern Africa
COP	Conference of parties
CSDH	Commission on Social Determinants of Health
CS	Civil society
CSO	Civil society organization
CSR	Corporate social responsibility
DAC	Development Assistance Committee (OECD)
DALY	Disability-adjusted life years
DDR	Doha Development Round
DFID	Department for International Development (UK)
DPAS	WHO Global Strategy on Diet, Physical Activity and Health
DNDi	Drugs for Neglected Diseases initiative
EB	Executive board
EC	European Community
EFC	European Foundation Centre
EPGH	European Partnership for Global Health
EU	European Union
FAO	Food and Agriculture Organization of the UN

FCA	Framework Convention Alliance
FCTC	Framework Convention on Tobacco Control
FDI	Foreign direct investment
FTA	Free trade agreement
GAP	Global AIDS Program (of CDC)
GATS	General Agreement on Trade in Services
GATT	General Agreement on Tariffs and Trade
GAVI	Global Alliance for Vaccines and Immunization (now known as the GAVI Alliance)
GBC	Global Business Coalition on HIV/AIDS
GDP	Gross domestic product
GFATM	Global Fund to Fight AIDS, TB and Malaria (also Global Fund)
GHG	Global health governance
GHI	Global health initiative
GHP	Global health partnership
GIIC	Global Information Infrastructure Commission
GPA	Global Programme on AIDS (WHO)
GPG	Global public good
GPGH	Global public goods for health
GOARN	Global Outbreak & Response Network
GPPP	Global public-private partnerships
H8	Health 8
HAART	Highly active antiretroviral therapy
HAI	Health Action International
HIC	High-income country
HIV	Human immunodeficiency disease
HR	Human resources
IAVI	International AIDS Vaccine Initiative
IBFAN	International Baby Food Action Network
ICC	International Chamber of Commerce
ICRC	International Committee of the Red Cross
IFF	International Finance Facility
IFF(Im)	International Finance Facility for Immunization
IFM	International Monetary Fund
IFPMA	International Federation of Pharmaceutical Manufacturers and Associations
IGM	Inter-governmental meeting
IGO	Inter-governmental organization
IGWG	Inter-governmental working group
IHG	International health governance
IHP	International Health Partnership
IHR	International Health Regulations
ILO	International Labour Organization
ILSI	International Life Sciences Institute

IMF	International Monetary Fund
INFACT	Infant Formula Action Coalition
INGOs	International non-governmental organizations
IP	Intellectual property
IPC	Intellectual Property Committee
IPR	Intellectual property rights
ISO	International Organization for Standardization
LFA	Local fund agent (GFATM)
LMIC	Low- and middle-income country
LN	League of Nations
LNHO	League of Nations Health Organization
LRCS	League of Red Cross Societies
MAP	Multi-Country HIV/AIDS Programme (World Bank)
M&E	Monitoring and evaluation
MDGs	Millennium Development Goals
METAG	Monitoring and Evaluation Technical Advisory Group
MOPH	Ministry of Public Health
MRA	Mutual recognition arrangements
MSF	Médecins Sans Frontières
NAM	Non-Aligned Movement
NCD	Non-communicable disease
NGO	Non-governmental organization
NHG	National health governance
ODA	Official development assistance
OECD	Organization for Economic Cooperation and Development
OHIP	Office International d'Hygiène Publique
OR	Official relations
PASB	Pan American Sanitary Bureau
PEPFAR	President's Emergency Plan for AIDS Relief (USA)
PHC	Primary health-care
PHM	People's Health Movement
PR	Principal recipient (GFATM)
PROPER	Programme for Pollution Control, Evaluation and Rating (Indonesia)
PRSP	Poverty Reduction Strategy Paper
R&D	Research and development
RBM	Roll Back Malaria
RF	Rockefeller Foundation
SARS	Severe acute respiratory syndrome
SOP	Standard operating procedure
SPHC	Selective primary health care
SPS	Agreement on the Application of Sanitary & Phyto-sanitary Measures
SPT	Sustained Patent Treaty

Stop TB	Global Partnership to Stop Tuberculosis
SWAp	Sector-wide approach
TAC	Treatment Action Network
TB	Tuberculosis
TBT	Agreement on Technical Barriers to Trade
TNC	Transnational corporation
TNPC	Transnational pharmaceutical companies
TPRM	Trade Policy Review Mechanism
TRIPS	Agreement on Trade-Related Aspects of Intellectual Property Rights
UIA	Union of International Associations
UK	United Kingdom
UN	United Nations
UNAIDS	United Nations Programme on HIV/AIDS
UNDP	United Nations Development Programme
UNESCO	United Nations Educational, Scientific, Cultural Organization
UN-HABITAT	United Nations Human Settlements Programme
UNICEF	United Nations Children's Fund
UNFPA	United Nations Population Fund
US	United States of America
USAID	United States Agency for International Development
WDR	World Development Report
WFPHA	World Federation of Public Health Associations
WHA	World Health Assembly
WHO	World Health Organization
WIPO	World Intellectual Property Organization
WTO	World Trade Organization

About the Contributors

Sonja Bartsch is a research associate at the GIGA German Institute of Global and Area Studies in Hamburg, and a member of the research programme 'Transformation in the Process of Globalization'.

Virginia Berridge is Professor of History and Head of the Centre for History in Public Health at the London School of Hygiene and Tropical Medicine. She is a historian who works on the contemporary history of health policy and public health.

Scott Burris is Professor of Law at Temple Law School and Associate Director of the Centers for Law and the Public's Health: A Collaborative at Johns Hopkins and Georgetown Universities.

Kent Buse is a Senior Adviser to the Executive Director, UNAIDS. He has taught at Yale University and the London School of Hygiene and Tropical Medicine and worked and consulted for think-tanks, multilaterals and major health partnerships. He is a political-economist working on policy processes in the health sector in lower income countries.

Gilberto Calcagnotto, MA (Sociology) and Lic. Phil. (philosophy), has since 1981 been a researcher at the Institute of Latin American Studies, Hamburg, with an emphasis on Brazil and Mercosur, concerning critical issues of social, economic and political development.

Benedikte Louise Matre Dal is a technical officer and team leader of the Trade, Foreign Policy, Diplomacy and Health unit at WHO. Her work focuses on issues related to globalization, trade and health, including global health governance, global health diplomacy, foreign policy and health, international trade and trade agreements.

Nick Drager, MD, PhD (Econ), is Director of the Department of Ethics, Equity, Trade and Human Rights at the World Health Organization. Prior to this he was Senior Adviser in the Strategy Unit, Office of the Director-General at WHO. His work focuses on current and emerging public health issues related to global change, global public goods for health, global health diplomacy, governing interdependence, foreign policy, international trade and health.

Andrew Harmer is a global health policy analyst with a background in politics and international relations. He has a specialist interest in global health partnerships and initiatives, global health governance, and health systems strengthening. He works for the consultancy Responsible Action, London.

Corinna Hawkes is a freelance consultant specializing in policies to address the global shift towards unhealthy diets and diet-related chronic diseases. She is a Visiting Research Fellow at the Centre for Food Policy, City University, London.

Wolfgang Hein is a Political Scientist at GIGA German Institute of Global and Area Studies, Germany. He teaches at Hamburg University, Germany, after having taught at the free University of Berlin, Germany, and the National University of Costa Rica. His research focuses on global governance (health, global politics), migration and sustainable development.

Matthias Helble is a Technical Officer in the Department of Ethics, Equity, Trade and Human Rights of WHO, Geneva. He holds a PhD in international economics and has worked for the WTO and World Bank. He has published in many prominent journals. His research interests lie in trade and trade-related health topics.

Rachel Herring is a Research Fellow at the Centre for History in Public Health, London School of Hygiene and Tropical Medicine. She is a social scientist with a long-standing interest in health and social policy.

Margaret Hilson was the Director of the Global Health Programmes at the Canadian Public Health Association and a former President of the World Federation of Public Health Associations. She is currently with the Masters of Public Health Programme at the Faculty of Health Sciences, Simon Fraser University, Canada.

Carmen Huckel Schneider is a Research Associate at the Centre for International Studies/Peace and Conflict Research, at the University of Tuebingen in Germany, and a member of the Research Training Group 'Global Challenges: Transnational and Transcultural Solutions'.

Nusaraporn Kessomboon is an Assistant Professor at the Faculty of Pharmaceutical Sciences at Khon Kaen University in Thailand. She has worked for the International Health Policy Programme in Thailand and was a technical officer to the WHO from 2007–08.

Ilona Kickbusch is the Director of the Global Health Programme at the Graduate Institute of International and Development Studies, Geneva and serves as senior health policy adviser to the Swiss Federal Office for Public Health. Prior to directing the Division of Global Health, School of Public Health at Yale University she worked for the World Health Organization.

Lars Kohlmorgen, PhD, is Senior Research Fellow at the Centre for Globalization and Governance at the University of Hamburg and Research Associate at the GIGA German Institute of Global and Area Studies, Hamburg.

Kelley Lee is Reader in Global Health at the London School of Hygiene and Tropical Medicine. Her research focuses on the impacts of globalization on communicable and non-communicable diseases, and the potential for global health governance to protect and promote population health.

Graham Lister, MSc, PhD, is Senior Associate of Judge Business School, Cambridge, Visiting Professor in Health and Social Care at London South Bank University. He was health-care partner for an international consulting firm. He has worked with the Nuffield Trust, the European Foundation Centre and the Aga Khan Foundation as well as with the WHO and the World Bank.

Kelly Loughlin was formerly a lecturer in the Centre for History in Public Health at the London School of Hygiene and Tropical Medicine. Her research interests are in the role of the media in health.

David McCoy is a physician and public health specialist based at the Centre for International Health and Development in University College London. He has previously worked as Director of Research at the Health Systems Trust in South Africa, and is a member of the Steering Council for the Peoples Health Movement.

Emily Mok is a DPhil candidate at the University of Oxford's Centre for Socio-Legal Studies and a Visiting Researcher at Georgetown University Law Center's O'Neill Institute for National and Global Health Law. She is a graduate of the University of Pennsylvania (BAS, MBE, MGA) and the University of Oxford (MSt Law).

Chris Naylor is a researcher with interests in health policy, public health and mental health. Before joining the King's Fund, London, he worked at the Sainsbury Centre for Mental Health and studied at the London School of Hygiene and Tropical Medicine.

John Wyn Owen, CB, is Chair of the University of Wales Institute, Cardiff, member of the Administrative Council, Madariaga European Foundation, Brussels, member of the board, UK Health Protection Agency and Chair of its Committee on Global Health. He is also an Adjunct Professor of the Australian Institute for Health Policy, University of Sydney.

Clifford Shearing is Chair of Criminology and the Director of the Centre of Criminology at the Law Faculty, University of Cape Town, where he also holds the South African National Research Foundation Research Chair in African Security and Justice. His most recent books are *Imagining Security* (2007) and *Lengthening the Arm of the Law* (Cambridge).

Richard D. Smith completed studies in economics and health economics at York University, and worked in Sydney, Cambridge, Bristol, Melbourne and Norwich before joining the London School of Hygiene and Tropical Medicine in 2007. He holds honorary positions at the universities of Hong Kong and East Anglia.

Neil Spicer, Lecturer in Health Policy at the London School of Hygiene and Tropical Medicine, he has previously worked as a researcher at the University of Birmingham and Goldsmiths College, University of London. He is part of a team coordinating studies on the effects of global HIV/AIDS initiatives health systems: http://www.ghinet.org/.

Sally Stansfield is the Executive Director of the Health Metrics Network. Prior to 2006 she was the Associate Director for Global Health Strategies of the Bill and Melinda Gates Foundation. She draws upon more than 30 years of clinical and public health practice, experience in research agencies, universities, governments, non-governmental organizations and multilateral agencies.

David Stuckler is a doctoral candidate in sociology at the University of Cambridge and King's College. He holds an MPH in health policy from Yale. His research integrates political economy and public health to explain the unprecedented mortality crisis in post-communist countries that occurred after the collapse of the Soviet Union. From October 2008 he has been a junior research fellow at Christ Church in Oxford.

Christian von Soest is Senior Research Fellow at the GIGA German Institute of Global and Area Studies in Hamburg. His areas of research include statehood and governance in southern Africa as well as African states' relationships with global actors.

Nina Veenstra, MPH, PhD, is a Research Associate with the Health Economics and HIV/AIDS Research Division at the University of KwaZulu-Natal. Her research interests centre around the impact of HIV/AIDS on health systems in sub-Saharan Africa.

Gill Walt is Professor of International Health Policy at the London School of Hygiene and Tropical Medicine. She has a special interest in the role of international organizations in health. Research interests are on health policy transfer between international and national jurisdictions, especially in relation to infectious diseases, global governance, and the growth of global public-private partnerships in health.

Alan Whiteside, MA, D.Econ, is the Director of the Health Economics and HIV/AIDS Research Division at the University of KwaZulu-Natal. He has written extensively on HIV/AIDS and development, most recently *HIV/AIDS: a Very Short Introduction* (2008).

Dr Jan Peter Wogart is an economist, a senior research associate at GIGA, and a lecturer at the University of Applied Sciences in Bremen. From 1976 to 2000 he worked for the World Bank and the International Finance Corporation.

Derek Yach is Vice President of Global Health Policy at PepsiCo. Previously he has headed global health at the Rockefeller Foundation, been Professor of Public Health and Head of the Division of Global Health at Yale University, and is a former Executive Director of the World Health Organization.

1
Global Health Governance: the Emerging Agenda

Kent Buse, Nick Drager, Wolfgang Hein, Benedikte Dal and Kelley Lee

Toward the end of the millennium, there emerged widespread recognition that a variety of processes – often taking the shorthand of globalization – reconstituted and intensified both the risks of ill-health and the opportunities for addressing them. This recognition was accompanied by concern that existing institutional arrangements were not only increasingly constrained from addressing these risks, but also from taking advantage of emerging opportunities. The nation-state appeared to be under pressure from all sides in discharging its obligations to population health. The World Health Organization (WHO), alongside other organizations, faced increasing challenges in playing a leading and coordinating role, as mandated by its constitution.[1]

Globalization, it was becoming apparent, had led to fundamental changes in the determinants and burden of ill-health, in how global health ought to be addressed, as well as in the policy and institutional responses needed (Lee, 2003; Lee and Collin, 2005; Lee et al., 2002). Not only was this palpable within the health sector, it was also becoming unmistakable that with globalization, the determinants of health were increasingly affected by dynamics outside of the sector. For example, ministries of health are increasingly called on to recognize and act on the public health implications of international trade and trade rules related to access to drugs, health services and food safety (WTO and WHO, 2002). Yet the policy space of ministries of health was at times constrained as member states of the World Trade Organization (WTO) made binding commitments on trade liberalization. Volatile trade and investment flows have serious consequences on fiscal resources in many poor countries, which, in turn, affect budgetary allocation to health services. Transborder criminal activities, such as the trafficking of illicit drugs, tobacco, counterfeit medicines, organs and even people, have exacerbated health challenges. Climate change affected the spread of diseases, as well as marginal agricultural yields and thus affected the nutritional status of large populations and their vulnerability to ill-health. New transport and communication technologies facilitated much increased transborder activities, for example, the increased promotion and availability of junk foods.

One could cite a number of killer facts concerning each of the aforementioned trends, but to take the latter as a case in point, US$15 billion was spent on food marketing to children in 2002, an increase from US$6.9 billion in 1992 (Lobstein, 2006). By 2007 there were an estimated 177 million children threatened by obesity-related diseases worldwide, and approximately 230 million diabetic adults. The latter accounted for an estimated 3.5 million deaths as a result of diabetes, a figure which is expected to rise to 350 million by 2025 (WHO, 2008). Yet 80 per cent of Type 2 diabetes is preventable by changes in diet, physical activity and improved living environments (World Diabetes Foundation, 2008).

However, it is important to recognize that globalization, through a variety of processes and mechanisms described in greater detail in various chapters in this volume, has also contributed to improved health outcomes. Transborder flows of capital, ideas and research have accelerated technological advances in relation to health-care diagnostics, drug discovery and delivery mechanisms – for example through telemedicine. The internet has enabled the consolidation of a networked group of professional and amateur epidemiologists and others who can instantaneously share information worldwide on suspected disease outbreaks, thereby enabling more rapidly coordinated global, regional and national responses. The globalized media can be a force for good in expanding coverage – and thus raising public awareness – of health concerns requiring public attention, and it has played a significant role in alerting the public's perception of the moral imperative to address AIDS and malaria. Processes associated with globalization have also fostered closer collaboration between individuals and groups hitherto excluded from or disadvantaged within formal decision-making forums, in the process creating opportunities to challenge powerful and entrenched interests. Herein lies the potential for globalization to change the nature and distribution of political power to embrace broader and more representative constituencies. So far, much of the potential for globalization to deliver substantial benefits to health remains untapped and deserves far greater exploration.

In this book, we understand globalization as the intensification of flows of people, goods and services, capital, information and ideas across national borders, although recognizing that the concept also applies to other dimensions of transnationalization (Held et al., 1999). We argue that, given evidence of the consequences of these flows, globalization demands more effective collective action by governments, business and civil society in order to enable its opportunities to be harnessed and shared, thus ensuring a more sustainable future. This quest, to better manage the risks and opportunities of globalization, is leading scholars and policymakers to reassess the rules, norms, institutions and organizations that govern health, as well as health policy and practice, at the sub-national, national, regional and global levels – in the health sector and beyond.

In light of the increasingly widespread recognition of the impacts of globalization on health, the past fifteen years have witnessed a profound transformation of the institutional response, a wide range of problems and ideas discussed, norms and rules agreed, reforms instigated, and activities and initiatives launched. New organizations and networks have been formed to address global health issues, hitherto unprecedented levels of funding have been mobilized – some from unconventional sources, new ways of delivering health aid have been devised, and bold experiments have been implemented: a thousand flowers appear to have bloomed. This dynamic environment constitutes what we call global health governance. The past decade, in particular, has been marked by a paradigm-like shift in our approach to dealing with global health. It is timely therefore to assess this transformation.

We thought long and hard about whether or not to include the word 'governance' in the title of this book. The term seemed overused and the concept abused. On the one hand, governance can be used very loosely to describe any type of steering or coordination of action – for good or for bad – so as to encapsulate almost all collaborative human endeavours. On the other hand, extended to 'good governance', the concept has been captured in the aid community to define a normative agenda concerned – when narrowly interpreted – with quantitative assessments of issues such as safety and security, rule of law, transparency and corruption (for example, the World Bank's Country Policy and Institutional Assessments or its Institute's World Governance Indicators). While concerned about framing the book around vague notions – and potentially misleading those concerned with governance assessments in the health sector (along the lines of the World Health Report of 2000 which ranked health systems) – we could find no adequate alternative to the word governance – and so it stuck.

We follow Rosenau (1995) who reminds us that governance is concerned with 'how a society or organization steers itself'. Consequently, our concern in this book is with the 'rules of the game' – how the priorities are set, funds raised and allocated, disputes settled and so on – which impact on health outcomes. In addition to institutions, which reflect the rules of the game, we are equally interested in examining the structures, agency and politics – who gets what, where and when – which determine the rules, and the resulting relationships, including those of participation in decision-making and accountability. The question of how to define and explain governance conceptually and practically as related to global health governance will be taken up in various chapters of this book.

In the following chapters, a group of authors from very different backgrounds describe and take stock of the changes to the manner in which global health is governed, assess whether or not these changes have been adequate and appropriate, reveal some of the unanticipated consequences, and, importantly, make recommendations as to what could and should be done differently. These policy-oriented recommendations are addressed to civil society, business, government ministries, international and intergovernmental organizations and the range of networks and partnerships which increasingly govern the global health commons. In so doing, the authors aim to inspire and inform the evolving realm of global health governance so as to deliver better and more equitable health outcomes. As such, this book is geared towards the range of actors involved in global health governance as well as to students and scholars thereof.

This introduction sets the scene in the following way. We begin by outlining why global health has achieved the impressive profile that it has, we then enumerate some of the key developments that constitute global health governance over the past decade and present the key messages emerging from this volume. Thus before introducing each of the chapters in the book, we highlight some of the major achievements as well as the opportunities and challenges shaping the path ahead.

Ill-health: of growing global concern

The spreading web of social relationships that characterizes contemporary globalization has important consequences in terms of the speed and reach of disease transmission, the distribution of health and disease patterns worldwide, and for the ways in which health status in turn impacts on social and economic well-being. A few examples readily explain why health has become of such global concern:

- An accelerated dispersion of health problems is discernable. This is the result of the expansion and acceleration of global mobility, which impacts particularly on the spread of infectious disease. The ongoing HIV crisis and potential influenza pandemic represent global threats, while hitherto unknown diseases, such as Ebola and Severe Acute Respiratory Syndrome (SARS), are being viewed as examples of new global health risks. The globalization of certain lifestyles and behaviours, as a consequence of global advertising and cultural change, spreads other health determinants (see Stuckler et al., Chapter 13, for example, concerning smoking, dietary patterns and alcohol use).
- The increasing resistance of pathogens to antibiotics holds great dangers. Drug resistance is the result of inappropriate use of medicines, often among the middle and upper classes, and of incomplete courses of treatment among poorer people as well as the widespread use of antibiotics in industrial livestock production. The emergence of pathogens resistant to most antibacterial agents has now become a serious problem in the treatment of both malaria and tuberculosis (TB), particularly extremely drug resistant tuberculosis (XDRTB).

- The accelerated spread of drugs and medical technology to virtually all corners of the globe has the potential to help the fight against disease worldwide, yet is increasingly posing ethical dilemmas. For example, income-based inequalities in health-care are becoming ever more pronounced while some technologies are used in questionable ways (for example, innovative technologies for cosmetic reasons, lifestyle drugs or the use of ultrasound to enable sex-selective abortions in India). The unacceptable nature of these inequities has implications beyond the health sector. Witness the manner in which progress on international trading rules was disrupted by activists in Doha protesting the patent protection regime in 2001 (see Helble et al., Chapter 8).
- Since the mid-1990s, there has been evidence of growing apprehension about the vicious circle of rising poverty and greater vulnerability to health problems in an increasingly global world. People are becoming ill more frequently because they are poor, while the illness in turn makes them even poorer – particularly where there is no adequate public health service or there are other barriers to access. HIV may have played some role in drawing attention to this circle within the business sector which increasingly plays a more proactive role in responding to the threat of the epidemic among its workforce and the communities in which it operates in low- and middle-income countries (Davis et al., 2007).
- Governments of rich countries (such as the members of the Organization for Economic Cooperation and Development – OECD) are becoming ever more concerned about the possible economic and political instability that might be associated with a high incidence of poverty-related disease in some regions of the world. This concern probably underlies the salience accorded to health at the historic discussion and resolution on HIV at the UN Security Council in 2000 and at subsequent meetings of the UN General Assembly, and G7 and G8 summits.
- Governments in a range of countries are increasingly sensitive to the real and potential effects of disease outbreaks on their economies (for example, through trade or tourism). It is estimated that the 2002–03 SARS outbreak cost the Asian region around US$50 billion (with some estimates as high as US$150 billion). This has generated new interest in the business community in effective measures to deal with global outbreaks of disease, framed within terms such as global health security. The security implications of health threats, in a range of guises, have also raised the global profile of health and stimulated increased emphasis on global health diplomacy, resulting in a UN resolution on global health and foreign policy in November 2008 (Prins, 2004; Morrison, 2006; Fidler and Drager, 2006).

These six observations reflect the reality that health issues are increasingly central – rather than merely tangential – to a range of issues on the global policy agenda.

The realm of global health: in search of improved governance

With increasing global concern for the state of ill-health and the inequalities that fuel it, from the mid-1990s, the sector witnessed a rash of developments and initiatives to respond to new challenges and fill gaps unattended by established organizations. The period witnessed a growing consciousness of *global* responsibility for *global* health – sometimes in the narrow discourse of the Millennium Development Goals and at others in bold calls for universal access to a range of treatments. This new-found consciousness was reflected in far-reaching innovations in global health governance.

Various new financing arrangements emerged – largely as a result of a new breed of philanthropists with interests in global health, epitomized by the Bill and Melinda Gates Foundation. In part fostered and incubated by the Gates Foundation, new mechanisms to raise and disburse finance were established. These included the Global Fund to Fight AIDS, Tuberculosis and Malaria (GFATM) and the GAVI Alliance and later instruments such as the International Finance Facility – Immunization (IFFIm) and Advanced Market Commitments (see Smith, Chapter 6). Although it has not developed into a coherent arrangement for resource transfers, a 'system' of global health governance per se, considerable volumes of new resources have been mobilized and agreements on how to allocate, disburse and account for them have been agreed among a surprisingly wide and diverse group of stakeholders. Moreover, large networks of independent actors perform the role of watchdogs pressing donor countries to disburse promised resource transfers and recipient countries to make use of these transfers according to accepted norms. Certainly, the results depend upon power structures and are subject to conflicting interests and perceptions, according to the anarchic character of the constantly evolving field of institutions.

Innovative financing arrangements have been accompanied by the establishment of novel organizational arrangements to tackle select health problems – particularly through global health partnerships (see Buse and Harmer, Chapter 12). More specifically, a number of such partnerships attempt to address the absence of research and development on neglected diseases and products (for instance, the Medicines for Malaria Venture, the Global Alliance for TB Drug Development, the International AIDS Vaccine Initiative, the Foundation for Improved Diagnostics). A different group of partnerships have been established to address lack of access to existing medicines. These initiatives include drug donation programmes (Mectizan, Diflucan and Malarone), as well as those aiming to reduce the costs of medicines (for example, the Green Light Committee for TB medicines). Yet another cluster of alliances aimed to catalyze action and improve coordination on a range of issues from TB (the Stop TB Partnership) and malaria (the Roll Back Malaria Partnership) to health measurement (the Health Metrics Network) and the crisis in human resources for health (the Global Health Workforce Alliance).

What is striking about these partnerships is the increasingly structured and sustained level of interaction that they engendered between intergovernmental organizations, states and a burgeoning number of advocacy and service-delivery non-governmental organizations. Collectively, these actors discovered new ways of meeting new and old challenges – as evidenced for example through the coalition-building efforts of MSF to ensure access for all to medicines. From 2000 onwards, we have also observed a series of significant developments in the field of global health that gave expression to the increasingly intense interaction between representatives of sectors which had hitherto operated in a less networked manner.

Over the same period, a number of international agreements relevant to global health were concluded. These include, among others, interpretations of specific measures within multilateral trade agreements. The Declaration on the TRIPS Agreement and Public Health agreed in Doha, Qatar in November 2001, and the Decision on Paragraph 6 of that Agreement issued in August 2003 by the General Council of the WTO, reaffirmed the right of member states to use flexibilities (for example, compulsory licences and parallel imports) within the Agreement on Trade-Related Aspects of Intellectual Property Rights (TRIPS) to protect public health and promote access to medicines. Thailand issued compulsory licences in 2007 on medicines for AIDS and heart disease, demonstrating the growing confidence of some developing country governments in using the available flexibilities. The Framework Convention on Tobacco Control (FCTC), which entered into force in 2005, can be seen as a landmark treaty. For the first time, the WHO used its position as an intergovernmental organization to create the basis of international law for cooperation on a global health issue. In 2005 an agreement on revised International Health Regulations (IHR) was also concluded. They no longer relate only to specific infectious diseases but to all 'public health emergencies of international concern'. The IHR provide an important role to non-state actors, by incorporating non-governmental sources of information into the surveillance process (Fidler, 2005: 374), and also bestow new roles and responsibilities upon the WHO. Most critically, the regulations provide the WHO with the flexibility to make public the recommendations it provides to member states, enabling other bodies to act where warranted and in a more coordinated manner in the event of a global health crisis. In a number of respects, the successful fight against the SARS epidemic in 2002–03 anticipated various forms of cooperation reflected in the new IHR (Fidler, 2005: 354–5).

In addition, new processes were established to address some key global health issues. The International Health Partnership (IHP+), for example, embraced not only previously agreed soft-norm (that is, non-legally binding) commitments on aid effectiveness[2] but also renewed global commitments to strengthening health systems[3] in poorer countries, which constitute the weakest links in global health governance. Other weak links were also the subject of concerted international efforts. For example, following the publication of the report of the WHO Commission on Intellectual Property Rights, Innovation and Public Health (CIPIH) in April 2006, a consensus began to emerge on the need for changes in the global system of innovation for medicines and for health research more generally. This led to the establishment of the Intergovernmental Working Group on Public Health, Innovation and Intellectual Property (IGWG) under the auspices of the WHO. This group, open to all interested member states, and including civil society actors,[4] was mandated to draw up a global strategy and plan of action. Its aim is to provide a medium-term framework to secure an enhanced and sustainable basis for needs-driven, essential R&D relevant to diseases that disproportionately affect developing countries by proposing clear objectives and priorities for research and development and estimating funding needs in this area. This global strategy and plan of action was adopted in a resolution passed at the World Health Assembly in May 2008 (WHA 61.21). On another front, in 2005, the WHO established the Commission on Social Determinants of Health (CSDH) which steered the focus of the international community to the importance of the social and environmental contexts which generate health and ill-health, including how they are governed through fields beyond a narrow purview of global health governance (GHG), such as trade, labour markets and debt management. The aim of the commission is to build a worldwide movement to address such determinants – many of which are global in nature.

The past few years have witnessed a renewed battle over what norms should define global health governance. Norms are invariably embedded within any form of global governance, with different norms competing for policy space and supremacy. Some global norms, such as nondiscrimination by virtue of race, religion or gender, are embedded within a wide range of international commitments. More contested is the dominance of market-based norms (for example, concerning the importance of growth versus equity). Such economism has underpinned a range of health sector reforms in recent decades across the global south (Lee and Goodman, 2002). In direct response to these norms, there has been a resurgence of support for human rights-based approaches. Reminiscent of the Health for All movement of the late 1970s, debates concerning access to medicines, led by countries such as South Africa, Thailand, Brazil and India, and supported by NGOs, have sought to elevate the norms of social justice and equity within global health governance. Similarly, the Declaration of Commitment on HIV/AIDS by the UN General Assembly in June 2001(including prevention, care, support and treatment), and the 're-discovery' of the importance of economic, social and cultural rights and the demands for the human right to the highest attainable standard of health, as interpreted in May 2000 in the General Comment No. 14 of the UN Committee on Economic, Social and Cultural Rights and taken up by a growing number of human rights organizations, stress the collective responsibility of an emergent global society for the world's health. Another set of norms, which have informed global health governance, challenge the primacy of state sovereignty. The revised IHRs have been prompted in part by the need to ensure the collective interests of the global community when dealing with 'public health emergencies of potential international concern'. Similar questions about the inviolability of state sovereignty have been raised in international law where natural or manmade disasters or abuses of state power lead to large-scale human suffering. The norm of non-intervention in another state's affairs has been eroded as greater value has been given to humanitarian need or protection of the global commons.

The emerging GHG agenda

The select developments in the field of global health listed above might be viewed as an initial set of governance responses to an emerging global health agenda. These responses have arisen from the interactions of intergovernmental organizations with a diverse set of member states and non-state actors. Three policy goals, which aim to tackle new patterns of health and disease, and their unequal distribution across populations, particularly affecting the poor, are central to this global health governance agenda:

- *Controlling global public 'bads' while promoting and delivering global public 'goods'.* The former category includes addressing and regulating harmful marketing, tobacco, alcohol, food risks and safety, environmental contamination, climate change and so on; while the latter includes disease surveillance, knowledge management, research and development on global public goods.
- *Strengthening health systems.* Health systems encompass a number of components to ensure more equitable and sustained improvements in service outputs and outcomes. These include health workforce mobilization, distribution, and motivation; drugs, equipment and infrastructure supply, distribution and maintenance; organization and management of health services; leadership and stewardship; health financing systems (collection, pooling, purchasing); and national information and monitoring systems. Health systems are access goods required to turn knowledge into health outcomes.
- *Ensuring policy coherence across sectors for improved public health.* Working more effectively with other policy sectors such as trade, development, environment and security to control 'bads' and promote those goods which affect health determinants and outcomes.

A range of functions are involved in governing these different themes. Such GHG functions include: (i) generating and reviewing evidence; (ii) developing norms and standards; (iii) undertaking advocacy and disseminating information; (iv) mobilizing resources; (v) supporting service delivery in fragile and poor states; (vi) intervening in market failures; (vii) monitoring and evaluation; and (viii) implementing accountability mechanisms. Illustrative examples of initiatives to address the various areas of the global health governance agenda are presented throughout the book. An illustration of the roles and responsibilities adopted by some institutions and actors is presented in Table 1.1.

Building progressive global health governance: key messages

Given recent efforts to strengthen global health governance, the emerging agenda and the findings presented later in this book, we see a number of key messages emerging for public health advocates, researchers and policymakers at a variety of levels with responsibility for health.

An opportunity as never before

Health in developing countries has a new-found and privileged position in the eyes of the general public and the world's political leadership – even the so-called Elders (Kofi Annan, Nelson Mandela, Mary Robinson, Jimmy Carter and so on) have identified health as one of their priorities. Health challenges now factor in national security strategies, appear regularly on the agenda of meetings of leading economic powers, affect the bilateral and regional political relationships between developed and developing countries and influence strategies for United Nations reform. The connections between health and the environment, trade, economic growth, social development, national security and human rights and dignity have been made and are seen as affecting both developed and developing country interests. Given the political profile, the global health community faces a unique opportunity to address the unconscionable and inequitably distributed burden of ill-health globally. This opportunity needs to be seized, not forfeited.

To leave governance to chance is to invite neglect

The heightened interest in global health is related to globalization and increasing interdependence. Economic integration appears to have outpaced society's collective ability to manage this interdependence, but its governance, and its consequences, should not be left to the market (much of which may be happening by default) or to chance, as either of these options leads to sub-optimal health outcomes. There are grounds for much more proactive approaches in identifying collective solutions to collectively identified problems. Past efforts have too readily dismissed the possibility of reinvigorating and reforming existing institutions and have been overly ad hoc and disjointed. Thus we need to deliberatively assess the relevance and adaptability of existing institutions and where necessary develop and refine those institutions, legislation, rules, norms, principles and decision-making

Table 1.1 The global health governance agenda: illustrative roles and responsibilities

GHG functions	Governance agenda			
	Controlling global bads	Promoting global goods	Strengthening health systems	Policy coherence
Reviewing evidence	WHO expert groups; UNAIDS; CODEX/SPS	WHO expert groups (e.g, *SAGE*); World Bank HNP; Global Health Watch; Kaiser Family Foundation	Health systems knowledge network; HMN; HSAN; IHME; World Bank HNP HSFG; MDGs	Multi-sector expert groups (e.g., CIPIH); UNAIDS
Agreeing priorities	FCTC; IGWG	WHA; GAVI	IHP+; HMN; GHWA	CSDH; World Health Assembly
Developing rules and norms and crafting instruments (e.g., treaties)	FCTC; IHR	UN Human Rights System	HMN	WHA; WTO; PHA; Trade and Health Diagnostic Tool
Advocacy and information	IBFAN; UNAIDS	Access Movement, NGOs, UNICEF	GHWA; HSAN	Global Forum for Health Research
Resource mobilization and financing	Bloomberg	GAVI; GFATM; Gates Foundation; IFFIm; Monterrey Consensus	IHP+; World Bank; GFATM; GAVI; NGOs	Paris Declaration on Aid Effectiveness; Monterrey Consensus
Service delivery in fragile and poor states	NGOs; Bilaterals;	NGOs; Bilaterals;	Merlin and other NGOs;	Global Health Council;

(*Continued*)

Table 1.1 (Continued)

GHG functions	Governance agenda			
	Controlling global bads	Promoting global goods	Strengthening health systems	Policy coherence
	UNICEF; WHO; World Bank	UNICEF; WHO; World Bank	Bilaterals; UNICEF; WHO; World Bank	ICRC
Intervening in market failures (including R&D)	Countries; WHO essential drug list	Medicines for Malaria Venture; DNDi	Countries; NGOs	CIPIH; IGWG
Surveillance, monitoring and evaluation	FCA; IBFAN; IHR	GOARN	IHR implementation; Consortium for Research on Equitable Health Systems	Paris Declaration on Aid Effectiveness
Accountability and enforcement	IHR	NGOs (blaming and shaming)	Countries; GFATM	Transparency International

Notes: CIPIH = Commission on Intellectual Property Rights, Innovation & Public Health; CODEX/SPS = FAO/WHO Codex Alimentarius Commission – Sanitary and Phyto-Sanitary Measures Agreement; CSDH = Commission on Social Determinants of Health; DNDi = Drugs for Neglected Diseases initiative; FCA = Framework Convention Alliance; GAVI = Global Alliance for Vaccines and Immunization; GFATM = Global Fund to Fight AIDS, TB and Malaria; GHWA = Global Health Workforce Alliance; GOARN = Global Outbreak Alert and Response Network; HMN = Health Metrics Network; HNP = Health, Nutrition and Population (Department of the World Bank); HSAN = Health Systems Action Network; HSFG = Health Systems and Financing (Department of the World Bank); IBFAN = International Baby Food Action Network; ICRC = International Committee of the Red Cross; IFFIm = International Finance Facility for Immunization; IGWG = Intergovernmental Working Group on Public Health, Innovation and Intellectual Property; IHME = Institute for Health Metrics and Evaluation; IHP = International Health Partnership; IHR = International Health Regulations; PHA = People's Health Assembly; SAGE = Strategic Advisory Group of Experts; WHA = World Health Assembly procedures that bring order and thus shepherd this collective action to improve health outcomes for all – that is, build a robust system of global health governance.

Remedies must cope with complexity

Seizing the opportunity to develop governance solutions is not as straightforward as one might hope. There are an exponentially increasing number of determinants of ill-health and components of health-care systems and, hence, an increasingly dense web of actors and initiatives that are involved in and impact on global health. Balancing the demands of sovereignty with those of a shared responsibility for global health as well as the self-interest of a range of groups and organizations is daunting. Yet to craft health policy today, governments, international organizations and non-governmental organizations must find mechanisms to manage health risks that spill into and out of every country. Many solutions require investments at international and national levels and cooperation across a very wide range of sectors and actors.

Address the weaknesses of past GHG initiatives

Past attempts to bring increasing order to the chaos (new organizations, principles and so on) have been marked by a number of weaknesses. They have often been responsive as opposed to pre-emptive, entailed a significant time lag between the identification of a problem and the implementation of a response, have been ad hoc and selective (a fund for only three diseases, an R&D effort for a drug for another disease, voluntary financing mechanisms without adequate incentives and so on) and have at times placed undue attention on structure while often failing to address agency, interests and the political dimensions of the reforms required. As a result, there has been a disproportionate emphasis on some problems (for example, AIDS and other communicable diseases) and approaches (for example, care and treatment) which deflects attention from other problems and approaches (for example, strengthening health systems, disease prevention, non-communicable diseases). Apparently, we still lack a forum to bring a necessary degree of order to this chaos (in setting priorities or even linking at the most basic level the burden of ill-health with investment decisions in the public sector).

Ensure that emerging mechanisms of GHG are underpinned by and advance a common set of principles and values

There remains the need for international forums that are legitimate, credible and effective in decision-making. Within these forums, national public interests will need to be effectively and proportionally represented – a new health diplomacy – and the power asymmetries between north and south and between governments and civil society will need to be acknowledged and addressed. In the quest for global health justice, the institutional arrangements need to be buttressed by a commonly accepted normative framework drawing on existing international norms concerning universalism, health as a human right, justice and dignity, health security, health and development, legitimacy, representation, fairness, value-for-money, accountability and so on. These principles need to be applied to intergovernmental organizations, foundations, global health partnerships, NGOs, networks and other sites of governance – and in the case of the WHO calls for a WHA+ type arrangement (that is, a more structured voice for non-state actors – see Kickbusch, Chapter 15).

Support the foundations of progressive global health governance that are currently being laid

A number of developments provide reasons for hope and foundations upon which to build, including:

- A number of countries are building networks of a new multilateralism. There is a new-found confidence in some developing country governments – particularly those of the BRICS (Brazil, Russia, India, China and South Africa) and Thailand – to join forces, to undertake joined-up trade-foreign-health policy (that is, to seek policy coherence) and to protect their interests in the development of international rules. For example, the ministers of foreign affairs of Brazil, France, Indonesia, Norway, Senegal, South Africa and Thailand joined together in September of 2006 to create the Oslo Initiative on Global Health and Foreign Policy, and the so-called Rio Group, led by Brazil, formed a bloc in the IGWG.[5] At times, as was the case in the campaigns to increase access to antiretroviral therapy in Brazil and South Africa, national actors have also joined forces through global coalitions and have spoken truth to the power of the pharmaceutical companies. The new multilateralism now needs to become more inclusive of low-income countries and fragile states.
- An increasing number of innovative governance mechanisms include greater numbers of under-represented interests (for example, some civil society groups are represented on the GFATM and GAVI Alliance boards) and more inclusive approaches to decision-making.
- A tremendous amount of consultation, negotiation and compromise has led to consensus on difficult issues (from MDGs to aid practices to debt-relief and so on) which provides lessons for future consensus-building processes.
- New global rules on infectious disease control and tobacco control have been reached, pushing the frontiers of possibilities. Following on the heels of these successes there are new and ongoing international efforts to develop rules related to the migration of health professionals, trade and

healthy diets, as well as to innovation, intellectual property and public health.
- Innovative financing mechanisms to fund GPG are being debated and established and are channelling larger volumes of resource transfers to build systems in the south.

Move beyond picking the low-hanging fruit

Despite considerable achievements over the past decade, it is clear that some of the agreements are not being implemented as anticipated (for example, the Paris Declaration on Aid Effectiveness). Moreover, it is patently the case that there are more complex and contentious issues on the GHG agenda, including climate change, alcohol abuse and bilateral trade regimes. The future will see the pitting of public health advocates and ministries of health against powerful interests where win-win situations may be more difficult to identify and negotiate.

Enable ministers of health to deliver joined-up, coherent, and evidence-informed policy

To best influence global negotiations on governance issues affecting health outcomes, public health advocates must define the problem and the terms of the collective debate early in the process. Researchers need to interact more with health policymakers and equip them with evidence that is easy to communicate to diplomats, defence attachés, trade negotiators and development specialists so as to ensure that health concerns and interests are better reflected in foreign policy and international trade initiatives. Much can be learned from new approaches to the exercise of influence – not through vertical hierarchical channels – but through more horizontal, consultative approaches emphasizing soft power and the importance of the framing of issues.

Support research and capacity-building to ensure effective governance

The foregoing suggests the need for greater investment in: (i) analysis of the globalizing determinants of health and ill-health, the impacts of governance responses (including private corporate governance), and opportunities for forward movement; (ii) capacity-building in the south (in health and other ministries) on issues as diverse as trade and health negotiation (to be effective, there needs to be closer interaction between research and policymaking in this fast-evolving environment); and (iii) investment in consultative processes – including those bringing in under-represented voices to consultation forums and negotiating tables. In making these investments, priority ought to be placed on capacity and systems-building in the south – and concomitantly less emphasis on the meetings and initiatives which are driven from and largely involve discussions in Geneva, New York and

Washington DC – and the introduction of mutual accountability systems that actually work.

This book examines these challenges in greater depth, from a variety of perspectives, and presents plausible ways forward – on a continuum from order (norms, standards, rules) to anarchy – which will better harness the power of globalization to improve public health in particular for poor and vulnerable populations. The essence of each chapter is set out below.

Book overview

As noted above, increasing interest in global health has led to increasing numbers of actors and increasingly complex patterns of relationships between them. In the context of such complexity in negotiation, decision-making and coordination, the concept of global health governance has emerged as a subject of interest and debate in the field of international health and beyond. Early publications introduced the concept of global health governance and the issues at stake, including the health impacts of globalization (Lee, 2003), the impact of globalization on health policymaking (Lee et al., 2002), the growing role of public-private partnerships in health (Buse and Walt, 2000a, 2000b), and global public goods for health (Smith et al., 2003). Since 2003, a substantial literature has been produced on: (i) global health and GHG in general (Thomas and Weber, 2004; Aginam, 2005; Walt and Buse, 2005; Cooper et al., 2007; Fidler, 2007; Labonté and Schrecker, 2007; Hein and Kohlmorgen, 2008; Zacher and Keefe, 2008); (ii) global health partnerships (Buse, 2004; Buse and Harmer, 2007); (iii) specific institutional mechanisms like the new International Health Regulations (Fidler 2004, 2005); (iv) chronic diseases governance (Yach et al., 2004); (v) WTO, trade and global health (Abbott, 2005; Mackintosh and Koivusalo, 2005; Blouin et al., 2006; Kimball, 2006); (vi) health and security (McInnes and Lee, 2006); (vii) governance processes related to HIV/AIDS (Poku et al., 2007; Hein et al., 2007); (viii) civil society's role in GHG (Seckinelgin, 2005; Doyel and Patel, 2008); and (ix) the WHO in a context of globalization (Lee, 2008), among other topics. More recently the topic of global health diplomacy has gained increasing attention (Kickbusch et al., 2007). Scholarly and policy interest in the subject has been reflected in the appearance of new international journals on the topic, notably *Global Public Health*, *Globalization and Health* and *Global Health Governance*.

The contribution of this volume to this literature is threefold. First, it builds on a series of papers published by the WHO, which formed the first detailed analysis of global health governance, which have subsequently been discussed by the contributors to this volume and some of which have been significantly revised and appear here. Second, this book is both unique and unconventional in bringing together leading scholars and policymakers involved in important GHG mechanisms, and in taking an interdisciplinary approach to the analysis of global governance. Third, the work is not merely an academic exercise but is also a practical one in which academics and practitioners were challenged to produce evidence-informed, specific, policy-relevant and feasible recommendations for improving the practice (and to some extent the analysis) of global health governance. Consequently, the authors eclectically but systematically unfold analyses of various dimensions of the field of GHG, of the specific problems and opportunities inherent in the present transformation in the sector, and make specific recommendations for further analysis and action to strengthen the effectiveness of governance to improve world health. Draft versions of many of the contributions to this book were presented and discussed at a workshop in Hamburg in February 2006 and subsequently revised. The authors come from a variety of walks of life, from the key organizations involved in global health governance as well as leading centres of learning, and thus bring diverse perspectives to the analysis of global health governance and suggestions on how best to strengthen it.

This volume sets out a range of global health challenges, where cooperation between national governments and intergovernmental organizations have failed to succeed, and where collective transborder efforts have been made to address them. The emerging complex web of global (health) governance reflects the interactions of two different structures of conflict: those between nation-states still reflecting the era of Westphalian international relations and those between other transnational actors characterizing the post-Westphalian era.[6] Despite the increasing weight of non-state actors in GHG, nation-states and territorially defined rule remain integral in a globalizing world. National egoisms prevent the necessary transfers of authority and the development of international regulations which might endanger the position of industries and institutions on which a privileged position of one or another nation in global society might be based. Furthermore, organized health systems – what Fidler (2007: 13) calls 'the hardware of global health governance' – are still based on the organizational and financial capability of nation-states. On the whole, the rise of global health governance reflects an increasing acceptance of global responsibility for health, which constitutes the common normative basis of all the contributions to this volume. Yet the success of the transformation may well depend on a shift of power, not least of which could be in north-south relations.

The volume begins by seeking to establish the historical dimensions of GHG, mapping out the actors and the mechanisms through which they interact, clarifying GHG's theoretical and conceptual contours, and setting out what is particular and specific to health. The chapters review and prescribe an ambitious agenda for the further development of GHG and reiterate the normative principles which ought to underpin it. Various chapters illustrate the drivers of GHG, the contributions of different actors and sectors and the mechanisms through which they wield influence. The authors discuss the potential and limitations of various tools of global health governance. In so doing, a range of weaknesses and opportunities are identified and recommendations are elaborated. The authors of the volume hope that its readers will find herein solutions to problems that they confront and which they can apply as they strive to do their part in fulfilling the universal right to health in an era marked by increasing inequality and ill-health. As such, we hope the volume serves as a useful resource to policymakers and policy-influencers as well as those with an interest in understanding and shaping the architecture of global health governance.

International cooperation in health dates back well into the nineteenth century, with the International Sanitary Conferences which took place from 1851 onwards generally viewed as the start of institutionalized arrangements. In the early phases of such cooperation, under specific circumstances, non-governmental organizations played an important role as is illustrated, for example, by the International Red Cross, professional associations, and the contribution of the Rockefeller Foundation in financing the League of Nations Health Organization. In Chapter 2, Virginia Berridge, Kelly Loughlin and Rachel Herring analyse the salient historical dimensions of global health governance and point to recent changes in the governance of international health concerns due to the extension of social and political spaces between and beyond states. These changes have given rise to a transformation of analytical focus from 'international health governance' to 'global health governance'. The authors stress, however, that many of the seemingly new themes and issues are in fact not that new; the role of non-state actors and of international philanthropy in health can be traced back for well over a century. Therefore, the concept of globalization itself 'should be subject to historical scrutiny' to allow a critical discussion of the 'aura of 'newness' which has been part of the WHO's refashioning in the 1990s as well as that of many other global health initiatives.

In the following chapter, 'Mapping the Global Health Architecture', Gill Walt, Neil Spicer and Kent Buse provide an overview of the growing multiplicity of actors in global health governance since the 1960s; a development which has led to calls for a 'new' global health architecture. The authors argue that such calls stem from two realizations: the increased multiplicity and diversity of actors involved in health and the weaknesses of traditional rules and decision-making structures to coordinate global health action.

But is 'architecture' the right analogy? Walt and colleagues suggest it may actually constrain our thinking on governance. Rather than looking at solid, permanent architectural or organizational structures they argue that efforts should be made to explore the changing and fluid interests and interrelations of the many different actors involved in global health. They do this by mapping changes in the actors involved in global health and their global institutions over time, paying attention to relational and structural power.

The authors focus on the major political and social ideas and events that affected discourse and actions and those actors who promoted them during particular periods. The chapter points to the recent proliferation of actors, the mobilization of considerable new resources, the attendant problems of coordination and decision-making and the blurring structures of accountability. The chapter concludes with a discussion of what is missing in the architecture metaphor, arguing that too much attention has been paid to structure and form – to the neglect of agency; and that the spotlight falls too strongly on *global* strategy to the detriment of *local* implementation. To reform the global health architecture, it is argued that it is necessary to focus much more on process and agency.

Wolfgang Hein, Scott Burris and Clifford Shearing discuss the 'Conceptual Models for Global Health Governance' based on the concepts of 'nodal governance' and 'interfaces'. Different perspectives are taken to address the central characteristics of GHG – the multiplicity of actors, flexibility of institutional arrangements and fluidity of relationships. The 'nodal governance' framework is 'an elaboration of contemporary network theory that explains how a variety of actors operating within social systems interact along networks to govern the systems they inhabit' (Burris et al., 2005: 33). The concept of 'interface' attends to the 'critical point of interaction or linkage between different social systems, fields or levels of social order where structural discontinuities based upon differences of normative values and social interest, are most likely to be found' (Long, 1989). Independently, these concepts can help us to understand what constitutes the binding forces and the types of power mobilized among the multitude of actors in global health governance. Taken together, they illuminate key challenges to good GHG: improving democracy, efficacy and coordination. Through a discussion of the global governance of HIV/AIDS, the usefulness of this approach in the interpretation of the dynamics of politics and institutions in the field of global health is demonstrated.

Even if we understand the new organizational forms of global governance as described in the previous chapters, the proliferation of state and non-state actors linked through complex relationships – including those of unequal power resources – raises many questions, including those concerning effectiveness, legitimacy and accountability. Using key concepts from political science and international relations theory, in Chapter 5, 'Governance Norms in Global Health', Sonja Bartsch, Carmel Huckel Schneider and Lars Kohlmorgen advance the argument that all actors involved in GHG ought to strive to ensure that their actions are effective, legitimate, accountable and serve to redistribute power. The authors unpack each of these constructs and discuss the relevant theoretical foundations upon which they rest. After presenting a normative case for each of these governance standards, the authors provide examples of how they are operationalized in practice. Finally, a series of recommendations are laid out for improving the quality of GHG through the application of these standards. The authors argue that we need to be able to identify costs which can be applied to power-wielders who fail to take into account the needs and preferences of those affected by their decisions. Furthermore, all actors – regardless of organizational type – should uphold standards of legitimacy based on both inputs and outputs, and their effectiveness should be more systematically monitored. Importantly, we need a better understanding of how to empower those who have the greatest stake in global health policy as their societies are too poor to deliver adequate health services. While the examples in this chapter focus on the WHO and GFATM, other chapters in this volume apply these standards critically to other actors – for example, Buse and Harmer to global health partnerships, Buse and Naylor to the commercial sector and McCoy and Hilson to CSOs.

In many parts of the world, during much of the twentieth century, the responsibility for the provision of basic conditions for a healthy life and of health-care was a central element of the nation-state's provision of public goods. Richard D. Smith's chapter, 'Global Health Governance and Global Public Goods', is based on the observation that globalization has increasingly turned health and health-care into cross-national issues, raising questions as to which collective action problems to prioritize as well as how to mobilize and coordinate the numerous actors who have some potential, yet critical role, in delivering collective solutions. Global public goods – goods for which there is a strong rationale toward universal consumption and where exclusion of an individual nation would be irrational – are increasingly necessary to achieve health globally. After summarizing the institutional problems of collective action in the field of global governance, and in particular the cooperation required for the optimal production of global public goods for health, Smith turns to the critical question of finance. He refers to the concept of 'new public finance' (Kaul and Conceição, 2006), concerned with 'the multifarious means to channel resources from ... various actors under various regulatory and monitoring structures and institutions'. While there has been some growth in such finance, Smith calls for more public-private partnering and more appropriate incentives for global cooperation, including various groups of non-state actors. As most resources will have to be provided voluntarily, the levels and forms of participation are crucial and the chapter concludes with the argument that the incentives need to be right and that both public and private participation in these funding mechanisms are required to make them effective and legitimate.

Access to medicines – such as antiretroviral therapy (ARV) for HIV/AIDS – constitutes an important field of conflict and offers a pertinent example concerning the provision of global public goods. Chapter 7, 'AIDS and Access to Medicines: Brazil, South Africa and Global Health Governance' by Jan Peter Wogart, Gilberto Calcagnotto, Wolfgang Hein and Christian von Soest, tries to unravel the dynamics of these conflicts by focusing on different types of actors (transnational pharmaceutical companies, transnational and national civil society organizations, national governments and legal institutions) and their respective roles at the interfaces between global and national politics. Based on the analysis of conflicts centring on Brazil and South Africa, the authors conclude that it is possible to develop a countervailing power to seemingly dominant transnational corporations and to the drive towards the creation of global markets through WTO agreements. This is based on the discursive power of global civil society in the field of basic human rights and strong national politics in these larger and middle-income developing countries. Global discourses unified Brazilian and South African governments with a range of global civil society allies in their respective struggles for affordable medicines. Yet, global discourses also had a decisive impact on forcing South Africa to accept treatment as a norm to address HIV/AIDS. The innovative and norm-building capacity of global civil society has, in some contexts, been sufficiently powerful to make governments as well as transnational corporations more responsive to human rights, at least in the fight against HIV/AIDS.

The conflicts over access to ARVs for the treatment of HIV/AIDS, analysed in Chapter 7, reveal how closely different fields of global governance are linked and how they can have beneficial or deleterious impacts on health depending on how, by whom and where they are managed. Trade rules in particular have an important impact on many GHG issues, but so far there have been hardly any governance arrangements to deal with conflicts arising between the international trade regime and the regime of health. Chapter 8, 'International Trade and Health: Loose Governance Arrangements across Sectors' by Matthias Helble, Emily Mok, Benedikte Dal, Nusaraporn Keesomboon and Nick Drager, focuses on the questions of coordination and cooperation between the two regimes, which until the mid-1990s was not seen as a particularly urgent issue.

The later chapters of the book discuss the roles of specific types of actors active in global health governance, further elaborating on some of the themes presented by Walt and colleagues in Chapter 3. These chapters define their units of analysis and then proceed to analyse their resources and strategies to influence GHG. There has been a great deal of debate and acrimony over the role of commercial organizations in global governance. The global shift in the health sector to a more private-friendly environment since the 1990s is seen by some as a pernicious trend threatening to corrupt governance systems, with social objectives being subverted by commercial ones. Others argue that the vast resources and global reach of some commercial actors makes them indispensable partners in addressing social concerns – including those of ill-health.

In Chapter 9, 'Commercial Health Governance', Kent Buse and Chris Naylor examine three ways in which the commercial sector is involved in global health governance – through establishing private regulatory systems, through attempting to influence public regulation, and more recently through 'co-regulation' with the public sector. They illustrate how the involvement of the commercial sector has had both beneficial and detrimental consequences for global public health. In different situations, commercial sector actors have demonstrated willingness both to defend their own interests to the detriment of public health and to work constructively with the public sector in developing countries. The authors argue that some form of involvement is both inevitable and desirable. The challenge is to engage the commercial sector in ways which will lead to the most positive outcomes. When self-regulation fails to do this, public health advocates should attempt to draw industry into co-regulatory arrangements. Where these also prove inadequate, formal public sector governance may be required.

During the last decades, civil society organizations (CSOs), an umbrella term for such diverse groups as NGOs, research organizations, faith-based organizations and private foundations, have rapidly increased their presence and their impact on global health governance. David McCoy, one of the authors of the Global Health Watch (2005) report, and Margaret Hilson, an activist in the Canadian Public Health Association, begin their chapter, 'Civil Society, its Organizations, and Global Health Governance', with a short overview on the disparate roles that different sectors of civil society play in GHG, concluding that a 'careful navigation through a landscape populated with a diverse range of actors and institutions' is needed. The authors identify five sets of activities undertaken by CSOs in global health: (i) participation in the decision-making structures of global institutions; (ii) lobbying and influencing decision-making structures; (iii) improving transparency and accountability; (iv) supporting the capacities of the south in more effectively participating in intergovernmental governance; and (v) opposing certain policies of global institutions. The final section of the chapter analyses the ambivalent relationship between CSOs and the WHO as expressed in the reluctance of the WHO to extend and include CSOs more formally in the governance of the organization and in the struggle between CSOs and corporate actors concerning the influence of such actors on the WHO. Reference to the People's Health Movement, the access to treatment campaign and the Framework Convention on Tobacco Control illustrates the growing impact of CSOs on global health governance.

Foundations as philanthropic organizations can be seen as part of civil society, but while CSOs were discussed by McCoy and Hilson largely in relation to their advocacy functions, foundations have played a more prominent role in the financing of health activities. Lately – in particular but not only through the largesse of the Bill and Melinda Gates Foundation – these organizations have gained a very prominent role in GHG. Chapter 11, 'The Role of Foundations in Global Governance for Health', by John Wyn Owen, Graham Lister and Sally Stansfield, discusses the heterogeneous 'landscape' of foundations and describes their efforts to promote innovation, contribute to global redistribution and complement government activities. Recent attempts to consolidate European cooperation between foundations with a global health remit are presented and efforts to develop standards of good practice and an integrated legal framework for foundations are compared with activities in the USA. Foundations have already played an important role in incubating and supporting global health partnerships, and the authors are among those who see the value in improving the alignment and harmonization of these initiatives as evidenced by the participation of the Bill and Melinda Gates Foundation in the IHP and H8 (the Health 8, an informal group of eight important health organizations). The authors argue that the contributions of foundations to GHG could be strengthened by extending cooperation with other organizations at regional and global levels, improving accountability and operating principles, and pressing for an appropriate international legal framework while continuing their good work as 'charitable venture capitalists'.

In the vernacular of music culture, energetic, expressive dancing is best done in a 'mosh pit', the crowded area in front of the stage at a gig. Global health governance needs a mosh pit: a less structured, non-hierarchic forum where multiple actors with different interests and ideas can come together and 'thrash-out' global health issues. In Chapter 12, Kent Buse and Andrew Harmer argue that global health partnerships (GHP) perform this function. The results have been impressive, and are documented in this chapter: innovative finance mechanisms, new forms of cooperation, respected norms of good governance and radical shifts in behaviour, all of which have led to a re-orientation of global health priorities – the litmus test of global health governance. But as anyone who has hurled themselves into a mosh pit will testify, the experience can be bruising: alignment and harmonization are problematic; roles and responsibilities left in the cloakroom; and an overstretched, under-resourced, mosh pit staff lost in the crowd. The authors recommend protective clothing: embrace the Paris agenda; adopt standard operating procedures; improve oversight; and acknowledge the 'invisible P' – the people – of partnerships. Dressed in appropriate attire, the mosh pit is an exhilarating and necessary arena for global health governance to provide better health for all.

The 'Governance of Chronic Diseases' by David Stuckler, Corinna Hawkes and Derek Yach, adds to a growing body of evidence that the global rise of chronic noncommunicable diseases has not been met with a policy response proportionate to the size of the problem. In the analysis, the authors introduce a novel 'input-output' model of governance to set up criteria for governance success and failure. The authors first point to a set of political-economy factors (or what they term 'inputs' to policy) – the historical orientation of health systems toward acute infectious care, the slow and steady rise versus the rapid and variable outbreak of infectious disease, low levels of public awareness – that are weakening the response to chronic diseases by civil society, market, state and global players. Next, they systematically review the actions of these relevant chronic disease actors (or what they term 'outputs' of policy), revealing incoherence across the WHO and other UN bodies that is perpetuated between health and non-health ministries and among NGOs. The chapter proposes that the WHO is the best positioned organization to correct the observed failures in chronic disease governance, but that it must first address the political-economy problems that are driving the insufficient prioritization of chronic diseases as well as resolve its own lack of coordination on chronic disease control. Building upon the strategies used in the WHO Framework Convention on Tobacco Control, an example of a successful global chronic disease governance intervention, the authors suggest, would be a good place to start.

In Chapter 14, 'Fighting HIV/AIDS and the Future of Health Systems', Nina Veenstra and Alan Whiteside also look beyond infectious diseases. They critically discuss the frequent assumption that the rising resources made available in vertical strategies of GHG (focusing on HIV/AIDS) might also contribute to the strengthening of health systems in the recipient countries. Based largely on the case of South Africa, Veenstra and Whiteside offer a systematic analysis of this hypothesis and look at the synergies which exist between resources to fight HIV/AIDS and the strengthening of national health systems as well as the many unintended effects which rather tend to undermine national systems. They conclude that poor countries face difficulties in absorbing large quantities of resources transferred by a great number of donors (coordination, corruption, inducing aid dependency). There is also a tendency for global policy networks to create an 'influential global policy elite' that at times pursues interests different to those held by the people affected by policy changes, drawing attention to the issues of 'legitimacy and appropriateness of reforms'. Yet, there are also opportunities for (re-) constructing health systems if the effects on national structures are taken into account in all vertical programmes – and the authors conclude that effectively addressing the AIDS epidemic will require such an approach (that is increasingly termed 'diagonal').

Ilona Kickbusch concludes the analysis of global health governance with a forward-looking chapter focusing on two dimensions of the global health action sphere: development and interdependence. 'Moving Global Health Governance Forward' argues that a new geography of power has emerged which is very different from the short unilateral period following the collapse of the Soviet Union. At present, global health governance is being conducted in a non-polar world of 'unstructured plurality'. This context provides a new dynamic for multilateral institutions, as they can strengthen their role as platforms and brokers between the myriads of actors as well as gaining acceptance for strengthening international law for health. The emerging economies and new power centres are also increasingly using the existing institutions – such as the WHO – to increase their own influence on global decision-making for health. In addition to this role for the WHO, Kickbusch calls for a new treaty on the provision of global public goods for health and for increased capacity-building for health diplomacy, so as, among other things, to ensure that foreign policy is viewed through a public health lens, and ensuring more joined-up policymaking across sectors where health outcomes are affected. For Kickbusch, as for most other contributors to this volume, it is essential that all future efforts are geared to the view of health as a right of all people.

Notes

1. '... to act as the directing and co-ordinating authority on international health work' (Chapter II, Article 2(a))
2. Agreements on improving the aid environment, particularly the Paris Declaration on Aid Effectiveness (2005) and the Global Task Team on improving AIDS coordination among multilateral and international donors (2005) were negotiated as reciprocal commitments with obligations for both donors (particularly multilaterals) and recipient governments.
3. The complexity of the GHG landscape, particularly the proliferation of global initiatives which channel funds through multiple mechanisms and often promote disparate or competing policy priorities and approaches, makes it difficult for national health systems to make an efficient use of external resources. All these organizations demand the attention of local administrations, dedicated reports and, as a whole, create a flexible but chaotic and onerous arrangement for developing countries.
4. For example, Médicins Sans Frontières (MSF), Knowledge Ecology Institute, Third World Network, Drugs for Neglected Diseases initiative (DNDi), the International Federation of Pharmaceutical Manufacturers and Associations (IFPMA).
5. The Rio Group comprises 13 countries: Argentina, Brazil, Bolivia, Chile, Costa Rica, Cuba, Ecuador, El Salvador, Honduras, Peru, Suriname, Uruguay and Venezuela.
6. The 'Westphalian system of international relations' refers to the role of the Westphalian Peace in 1648 in the development of a system of international relations between sovereign nation-states. Discussion on global governance has contributed many elements towards understanding the (still incomplete) transformation of traditional international relations towards a system of post-Westphalian global politics. This is characterized by an increasing transnational cooperation of non-state actors leading to dynamics and opportunities which increasingly limit the political options of nation-states (see Linklater, 1996; Fidler, 2004).

References

Abbott, F.M., 'The WTO Medicines Decision: World Pharmaceutical Trade and the Protection of Public Health', *American Journal of International Law*, 99 (2005): 317–58.
Aginam, O., *Global Health Governance: International Law and Public Health in a Divided World* (Toronto: Toronto University Press, 2005).
Blouin, C., N. Drager and R. Smith (eds), *International Trade in Health and Services and the GATS: Current Issues and Debates* (Washington, DC: The World Bank, 2006).
Burris, S., P. Drahos and C. Shearing, 'Nodal Governance', *Australian Journal of Legal Philosophy*, 30 (2005): 30–58.
Buse, K., 'Governing Public-Private Infectious Disease Partnerships', *Brown Journal of World Affairs*, 10 (2) (2004): 225–42.
Buse, K. and A. Harmer, 'Seven Habits of Highly Effective Global Public-Private Health Partnerships: Practice and Potential', *Social Science and Medicine*, 64 (2) (2007): 259–71.

Buse, K. and G. Walt, 'Global Public-Private Partnerships: Part I – A New Development in Health?', *Bulletin of the WHO*, 78 (4) (2000a): 549–61.
Buse, K. and G. Walt, 'Global Public-Private Partnerships: Part II – What are the Health Issues for Global Governance', *Bulletin of the WHO*, 78 (5) (2000b): 699–709.
Cooper, A.F., J.J. Kirton and T. Schrecker (eds), *Governing Global Health: Challenge, Response, Innovation* (Aldershot: Ashgate, 2007).
Davis, M., F. Samuels and K. Buse, 'AIDS and the Private Sector: the Case of South Africa', Overseas Development Institute Briefing Paper 30, ODI, London, 2007.
Doyel, C. and P. Patel, 'Civil Society Organisations and Global Health Initiatives: Problems of Legitimacy', *Social Science and Medicine*, 66(9)(2008): 1928–38.
Fidler, D.P., *SARS, Governance and the Globalization of Disease* (Basingstoke: Palgrave, 2004).
Fidler, D.P., 'From International Sanitary Conventions to Global Health Security: the New International Health Regulations', *Chinese Journal of International Law*, 4 (2) (2005): 325–92.
Fidler, D.P., 'Architecture amidst Anarchy: Global Health's Quest for Governance', *Global Health Governance*, 1 (1) (2007): 1–17.
Fidler, D.P. and N. Drager, 'Health and Foreign Policy', *Bulletin of the WHO*, 84 (9) (2006): 687.
Global Health Watch, *Global Health Watch 2005/2006 – An Alternative World Health Report* (London and New York: Global Health Watch, 2005).
Hein, W. and L. Kohlmorgen, 'Global Health Governance: Conflicts on Global Social Rights', *Global Social Policy*, 8 (1) (2008): 80–108.
Hein, W., S. Bartsch and L. Kohlmorgen, *Global Health Governance and the Fight against HIV/AIDS* (Basingstoke: Palgrave, 2007).
Held, D., A. McGrew, D. Goldblatt and J. Perraton, *Global Transformations: Politics, Economics and Culture* (Oxford: Polity Press, 1999).
Kaul, I. and P. Conceição (eds), *The New Public Finance: Responding to Global Challenges* (Oxford: Oxford University Press, 2006).
Kickbusch, I., G. Silberschmidt and P. Buss, 'Global Health Diplomacy: the Need for New Perspectives, Strategic Approaches and Skills in Global Health', *Bulletin of the WHO*, 85(3) (2007): 230–2.
Kimball, A.M., *Risky Business: Infectious Disease in the Era of Global Trade* (Aldershot: Ashgate, 2006).
Labonté, R. and T. Schrecker, 'Globalization and Social Determinants of Health', *Globalization and Health*, 3 (5) (2007): 1–10.
Lee, K. (ed.), *Health Impacts of Globalization: Towards Global Governance* (Basingstoke: Palgrave, 2003).
Lee, K., *World Health Organization* (London: Routledge, 2008).
Lee, K. and J. Collin (eds), *Global Change and Health* (Milton Keynes: Open University Press, 2005).
Lee, K. and H. Goodman, 'Global Policy Networks: the Propagation of Health Care Financing Reform since 1980', in K. Lee, K. Buse and S. Fustukian (eds), *Health Policy in a Globalising World* (Cambridge: Cambridge University Press, 2002), pp. 97–119.
Lee, K., K. Buse and S. Fustukian (eds), *Health Policy in a Globalising World* (Cambridge: Cambridge University Press, 2002).
Linklater, A., 'Citizenship and Sovereignty in the Post-Westphalian State', *European Journal of International Relations*, 2 (1) (1996): 77–103.
Lobstein, T., 'Marketing to Children: Understanding the Need for International Standards', International Obesity Task Force Briefing Paper, London, 2006,

http://www.iotf.org/documents/iotfmarketingbriefsep2006.pdf (accessed 26 May 2008).

Long, N., *Encounters at the Interface* (Wageningen: Wageningen Studies in Sociology, 1989).

Mackintosh, M. and M. Koivusalo (eds), *Commercialization of Health Care: Global and Local Dynamics and Policy Responses* (Basingstoke: Palgrave, 2005).

McInnes, C. and K. Lee, 'Health, Security and Foreign Policy', *Review of International Studies*, 32 (2006): 5–23.

Morrison, S.J., 'What Role for U.S. Assistance in the Fight against Global HIV/AIDS?' Working Paper, the Brookings Institution, Washington, DC, 2006.

Poku, N., A. Whiteside and B. Sandkjaer (eds), *AIDS and Governance* (Aldershot: Ashgate, 2007).

Prins, G., 'AIDS and Global Security', *International Affairs*, 80 (5) (2004): 931–52.

Rosenau, J., 'Global Governance in the Twenty-First Century', *Global Governance*, 1(1) (1995): 13–43.

Seckinelgin, H., 'A Global Disease and its Governance: HIV/AIDS in Sub-Saharan Africa and the Agency of NGOs', *Global Governance*, 11 (3) (2005): 351–68.

Smith, R., R. Beaglehole, D. Woodward and N. Drager (eds) *Global Public Goods for Health: Health, Economic, and Public Health Perspectives* (Oxford: Oxford University Press, 2003).

Thomas, C. and M. Weber, 'The Politics of Global Health Governance: Whatever Happened to "Health for All by the Year 2000"?', *Global Governance*, 10 (2004): 187–205.

Walt, G. and K. Buse, 'Global Cooperation in International Public Health', in M. Merson, D. Jamison and A. Mills (eds), *International Public Health* (Boston: Jones and Bartlett, 2005), pp. 649–80.

Werner, D. and D. Sanders, *Questioning the Solution: the Politics of Primary Health Care & Child Survival* (Palo Alto: Healthwrights, 1997).

World Diabetes Foundation, 'Factsheet', 2008, http://www.worlddiabetesfoundation.org/composite-35.htm (accessed 9 June 2008).

WHO, 'Evidence and Health Information', 2008, http://www.searo.who.int/EN/Section1243/Section1382/Section1386/Section1898_9438.htm (accessed 9 June 2008).

WTO/WHO, *WTO Agreements & Public Health: A Joint Study by the WHO and the WTO Secretariat* (WTO/WHO: Geneva, 2002), http://www.wto.org/english/res_e/booksp_e/who_wto_e.pdf (accessed 26 February 2008).

Yach, D., C. Hawkes, C.L. Gould and K.J. Hofmann, 'The Global Burden of Chronic Diseases: Overcoming Impediments to Prevention and Control', *Journal of the American Medical Association*, 291 (2004): 2616–22.

Zacher, M.W. and T.J. Keefe, *The Politics of Global Health Governance* (Basingstoke: Palgrave, 2008).

2
Historical Dimensions of Global Health Governance

Virginia Berridge, Kelly Loughlin and Rachel Herring

Introduction

This chapter aims to highlight the potential of historical analysis as a means to provide context for the concepts and definitions mobilized in discussions of global health governance (GHG). We argue that many aspects of current debates and activities were inherent in the nineteenth and twentieth centuries and in the role of international organizations. The recent discourse of 'globalization' represents changed forces within international health and, as such, deserves unpacking as a political construct and as a subject for contemporary history.

History and global governance

The ideas and claims embedded in the concept of global health governance can be usefully broken down into *globalization* and *global health governance*. Globalization is a much debated and contested concept. It has been described as the 'widening, deepening and speeding up of the world interconnectedness in all aspects of contemporary life' (Held et al., 1999: 2). Held et al. (1999: 1) argue that:

> the world is rapidly being moulded into a shared social space by economic and technological forces... [and] developments in one region of the world can have profound consequences for the life chances of individuals or communities on the other side of the globe. For many globalization is also associated with a sense of political fatalism and chronic insecurity in that the sheer scale of contemporary social and economic change appears to outstrip the capacity of national governments or citizens to control, contest or resist that change. The limits of national politics, in other words, are forcefully suggested.

The consequences of globalization for health are the subject of much analysis (for example, Lee, 2003a, 2003b; Lee and Collin, 2005; Labonté and

Schrecker, 2006). The debates around GHG arise because globalization is seen to have specific health consequences that cannot be effectively addressed by existing forms of health governance. The emergence or intensification of transborder health risks such as global climate change or the role of international corporations appears to challenge existing forms of international health governance (IHG) which are defined by national borders. Global issues, it is argued, may be partly or wholly beyond the control of governments (Lee, 2003a). The potential weakness associated with forms of governance anchored around the cooperation of nation-states points to the growth in number and influence of non-state actors in the national, international and global arenas, for example, civil society groups, non-governmental organizations (NGOs), social movements and private companies.

Like globalization, global health and global health governance are 'slippery' concepts which have eluded attempts to define them with any degree of clarity. Health governance refers to 'the actions and means adopted by a society to organize itself in the promotion and protection of the health of its population' (Dodgson et al., 2002: 6). Such organization can be formal or informal, the mechanisms of governance can be local, regional, national or international, and health governance can be public or private or a combination of the two. This description of global health governance is difficult to operationalize historically, because of its almost boundless nature. The associated idea of good governance, which emphasizes the need for governance mechanisms and organizations that are appropriate, representative, accountable and transparent, is more specific and clearly located in a historical trajectory – the emergence and expansion of concepts of liberal democracy. Historically speaking these concepts are associated with the development of the European nation-states, a feature implicit within the above definition of health governance (the way society organizes itself to protect its population). And herein lies a key element in the emerging paradigm of GHG, and an important claim concerning the distinction from existing forms of international health governance (IHG).

Ideas of good governance (representative, accountable) fit well with the nation-state and with forms of IHG that are anchored in the cooperation of states and therefore still serve discrete constituencies. However, are such concepts applicable to the kind of social and political spaces that now exist between and beyond states? According to the literature on GHG, the proliferation of such spaces is a recent phenomenon, both a consequence of and a response to globalization. The increased number and influence of non-state actors operating in these spaces, individually or in association with a range of other state and non-state actors, is considered a defining feature of the transition from international to global health governance and one requiring the implementation or adaptation of recognized concepts of good governance. Our following survey, however, indicates that many of those issues – the mix of public and private in international health, the influence of groups and organizations not formally associated with the state and the health consequences of globalization – are not new but recognizable from the past.

The development of international health governance

The development of international cooperation in health can be considered over four periods:

1. The nineteenth century and the first international sanitary conferences.
2. The interwar period, with the establishment of international organizations, such as the League of Nations (LN), and the rise of the American foundations.
3. The immediate post-war era, dominated by the history of the World Health Organization (WHO).
4. The more recent period since the 1970s with the proliferation of new players at the international level.

The international sanitary conferences, 1851–1903

The beginning of international health cooperation (that is, cooperation between two or more states) is traditionally located in the series of international sanitary conferences held between 1851 and 1903 (Goodman, 1971; Howard-Jones, 1975). Harrison has, however, argued that a cut-off point came in 1815. Prior to that date, quarantine was used for objectives other than public health, but afterwards the nature of international relations changed (Harrison, 2005).[1] The spread of epidemic diseases, especially cholera and yellow fever, was an important motive force. The two cholera pandemics that engulfed Europe between 1830 and 1847 were facilitated by the increased movement of goods and people between east and west that accompanied developments in international commerce: steamships, rail, and later the construction of the Suez Canal. The long-established response to epidemic disease, such as the plague, was to close ports and impose quarantine, but that proved difficult to sustain in the age of international commerce. Quarantine measures and disruption to shipping served to undermine the maritime economies of nations like Britain and France, whereas the speed of steamships meant that people and goods would have disembarked before a disease declared itself. The international sanitary conferences emerged as a mechanism for responding to the political and economic threats which a new epidemic disease such as cholera posed to the European powers.

Political and commercial issues were the primary concerns of the first conference held in Paris in 1851 and attended by diplomatic and medical representatives of twelve governments. Commerce and competition were high on the agenda. The Middle East stimulated much of the debate; it was not only the area through which epidemics reached Europe, but was also the key arena in which European powers had jostled for position since the 1830s. Economic and imperialist conflicts surfaced at regular intervals throughout the subsequent conferences convened between 1859 and 1903. For example, the 1885 Rome conference was provoked largely by Franco-British tensions in Egypt. Britain occupied Egypt in 1881 and dominated the 'sanitary council' of Alexandria (one of a series of regional councils). Italy and France resented Britain's anti-quarantine stance when cholera broke out in Egypt in 1893. Britain retaliated by threatening to divert shipping away from the French-run Suez Canal because of French claims that cholera was being introduced from British India.

The conventions and regulations that emerged from the majority of these conferences were never successfully ratified by participating governments. But in 1903 a conference held in Paris produced what Goodman describes as the 'first effective convention' (Goodman, 1971: 23). The 1903 convention formed the basis of the regulations governing quarantine on land and sea until the Second World War. In 1903, representatives of twenty governments including the USA, Egypt, Persia and Brazil, as well as European nations, recommended the establishment of an International Office of Public Health. The Office International d'Hygiène Publique (OIHP) was established in 1907. It was based in Paris but maintained close communication with the regional sanitary councils and the health authorities in various countries. The primary function of the OIHP was the collation and dissemination of epidemiological intelligence. Governments were obliged to inform the office of the steps being taken to implement the sanitary conventions and the office could suggest modifications. The OIHP's coordination through regional councils and its focus on the health authorities of states prefigures the organizational emphasis of later bodies such as the WHO.

The establishment of the OIHP marked the transition from the era of international conventions to that of permanent international health organizations, of which the Pan American Sanitary Bureau (PASB) was the first in 1903. The idea of an international commission for the notification and exchange of information on epidemics had first been proposed at a sanitary conference in 1874. The consensus that began to emerge at the close of the century is best understood in relation to a range of forces, the most immediate of which were the cholera epidemics of 1883 and 1897. However, the development signalled by the emergence of the first international health organizations was part of a broader movement toward international cooperation, which had been growing in range and complexity throughout the nineteenth century. And it is in this broader movement that key aspects of the debate on GHG have some resonance.

The broader context of international cooperation

The century from the Congress of Vienna (1815) to the outbreak of war in 1914 saw the emergence of wide-ranging international cooperation in many

Table 2.1 Development of international organizations, 1815–1914

	INGOs* created	Still active at mid-20th century	IGOs** created	Still active at mid-20th century
1815–49	4	4	1	1
1850–54	1	1	0	0
1855–59	4	1	2	0
1860–64	6	3	1	0
1865–69	9	4	5	3
1870–74	8	6	3	1
1875–79	17	9	2	2
1880–84	11	6	3	2
1885–89	29	16	2	1
1890–94	35	19	3	3
1895–99	38	20	2	1
1900–04	61	22	5	2
1905–09	131	42	4	1
1910–14	112	38	4	3
Total	466	191	37	20

Notes: * International non-governmental organizations; ** Intergovernmental organizations.
Source: Lyons (1963: 14).

areas: law, economics, labour, religious and intellectual movements, social and welfare organizations and humanitarian causes. According to Lyons (1963: 12), there were nearly 3000 international gatherings in this period and the creation of more than 450 private or non-governmental international organizations (INGOs) and over 30 governmental ones. Developments in transport and communication facilitated this level of international activity, and national governments vied for the patronage of international conferences. Many of these gatherings and organizations addressed health issues, broadly defined, and as Table 2.1 suggests, non-state actors played an important role in nineteenth-century internationalism.

Developments that can be considered as having a health dimension can be broken down into two fields: intellectual cooperation and consensus in science and social, religious and humanitarian movements.

Disputes concerning the aetiology of diseases such as cholera bedevilled many of the early international sanitary conferences. Scientific developments, such as Snow's work in London and Koch's in Germany, had no impact on the conferences that followed these discoveries (1859 and 1885 respectively). But effective cooperation in areas of science and medicine did make progress through the century (Crawford, 1992). Initially this took the form of international congresses on specific areas, for example, the first statistical congress (1853), the first congress of ophthalmologists (1857), the first congress of chemists (1860). Many of these went on to form international committees and associations. The statistical congress of 1853 initiated the preparation of a nomenclature of the causes of death that would be applicable to all countries. This was adopted and revised at subsequent meetings and taken forward by the International Statistical Institute formed in 1890. International associations that cut across different areas of specialization also began to emerge, such as the Association of Academics (1900) which brought together leading national scientific associations. Intergovernmental cooperation in areas such as measurement and mapping developed largely from these international initiatives, for example, the International Geodetic Association (1867), and the International Agreement on the Unification of Pharmacopoeial Formulas for Potent Drugs (1906).

At the close of the century the momentum for cooperation between non-state actors, and later between states, focused on the exchange of information, and represented the first moves towards an international vocabulary (standards, classification) in medicine and science. The social, religious and humanitarian movements that emerged in the nineteenth century were more complex and diverse in their development. Many were characterized by popular and even mass support but there was also the pattern of conferences leading to more permanent committees or organizations. A burgeoning middle class and the spread of missionary activities supported many of the activities, whereas the shared experience of industrialization and urbanization spawned common social problems across a number of states. The first of four International Congresses of Charities, Correction and Philanthropy met in Brussels in 1865. These were followed in 1869 by a new series of international congresses on public and private charity that met at irregular intervals up to 1914. According to Lyons, these meetings were attended by representatives of a wide range of philanthropic organizations and the discussions covered a broad spectrum of issues: food production, alcoholism, prison conditions, medical assistance to the poor, rehabilitation, infant mortality and the protection of women and girls (Lyons, 1963: 264). In 1900 an international committee was formed and a bureau of information and studies followed in 1907. This umbrella association emphasized the need for information exchange and an increasing number of governments sent representatives to its conferences.

A number of international 'single issue' reform movements also came to the fore, a development seen as early as 1840 with the International Anti-Slavery Conference and later the International Committee of the Red Cross (1864). In the health and welfare field these associations could be popular in orientation or focused on specialist expertise. Some, such as the congresses on alcohol, and the resultant International Temperance Bureau (1906), mingled both activism and science (Bruun et al., 1975), as did the international Central Bureau for the Campaign against Tuberculosis (1902), which emerged from a series of international conferences dating back to the 1860s. The pattern here seems to be one of initial activity by non-state actors in the international arena leading to greater intergovernmental involvement. The relationship between national associations and national governments would need to be explored in greater detail to understand the mechanisms involved. Interestingly, it seems that many of these movements were characterized by a mix of governmental, voluntary and local activity, such as the policing conventions around the 'white slave trade', which stemmed from the 1899 International Bureau for the Suppression of Traffic in Women and Children (Lyons, 1963: 274–85).

A significant development at the close of this period was the establishment of a platform organization, the Central Office of International Associations in Brussels (1907), an organization that changed to the Union of International Associations (UIA) at the first World Congress of International Organizations in 1910. This coordinating centre for international activity produced a wealth of documentation, including annual indices, which provides the most comprehensive guide to international activity at the turn of the century, although it has yet to receive sustained historical investigation (Seary, 1996).

The interwar period

The interwar period was characterized by two interrelated developments, the rise of a new style of international corporate philanthropy, such as that developed by the Rockefeller Foundation (RF) and the establishment of permanent international organs, in particular the League of Nations (LN). The interwar developments have received detailed historical investigation and in discussing the main developments of the time (corporate philanthropy and the LN) the depth and degree of interlinking between them should be noted, in terms both of financial support and personnel. For example, the League of Nations Health Organization (LNHO) drew between a third and a half of its budget from the RF (Weindling, 1995: 137). Indeed, the relationship is described by Dubin as symbiotic and tied to the creation of an elite of biomedical and health specialists at the centre of a worldwide biomedical/public health episteme:

> The RF helped Rajchman [the League's medical director] recruit staff; awarded travel grants to individuals visiting Geneva; recommended persons for expert bodies; made its own staff available for special purposes; helped assess requests for technical assistance; provided additional help to governments receiving LN assistance; and funded its own schools, laboratories and institutes of persons engaged in the LNHO.
>
> (Dubin, 1995: 72)

This level of involvement by the RF and the creation of an international cadre of public health expertise is subject to ongoing historical debate. Historians have discussed how best to interpret the role of American foundation involvement in international health during a period of US political isolationism – was it benign philanthropy or American imperialism by private means? And how does one interpret 'social medicine'? As a movement to place medicine on a socio-economic and humanitarian basis or as the spearhead of professional imperialism? These debates echo concerns raised in the GHG literature, especially in relation to the contemporary role of corporate philanthropy and public-private partnerships (see Owen et al. in Chapter 11 and Buse and Harmer, Chapter 12 below).

The role of American foundations

The years between 1901 and 1913 witnessed the emergence of a new form of philanthropy, characterized by the RF and other largely American institutions – the Milbank Memorial Fund, Commonwealth Fund, Sage Foundation (Bulmer, 1995). This new form of philanthropy developed a research-oriented view of social improvement and introduced a wider, international dimension to research and sponsorship activities, especially in the area of science and medicine. The scale of the RF's financial input into the LNHO has already been noted, but the foundation also developed its own initiatives through its International Health Commission (1913) and through support for clinics, training schemes, schools of public health and laboratory services through the world (Berliner, 1985; Farley, 1995). Importantly, the RF pursued a much more interventionist and ameliorative programme than the American government was willing to contemplate at the time (that is, the RF backed the LNHO although the USA was not a member state). For some historians, however, the RF is seen as a stalking horse for wider American political interests, and as a central agent of biomedical imperialism – exporting a US model of public health across the world (Arnove, 1980; Birn and Solorzano, 1999).

More recently however the complexity of the RF, and its degree of autonomy from the American administration, and awareness that its programmes changed over time have come to the fore. Undoubtedly, US political interests were furthered by RF involvement in the LN and through its programmes, for example in the Far East (Manderson, 1995) and in Latin America (Cueto, 1995, 1997). According to Gillespie's work on Australia and the Pacific Islands, 'There was no simple imposition of an American model on compliant local populations... [but] a complicated process of bargaining and compromise [that] led to local interests dominating the implementation of the Rockefeller programme' (Gillespie, 1995: 382). Moreover, Weindling emphasizes the relative freedom of the American foundations, as they were without public or political constraints and had no need to placate the interests of the medical profession as such (Weindling, 2002). For example, in the aftermath of the First World War, RF support helped develop a system of socialized primary health-care in Serbia, and contributed to primary health-care initiatives in the USA and abroad. This relative freedom also enabled the foundations to support 'unpopular' health issues. For example, the RF provided backing for child guidance and mental hygiene, and the Commonwealth Fund targeted mental health during the interwar period (Thomson, 1995).

Through its focus on training and institution-building the RF was fundamental in creating an international network of public health experts. Drawing on the universalism of science, the RF emphasized technology transfer and the exchange of trained personnel. During the interwar period instruments developed in America to measure community health performance were transferred to Europe via the RF (Murard, 2005). As Murard notes it was not a simple case of applying the American 'Appraisal Form for Community Health Work' to European nations, but rather involved reframing and transforming the instrument into the League of Nations' collection of 'Life, Environment and Health Indices', a much broader instrument than its American 'parent'. This approach is seen by some to accompany the scientization of social policy on the one hand and the primacy of professionalized, increasingly technocratic solutions to public health on the other – noting how the RF's disease eradication campaigns in Australia, the Pacific Islands and Latin America became increasingly laboratory-based (see Gillespie, 1995; Farley, 1995 for this transition).

International health and the League of Nations

The technical agencies of the League of Nations, the Health Organization, and the International Labour Office (ILO) followed a similar pattern to that noted in the RF programmes – a narrowing of focus. Initially the ILO had an expansive vision of its role in health and welfare, legitimized by the Treaty of Versailles which assigned it the role of protecting 'the worker against sickness, disease and injury arising out of his (sic) employment' (Weindling, 1995: 139). But the broad vision was restricted early on. Weindling comments: 'in seeking to justify its reformist demands in the universalist terms of science, it had to devolve initiatives to scientific experts whose empirically based approaches were necessarily limited to what could be proven in the laboratory' (ibid.). Consequently, the focus of the ILO became overly technical, anchored around the production of scientific evidence of the health effects of particular hazards. Moreover, despite its overall premise that welfare was determined by socio-economic conditions, no attempt was made to correlate economic trends with the mortality and morbidity data present in its labour statistics.

The LNHO, the agency with responsibility for public health and social medicine showed a similar narrowing of focus, signalled by its separation from the Social Section in 1920 (Miller, 1995).[2] The primary concern of the LNHO in the 1920s was the scientific universalism of standard-setting, in terms of biological and morbidity/mortality statistics (Sizaret, 1988; Cockburn, 1991; Mazumdar, 2003). Indeed, by 1937 approximately 72 per cent of the world's population was covered by LNHO statistics. This emphasis on international standards did, however, provide leverage for broader health debates during the economic depression of the 1930s. The LNHO developed cooperative programmes with the ILO that focused on developing social medicine on economic bases – how diet, housing and economic conditions shaped health were key areas of research. Scientific expertise served radical reform in areas like nutrition, as British scientists criticized their government by invoking nutrition standards endorsed by the LNHO/ILO – forcing it to raise the minimum standards used in calculating unemployment and maternity benefits.

The international health section of the LN was, as would be its successor the WHO, anchored around the health ministries of participating national governments. However, through the 1930s the LNHO sought greater autonomy, aided by RF money. In moving towards independent research initiatives and settling optimum standards it hinted at the kind of autonomy condemned by some contemporaries: the LNHO should not presume to 'constitute itself as super-health authority which supervises or criticises the public health administrations of the world' (Sir George Buchanan 1934, quoted by Weindling, 1995: 143).

'Unpopular' issues, such as sexually transmitted infections, were championed by voluntary initiatives and kept at a distance from arenas dominated by state actors (Weindling, 1993). It has already been noted that the RF did provide support for mental health initiatives, whereas the ILO focused primarily on economically productive sectors of the population (not the elderly, disabled or mentally ill), and the LNHO avoided the politically controversial issue of birth control. In one case, that of illicit drugs, a separate system emphasizing control of trade, although in the interests of health, was set up in the interwar period. A series of international conventions following the Geneva Convention (1925) established and extended an import certificate system together with limitation of manufacture (Berridge, 2001).

Historically, a particularly interesting aspect of international health in the early twentieth century is that initially there were voluntaristic models for a world health authority, led by the League of Red Cross Societies (LRCS). In line with the new form of philanthropy epitomized by the RF, the LRCS, an off-shoot of the American Red Cross, sought to move away from sporadic relief towards securing community-based welfare (Hutchinson, 1995, 1996). In relation to the LN and its technical agencies, the LRCS was involved early on but later this relationship changed to one where the LN was less interested in NGO opinion (Seary, 1996: 23). This distancing process can also be seen in the reorganization of the LN's Committee on Social Questions, which became entirely governmental in 1936. The UIA, mentioned above, was also sidelined by the development of the LN, which moved the focus of INGOs to Geneva and away from Brussels (the home of the UIA). In 1929 the Federation of International Institutions came into being in Geneva and by 1938 grouped together 42 INGOs, addressing technical matters on the running of INGOs (taxes). In general it was far less ambitious than the UIA.

War, the United Nations and the World Health Organization

The history of international health in the second half of the twentieth century represents the largest and most organizationally complex era of developments in this field. The key difference in the post-war context is one of scale, mainly the scale of participation involving a significant rise in the number of states, the number of intergovernmental organs and specialized agencies and the number of NGOs. This rise in scale and complexity has been intimately related to fundamental shifts in geopolitical structures, such as the dismantling of nineteenth-century colonial empires and the rise and fall of the Soviet bloc. Other significant developments, more specifically related to health and medicine, have also marked the post-war decades, such as the rise of the pharmaceutical and biotechnology sectors, and the emergence of new health threats like atmospheric pollution, and emerging and re-emerging infectious diseases such as HIV and TB.

The most significant and well-documented event in the organization of post-war international health was the creation of the World Health Organization (WHO) as a specialized agency of the United Nations (UN) in 1948. The origins and development of the WHO are covered in a series of 'in-house' or 'insider' histories covering the central agency and the regional offices (WHO, 1958, 1968, 1998; Howard-Jones, 1981; Manuila, 1991). More critical 'outsider' accounts by Siddiqi (1995), Lee (1997) and Brown et al. (2006) have considered the various roles played by the WHO in the shift from international health to global health. This is now an expanding area of historical interest (AHA, 2008; Global Health Histories, 2008). A number of interrelated themes emerge, for example, regionalization, the emergence of political blocs, the issues of politicization and the shifting paradigms of disease eradication, primary health-care, and health sector reform. The issues raised in the literature tend to focus on the role of international health in the context of development. However, it is arguable that international organizations have also been of great policy importance in relation to the policy agendas of developed countries. The WHO's Global Programme on AIDS, for example, disseminated an international ethos of human rights in both developed and developing countries. Concepts of drug and alcohol addiction and dependence gained authority through their association with WHO expert committees (Berridge, 1996; Room, 1984).

The regional structure of the WHO is largely a historical legacy, in that pre-existing regional organizations were absorbed into the new specialized health agency. The six regions (Eastern Mediterranean, Western Pacific, Europe, Americas, Africa, South East Asia) developed from earlier regional structures like the Pan American Sanitary Organization. Siddiqi (1995) argues that this decentralized structure, which delineated broad areas and assigned countries to particular regions was problematic from the start. At the founding of the WHO there was no discussion of potential problems, such as the peculiar delineation of compact geographical boundaries, or the possibility that regional organizations would come under the influence of regional blocs. For example, Pakistan chose to be in the Eastern Mediterranean rather than in South East Asia with India and Afghanistan.

Independence movements and the political nature of regional alliances have been fundamental forces operating within the UN system and its agencies since their inception (Amrith, 2006). For example, the WHO had 48 full members in 1948 and this had risen to 183 full and two associate members by 1993. Although the action of political blocs was not new (for example, the mass withdrawal of socialist states in 1949–50), the structural and political inability of the WHO to absorb the newly emerging post-colonial nations meant that new formations, based on differences in wealth, joined established Cold War ideological distinctions. In response to what was seen as a disparity between voting strength and financial contribution between rich and poor nations (Talbot, 1994; Siddiqi, 1995), the 1960s and the 1970s saw the emergence of blocs, such as the Geneva Group (made up of states that contributed the majority of funds to UN/WHO) and the Group of 77 (an international interest group representing developing countries). North-south (donor/recipient of aid) became a new axis of political and ideological conflict in post-war international health.

The 1970s onwards

This axis structured debates around the 'politicization' of the WHO in the 1970s and 1980s, such as in the 1985 World Health Assembly (WHA) resolutions on Arab health in the territories occupied by Israel, and the health impacts of economic sanctions on Nicaragua. The alignment of developed–developing countries was clear in the subsequent passing of resolutions WHA 38.15 and WHA 38.17, as the USA, Israel and most western countries voted against (Siddiqi, 1995: 8–9). It was also reflected in the attack on the marketing policies of transnational corporations when the WHA adopted an International Code for the Marketing of Breast-Milk Substitutes. This was the culmination of international protest on the issue, and followed an earlier WHA resolution (1974) and the call for a boycott of Nestlé products by the Infant Formula Action Coalition (INFACT) in 1977. NGO-led activism of this kind was a development from nineteenth-century single issue concerns. The ability to generate a consumer boycott of a global product range on a health/development issue was new (Walt, 1993).

A broad-based philosophy of health, which was more sensitive to local requirements and distinctions and was anchored around the provision of primary health-care gained ground at the WHO in the 1970s (Cueto, 2004). The clearest expressions of this development were the Declaration of Alma Ata (1978) which emerged from the International Conference on Primary Health Care, and 'Health for All by the Year 2000', a global strategy emphasizing social justice, equity and the link between health service provision and a nation's socio-economic development (Koivusalo and Ollila, 1997: 109–36). Historically, one can see echoes of the LNHO's work in the 1930s in the developments of the 1970s (Siddiqi, 1995: 193–5). In the 1930s and in the 1970s international health organizations began to emphasize primary health-care (PHC) and an understanding of the economic underpinnings of health. The terminology of 'new public health' and 'health promotion' also began to spread in developed countries through international initiatives such as the Ottawa Charter (1986) (Kickbusch, 2003; Berridge et al., 2006). Economic crisis formed the backdrop to developments in both decades, although the new post-war axis of north-south and the greater representation of poor nations in the machinery of intergovernmental organizations led developing countries to demand a New International Economic Order (supported by the Alma Ata Declaration).

PHC also followed on from critiques of the vertical (disease-specific) programmes developed by the WHO in the 1950s and 1960s, such as the Malaria Eradication Programme (Sidiqqi, 1995; Lee, 1998) and the Smallpox Eradication Programme in India (Bhattacharya, 2004, 2006). Greenough (1995) argues that the use of coercion and intimidation in the final stages (1973–75) of the Smallpox Eradication Programme in South East Asia led to local resistance amongst both health professionals and public to later vaccination campaigns. One of the engines behind PHC was the evidence of successful, low-technology community health-care provided by China's 'barefoot doctors' (China gained membership of the WHO in 1973). According to Lee (1997), the examples of China and Cuba, which were successfully mobilized by the Soviet Union, challenged the prevailing ideology of the WHO, rooted as it was in biomedicine. This challenge also encouraged a renewed interest in traditional medical practices and personnel and during the WHA of 1974 delegates from a range of developing countries began speaking of their traditional medicine as a positive affirmation of their native cultures (Lee, 1997: 38). Moreover, the renewed interest in horizontal programmes (health systems concerns as a whole, rather than disease specific programmes) and the emphasis on appropriateness and community involvement pointed to a more inclusive disciplinary mix in international health. As a former WHO official noted in 1975, in reference to the Malaria Eradication Programme, 'money, time and effort has been unstintingly spent in the belief, seemingly, that the basic laws of ecology and social anthropology would be lifted to allow a magical disappearance of the disease' (quoted in Lee, 1997: 29). However, despite Lee's somewhat romantic account of the WHO's re-orientation it should be noted that while the organization's regular budget was frozen in the early 1980s, the majority of extra-budgetary funds were still directed to disease-specific or technology-specific programmes (Koivusalo and Ollila, 1997: 115–19). Selective primary care, supported by UNICEF, the Rockefeller Foundation and heavily influenced by the USA, began to replace the more inclusive version (Brown et al., 2006).

Although 'Health for All' may have provided a new ideological touchstone for international health, Alma Ata was still based largely on the assumption that states would play the major role in health provision and health development; Alma Ata did not highlight NGOs and non-state organizations more generally. The primacy now accorded to NGOs developed in the 1980s and during a period when major donor countries pursued anti-statist policies in their domestic health sectors. On the international plane this found echoes in the policies of structural adjustment pursued by the International Monetary Fund (IMF) and the World Bank, whose health funding eclipsed that of the WHO in the 1990s. Downsizing and sustainability climbed policy agendas in the 1980s, along with health sector reform. The emphasis on NGOs arose in a climate where public sector health provision was often characterized as inefficient, centralized and unaccountable (Green and Mathias, 1997). In this context there was a growing awareness of the financial capacity of NGOs and their experience in funding systems at a local level. Sollis also points to the heightened media profile of NGOs through their involvement in emergency and disaster relief during the 1980s and 1990s (Sollis, 1992; see also, Philo, 1993, 1999). NGOs also attracted the attention of donors in relation to concepts of good governance and plurality. Industrialized donor countries began to criticize not only the efficiency of recipient states, but also their legitimacy, on the grounds of a lack of democratic process or accountability. There is no historical evidence on which to base these claims of accountability (Green and Mathias, 1997: 15).

The WHO had refashioned itself in order to survive the growing influence of new and powerful actors such as the World Bank. Its essential drugs programme in the 1980s had incurred the opposition of the USA and American pharmaceutical companies. In the 1990s it set itself up as coordinator, strategic planner and leader of global health initiatives working in partnerships with the new players. In part this was in response to the Children's Vaccine Initiative, seen in the organization as an attempt by UNICEF, the World Bank, the UN Development Programme and other players to wrest away control of vaccine development (Brown et al., 2006). New mechanisms, institutions and targets emerged with the new actors. New 'hybrid' institutional actors appeared, bringing together different combinations of state, market and civil society actors in innovative institutional arrangements (Lee et al., 2009 forthcoming). Since the early 1990s there have been a proliferation of initiatives that bring together state, market and civil society actors; these global public-private partnerships (GPPPs) have focused on specific targets. Key examples are the Global Fund to Fight AIDS, Tuberculosis and Malaria (GFATM) and the GAVI Alliance. GPPPs have involved for-profit organizations directly in decision-making and the appropriateness of this approach has been questioned (Buse and Walt, 2000; Ollila, 2003; Richter, 2004). Contemporary philanthropic foundations, in particular the Bill and Melinda Gates Foundation, have become major actors in GPPPs (see Buse and Harmer in Chapter 12 below). The Gates Foundation is currently among the three biggest donors to global health (for example, to GFATM and GAVI Alliance). New targets have also been set. The UN Millennium Development Goals set eight targets to be met by 2015, including halving extreme poverty and providing universal primary education. According to reports in 2007 progress has been mixed, with few inroads in some areas, for example in reducing poverty in sub-Saharan Africa (UN, 2007a, 2007b).

Conclusions: old wine in new bottles? Strengthening our understanding of GHG

We can see from this overview that many of the themes and issues considered 'new' in GHG are in fact not new at all. In the nineteenth century, the need to mobilize internationally to confront pandemics and epidemics also preoccupied states, and conditions of trade and economy were important determinants of the nature of the response. Non-state actors and organizations proliferated in influence and in organization, and so did rapid technological change. The interwar years likewise have much to offer to consideration of the present. The history of international philanthropy in the interwar years, with the work of Rockefeller and the other foundations, should speak directly to today's assessment of the role of public-private partnerships. The relationships between the LNHO and RF, were in essence a public-private partnership. As Dubin has argued 'They penetrated deeply into national societies drawing domestic administrative, research and educational agencies into a transboundary biomedical/public health infrastructure' (Dubin, 1995: 73). This early dominance of the biomedical paradigm at the international level is mirrored in today's criticisms of reliance on technical solutions such as vaccination or medicines. Other features of the interwar period are also worthy of note. It was the 1930s that witnessed the first single issue cooperation between INGOS – in 1932 around 30 international peace and disarmament organizations formed an International Consultative Group to promote 'cooperative action and coordinated policies' (Seary, 1996: 21–2).

Globalization itself should be subject to historical scrutiny. Brown et al. (2006) have argued persuasively that the WHO focus latterly on the global and on global health governance with its aura of 'newness' was part of the organization's refashioning of itself in the 1990s as coordinator and planner of health initiatives involving the much wider range of key players who had come onto the scene. They see Brundtland's tenure at the WHO as key to this repositioning. The term 'globalization' also gained support from interests who had opposed nuclear war and who, as this threat receded in the 1990s, transferred their attention to environmentalism. Some other features of this repositioning, hailed as new, are also redolent of the past. Take, for instance, the WHO's Framework Convention on Tobacco Control of 2005, or the current moves to develop a similar convention for alcohol (*Lancet*,

2007). These initiatives can be located in the history of international moral and scientific health activism and have their antecedents in the history of international drug control, with its origins in the early twentieth century (Berridge, 2001). The rise, fall and refashioning of terminology always carries with it a broader political significance beyond a simple representation of 'reality'. It is tempting to see everything as new. This chapter has argued that this is not entirely the case: the earlier history of international health governance offers case studies which speak to today's concerns. We now need to move to a contemporary history, the history of the emergence of the concept of 'globalization' itself and the interests which have supported it.

Notes

This chapter is a substantially updated and revised version of K. Loughlin and V. Berridge, 'Global Health Governance: Historical Dimensions of Global Governance', WHO and London School of Hygiene and Tropical Medicine, 2002.
1. Although objectives of a non-public health nature, such as facilitating trade, persisted.
2. The Social Section was responsible for the traffic of women and children, the traffic of opium and other dangerous drugs and from 1924 the residual aspects of child welfare not covered by the LNHO and ILO. A separate opium section was created in 1930.

References

AHA, '122nd Annual Meeting of the American Historical Association', 3–6 January 2008, Washington DC, www.historians.org/annual/2008/index.cfm (accessed 16 January 2008).
Amrith, S., *Decolonizing International Health: India and South East Asia, 1930–65*, (London: Palgrave Macmillan, 2006).
Arnove, R.F. (ed.), *Philanthropy and Cultural Imperialism: the Foundation at Home and Abroad* (Boston: G.K. Hall, 1980).
Berliner, H., *A System of Scientific Medicine: Philanthropic Foundations in the Flexner Era* (New York: Tavistock, 1985).
Berridge, V., *AIDS in the UK: the Making of Policy, 1981–1994* (Oxford: Oxford University Press, 1996).
Berridge, V., 'Illicit Drugs and Internationalism: the Forgotten Dimension', *Medical History*, 45 (2001): 282–8.
Berridge, V., D. Christie and E. M. Tansey (eds), *Public Health in the 1980s and 1990s: Decline and Rise?* (London: Wellcome Centre, 2006).
Bhattacharya, S., 'Uncertain Advances: a Review of the Final Phases of the Smallpox Eradication Programme in India, 1960–1980', *American Journal of Public Health*, 94 (2004): 1875–83.
Bhattacharya, S., *Expunging Variola: the Control and Eradication of Smallpox in India, 1947–77* (New Delhi/London: Orient Longman India Ltd/Sangem Books UK, 2006).
Birn, A.E. and A. Solorzano, 'Public Health Policy Paradoxes: Science and Politics in the Rockefeller Foundation's Hookworm Campaign in Mexico in the 1920s', *Social Science and Medicine*, 49(9) (1999): 1197–213.

Brown, T.M., M. Cueto and E. Fee, 'The World Health Organization and the Transition from International to Global Public Health', *American Journal of Public Health*, 96 (2006): 62–72.

Bruun, K., L. Pan and I. Rexed, *The Gentleman's Club: International Control of Drugs and Alcohol* (Chicago: University of Chicago Press, 1975).

Bulmer, M., 'Mobilizing Social Knowledge for Social Welfare: Intermediary Institutions in the Political Systems of the United States and Great Britain between the First and Second World Wars', in P. Weindling (ed.), *International Health Organizations and Movements, 1918–1939* (Cambridge: Cambridge University Press, 1995), pp. 305–25.

Buse, K. and G. Walt, 'Global Public-Private Partnerships: Part I – A New Development in Health?' *Bulletin of the World Health Organization*, 78(4) (2000): 549–61.

Cockburn, W.C., 'The International Contribution to the Standardisation of Biological Substances: Biological Substances and the League of Nations, 1921–1946', *Biologicals*, 19 (1991): 161–9.

Crawford, E., *Nationalism and Internationalism in Science, 1880–1939* (Cambridge: Cambridge University Press, 1992).

Cueto, M., 'The Cycles of Eradication: the Rockefeller Foundation and Latin American Public Health, 1918–1940', in P. Weindling (ed.), *International Health Organizations and Movements, 1918–1939* (Cambridge: Cambridge University Press, 1995), pp. 222–43.

Cueto, M., 'Science under Adversity: Latin American Medical Research and American Private Philanthropy, 1920–1960', *Minerva*, 35(1997): 233–45.

Cueto, M., 'The Origins of Primary Health Care and Selective Primary Health Care', *American Journal of Public Health*, 94 (2004): 1864–74.

Dodgson, R., K. Lee and N. Drager, 'Global Health Governance: a Conceptual Review', Discussion Paper No.1, WHO, Geneva (2002), http://whqlibdoc.who.int/publications/2022/a85727_eng.pdf (accessed 12 January 2008).

Dubin, M., 'The League of Nations Health Organization', in P. Weindling (ed.), *International Health Organizations and Movements, 1918–1939* (Cambridge: Cambridge University Press, 1995), pp. 56–80.

Farley, J., 'The International Health Division of the Rockefeller Foundation: the Russell years, 1920–1934', in P. Weindling (ed.), *International Health Organizations and Movements, 1918–1939* (Cambridge: Cambridge University Press, 1995), pp. 203–21.

Gillespie, J., 'The Rockefeller Foundation and Colonial Medicine in the Pacific, 1911–1929', in L. Bryder and D. Dow (eds), *New Countries and Old Medicine* (Auckland: Pyramid Press, 1995) pp. 380–6.

Global Health Histories (2008), www.who.int.global_health_histories/en (accessed 10 January 2008).

Goodman, N.M., *International Health Organizations and their Work*, 2nd edn (Edinburgh: Churchill Livingston, 1971).

Green, A. and A. Mathias, *Non-Governmental Organizations and Health in Developing Countries* (Basingstoke: Macmillan Press, 1997).

Greenough, P., 'Intimidation, Coercion and Resistance in the Final Stages of the South Asian Smallpox Eradication Campaign, 1973–1975', *Social Science and Medicine*, 41 (1995): 633–45.

Harrison, M., 'Disease, Diplomacy and International Commerce', annual Centre for History in Public Heath lecture, London School of Hygiene and Tropical Medicine, 24 November 2005.

Held, D., A. McGrew, D. Goldblatt and J. Perraton, *Global Transformations: Politics, Economics and Culture* (Oxford: Polity Press, 1999).

Howard-Jones, N., *The Scientific Background of the International Sanitary Conferences, 1851–1938* (Geneva: WHO, 1975).
Howard-Jones, N., *The Pan American Health Organization: Origin and Evolution* (Geneva: WHO, 1981).
Hutchinson, J.F., 'Custodians of the Sacred Fire: the ICR and the Postwar Reorganization of the International Red Cross', in P. Weindling (ed.), *International Health Organizations and Movements, 1918–1939* (Cambridge: Cambridge University Press, 1995), pp. 17–35.
Hutchinson, J.F., *Champions of Charity: War and the Rise of the Red Cross* (Boulder: Westview Press, 1996).
Kickbusch, I., 'The Contribution of the World Health Organization to a New Public Health and Health Promotion', *American Journal of Public Health*, 93(3)(2003): 383–8.
Koivusalo, M. and E. Ollila, *Making a Health World: Agencies, Actors and Policies in International Health* (London: Zed Books, 1997).
Labonté, R. and T. Schrecker, 'Globalization and Social Determinants of Health: Analytic and Strategic Review Paper', WHO Globalization Knowledge Network (Ontario/Geneva: Institute of Population Health/WHO, 2006), www.who.int/social_determinants/resources/globalization.pdf (accessed 22 January 2008).
Lancet (Editorial), 'A Framework Convention on Alcohol Control', *Lancet*, 370 (2007): 1102.
Lee, K., *Historical Dictionary of the World Health Organization* (London: Scarecrow Press, 1998).
Lee, K., *Globalization and Health: an Introduction* (London: Palgrave Macmillan, 2003a).
Lee, K. (ed.), *Health Impacts of Globalization* (London: Palgrave Macmillan, 2003b).
Lee, K. and J. Collin (eds), *Global Change and Health* (Milton Keynes: Open University Press, 2005).
Lee, K., M. Koivusalo, E. Ollila, R. Labonté, T. Schrecker, C. Schuftan and D. Woodward, 'Globalization, Global Governance and the Social Determinants of Health: a Review of the Linkages and the Agenda for Action', in R. Labonté, T. Schrecker, C. Packer and V. Runnels (eds), *Globalization and Health: Pathways, Evidence and Policy* (London: Routledge, forthcoming 2009).
Lee, S., 'WHO and the Developing World: the Contest of Ideology', in A. Cunningham and B. Andrews (eds), *Western Medicine as Contested Knowledge* (Manchester: Manchester University Press, 1997), pp. 24–45.
Lyons, F.S.L., *Internationalism in Europe, 1815–1914* (Leyden: A.W. Sythoff, 1963).
Manderson, L., 'Wireless Wars in the Eastern Arena: Epidemiological Surveillance, Disease Prevention and the Work of the Eastern Bureau of the League of Nations', in P. Weindling (ed.), *International Health Organizations and Movements, 1918–1939* (Cambridge: Cambridge University Press, 1995), pp. 109–33.
Manuila, A. (ed.), *EMRO Partner in Health in the Eastern Mediterranean, 1949–1989*, (Alexandria: WHO Regional Office for the Eastern Mediterranean, 1991).
Mazumdar, P., ' "In the Silence of the Laboratory": the League of Nations Standardizes Syphilis Tests', *Social History of Medicine*, 16 (2003): 437–59.
Miller, C., 'The Social Section and Advisory Committee on Social Questions of the League of Nations', in P. Weindling (ed.), *International Health Organizations and Movements, 1918–1939* (Cambridge: Cambridge University Press, 1995), pp. 154–75.
Murard, L., 'Atlantic Crossings in the Measurement of Health: from US Appraisal Forms to the League of Nations' Health Indices', in V. Berridge and K. Loughlin (eds), *Medicine, the Market and the Mass Media* (Abingdon/New York: Routledge, 2005).

Ollila, E., 'Health Related Public-Private Partnerships and the United Nations 2003', in B. Deacon, E. Ollila, M. Koivusalo and P. Stubbs, *Global Social Governance: Themes and Prospects* (Helsinki: Ministry for Foreign Affairs, 2003), pp. 36–78.

Philo, G., 'From Buerk to Band Aid: the Media and the 1984 Ethiopian Famine', in J. Eldridge (ed.), *Getting the Message: News, Truth and Power* (London: Routledge, 1993).

Philo, G. (ed.), *Message Received: Glasgow Media Group Research, 1993–1998* (London: Longman, 1999).

Richter, J., *Public-Private Partnerships and International Health Decision Making: How to Ensure the Centrality of Public Interests?* (Helsinki: Ministry of Foreign Affairs, 2004).

Room, R., 'The World Health Organization and Alcohol Control', *British Journal of Addiction*, 79 (1984): 85–92.

Seary, B., 'The Early History: from Congress of Vienna to the San Francisco Conference', in P. Willetts (ed.), *The Conscience of the World: the Influence of Non-Governmental Organizations in the UN System* (London: Hurst and Co., 1996), pp. 15–30.

Siddiqi, J., *World Health and World Politics: the World Health Organizations and the UN System* (London: Hurst and Company, 1995).

Sizaret, P., 'Evolution of Activities in International Biological Standardization since the Early Days of the Health Organization of the League of Nations', *Bulletin of the World Health Organization*, 66 (1988): 1–6.

Sollis, P., *The Origins of the World Health Organization: a Personal Memoir, 1945–1948* (Boca Raton, Fla: LISZ Publications, 1982).

Sollis, P., 'Multilateral Agencies, NGOs and Policy Reform', *Development in Practice*, 2(3) (1992): 174.

Talbot, R.B., *The Dictionary of the International Food Agencies, FAO, WFP, WFC, IFAD* (London: Scarecrow Press, 1994).

Thomson, M., 'Mental Hygiene as an International Movement', in P. Weindling (ed.), *International Health Organizations and Movements, 1918–1939* (Cambridge: Cambridge University Press, 1995), pp. 283–304.

UN, *The Millennium Development Goals Report 2007* (New York: UN, 2007a), www.un.org/millenniumgoals/pdf/mdg2007.pdf (accessed 22 January 2008).

UN, *Africa and the Millennium Development Goals 2007 Update* (New York: UN, 2007b), www.org/millenniumgoals/docs/MDGafrica07.pdf (accessed 22 January 2008).

Walt, G., 'WHO under Stress: Implications for Health Policy', *Health Policy*, 24 (1993): 125–44.

Weindling, P., 'The Politics of International Co-ordination to Combat Sexually Transmitted Diseases, 1900–1980s', in V. Berridge and P. Strong (eds), *AIDS and Contemporary History* (Cambridge: Cambridge University Press, 1993), pp. 93–107.

Weindling, P., 'Social Medicine at the League of Nations Health Organization and the International Labour Office Compared', in P. Weindling (ed.), *International Health Organizations and Movements, 1918–1939* (Cambridge: Cambridge University Press, 1995), pp. 134–53.

Weindling, P., 'From Moral Exhortation to the New Public Health, 1918–45', in E. Rodríguez-Ocaña (ed.), *The Politics of the Healthy Life: an International Perspective* (Sheffield: European Association for the History of Medicine, 2002), pp. 113–30.

WHO, *The First Ten Years of the World Health Organization* (Geneva: WHO, 1958).

WHO, *The Second Ten Years of the World Health Organization* (Geneva: WHO, 1968).

WHO, *Fifty Years of the World Health Organization in the Western Pacific Region* (Manila: WHO Regional Office for the Western Pacific, 1998).

3
Mapping the Global Health Architecture

Gill Walt, Neil Spicer and Kent Buse

It is widely perceived that the increased diversity and numbers of actors involved in global health has challenged existing rules and decision-making structures, and that the coordinated governance of the institutions and organizations that fund, direct and implement health activities worldwide needs rethinking. The call for a new global health architecture stems from this acknowledgement.

However, in this chapter we argue that the global health architecture analogy constrains new thinking. This is because 'architecture' is usually defined in terms of solid or permanent organizational structures, rather than the changing, fluid interests and interrelations between architects, investors, builders and building users. While there is considerable discourse around an improved architecture for global health governance, most commentators stress the forms and functions of both 'global health governance' and 'architecture' and neglect agency, that is, the interaction and interests of the many actors involved, their ideas, values, motivations and exercise of power (Godal, 2005; Shakow, 2006; Cooper et al., 2007). What is neglected is discussion on the incentives and disincentives that influence actors in moving towards such new organizational and institutional structures. Fidler (2007) also doubts the usefulness of the architectural metaphor because he sees it as focusing too much on the state as central actor, promoting rationalization, centralization and harmonization. He argues that the state is no longer the central actor amongst a plurality of actors, and proposes 'open source anarchy' as a more fluid and dynamic conceptualization of contemporary and future global health governance in which non-state actors are intimately involved in health decision-making and activities.

In this chapter we explore the call for a new global health architecture, but place the emphasis on the relations between the actors affected. First we trace the change in the actors involved in global health and their global institutions over time, paying attention to relational and structural power. Second, since the relationship between power and agency cannot be separated from the context within which they are exercised, we focus on the major political and social ideas and events that affected discourse and actions and those actors who promoted them during particular periods in relation to global health policies. We draw on a number of developments in the field of AIDS, which has gained substantial attention at the global level since the 1990s, leading to the establishment of new governance mechanisms.

Finally, we return to global health architecture as defined and debated by scholars and identify what is missing in this particular metaphor. As well as the argument that attention has been paid to the structure and form of global architecture while neglecting agency, that is, the underlying ideas and values as well as the practices (exercise of power) and motivations of different actors, we also argue that far too much attention is paid to *global* strategy to the detriment of *local* implementation, with the emphasis on global agenda-setting and policy formulation rather than on local implementation processes. We conclude that it is important to understand agency and process if any progress is to be made in reforming the global health architecture for the better.

Throughout the chapter the discussion is informed by 'the policy triangle', a framework that takes account of actors, processes and context (Walt and Gilson, 1994) and draws on concepts of power, ideas and institutions to help explain how and why the shift towards (and within) global health took place. In so doing, we take several liberties – drawing eclectically from a broad literature and setting boundaries to periods where no such boundaries existed – in the quest to clarify and simplify a dazzling kaleidoscopic environment. Thus we arrange our analysis over three time periods: 1970s–mid-1980s; mid-1980s–mid-1990s; and mid-1990s–2008. The first period is characterized as the era of primary health-care, the second period as the era of health reforms, and the third period as the era of global partnerships.

Primary health-care: 1970s–mid-1980s

With the establishment of the United Nations (UN) in the late 1940s, the World Health Organization (WHO) was designated the UN's special agency to direct and coordinate health activities worldwide. In this role the WHO was highly regarded – especially after leading the worldwide campaign to eradicate smallpox over the years 1952–79. Its normative work on regulations and standard-setting was informed by, and relevant to, high-, middle- and low-income countries. However, much of its legitimacy was derived from its focus on the needs of middle- and low-income countries. The only other UN agency to work closely with the WHO during this period was UNICEF, which played a largely supportive role in relation to immunization against childhood diseases. Outside the UN, bilateral agencies provided substantial aid for health activities and a few foundations, such as the Rockefeller Foundation were active in health, albeit largely in disease control measures (Birn, 1996). This was a period in which most UN and bilateral donors (for example, the United States Agency for International Development) interacted with governments of donor and recipient countries rather than non-governmental organizations, and policies were largely focused on public sector health delivery, although private for-profit insurance systems flourished in a few countries, as did private practice, and in Latin America social insurance schemes dominated health-care.

Contested discourses of primary health-care

In the 1960s the WHO was a largely technocratic agency focused on disease control, but this changed as scholars and professionals began to question biomedical solutions to health problems caused by social, political or economic factors (Illich, 1975) and the relevance to poor countries of organizing health services based on western models (King, 1966). By the mid-1970s there was a major movement away from disease control towards the promotion of what became known as the primary health-care (PHC) approach. Launched by the WHO and UNICEF at Alma Ata in 1978, PHC became central to the WHO strategy, 'Health for All by the Year 2000' (Maciocco, 2008; Walt, 2001).

Alma Ata was a critical meeting because it included representatives from over 150 WHO member states, it addressed the needs of health systems in the poorest countries and articulated an international health policy 'vision'. Its focus on PHC shifted attention from disease control to the promotion of health, from medical decision-making to empowering people to make decisions about their health and health-care, and from technical interventions to tackling the structural and social factors underlying ill-health (such as poor nutrition, lack of water, or social class and gender). It sharpened a long-standing tension in health (van Praag et al., 2006) between those who emphasized selected disease control interventions and those who were concerned with health promotion to ameliorate inequities in health. This tension was played out in a controversial discourse between 'selective' and 'comprehensive' PHC (Walsh and Warren, 1980; Rifkin and Walt, 1986). The former involved a series of programmes which focused on specific, low-cost interventions such as oral rehydration salts for children with diarrhoeal disease; the latter included the training of village health workers to promote healthy behaviour. Policies emanating from both discourses were supported by bilateral donors and UN agencies and put into practice at country level. They led to many successful public sector programmes – for example, immunization against childhood diseases and rural health service expansion involving community participation (Walt, 2001).

The WHO promoted and coordinated the PHC approach. Its power to do this was legitimized through a vertically representative decision-making structure. Member states sent delegations representing health ministries to meetings at the WHO headquarters in Geneva each year, at which policies would be decided by those delegations. Delegates then returned to their own countries, with an international remit to implement the decisions made – although the final decision rested with country governments themselves. The financing of the PHC approach was assumed to be through the government's public sector budget and infrastructure, and therefore depended on the health ministries making the case to the government (or donors) for increased expenditure on the health system.

Most countries placed considerable store on WHO authority and leadership. Indeed, the organization's influence and confidence was sufficiently strong in this period for it to challenge powerful industry interests when these threatened PHC activities. For example, from the mid-1970s, the WHO and other UN organizations were engaged in discussions about pharmaceutical policies to make safe and effective medicines more affordable and available to low-income countries and populations. In 1977, the WHO published the first essential drugs list and in 1981 approved the International Code on Marketing of Breast-Milk Substitutes, in spite of strong protests from the respective transnational industries (Kanji et al., 1992; Sikkink, 1986). In later years, as the discourse changed, and as the WHO's power diminished, it took a more cautious approach in its dealings with industry (Lee, 2008).

However, by the early 1980s, even as PHC activities were being put into effect in low- and middle-income countries, the discourse was already shifting among the main actors. There was growing conflict between the two promoters of the Alma Ata conference, with UNICEF rejecting the 'comprehensive' PHC approach of WHO, and advocating and funding more 'selective' interventions such as the use of infant growth monitoring charts, oral rehydration therapy, breast-feeding and immunization. For many this was a step in the wrong direction. Maciocco (2008: 38) quotes Ken Newell, an early protagonist of PHC declaring that 'Selective PHC is a threat … Attractive to professionals, financing agencies and governments that are seeking results in the short term, but it is a pure illusion.' Indeed, economists, funding agencies and some governments lauded UNICEF's promotion of selective interventions, and many bilateral organizations followed suit, financing vertical programmes and interventions addressing specific child and maternal health issues in low-income countries. This period can be seen as the beginning of the retreat from comprehensive support for health systems by global actors. As the US government expressed its impatience with the WHO's challenge to industry through its International Code on Breast-Milk Substitutes and its publication of an essential drugs list (by withholding or delaying its mandatory financial contributions to the WHO budget), and as the World Bank began to focus on health financing and reforms to the health sector, the WHO became isolated from an increasingly US and World Bank-dominated discourse on health policy.

The 1980s and early 1990s was also the period in which criticism of the state's role in health grew, especially in the USA. Scholarly papers and reports objected to what was perceived as over-expanded, over-extended and bloated state institutions in developing countries. The huge debts incurred by poor countries in the late 1970s and early 1980s were seen as evidence of inefficient, failing governments rather than weak governance among creditors such as private banks. As the neo-liberal economic policies of US President Reagan and UK Prime Minister Thatcher began to take hold, there was a clear shift from the ideas that had stimulated PHC and policies that looked at the whole health system to sober reflections on how to finance health by reducing public expenditure, drawing in non-state actors, and focusing on specific issues or diseases rather than on systems.

Health reforms: mid-1980s–late 1990s

The 1980s saw the entry of a powerful new actor into the health arena. Until then the World Bank had financed small health projects as components of development programmes. With the publication of its *Health: Sector Policy Paper* (1980) the Bank's influence grew. By 1984 it was shifting the discourse from the implementation of PHC to concerns about how to finance the health sector, and suggesting policies such as user fees to mobilize greater resources (Lee and Goodman, 2002). By 1993, when the World Bank published *Investing in Health*, PHC was largely absent from international health agendas. The health reform era focused on effectiveness and efficiency: how to finance and better manage health-care, delimiting the role of the state, and promoting the role of the market (Buse, 1994; Zwi and Mills, 1995). *Investing in Health* recommended four ways of improving government spending: by reducing government expenditures on tertiary facilities; by shifting attention to public health interventions that presented significant positive externalities – for example infectious disease control; by providing only an essential package of clinical services; and by improved management, including decentralization and contracting out of services (p. 6).

While the change in discourse did not go unchallenged – some European donors, and indeed, the WHO, were critical of the neo-liberal directions proposed for health – many bilateral donors supported World Bank recommendations and promoted collaboration with the private sector as a way of introducing health reforms (Skaar, 1998; Brugha and Zwi, 2002). The Bank's expertise on public sector reform and analytical capacity as well as its financial resources gave it considerable power during the 1980s and 1990s, both to influence other actors and to shrug off criticisms of its structural adjustment policies (Stiglitz, 2000).

Another group of actors that grew in prominence was the non-governmental community. Although the UN agencies were relatively slow to acknowledge their importance, many bilateral organizations supported the notion of democratizing decision-making through including the views and experience of non-governmental or civil society organizations (NGOs or CSOs). These groups, in turn, began to pay more attention to international policy and to demand a voice in policy dialogue. Non-government organizations active in implementing health programmes proliferated as aid was increasingly channelled through them rather than to governments.

One of the main catalysts for change was the AIDS epidemic, in which NGOs played a significant part. Although it took time for AIDS to be recognized as a global threat, by the early 1990s a vibrant and active group of non-government organizations was becoming highly vocal, drawing attention to the needs of people living with the virus or with AIDS, and to the lack of access to drugs, especially for those in poor countries. In 1996, the WHO's global programme on AIDS was replaced with a new multi-sectoral agency, the Joint United Nations Programme on AIDS (UNAIDS), to address the crisis.

Throughout this period, the WHO struggled to maintain its leadership in global health policy, damaged by a degree of criticism that would have been unthinkable in the early 1970s (see for example the series by Fiona Godlee in the *British Medical Journal* in 1994; Godlee 1994a–d). Increasingly it was the World Bank's discourse on health reforms, financing, effectiveness and efficiency that led thinking on health, in spite of trenchant criticisms of its macroeconomic policies, such as structural adjustment, which had led to reductions in the standards of living in Africa and elsewhere, thereby undermining health gains of previous decades. By the mid-1990s, the neo-liberal economic agenda dominated thinking on health. Negotiations on trade had opened the doors to private for-profit players in insurance and health-care delivery; and privatization of traditionally public utilities (such as communications and energy) introduced new market players. As markets expanded, industry increasingly recognized the benefits of alliances with the UN and other intergovernmental groups as a way of gaining access to decision-making processes and penetrating emerging markets (Buse and Walt, 2002). Policy discussion and even decision-making forums were opened up to many new, private sector players (Lee et al., 1997).

Technological advances in communication and travel associated with globalization heightened awareness of increased interdependence between sectors and countries and facilitated the establishment of global networks. Some of these were quite technical: based on acknowledgement of global interdependence in relation to epidemics such as SARS or influenza, for example, and the need to collect and share data on particular hazards.

Communication technologies also encouraged the spread of networks for advocacy and empowered non-government organizations to use the internet for exchange of ideas and to organize collective action (see Box 3.1). Campaigns to decrease the cost of antiretroviral drugs and to challenge the pharmaceutical industry position on patents were examples of relatively powerless non-state organizations (sometimes working with state groups) joining forces globally through technology to challenge industry interests. The best known examples are those of the Treatment Action Campaign (TAC) in

> **Box 3.1 The Global Outbreak Alert and Response Network (GOARN)**
>
> The Global Outbreak Alert and Response Network (GOARN) was formed in 2000 in recognition that no individual country or organization is capable of responding alone to major global health threats such as SARS or avian influenza. It is a collaboration between representatives of technical institutions, organizations and networks in global epidemic surveillance and response, who pool expertise and resources to identify the threat of epidemics, alert the international community and support appropriate responses. It is also contributing to longer-term capacity-building for epidemic preparedness. The network consists of over 400 experts who work in 40 countries. Although the network is hosted by the WHO, which provides a project manager and secretariat services, members self-fund their participation. Its guiding principles include the following:
>
> - The WHO ensures outbreaks of potential international importance are rapidly verified and that information is quickly shared within the network.
> - There is a rapid response coordinated by the Operational Support Team to requests for assistance from affected state(s).
> - The most appropriate experts reach the field in the least possible time to carry out coordinated and effective outbreak control activities.
>
> *Source*: http://www.who.int/csr/outbreaknetwork/en (accessed 4 February 2009).

South Africa (Friedman and Mottiar, 2004) and Médecins Sans Frontières' Campaign for Access to Essential Medicines[1] (see Box 3.2). Epistemic and other types of networks, including trans-governmental actors – government policymakers working across state borders – were also able to capitalize on the opportunities offered by electronic communication. For example, although many groups in South Africa embraced global concerns to prioritize attention and resources for HIV/AIDS, in the early 2000s President Mbeki's policies did not translate this concern into action. It was the actions of South African civil society, networking internationally, that brought pressure to bear on the South African government to address the issue (von Soest and Weinel, 2007).

What characterizes this period is the shift towards a more horizontal decision-making environment, with a larger number of actors and networks at the global level influencing or participating in information exchange, policy debate and decision-making. Although for much of the period the World Bank was regarded as an extremely powerful player in health – 'the 800lb gorilla' (Abbasi, 1999: 866) – not only for its ability to mobilize resources but also for its analytical expertise and access to finance and planning ministers,

> **Box 3.2 Treatment Action Campaign: a local network that mobilized global action**
>
> The Treatment Action Campaign (TAC) is a South African AIDS activist organization founded in 1998. With visionary leadership TAC grew rapidly into a broadly-based group, with chapters in many regions of the nation and a largely black and poor constituency. The group campaigns for greater access to HIV treatment for all South Africans by raising public awareness and understanding about issues surrounding the availability, affordability and use of HIV treatments. In the early 2000s TAC confronted the South African government for failing to ensure that programmes to prevent mother-to-child transmission (PMTCT) were available. The campaign won this case on the basis of the South African constitutional guarantee of the right to health-care, and the government was ordered to provide PMTCT programmes in public clinics.
>
> A study by Friedman and Mottiar (2004) suggests that TAC's most strategically important alliance may have been that with international allies. International support helped TAC assist its own government by defending it in the case brought against it by the pharmaceutical industry. Campaigning with others worldwide, TAC helped to bring down the price of anti-retroviral medicines. A key feature of international alliances in the era of electronic communication is that they can be sustained without significant resources – 'we don't need a direct presence abroad to build international support'. TAC's most consistent international ally has been the Belgian NGO Médicins Sans Frontières (MSF), which, with the activist group Act Up, put pressure on political leaders and their policies on HIV/AIDS. By around 2005, TAC was seeking to broaden its international base by strengthening a Pan-African network of AIDS treatment activists, passing on experience in coalition-building. The network engages the secretariat of the Southern African Development Community and the African Union, potentially creating new momentum towards treatment in South Africa and other countries.
>
> *Source*: Friedman and Mottiar (2004).

even the Bank could not escape the increasingly relentless onslaught of commentators on the United Nations as a whole and the need to recognize the growing importance of non-state actors.

Observers and scholars alike criticized the UN and its many agencies, with reason in some cases. Although reforms of the UN system and its specialized agencies were addressed to some extent during the 1990s (enunciated for example, in two reports in 1992 and 1994, respectively, *An Agenda for Peace*, and *An Agenda for Development*) change was slow, and insufficient to stem the tide of criticism or the increasing power of the corporate sector in the UN.

In 1998 the UN Secretary-General proposed a 'Global Compact' to provide a framework for businesses to align their strategies to a set of principles, and opened the opportunities for more corporate involvement in the UN.

The World Bank also began to invite non-state actors to sector-wide discussions in this period. Scholarly debates about the shrinking of the state (actively contributed to by World Bank policies) or its 'withering away' (Ohmae, 1995) observed that global changes had weakened sovereign states' abilities to exert power, and that, in an age of increasing interdependence, even powerful organizations such as the World Bank depended on other actors to respond to problems, to make and shape policy.

By the turn of the century, scholars were describing the shift from *international health* policy to *global health* policy. Where once international policy processes had involved vertical representation and relations between sovereign states and intergovernmental organizations, such as the UN agencies, now global health policy processes were increasingly horizontal, involving many different types of actors operating at the global level, with no clear hierarchy, limited accountability and with different power resources, interests and values in relation to global health. These policy processes were marked by a broad range of non-state actors, including the corporate sector and networks – many of whom were interacting across national borders (Brown et al., 2006). The implication was that traditional roles had changed: no actor in health could now wholly dominate the policy process, or certainly could not attempt change, without conferring and consulting with a very broad range of actors whose power and influence came from different means including financial resources, traditional political authority, access to knowledge and the ability to generate it, and the ability to mobilize the media and the public in support of or in opposition to particular policies.

Roles had also changed among traditional actors. Bilateral donors increased their engagement with civil society and with the corporate sector. For example, deregulation opened public sector research to private for-profit companies, and bilateral organizations increasingly channelled research funds to consultants or private research groups, and aid monies to services run by nonprofit NGOs. Transnational corporations were also participating in global health policymaking by shaping agreements made under the auspices of the General Agreement on Tariffs and Trade (GATT) and the World Trade Organization (see Buse and Naylor, Chapter 9 below). A series of major mergers and business alliances between transnational pharmaceutical corporations in the 1980s and 1990s concentrated ownership and power among an increasingly small number of large private sector actors able to mobilize formidable resources. NGOs moved from traditional service delivery functions to play policy advice and campaigning roles across borders; campaigns on debt, access to medicines, and landmines, among others, were successful in changing policies among the various actors involved. Rowson (2005) noted nine different types of activities in which NGOs engaged, among which were representing the 'voice of the people', advocacy and lobbying, research and policy analysis, or acting as 'watchdogs'. Through engagement in global governance mechanisms (having a seat on the board of the GFATM, for example), civil society organizations or networks of CSOs increasingly had opportunities to influence health policy processes at the global, national and sub-national levels, where they had a country presence (see McCoy and Hilson, Chapter 10).

As all these traditional roles shifted, so too did traditional mistrust between public and private sectors. Dialogue began, for example, between some members of the pharmaceutical industry and public sector bodies in an attempt to tackle market failure in research and development for medicines and allied products in order to address the burden of disease among the poor, or on how to address the AIDS epidemic among employees and their families. By the end of the 1990s, there was a great deal of cautious discourse about partnership between the private and public sectors which finally took off with the advent into the global health field of the Bill and Melinda Gates Foundation. The era of partnerships had arrived.

The era of partnerships: late 1990s–2008

If the World Bank had been the new actor on the international health stage in the mid-1980s, the Bill and Melinda Gates Foundation was a shooting star in the skies of the new millennium. Founded in 2000 with an initial US$1 billion, a huge injection of funds from Warren Buffet in 2007 meant that the Gates Foundation became the world's most powerful financial investor in health and other activities, far surpassing the budget of the WHO.

From the beginning, the Gates Foundation emphasized the value of public-private partnerships. Although partnerships between the two sectors had existed before, it was only in the late 1990s that the concept really took hold, with powerful actors strongly promoting it. One of the first partnerships established with Gates Foundation funding was the GAVI Alliance, initially established as the Global Alliance for Vaccines and Immunizations. Launched in 2000, with US$750 million from the Gates Foundation, GAVI's board members came from the private vaccine sector as well as UN agencies, governments and NGOs. The GAVI Alliance aimed to promote the development and introduction of new vaccines and to increase coverage and use of vaccines in poor countries. The Gates Foundation rapidly became a partner in many global public-private partnerships, from the Roll Back Malaria partnership initiated by WHO, UNICEF, UNDP and the World Bank, to the Global Alliance for Improved Nutrition (see Buse and Harmer, Chapter 12 below).

The number of such partnerships grew exponentially. Initially these partnerships were defined as 'Collaborative relationships which transcend national boundaries and bring together at least three parties, among them a corporation and an inter-governmental organisation, so as to achieve a shared health creating goal on the basis of a mutually agreed and explicitly defined division of labour' (Buse and Walt, 2000: 699), and much early scholarly work focused on their governance aspects, showing them to be extremely varied (Buse and Walt, 2000). Many of these partnerships were dedicated to developing new products such as medicines or vaccines, others were raising funds to increase access to specific treatments (for AIDS or trachoma), while still others were devoted to raising consciousness or campaigning. While all were called 'partnerships' (between state and non-state, private and public sector representatives) in fact only 22 out of a purported 100 or so had representatives from both the corporate and state sectors (Buse and Harmer, Chapter 12 below), and the financial resources they were expected to mobilize from the private sector were on the whole disappointing. What they had in common, however, was their focus on a single issue.

While most of these partnerships were welcomed as bringing new attention for health issues and for providing new resources and expertise from the private sector to the public sector, there were also many who were cautious about their effects, raising governance questions about accountability and sustainability, and the extent to which these were truly partnerships, among other things (Buse and Walt, 2000; Buse and Harmer, 2004; Richter, 2003, 2004).

What is particularly significant about this era for the discussion of architecture is the nature of partnership interaction: intense and unprecedented levels of ongoing exchange between partners (and often a secretariat) at a variety of organizational levels. While partners may share an explicit common goal and have some overlapping areas of mandate or interests, they often have distinct or even competing interests. The picture today is of a delicate, complicated web of partnerships and networks which aim to deliver a measure of consensus between organizations – through formal board and working committees, but also through less formal, time-limited task teams and sub-groups. They in turn, often draw on individuals and groups that are not formally involved in the partnership.

However complex the interactions between these different networks and organizations, it seems clear that an elite is emerging: the H8 (the Health 8), perhaps taking over from the G8, once referred to as the 'global-health governor' (Kirton et al., 2007: 192). The H8 is made up of the heads of the WHO, the World Bank, the GAVI Alliance, UNICEF, UNFPA, UNAIDS, the Global Fund to Fight AIDS, Tuberculosis and Malaria, and the Bill and Melinda Gates Foundation, who pledged in 2007 to meet biannually, on an informal basis, to discuss challenges to scaling-up health services and improving health-related Millennium Development Goal outcomes.

Global health governance today: chaos or consensus?

For many, the proliferation of new global health actors and shifts in the relative importance and roles of existing actors is to be welcomed. For others, this multitude of diverse actors and networks indicates continuing and growing fragmentation and chaos at global and national levels. Nonetheless, there are clear signs of a growing consensus about the need for cooperation and coordination between these different organizations and networks. These issues are discussed below.

Mitigating chaos and fragmentation?

We have introduced some of the myriad of new actors engaged in the health sector, including global public-private partnerships and global initiatives, transnational research, campaigning and knowledge exchange networks, global civil society groups and networks, and the corporate sector. Organizationally, there are many different bodies involved in quite similar activities, both at global and national levels, and it has been observed that this can result in duplication or even conflict in terms of the approaches or technical strategies they advocate or the activities that they are willing to fund (Garrett, 2007). For example, some donors promote a move towards general budget support to countries, others are cautious about it; some donors fund broad reproductive and sexual health programmes, others, such as the USA, refuse resources to any organization offering abortion. There is also a plethora of values, theories and core interests held by these different actors. Health policymaking has broadened from being undertaken predominately by medical professionals, to include economists, social scientists, legal professionals, IT specialists and management consultants (Lee et al., 2002; Kumaranayake and Walker, 2002). Different disciplines bring contrasting insights to health planning and policy, but these can also conflict (for example, economists' concern with efficiency versus public health professionals' concern with equity). Equally the World Bank view of health has tended to be more market-oriented than that of the World Health Organization.

Quite aside from the kaleidoscope of potential differences in policy approaches, attitudes and values regarding health and health-care systems between the different actors, there are very practical problems in processing all their interactions. So, while many have perceived the proliferation of new agencies as reflecting greater democracy, flexibility, release of new resources and creative thinking, there has also been awareness of the potential for conflict in the resulting fragmentation. At the launch of the International Health Partnership (IHP), the UK's Department for International Development enumerated the problem under 'health facts': global policy development and implementation involved 40 bilateral donors, 26 UN agencies, 20 global and regional funds, and 90 global health initiatives (DFID, 2007). All these actors compete for attention and space not only with each other, but also with traditional actors such as the World Bank and the WHO, which have shaped global health policies for so long. Indeed, debates have been ongoing for many years about the interactions between the different actors, focusing on ways to ensure democratic and inclusive processes, rules, representation and accountability, and how to reform traditional policy processes (Walt and Buse, 2005). Without consensus and coordination between these ideas and the actors that put them into effect, new forms of governance remain elusive.

In recognition of this, there have been many attempts to bring some sense of coherence to global health havoc. Global actors themselves have displayed considerable adaptability in trying to reform old systems and forge some consensus within the increasingly crowded global health community. Dialogue and discussion during the 1990s resulted in a number of events and global policies which were significant in terms of the number of governments and other actors who signed up to a more coordinated and concerted effort in the development arena.

For example, the International Conference on Finance for Development held in Mexico in 2002 produced the Monterrey Consensus. The consensus was adopted by over 50 heads of state; 200 ministers of finance, foreign affairs, development and trade participated in the event, as well as the heads of the United Nations, the International Monetary Fund, the World Bank, the World Trade Organization and prominent business and civil society leaders. New development aid commitments from the United States and the European Union and other countries were made at the conference. Among its aims, the more important were to mobilize larger amounts of international finance for development, to reform global governance and to secure greater coherence in development. The Monterrey Consensus was seen as an important way of meeting the Millennium Development Goals, which had been agreed in 2000 by 189 countries of the United Nations, with the support of the IMF, the World Bank, the Organization for Economic Cooperation and Development, and the G7 and G20 countries. Of the eight goals, three were directly related to health, and each had a number of targets and indicators by which achievements could be assessed in 2015.

Global agreements are examples of the global community attempting to work together to secure greater policy cohesion. Other agreements have included attempts to achieve greater coherence at the country level. For example, the Paris Declaration on Aid Effectiveness, endorsed in 2005, was signed by development officials and ministers from 91 countries, 26 donor organizations and partner countries, representatives of civil society organizations and the private sector. It committed participants to increase efforts in harmonization, alignment, aid management and mutual accountability.[2] It included a set of indicators which could be monitored (measuring the number of donors, for example, using the recipient countries' public financial management or procurement systems). Other attempts have also been made to improve donor alignment with national government priorities. For example, sector-wide approaches (SWAps), whereby donors agree activities and support within a plan developed by the recipient country and sometimes provide sector budget support or pool resources in a particular sector, were introduced to promote coordinated donor activities, rather than in tandem or even competitively, at country level (Walt et al., 1999). Although only operating in health sectors in approximately 20 countries, SWAps have been partially successful in getting a range of stakeholders around the table on an annual basis to review progress and commit to common objectives for the coming year. An effort to bridge aspects of SWAps and Paris Declaration intentions was manifest in the 2005 Global Task Team's report on improving AIDS coordination, which recommended promoting national leadership and ownership, improving alignment and harmonization of AIDS policies, more effective coordination of multilateral efforts and improved accountability and oversight (Global Task Team, 2005).

In 2007, as evidence accumulated that the global community was not on track to meet the health targets set out in the MDGs by 2015, another initiative was launched to accelerate joint efforts. Recognizing the need to strengthen poor countries' health systems, the International Health Partnership was unveiled in London, and a partnership agreement was signed by eight governments, several UN agencies, the GAVI Alliance, the Global Fund to Fight AIDS, TB and Malaria, the Gates Foundation, the African Development Bank and the UN Development Group. The IHP's goal was to encourage donors to work together more effectively and build strong and sustainable health systems. Eight countries agreed to be part of a 'pilot compact' to implement the IHP.[3] The heads of these eight agencies also formed the H8, and by 2008 were focusing attention on how the different agencies could work together to strengthen health systems. The growing discourse about health systems strengthening was contentious however, with criticisms from those who believed that resources would disappear into 'black holes' with little evidence of outcomes (for example, topping up of health worker salaries). Both the GAVI Alliance and Global Fund boards had heated debates about the value of funding for health systems, and only narrowly reached agreement to increase resources for this purpose. By mid-2008 many different meetings were being held on what sorts of actions would improve health systems, with increased attempts to find the synergies between different agencies to do just that. For example, the WHO held an expert consultation in May 2008, on 'positive synergies between Global Health Initiatives and health system strengthening.'

These examples provide considerable justification for the view that the global health community is seriously concerned about a lack of coherence and burgeoning competition between the proliferation of global actors. The number of initiatives demonstrates a degree of commitment to working towards better global coordination and consensus. However, there are questions as to whether global-level commitment is matched by practice on the ground. At least some of the donors have failed to institutionalize the kind of incentives that would be required to change modes of practice by their officials at the recipient country level. So the jury is out on many of these initiatives – some of which are being piloted in a small number of countries, and all of which will need considerable time to be established before assessments can be made of their strengths and weaknesses and lessons learned. It is difficult to see, for a restless, achievement-hungry, global health community that wants to demonstrate that funds have produced results that can be attributed to their own inputs, how these interests can be reconciled with more collaborative approaches to supporting health programmes.

There will also be considerable costs involved in collecting the evidence to show that different, complex initiatives work, and that success can be attributed to their particular inputs. Concern about shortfalls in health information systems and health knowledge, and the unsynthesized plethora of evaluations conducted by a huge variety of organizations, have led to the establishment of the Health Metrics Network (a WHO hosted partnership) and the Institute for Health Metrics and Evaluation (*Lancet*, 2007) and to calls for a 'common evaluation framework' (Murray et al., 2007).

Translating global agreements into local practice

Many would argue that in spite of the efforts made at the global level, evidence has accumulated to suggest that, at least at the country level, confusion and competition continue to affect health systems.

Examples from the AIDS field illustrate the continuing complexity at country level. At the same time as the global aid discourse started in Monterrey to focus on consensus and cooperation in order to increase the volume and improve the quality of assistance to countries, global commitments were up against significant obstacles at the country level. One challenge was simply the huge number of actors financing and implementing AIDS control programmes, the other was the size of the funding flowing in for HIV/AIDS programmes. The launch of the Global Fund to Fight AIDS, Tuberculosis and Malaria (GFATM) in 2000 offered countries the opportunity to apply for much larger grants than had ever been available for disease programmes. While the funds covered the three diseases, in the first years of the fund over 60 per cent of its expenditure went to support HIV/AIDS programmes. Two other initiatives also disbursed significant funds to address AIDS: the World Bank's Multi-Country AIDS Programme (MAP) and President Bush's Emergency Plan for AIDS Relief (PEPFAR). The initiatives worked in very different ways: the World Bank through governments and civil society, with grants; the GFATM, described as a financial mechanism, with no country presence, responded to funding proposals from countries which had established Country Coordinating Mechanisms for this purpose; and PEPFAR, a bilateral arrangement between the US government and selected countries, disbursed funds almost entirely to a vast array of non-government organizations and contractors, setting up its own processes of selection, disbursement and monitoring. Added to these organizations, many others were involved in supporting HIV/AIDS programmes, including the Clinton Foundation (which tended to work through governments), NGOs such as Médecins Sans Frontières, and UN agencies, including, among others, UNAIDS, WHO and UNFPA (see Veenstra and Whiteside, Chapter 14 below).

There was no one mechanism through which such huge resources from disparate sources flowed and were disbursed. Countries were rapidly flooded with very large amounts of money for one particular disease, and in the poorest African countries, AIDS monies very soon became larger than the whole budget for health.

As evidence accumulated of the fragmented landscape of AIDS programmes at country level, attempts were made to coordinate efforts. For example, from 2004, UNAIDS tried to persuade countries and other donors to support the strengthening of national AIDS responses through the 'Three Ones' initiative: one national AIDS coordinating authority, one national HIV/AIDS action framework, and one monitoring and evaluation system. The scheme was launched in 12 countries, and an evaluation in early 2007 reported some move towards rationalization within multilateral AIDS policies at country level, but noted many challenges remaining (Attawell and Dickinson, 2007). Furthermore, the terms of reference for the Global Task Team charged with delivering on the Three Ones focused only on ensuring an improved multilateral response, and did not consider the role played by the bilateral agencies, which exempted themselves from scrutiny.

There are other examples of attempts to improve country-level alignment and harmonization. For example, in 2006 the Government of Ethiopia, the GFATM, and PEPFAR entered into a memorandum of understanding to better coordinate and harmonize implementation of AIDS programmes in the country.[4] In mid-2007, a joint statement by PEPFAR and the GFATM announced that the two 'partners' were supporting life-extending antiretroviral treatment for a combined 1.58 million people living with AIDS worldwide. The statement also drew attention to the US government's role as founding member of the fund and as its largest contributor.[5]

How far such attempts go beyond policy intentions of goodwill and translate into coordinated action, however, is unclear. A report on coordination from Rwanda noted that:

> Regarding alignment, the preliminary point to note is that whilst some major donors refer to Rwanda PRSP in development programs, they do not, on the whole, align, at least not explicitly, to the basic policy instruments, namely the strategic lines defined in the National Strategic Framework and the Multisectoral National Plan 2002–2006.
> (MacKellar et al., 2005: n.p.)

A number of small independent studies have reported extremely weak collaboration between and within different agencies and national bodies[6]

(Murzalieva et al., 2008; Semigina et al., 2008) as well as competition between agencies and funders, with the result that although there may be a national plan, many donors continue to finance interventions which are off plan and off budget – and which are monitored through project-specific instruments. Similarly, one study showed that between 2003–06 project funding dominated aid for maternal, neonatal and child health (Greco et al., 2008). There are still few countries where *all* the major actors provide sector budget support, pool funds or adopt national or common reporting systems – even where they have entered into agreements to do so as noted above. We would argue that this is made even more difficult because emphasis has been put on some issues to the detriment of others.

Back to the drawing board: putting agency before architecture

Much of the discussion about the global health architecture has focused on the form and structure of interactions between a multiplicity of actors. However, there is a considerable gap between what has been achieved at the level of global rhetoric (even where this has been translated into goals, guidelines and indicators that can be monitored) and what has been achieved at the country level (see Veenstra and Whiteside, Chapter 14). This is partly because most attention has been on reaching a consensus on global goals and indicators on which a broad variety of partners can agree – and which are therefore couched in general and relatively anodyne terms. In terms of the literature on global architecture, the focus has been largely on global actors and their attendance at meetings to discuss or to agree new policies or initiatives. There has been much less attention played to their *agency*: the interaction of these different actors, how far their actions may be governed by their interests, and how these reflect and are reflected in their ideas, values, motivations and exercise of power and the ways in which these may be affected by any particular governance arrangement. For example, while governments, non-government organizations and private corporations might agree on the need for coordination and cooperation, they will each seek to satisfy their own constituencies by attributing success and change to their own actions and funds. This could mean that they are not easily prepared to share data and information, might prefer to seek their own publicity and media coverage, and more profoundly, might not agree on basic principles regarding the balance between equity and efficiency in health-care, or long- versus short-term gains. At an individual level, new directors of organizations or new heads of government seek to make their mark by introducing new initiatives even as older ones have not had time to be embedded. Such imperatives make it difficult to establish more effective and long-term support of national programmes (de Renzio et al., 2005; Coyle and Lawson, 2006).

It is because of the interests of global actors that major rationalization of the global health environment (and therefore its governance) has been so difficult. For example, there is a lack of agreement on what core functions define any one organization. Even among the UN agencies, it has been painfully difficult to introduce the notion of 'one UN' at the country level: one UN programme, one budgetary framework, one leader and one office. Eight countries are party to a pilot scheme to reach this goal, as recommended by the High-Level Panel on UN Systemwide Coherence in 2006. The aim of the initiative was to reduce duplication and transaction costs so that the UN could use resources more effectively to support partner countries to achieve their development goals.[7] However, attempts by the UN agencies to redefine their functions in relation to their comparative advantage have been thwarted by disagreement (Frenk et al., 1997; Shakow, 2006). Indeed, Rogerson et al. (2004) point out that in 50 years of aid, no major global health actor, including the UN agencies, has closed or merged with another. Debates continue with current dialogue among some of the global health initiatives (GAVI Alliance, GFATM) on how to extend their narrow focus on immunizations and diseases to strengthen health systems through what is called diagonal financing (GAVI, 2007; WHO, 2007), providing support to achieve disease-specific outcomes while also generating positive externalities which support health systems more broadly (for example, training HIV lab technicians to use HIV supported labs for screening for congenital syphilis). And by mid-2008 different agencies were positioning themselves to take a lead on strengthening health systems.

As the WHO was losing its international policy leadership role, a very different organization, the Bill and Melinda Gates Foundation, was gaining ascendancy in terms of shaping health policy through its funding decisions and presence at the global level. Many acknowledge the importance of this injection of funds and how Gates's ideas have opened up the participation in health to private sector actors who are attracted to the foundation's technological trajectory. Yet, in early 2008 the WHO's chief of malaria, Arata Kochi, criticized the extent of influence of the Gates Foundation, suggesting that it was stifling a diversity of views among scientists because many of the world's leading scientists are 'locked in a cartel' that has worked hard to maintain its position.[8] So, while 'Billanthropy' has transformed the health funding environment and brought new optimism and ways of working, some have suggested it is creating its own WHO, reflecting its own (or US) interests.

Focusing on global structures (or 'architecture') deflects attention from agency. However, any approach to understanding global health governance which stresses exclusively either structure or agency is limited: it is more useful to see the relationship as

> dialectical ... The actor brings strategic knowledge to the structured context and both that strategic knowledge and the structured context help shape ... action. However the process is one of almost constant iterations, as the action affects both the actor's strategic knowledge and the structured

context, which then, in turn, shape, but of course do not determine ... future action.

(Marsh and Smith, 2000: 5)

While changes to structure and form are important for identifying improvements in future global health governance, agency is also critical, helping to set in place the processes for open and inclusive decision-making, mutual accountability, fair representation and transparent financial and management systems; the success of agreed rules and norms will depend on the behaviour of actors and the incentives they face to change old habits.

In terms of agency we would argue that there has been insufficient attention paid to incentives for change and how the various actors' interests are affected by such changes, and how they therefore respond. Driving change from the global level when it is dependent on actors at the local level is complex. Even if individual government representatives have been party to a global agreement, they may not be able to persuade their government or civil servant colleagues to prioritize this particular agreement above many others. Incentives for coordination for example, may not be obvious at the country level, and sanctions against governments which play off one donor against another are seldom invoked. Even if governments favour coordination, donors seldom censure or condemn those donors who choose not to participate in coordination efforts. Where financial resources provide a strong incentive, change may be successful, although it might itself have unintended consequences. For example, donors have been successful in getting many countries to introduce governance changes in order to apply for large grants. Examples include the Millennium Challenge Corporation[9] and the GFATM's insistence on transparent financial disbursement and oversight monitored through the private sector (local fund agents) or broad decision-making bodies for proposal development (CCMs). Sanctions include withdrawing funds if conditions are breached or targets not achieved. Even so, there are examples where it has been difficult to apply sanctions, or where they have affected the very people they were aimed at helping (Kapiriri and Martin, 2006).

Financial incentives can also be misplaced, or introduce competition. It seems that this is one of the side-effects of PEPFAR funding, which is competitively awarded by contract to implementers, who have been perceived to be cautious in allowing outsiders to review data collected, and who may not want to share programmatic weaknesses or failures with others considered to be rivals. In such situations, collaboration and coordination are perceived as threats and not incentives. Establishing incentives that change behaviour and that do not rely on instrumental rewards is not easy, but examples include working in teams and sharing ideals and professional values – what Frenk has called promoting a renewed ethic of universal rights (Frenk, 2008).

Even where country level authorities are in favour of implementing the various global agreements in order to support alignment and harmonization, they do not always have the capacity and skills to do so. Sometimes this is the result of a lack of effective national leadership, or because some national officials gain from poorly coordinated, project-targeted aid, but sometimes it is because donors themselves do not adhere to global agreements or, as the US agencies often argue, cannot, because of US laws. It is notable that a great deal of space and dialogue is given to reform of UN agencies, and yet multilateral aid is only a quarter of all aid – the bilateral agencies are financially much more important and influential actors, and yet they are the least disciplined, the least accountable and the least likely to support coordinated efforts (with some notable exceptions). The debate regarding China's role in aid for Africa is just the latest manifestation of a long battle for position and power (Alden, 2007).

Conclusions

Given the somewhat unruly melange of actors at both global and national levels, it is difficult to know how the global confluences of different actors that now populate the health stage are able to provide overall coherence. It is perhaps no wonder that Fidler (2007) concludes that the result is a climate of 'anarchy'. Although it seems rational that coherence would be better established with one global health leader to drive changes and coordinate global health policy, it is difficult to see agreement on which of the current agencies would take this role. Some have suggested establishing a global health fund that transforms the best in the WHO, and possibly the GFATM, and establishes an overarching health agency that provides 'evidence-based and trustworthy guidance to a globalized world' (Yamey, 2002: 1298); an organization that replaces the current fragmented support to low-income countries and channels resources through one mechanism that is aligned to national interests. Others have suggested a world health insurance system (Ooms et al., 2006) that would spread the health risks and burden of healthcare between rich and poor states, and that would be organized through a mechanism to allocate resources to poor states and determine the contributions from rich states. Yet another suggestion has been that the WHO wrest back its leadership, and establish a committee 'C' to the existing Committees A and B at the World Health Assembly, which would provide an overall, more inclusive and democratic, transparent coordination of all aspects of international health (Silberschmidt et al., 2008). It is difficult to see, at this stage of global history, that the powerful H8 group would ever be able to reach agreement on the establishment of one mechanism or one leader on global health from among their own members. And given the difficulties of coordination, even with considerable existing goodwill establishing another global fund for health would probably meet with little enthusiasm.

There are, however, actions that could be taken to improve coordination and collaboration. Incentives need to be established to discourage one-off or annual evaluations of every initiative. Leaders need to be patient, and not want to prove that their own ideas or initiatives have been successful. Global evaluations need to be re-focused on alternative, country-based systems for monitoring, so that performance can be judged over time, implementers and their clients can be included in assessing services, and changes can be introduced iteratively rather than suddenly. New initiatives – especially when they are largely old ideas re-named and re-packaged (for example, the IHP) – should be minimized, with the balance moved towards consolidation and monitoring of progress over a realistic time period – seldom less than 10–15 years. National leaders, whether political or scientific, should be rewarded for staying in their own countries and contributing to the building of national capacity, rather than being encouraged to move to global organizations. Movements between national and global level organizations should be bounded by time and by commitment to ideals, not individual careers. There should be fewer global-level meetings and fewer global agreements, frameworks, guidelines and toolkits, and more time for open discussion and dialogue at country level and across countries, between the people who implement programmes, as well as their beneficiaries. Research institutions and civil society organizations should enhance and enlarge their 'watch' and 'synthesis' functions so that the big questions around intellectual property, trade, human rights, and so on are kept on the global agenda.

We have argued that deliverance from the chaos of global governance is being sought from the wrong stance: from a top-down global view focusing on structure, instead of a bottom-up country view with greater acknowledgement of agency and how to mobilize power to ensure action. We need more research to help understand the interests and incentives which govern the behaviour of the different actors, at both global and local levels before we can imagine how new global health structures will look, and how they might perform. We also need more financing at local level to support coordination efforts, whether SWAps, IHP compacts, or monitoring and evaluation systems. What we call for, in short, is an extended debate around global architecture that would be stimulated to think about agency as well as structure, and to focus more on ways of mobilizing and supporting agency, especially at the country level.

Notes

1. http://www.msf.org/ (accessed 15 December 2008).
2. www.aidharmonization.org/secondary-pages/Paris2005 (accessed 21 February 2008).
3. http://www.dfid.govt.uk/news/files/ihp/default.asp (accessed 20 February 2008).

4. http://www.theglobalfight.org/downloads/Releases/Newsletter_September2007.pdf (accessed 21 February 2008).
5. http://www.pepfar.gov/press/85885.htm (accessed 21 February 2008).
6. See www.ghinet.org (accessed 15 December 2008).
7. http://www.undg.org/?P=7 (accessed 28 May 2008).
8. http://www.nytimes.com/2008/02/16/science/16malaria.html? (accessed 18 February 2008).
9. See http://www.mcc.gov/selection/index.php (accessed 15 December 2008).

References

Abbasi, K., 'The World Bank and World Health: Changing Sides', *British Medical Journal*, 318(7187) (1999): 865–9.
Alden, C., *China in Africa* (London: Zed Books, 2007).
Attawell, K. and C. Dickinson, *Independent Assessment of Progress on Implementation of Global Task Team Recommendations in Support of National AIDS Responses* (London: HLSP, 2007).
Birn, A.E., 'Health or Public Menace? The Rockefeller Foundation and Public Health in Mexico: 1920–1950', *Voluntas*, 7(1) (1996): 35–56.
Brown, T., M. Cueto and E. Fee, 'The World Health Organization and the Transition from "International" to "Global" Public Health', *American Journal of Public Health*, 96 (2006): 62–72.
Brugha, R. and A. Zwi, 'Global Approaches to Private Sector Provision: Where is the Evidence?' in K. Lee, K. Buse and S. Fustukian (eds), *Health Policy in a Globalising World* (Cambridge: Cambridge University Press, 2002), pp. 63–77.
Buse, K., 'Spotlight on International Agencies: the World Bank', *Health Policy and Planning*, 9 (1) (1994): 95–9.
Buse, K. and A. Harmer, 'Power to the Partners? The Politics of Public-Private Health Partnerships', *Development*, 47(2) (2004): 43–8.
Buse, K. and G. Walt, 'Global Public-Private Partnerships: Part I – A New Development in Health?' *Bulletin of the World Health Organization*, 78(4) (2000): 549–61.
Buse, K. and G. Walt, 'Globalisation and Multilateral Public-Private Health Partnerships: Issues for Health Policy', in K. Lee, K. Buse and S. Fustukian (eds), *Health Policy in a Globalising World* (Cambridge: Cambridge University Press, 2002), pp. 41–62.
Cooper, A.F., J.J. Kirton and T. Schrecker (eds), *Governing Global Health: Challenge, Response, Innovation* (Aldershot: Ashgate, 2007).
Coyle, E. and A. Lawson, *World Bank Incentives for Harmonization and Alignment: Report to the World Bank* (London: ODI, 2006).
de Renzio, P., D. Booth, A. Rogerson and Z. Curran, 'Incentives for Harmonization and Alignment in Aid Agencies', Overseas Development Institute Working Paper 248, Overseas Development Institute, London, 2005.
Department for International Development, 'The International Health Partnership Launched Today' (2007), http://www.dfid.gov.uk/news/files/ihp/default.asp (accessed 20 February 2008).
Epstein, P. and G. Guest, 'International Architecture for Sustainable Development and Global Health', in G. Guest (ed.), *Globalization, Health and the Environment: an Integrated Perspective* (Lanham, MD: Altamira Press, 2005), pp. 239–58.
Fidler, D.P., 'Reflections on the Revolution in Health and Foreign Policy', *Bulletin of the World Health Organization*, 85(3) (2007): 243–4.

Frenk, J., J. Sepúlveda, O. Gómez-Dantés, M.J. McGuinness and F. Knaul, 'The Future of World Health: the New World Order and International Health', *British Medical Journal*, 314 (1997): 1404.

Frenk, J., 'Strengthening Health Systems: Towards New Forms of Global Cooperation', talk at meeting on Global Health and the United Nations, Carter Center, Atlanta, Georgia, USA, 8–9 May 2008.

Friedman, S. and S. Mottiar, 'A Moral to the Tale: the Treatment Action Campaign and the Politics of HIV/AIDS', Centre for Civil Society and the School of Development Studies, University of KwaZulu-Natal, South Africa, 2004.

Garrett, L., 'Do no Harm: the Challenge of Global Health', *Foreign Affairs*, 86 (1) (2007): 14–38.

GAVI, 'Health Systems Strengthening (HSS) Support Update' (2007), http://www.gavialliance.org/resources/HSS_Update_May07.pdf (accessed 4 February 2009).

Global Task Team, 'Global Task Team on Improving AIDS Coordination among Multilateral Institutions and International Donors: Final Report', UNAIDS, Geneva, 2005.

Godal, T., 'Do we have the Architecture for Health Aid Right? Increasing Global Aid Effectiveness', *Nature Reviews Microbiology*, 3 (2005): 899–903.

Godlee, F., 'WHO in Crisis', *British Medical Journal*, 309(6966) (1994a): 1424–8.

Godlee, F., 'WHO in Retreat: is it Losing its Influence?' *British Medical Journal*, 309(6967) (1994b): 1491–5.

Godlee, F., 'The World Health Organisation: the Regions – too Much Power, too Little Effect', *British Medical Journal*, 309(6968) (1994c): 1566–70.

Godlee, F., 'WHO at Country Level – a Little Impact, no Strategy', *British Medical Journal*, 309(6969) (1994d): 1636–9.

Greco, G., T. Powell-Jackson, J. Borghi and A. Mills, 'Countdown to 2015: Assessment of Donor Assistance to Maternal, Newborn and Child Health between 2003 and 2006', *Lancet*, 371 (2008): 1268–75.

Illich, I., *Medical Nemesis: the Expropriation of Health* (London: Marian Boyars, 1975).

Kanji, N., A. Hardon, J. Harnmeijer, M. Mamdani and G. Walt, *Drugs Policy in Developing Countries* (London: Zed Books, 1992).

Kapiriri, L. and D. K. Martin, 'The Global Fund Secretariat's Suspension of Funding to Uganda: How Could this have been Avoided?', *Bulletin of the World Health Organization*, 84(7) (2006): 576–80.

King, M., *Medical Care in Developing Countries* (Oxford: Oxford University Press, 1966).

Kirton, J., N. Roudev and L. Sunderland, 'Making G8 Leaders Deliver: an Analysis of Compliance and Health Commitments, 1996–2006', *Bulletin of the World Health Organization*, 85 (2007): 192–9.

Kumaranayake, L. and D. Walker, 'Cost-Effectiveness Analysis and Priority Setting: Global Approach without Meaning?' in K. Lee, K. Buse and S. Fustukian (eds), *Health Policy in a Globalising World* (Cambridge: Cambridge University Press, 2002), pp. 140–56.

Lancet, 'Editorial: a New Institute for Global Health Evaluations', 369 (2007): 1902.

Lee, K., *World Health Organization* (London: Routledge Global Institutions Series, 2008).

Lee, K. and H. Goodman, 'Global Policy Networks: the Propagation of Health Care Financing Reform Since the 1980s', in K. Lee, K. Buse and S. Fustukian (eds), *Health Policy in a Globalising World* (Cambridge: Cambridge University Press, 2002), pp. 97–119.

Lee, K., D. Humphreys and M. Pugh, ' "Privatisation" in the United Nations System: Patterns of Influence in Three Intergovernmental Organisations', *Global Society*, 11(3) (1997): 339–57.
Lee, K., K. Buse and S. Fustukian (eds), *Health Policy in a Globalising World* (Cambridge: Cambridge University Press, 2002).
Maciocco, G., 'From Alma Ata to the Global Fund: the History of International Health Policy', *Social Medicine*, 3 (2008): 36–48.
MacKellar, L., T. Antony and J.B. Nahabakomeye, 'Donor Coordination of HIV/AIDS Assistance in Rwanda: Study Report', Government of Rwanda, 2005.
Marsh, D. and M. Smith, 'Understanding Policy Networks: Towards a Dialectical Approach', *Political Studies*, 48(1) (2000): 4–21.
Murray, C., J. Frenk and T. Evans, 'The Global Campaign for the Health MDGs: Challenges, Opportunities, and the Imperative of Shared Learning', *Lancet*, 370 (2007): 1018–20.
Murzalieva, G., K. Kojokeev, A. Samiev, J. Aleshkina, N. Kartanbaeva, G. Botoeva et al., 'Tracking Global HIV/AIDS Initiatives and their Impact on Health Systems in Kyrgyzstan: Interim Report', Center for Health System Development, Bishkek 2008.
Ohmae, K., *The End of the Nation State* (New York: Free Press, 1995).
Ooms, G., K. Derderian and D. Melody, 'Do We Need a World Health Insurance to Realise the Right to Health?', *Public Library of Science Medicine*, 3(12) (2006): 2171–6.
Richter, J., ' "We the Peoples" or "We the Corporations"? Critical Reflections on UN-Business "Partnerships" ', International Baby Food Action Network and Geneva Infant Feeding Association, Geneva, 2003.
Richter, J., 'Public–Private Partnerships for Health: a Trend with no Alternatives?' *Development*, 47(2) (2004): 43–8.
Rifkin, S. and G. Walt, 'Why Health Improves: Defining the Issues Concerning "Comprehensive Primary Health Care" and "Selective Primary Health Care"', *Social Science and Medicine*, 23(6) (1986): 559–66.
Rogerson, A., A. Hewitt and D. Waldenburg, *The International Aid System 2005–2010: Forces for and against Change* (London: Overseas Development Institute, 2004).
Rowson, M., 'Health and an Emerging Global Civil Society', in K. Lee and J. Collin (eds), *Global Change and Health* (Maidenhead, Berkshire: Open University Press, 2005).
Semigina, T., I. Griga, D. Bogdan, I. Schevchenko, V. Bondar, K. Fuks et al., 'Tracking Global HIV/AIDS Initiatives and their Impact on Health Systems in Ukraine: Interim Report', Kyiv Mohyla Academy, Kyiv, 2008.
Shakow, A., 'Global Fund–World Bank HIV/AIDS Programs Comparative Advantage Study', GFATM/World Bank, Geneva, 2006.
Sikkink, K., 'Codes of Conduct for Transnational Corporations: the Case of the WHO/UNICEF Code', *International Organization*, 40(4) (1986): 814–40.
Silberschmidt, G., D. Matheson and I. Kickbusch, 'Creating a Committee C of the World Health Assembly', *Lancet*, 371 (2008): 1483–6.
Skaar, C.M., *Extending Coverage of Priority Health Care Services through Collaboration with the Private Sector: Selected Experiences of USAID Cooperating Agencies* (Bethesda, MD: Partnerships for Health Reform and Abt Associates, 1998).
Stiglitz, J.E., *Capital Market Liberalization, Economic Growth, and Instability* (Washington, DC: World Bank, 2000).
United Nations, *An Agenda for Peace* (1992).
United Nations, *An Agenda for Development* (1994).

van Praag, E., K. Kehne and V. Chandra-Mouli, 'The UN Response to the HIV Pandemic', in E.L. Beck, N. Mays, A. Whiteside and J. Zuniga (eds), *The HIV Pandemic: Local and Global Implications* (Oxford: Oxford University Press, 2006).

von Soest, C. and M. Weinel, 'The Treatment Controversy: Global Health Governance and South Africa's Fight against HIV/AIDS', in W. Hein, S. Bartsch and L. Kohlmorgen (eds), *Global Health Governance and the Fight against HIV/AIDS* (London: Palgrave Macmillan, 2007), pp. 202–25.

Walsh, J. and K. Warren, 'Selective Primary Health Care: an Interim Strategy for Disease Control in Developing Countries', *New England Journal of Medicine*, 14(2) (1980): 145–63.

Walt, G., 'Health Care in the Developing World, 1974–2001', in C. Webster (ed.), *Caring for Health: History and Diversity* (Milton Keynes: Open University Press, 2001), pp. 253–94.

Walt, G. and K. Buse, 'Global Cooperation in International Public Health', in M. Merson, D. Jamison and A. Mills (eds), *International Public Health* (Boston: Jones and Bartlett, 2005), pp. 649–80.

Walt, G. and L. Gilson, 'Reforming the Health Sector in Developing Countries: the Central Role of Policy Analysis', *Health Policy and Planning*, 9 (1994): 353–70.

Walt, G., E. Pavignani, L. Gilson and K. Buse, 'Managing External Resources in the Health Sector: are there Lessons for SWAps?', *Health Policy and Planning*, 14(3) (1999): 273–84.

WHO, *The Global Fund Strategic Approach to Health Systems Strengthening Report from WHO to the Global Fund Secretariat* (Geneva: WHO, 2007).

World Bank, *Health: Sector Policy Paper* (Washington, DC: World Bank, 1980).

World Bank, *World Development Report 1993: Investing in Health* (New York: Oxford University Press, 1993).

Yamey, G., 'Have the Latest Reforms Reversed WHO's Decline?', *British Medical Journal*, 325 (2002): 1107–12.

Zwi, A. and A. Mills, 'Health Policy in Less Developed Countries: Past Trends and Future Directions', *Journal of International Development*, 7(3) (1995): 299–328.

4
Conceptual Models for Global Health Governance

Wolfgang Hein, Scott Burris and Clifford Shearing

Introduction

Globalization has led to an appreciation of a system of global politics beyond the control of nation-states and the traditional system of international relations. Global politics is characterized by a pluralization of governance mediated by a constant effort to establish shared norms on global public goods and bads to constrain the exercise of power or, expressed in another way, to attain a more equitable access to power resources. Traditional state institutions of national and international governance have become more diversified as a reaction to their inherent limitations and the increasing power of new forms of governance built by private actors. Though the state remains a powerful, often dominant, actor in governance, it competes with and sometimes is itself governed by a diverse set of non-state actors, including corporations, foundations, religious groups, social advocacy organizations and 'dark networks', such as al-Qaeda or narcotics cartels. States and traditional institutions of international governance are increasingly seen as complex assemblages in and of themselves, comprised of more or less well-networked nodes operating somewhere on the spectrum between cooperation and competition. States have actively embraced this pluralization, seeking to increase or protect their power by vigorous use of governance devices such as privatization and partnerships.

These developments are clearly visible in the health sector, which has witnessed an institutional change from a structure that consisted primarily of independent national health systems and some international agencies devoted to controlling the cross-border effects of ill-health, towards a system of global health governance (GHG). Contemporary GHG is characterized by a polycentric, distributed structure and a substantive concern with issues that affect populations worldwide directly (for example, the global spread of infectious diseases or antibiotic resistance) or indirectly (for example, political instability and global insecurity arising from extreme socio-economic inequality). Global health governance now requires management not merely of specific transborder epidemics, like SARS or avian influenza, but of the host of issues in health that arise at the intersection of a globalized economy and lives lived in particular localities. Dealing with 'glocal' health challenges increasingly requires attention not only to 'horizontal' coordination of global politics, but also to more effective vertical integration of global-level governance with governance at the national and local levels.

Both practitioners and students of health policy require new conceptual tools to understand and influence GHG. During recent years, two models have been developed that, from different perspectives, address these characteristics of multiplicity of actors, flexibility of institutional arrangements and fluidity of relationships. The 'nodal governance' framework builds on network theories to describe distributed governance and the ways in which institutions project power across networks to govern the systems they inhabit (Burris et al., 2005: 33). The concept of 'interface', refers to 'a specific space, where two different social *systems* or *fields of social order* interact (here: global/national systems; institutional systems related to modes of regulation), which are characterized by specific institutions and specific backgrounds' (Bartsch et al., 2007: 29). Development aid, for example, typically presents substantial discontinuities between the preferences of recipients and the imperatives driving donors. Independently, the concepts of nodal governance and interfaces can help us to understand what constitutes the binding forces and the types of power mobilized among the multitude of actors in global health governance. Taken together, they illuminate key challenges to good GHG: improving democracy, efficacy and coordination. In this chapter we use these two frameworks to understand the emerging dynamics of GHG and then illustrate their usefulness through a discussion of the global governance of HIV/AIDS.

Global health governance: governors and good governance

The broad concept of governance has gained a central position in most social science disciplines as well as among practitioners (Burris et al., 2008). Immediate evidence is found in the sheer number of definitions of 'governance' being offered today. We adopt a simple one – management of the course of events in a social system. Central to this definition is a focus on the function of governing and an acknowledgement that governing has multiple forms and locations. There is broad agreement that governance is in a time of change, and that a major element of this change is the abandonment of the formal Westphalian premise of governments' monopoly on the governance of international affairs (Keohane, 2002; Fidler, 2004). It now makes more sense to describe governance as polycentric, with multiple agencies and sites of governance (Joerges et al., 2004; Slaughter, 2004).

We distinguish three different kinds of governors: public, private and hybrids. Public (or state) governance structures are typically characterized by at least a formally representative relation to the governed, by hierarchy, and by a claim to a monopoly on the legitimate exercise of governing power (including the use of force). Private or non-state governors, which include for-profit and charitable corporate entities, religious bodies and unrecognized groups such as criminal gangs, are heterogeneous in structure and internal management. They range from large hierarchical corporations to small, participatory non-governmental organizations (NGOs). Private governors may use force, but typically govern through economic and discursive methods. Hybrid forms, which constitute a notable element of new public management/reinventing government strategies, include public-private partnerships (PPPs) and other contractual structures in which some previously governmental function or service is devolved to non-state governors (Burris et al., 2008).

The Westphalian system was a means of addressing the lack of a central government authority in global governance. Treaty regimes, and the international institutions that managed them, mirrored the rule of law enjoyed by successful states. As state governance has changed, so there has been an increasing tendency to avoid the difficulties of managing international collective action by moving to the same sort of hybrid governance mechanisms being used to 'reinvent' governance at the national level. In the last fifteen years, in the field of global health alone, some 100 new PPPs have been established to coordinate the resources of pharmaceutical companies, philanthropic organizations and governments in various public health projects (Cohen 2006; see also Buse and Harmer, Chapter 12 below, for a critique of this claim).

Complexity, diversity and particularity drive accounts of governance today. The structure of governance is most commonly described in network terms. Governors are distributed throughout complex networks operating both horizontally and vertically. Writers point to phenomena as diverse as the internet, PPPs, markets, informal policy networks at the international level, and 'whole of government' (that is, joined-up) initiatives as examples of networked governance in action. The effective exercise of power increasingly depends upon enrolling nodes in responsive regulatory networks. State governors network formally (as in the Westphalian institutions or in PPPs) and less formally through networks established between individual ministries or agencies (Slaughter, 2001). Corporations use networks liberally to achieve their ends (Braithwaite and Drahos, 2000; Drahos, 2004), as do advocacy groups (Hurtig and San Sebastian, 2005) and even terrorists (Raab and Milward, 2003; Wood, 2006). It has become increasingly difficult to propose managing networked governance in a 'top-down' or centralized manner. Managing the complexity of social systems is, in significant part, a matter of effective adaptation, which gives an advantage to organizations that can effectively gather and rapidly analyse information. Likewise, the larger 'constitutional' project of evolving appropriate constraints upon governors (such as norms or forms of structural checks and balances) can neither be conceptualized nor pursued as a top-down, centralized activity (Fidler, 2004; Teubner, 2004). Rather, commentators emphasize the need for decentralized practices of governance experimentation (Lobel, 2004; Sabel, 2004).

These descriptive observations should be placed in an explicitly normative context: 'governance' is not synonymous with 'good governance'. Governance can be 'good' in at least two senses: it can deliver good results – in this case healthy public policies and good health – and it can work through processes and institutions that meet broadly accepted standards of democracy, justice and due process. Ideally governance is good in both of these ways, and, indeed, many people believe that governance that fails the second criterion will normally have difficulty delivering on the first. Any contemporary governance system may be inefficient, corrupt or unresponsive to the needs of the governed. Donor nations, development organizations and even individual philanthropists have taken action to promote good governance in the sense of honest government. This is important, of course, but there is increasing recognition of the need to apply traditional norms of good government – stability, accountability, transparency, efficiency, respect for human rights – to new governance institutions, particularly non-state and hybrid forms (Sinden, 2008). Norms of justice and fairness are also implicated. Networks make possible a global, information-based society, but not everyone is included. A marginalized social class comprised of the vast majority of the earth's population is relegated to informational black holes, cut off from the information flows that drive the knowledge economy and from the access necessary to participation in governance (Luhmann, 1997; Shearing, 2005). This problem of 'democratic deficits' has the potential to undermine the legitimacy of networked governance theory as a means of advancing health and render the GHG project an idle pastime that will never benefit the mass of the world's population.

Scholarship and activism in GHG are today generally aligned in their attention to structural inequalities in health and their impatience with what might be called 'Westphalian excuses' for their persistence. David Fidler has argued that GHG has begun to coalesce around a pursuit of 'global public goods for health' (GPGH) (Fidler, 2004: 264). The GPGH concept traduces the claim that health politics may be reduced to the pursuit of national self-interest in a global competition for power and resources. 'GPGH encompass more than state interactions and are sought for reasons beyond defending against exogenous threats and promoting national exports' (Fidler, 2004: 270). Moreover, as Gostin has powerfully argued, a post-Westphalian, human rights-based account of health requires governance mechanisms that actively constrain the pursuit of state and corporate self-interest in favour of substantial improvement in the level and distribution of health in the world's population (Gostin, 2008).

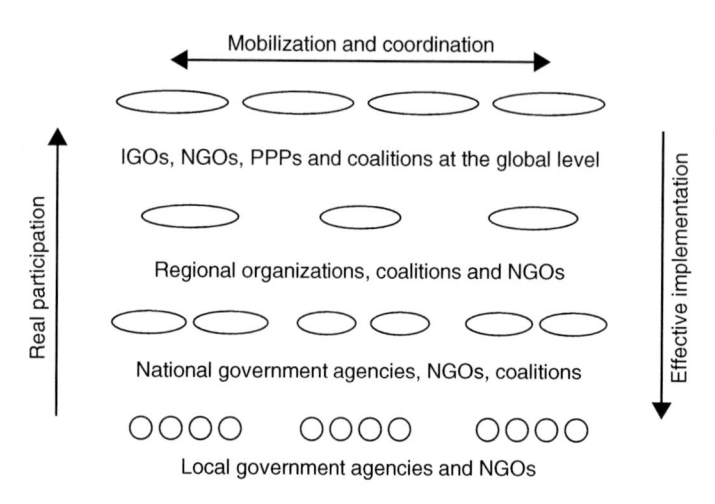

Figure 4.1 The virtuous circle of GHG

For the purposes of this chapter, we consider good GHG to be governance that operates in a manner that respects, defends and promotes the right of all people to the highest attainable health. In the tradition of public health, GHG is attentive to evidence, and has as its focus the improvement of the health and well-being of the population and the reduction of inequity in health and its determinants. As shown in Figure 4.1, good GHG would operate as a 'virtuous circle'. Governance at every level of social organization would be characterized by effective mobilization of resources and coordination of action by state, non-state and hybrid institutions. The concentration of resources and power at the global level would be mediated in two crucial ways through effective governance at the regional, national and local levels. First, better governance below the global level increases the chances that programmes designed and funded at the global level can be effectively implemented. Second, better governance increases the capacity of lower levels of the system to influence, inform and participate in global level decision-making, which can be expected to lead to global-level institutions that are both more legitimate and more effective. In this ideal model, power and information are shared by institutions of governance within and across the various levels of social organization.

Frameworks for the analysis of the interaction of actors in global health governance

Nodal governance

Governance today is characterized by a plurality of institutions forming more or less interconnected governance networks; a plurality of mechanisms that enable or constrain the exercise of power and rapid adaptive change. The concept of 'nodal' governance has emerged from diverse scholarship that has made networks a central element in governance theory (Castells, 2000; Dupont, 2004; Rhodes, 1997). Rather than centring governance in the state, this approach gives equal weight to the activities of non-state and hybrid actors in governance.

> Within a nodal conception of governance, no set of nodes is given conceptual priority. Rather, the exact nature of governance and the contribution of the various nodes to it are regarded as empirically open questions. It is assumed that the specific way in which governmental nodes relate to one another will vary across time and space. While these arrangements might very well become entrenched for considerable periods in many places, this should be regarded as an empirical state of affairs rather than an analytical constant.
>
> (Shearing and Wood, 2003: 404)

A node is any formal or informal institution that participates to any degree in a governance network. Governing nodes take many forms, from government agencies to foundations and NGOs to street gangs. From a nodal perspective, many large organizations can be seen as nodal assemblages rather than unitary institutions. For example, state governments are made up of many nodal assemblages (judiciary, legislature, executive) that in turn are themselves comprised of further nodes down to the level of a local constituent or enforcement office. This structure is what enables the sort of networked global governance arrangements among subordinate state nodes described by Slaughter (2004). Nodal governance reflects the role of networks in contemporary governance, in so far as governance is understood to be accomplished through networks and access to the network is a precondition for effective participation. It also, however, focuses attention on those points of a network – the nodes – where power is accumulated and from whence it is directed onto the network: their internal constitutions, their cultures, their resources, and the strategies they use to amass and project power (Burris et al., 2005; Dupont, 2004).

States aim ultimately to integrate their constituent networks. In governments, hierarchical lines of authority and political appointees are commonly used to try to coordinate or control the activities of ministries, agencies, bureaus and offices. 'Missions' and strategic plans are also common devices. Drahos has written extensively about the importance of a different type of node, termed a 'superstructural' node, that does not integrate networks, 'but rather is a structure that brings together actors who represent networks in order to concentrate resources and technologies for the purpose of achieving a common goal' (Drahos, 2004). His work documents, for example, the way in which intellectual property holders have created superstructural nodes like the Business Software Alliance to coordinate patent enforcement with US and European governments. Civil society organizations typically use a superstructural device – the coalition – to concentrate and project their power resources into governance. 'Superstructural nodes are the command centers of networked governance' (Drahos, 2004: 405).

The nodal governance literature has focused particularly on the powers that nodes use to govern others (Burris et al., 2005). Nodal systems make flexible use of the regulatory strategies typically described in international relations theory (Kooiman, 2003; Rosenau, 2004; Mayntz, 2005; Barnett and Duvall, 2005), depending on the types of power that they are able to control. *Economic power* and the *threat of force (coercive power)* continue to be reliable means of exerting state control, and give developed states a great deal of leverage. Economic power is widely used by non-governmental entities as well. Drahos and Braithwaite have shown how transnational corporations have used their considerable capacities to collect and analyse information to define their governance goals and target their efforts (Braithwaite and Drahos, 2000; Drahos, 2004). Information is often at the heart of the *discursive power* used by those without significant economic or military power. NGOs in health rely heavily on collecting data to define problems and priorities (for example, Global Health Watch) and to support the effort to constrain powerful actors through norms such as human rights. Through their links to state institutions and international organizations nodal systems can also use *organizational power* in decision-making bodies and *legal power* based on legal structures and laws.

The distributed nature of nodal systems makes 'forum shifting' a particularly useful and often employed device for all kinds of global actors (Braithwaite and Drahos, 2000; Helfer, 2004). This happens in many ways: transferring regulatory jurisdiction from one agency to another, simply withdrawing from participation or recognition of a governing node or network, creating a new node or network, or combining one or more of all these strategies (Braithwaite, 2004). For example, the World Trade Organization's Agreement on Trade-Related Aspects of Intellectual Property Rights (TRIPS) moved the international regulation of intellectual property rights away from the World Intellectual Property Organization (WIPO) to the World Trade Organization (WTO), allowing those dissatisfied with WIPO, such as the US government, to move the focus of political activity to more advantageous nodal arrangements.

The institutional focus of nodal governance links it to the work of thinkers like Roberto Unger (1996), Archon Fung (2004), Michael Dorf and Charles Sabel (1998) who have revived Dewey's notion of 'democratic experimentalism'. Reform may be practised on or within existing institutions, but building new institutions or new institutional arrangements is an equally potent strategy. Sabel writes, for example:

> If, as I and many other assume, there are no principals in civil society – not even the political parties that connect it to the agents in public administration – with the robust and panoramic knowledge needed for this directive role ... [t]hen the problem for reform is at least as much determining ways actors can discover together what they need to do, and how to do it, as determining which actors ought to be the principals in public decision making.
>
> (Sabel, 2004: 174–5)

Normatively, a nodal view de-centres the state; the aim of good governance becomes not just good government but the adaptation of widely accepted norms of transparency, accountability and human rights that have traditionally been laid upon the state to the demands of a world in which decision-making and social service delivery is dispersed in complicated ways between state, private and hybrid actors (Sabel, 2004; Burris et al., 2005; Sinden, 2008; Wood and Shearing, 2007). New norms are also called for to constrain and legitimize governing power, no matter what kind of node wields it. Braithwaite, for example, has argued that responsiveness in the exercise of power is not just a good strategy of regulation, but a normative good that fosters deliberation and democracy (Braithwaite, 2005).

Interfaces

Nodal governance offers a useful way of thinking about the 'power map' in a governance system and the key characteristics of effective governing nodes. The concept of interfaces can then be used to refine the study and analysis of the power relations between different nodes and/or networks. Although there has been some research on interactions within particular categories of nodes – for example non-state actors (Arts et al., 2001; Baker and Chandler, 2005) and international organizations (Rittberger and Zangl, 2006) – the linkages between these actors have, to date, not been well examined. Moreover, there are few theoretical approaches explicitly dealing with interactions in governance and global governance. Oran R. Young (1996; see also Stokke, 2001; Oberthür and Gehring, 2006) scrutinizes the 'institutional interplay' of regimes and their relations to their institutional environment – regimes seen as 'sets of ... principles, norms, rules, and decision-making procedures around which actors' expectations converge in a given area of international relations' (Krasner, 1983: 2). Our approach refers more to Jan Kooiman who defines interactions as 'mutually influencing relations between two or more actors or entities' (2003: 13) and differentiates between a structural and an intentional level of interaction. The intentional level is comprised of actors and their objectives and interests, whereas the structural level refers to the 'material, social and cultural context' (that is, institutions, social constructs, forms of communication, technological development, power relations) in which interactions take place.

In an attempt to develop a concept which allows us to integrate Kooiman's structural and intentional levels and at the same time open up the term 'institutional interplay' for more actor-oriented analysis, we propose to take up Norman Long's concept of 'interfaces' and to discuss its value in analysing the interactive process of institutional change in global health governance.

While the term 'interfaces' is often used loosely and can be found to describe meetings in coffee houses as well as interactions between the governing bodies of international organizations, Norman Long's concept of 'social interface' provides the first detailed conceptualization of this term. Long defines a social interface 'as a critical point of interaction or linkage between different social systems, fields or levels of social order where structural discontinuities based upon differences of normative value and social interest, are most likely to be found' (Long, 1989: 1–2).

Long – in an essentially constructivist perspective – explains that 'studies of social interfaces should aim to bring out the dynamic and emergent character of the interactions taking place and to show how the goals, perceptions, interests, and relationships of the various parties may be reshaped as a result of their interaction' (ibid.) Thus, interfacing both influences and might change the actors' original strategies (as described later in the chapter in relation to the pharmaceutical corporations in South African through their interactions with civil society over two court cases). There is always an interplay and a mutual influence on the actors' behaviour even if they are in an antagonistic relationship and if there are great disparities in power. This reciprocity might lead to a harmonization of conflicting strategies. If interactions continue, the development of boundaries and shared expectations is likely, which shapes the interaction and may constitute 'an organised entity of interlocking relationships and intentionalities' (Long, 2001: 69). Interfaces frequently entail complex processes particularly when a variety of actors with different interests, relationships and modes of rationality are clashing. Moreover, Long stresses that it is important to focus not only on one single interface and the related actors and institutions, in a kind of micro-perspective, but also to include the actors and institutions beyond this concrete interface in a macro-perspective. Interface analysis should be based on broader institutional frameworks and fields of power (Long, 2001: 66) and should not be understood as a mechanical point where two actors, programmes or other entities meet. In nodal terms, governance operates in a landscape of multifarious social interactions and conflicting or merging cultural and political habits and behaviours meeting in related sets of specific interfaces – the complex web of institutions and informal networks linked to GHG in Geneva serves as a good example.

Long applies the social interface approach mostly to interfaces between the global and the national/local level in the field of development, that is, to vertical interfaces. Most of the elements of Long's approach, however, can also be used for our approach to the analysis of global governance, including the analysis of horizontal interfaces between different types of actors at the global level. We will modify Long's approach by concentrating less on cultural practices and sociological aspects (though not denying their importance) and by focusing instead on the political processes and dynamics of power (that is, adapting it to institutionalist approaches of international relations theory).

Because of their specific institutional environments, interfaces allow the use of particular forms of power and, thus, we can distinguish them according to the types of power being primarily used. Discursive interfaces relate to interactions aiming at changing perceptions, concepts and norms held by different nodes of governance (for example, mass media, campaigns or expert commissions). Discursive power is linked to the central role of communication in the very production of social relations and thus is related not only to the acceptance of basic beliefs on specific issues but also to broad values such as human rights. Discursive power shapes the demands and perceptions of actors' interests. Resource-transfer interfaces involve the relationships between donors (countries, foundations) and recipients. Here the resources required to tackle problems are identified, mobilized and disbursed; they are frequently closely linked to organizational interfaces, where decisions on using resources are made. Organizational interfaces refer to decision-making structures linking different actors within relevant organizations and institutions. Actors who dispose of significant resources but do not see a chance within existing organizations to have them used in a way which serves their interest might try to establish new organizations to pursue their goals (consider the foundation of the Global Fund to Fight AIDS, Tuberculosis and Malaria (GFATM)). Finally, the level of legal interfaces (as a specific outcome of processes at state-based organizational interfaces) relates to the most highly formalized norms for regulating human relations and resolving social and political conflicts without recourse to violence. As, however, there is no effective legal system at the global level, the implementation of international law depends to a large extent upon conflicts at other types of interfaces (consider the role of popular mobilization – discursive interfaces – in the outcome of conflicts linked to TRIPS regulations discussed later in this chapter).

Different nodes are more or less powerful at different types of interfaces. For example, NGOs typically have been at their most powerful in discursive interfaces, while corporations are dominant at resource-based ones. In some states, though rarely at the international level, legal interfaces provide an opportunity for NGOs to exercise power against better-resourced entities and government itself. Thus the outcome of conflicts depends to a large degree on the types of interfaces at which conflicts are fought. These outcomes will be described in greater detail in the case study presented below.

Synthesis of node and interface concepts

Nodal institutions, but also individual actors, will try to have an impact on governance processes using all types of interfaces accessible and perceived as relevant to reaching a specific goal. Their success will depend upon their specific power resources, the appropriateness of their strategy and the specific characteristics of the policy field. The concept of interfaces is a tool for analysing the nature of relations between actors within and between governance systems. The nodal governance approach provides a framework for characterizing the distribution of power in dynamic systems of polycentric governance. Deploying the two together allows us to situate a more rigorous analysis of how actors and institutions interact within an account of governance competition and change. Given a set of nodes in a governance system, interface analysis uses the generic types of interaction defined above to understand the relations typical of different types of interfaces.

Several characteristics of the interface concept make it particularly useful for the analysis of links between nodes in GHG. It defines a specific plane of social space where governing nodes link and interact, but leaves a high degree of flexibility with regard to the types of interacting systems and the nature of the site of interaction. Thus the concept can be applied to both horizontal and vertical interactions (for example, World Health Organization–WTO, bilateral donor–recipient) and interactions between nodes of very different types and characteristics (for example, community-level NGO and global PPP). Interfaces may occur within or be constituted through institutions. For example, a superstructural node is normally created as an organizational interface to facilitate cooperation between nodes. But the notion of interface is relational, rather than institutional. Thus a case before the World Trade Organization is a legal interface which involves interactions within and between a wide variety of actors and institutions, including government ministries, corporations and so on. An interface, as suggested by Long's definition, is simply a site of recurrent interactions between nodes, so it encompasses a wide range of more or less formalized or recurrent relations. Interfaces might be organized by existing organizations, becoming 'repeated practices' leading to informal rule systems (Rosenau, 2004: 32), but they might also remain just spaces of informal interaction between actors belonging to different social systems.

Nodes and interfaces: governance of access to antiretroviral (ARV) medicines

Conflicts associated with HIV/AIDS have played a central role in the development of GHG. In this section, we analyse the fight against HIV/AIDS to show the value of the nodal/interfaces approach to understanding how GHG is constituted by networked nodes that claim the status of global actors and use that status as a tool of control and legitimization.[1] The impact of these nodes on shaping policies and results in global health governance depends on conflicts at the interfaces with other nodes, and to a large degree on whether they succeed in shifting conflicts to often newly created forums (interfaces between governing nodes) where they can make optimal use of their power resources (Braithwaite, 2004). As existing nodes continued to strive for influence after the mid-1990s, this strategy led to a proliferation of actors in global health. We will see that the chances for groups poorly represented in Westphalian international relations to have a voice in GHG have grown and that strong actors such as transnational pharmaceutical corporations (TNPCs) and powerful states were adapting to these new forms of governance to pursue their interests.

The governance of HIV/AIDS since the end of the 1980s exhibits an unmistakable nodal character. The recognition of HIV/AIDS as a global health challenge has been marked by repeated changes in governance with the entry of new nodes into the system, as governments and intergovernmental organizations failed to provide an adequate response to the pandemic. Governments have worked through a rapidly changing set of international and bilateral agencies (for example, the WHO, the United Nations Joint Programme on HIV/AIDS , the American President's Emergency Plan for AIDS Relief (PEPFAR[2]), PPPs (GFATM) and with private actors (NGOs, foundations)). Since the second half of the 1990s these developments have been increasingly influenced by interfaces with the nodal governance system of intellectual property rights (IPRs) over access to medicines.

Nodal governance of HIV/AIDS and a proliferation of actors

On the international level, institutional developments in the fight against HIV/AIDS began in 1986 when the WHO, the titular global health leader, set up what soon became the Global Programme on AIDS (GPA). The GPA pursued the fight against the epidemic in developing countries by linking international discourses on the disease with technical assistance for developing countries and the mobilization of donor countries for a multilateral response. Under the leadership of Jonathan Mann, the GPA broke away from the dry technical assistance discourse frequently found in WHO in those years. In the international guidelines on HIV/AIDS and human rights published by the Office of the United Nations High Commissioner for Human Rights and UNAIDS (1998), Mann deployed a rhetoric that had both discursive force and brought HIV into the ambit of the UN's legal interfaces.

The World Bank also developed a number of country-cooperation projects, including an AIDS Strategy for Africa (World Bank, 1988) and the Multi-Country HIV/AIDS Program (MAP) (World Bank, 2000). The World Bank constituted the first significant resource-based interface on the global level in relation to HIV/AIDS. Furthermore, the United Nations Children's Fund (UNICEF) concentrated on the prevention of mother-to-child transmission of the virus. Dissatisfaction with the WHO led major nations funding the HIV response to support the creation of the Joint United Nations Programme on HIV/AIDS (UNAIDS), a new organizational interface for HIV control. UNAIDS was designed by the UN system as a superstructural node coordinating the activities of several UN agencies substantially involved in HIV control. Poor in resources and dependent upon voluntary cooperation, it has never realized its potential to rationalize and coordinate UN actions.

The introduction of highly active antiretroviral therapy (HAART) gave new force to the discursive pressure for HIV treatment (and to a lesser extent prevention) wielded by NGO networks. The availability of HAART created a shift in emphasis from behavioural prevention to treatment and, as a result, increased the need to mobilize substantially more resources. NGOs, including Médecins Sans Frontières (MSF), took an increasingly aggressive and effective position in the governance of HIV/AIDS policy in the world's discursive interfaces and in the organizational interfaces of the UN system, supporting the human rights of the poor and vulnerable to access to medicines. G8 donors (especially the USA and Japan), under pressure to provide more money, were reluctant to give it to UNAIDS or the WHO. They chose instead to shift the forum for treatment funding by creating a new node, the GFATM. This entailed a new structure of interfaces. Unlike the WHO, where developing/recipient countries form a majority of member states, the GFATM is a partnership, with an equal representation of donors and recipients. Using the PPP vehicle created a powerful resource-based interface and largely eliminated legal interfaces associated with government and UN organizations. The constitution of the GFATM in a global PPP-like form thus helped to integrate private actors (and to accommodate conflicting interests between them) and to reduce the importance of the intergovernmental and nation-state interfaces as institutionalized in UN organizations. The Country Coordinating Mechanism (CCM) was a superstructural node meant to link key public and private organizations in the recipient country into a cohesive and coordinated network for proposals to apply for GFATM money.

The US government, dubious about multilateral entities and at the same time the only government powerful enough and with sufficient self-confidence in its global mission 'to go it alone', supported the GFATM but then also launched PEPFAR, a 'unilateral global' programme. PEPFAR reflected nodal governance in domestic US politics, arising as an interface at which several different networks could advance their interests. For social conservatives, PEPFAR was a means through which funding restrictions related to commercial sex work and abstinence could be projected into GHG. For treatment activists, PEPFAR was a vehicle for even greater expenditure for HIV/AIDS. The programme also brought money to TNPCs, which secured a provision favouring the procurement of brand-name drugs. For public health nodes within the US government, such as CDCs (Centers for Disease Control and Prevention) and the United States Agency for International Development

(USAID), PEPFAR was a means through which their existing international AIDS programmes could be strengthened in the face of 'competition' from the GFATM. By integrating faith- and community-based groups and by taking the lead in building a new PPP for paediatric HIV treatment, formulations and access (cooperating with TNPCs, the Elizabeth Glaser Pediatric AIDS Foundation and UNAIDS), PEPFAR reflects the nodal governance structure of GHG in a state-led endeavour.

Foundations are another important group of actors on the nodal map of GHG for HIV/AIDS. The unprecedented wealth of the Bill and Melinda Gates Foundation made it a strong player the moment it entered the field by supporting the International AIDS Vaccine Initiative in the late 1990s. The Clinton Foundation has acted as an interesting superstructural node. Without a substantial endowment, it has worked to connect government, corporate, UN and NGO nodes to facilitate negotiation on price and delivery of drugs.

This great diversity of actors in the global governance of HIV/AIDS is consistent with the nodal governance model: government and international organizations do not have the sole or even leading governing role on the full range of issues or priorities. In the control of this public health threat, state and international governors have often been second place or at least shared governance with private and hybrid entities. This change has allowed the participation of a much broader field of actors in GHG, which implies greater opportunities for advocacy of diverse perspectives and a higher degree of flexibility in GHG – but not necessarily more accountability nor effectiveness. The proliferation of actors and interfaces has made forum-shifting an even more important tool. In the ongoing dispute over access to medicines, weaker advocates, such as NGOs, have leveraged discursive power at organizational interfaces to influence the decisions made at legal interfaces such as the WTO and resource-based interfaces such as PEPFAR and the GFATM.

Interfaces between the governance of IPRs and the governance of HIV/AIDS

In the 1990s, the WHO, the World Bank and UNAIDS supported prevention as the best practice in the fight against HIV/AIDS in developing countries. This was seen as a matter of 'cost-effectiveness', because annual drug costs stood at about US$10,000 per person. Although prices of ARVs for treatment were at least one hundred times the production costs of the medicines, because of monopoly-pricing due to patent rights, intergovernmental organizations (IGOs) were slow to take action aimed at securing lower prices. In the late 1990s, however, a medical consensus on the efficacy of treatment coincided with the establishment of the TRIPS regime. Very quickly, NGOs and the IGOs in UNAIDS began to push on treatment access, and recognized that global IPR governance in the form of TRIPS was going to be a prime determinant.

Until the end of the 1990s the outputs of the systems of global health and global trade were structurally linked, but not yet linked by the emergence of an inter-systemic governance system. The conflict between IPRs and access to medicines took its present shape as a result of an earlier forum-shifting strategy engineered by the nodal governance system of transnational corporations in technology-intensive sectors (Sell, 1998, 2003). Dissatisfied with the degree of protection afforded by WIPO, IPR holders in the 1980s formulated and began to implement a plan to supplant the UN agency with the creation of a treaty on Trade-Related Intellectual Property Rights (TRIPS) within the WTO and linked to its system of dispute settlement, that is of trade rule enforcement. TRIPS changed the politics and the market for pharmaceuticals by strengthening the rights of patent holders, who gained a more effective enforcement regime, and placing substantial limitations on the production of generics by countries like India and Brazil. The impact of IPRs on drug prices and the related challenge to provide universal access to ARVs became one of the central points of conflict in the development of GHG, and significantly changed the interfaces between institutions of global economic and global health governance.

The battle for access revolved around the costs of medication and how they might be met. Strategies aimed at raising funds to pay for drugs and their delivery resulted in part in the creation of new nodes, PEPFAR and GFATM. Here we focus on the struggle over the production of low-priced generics under what came to be known as the 'TRIPS flexibilities' – compulsory licensing and parallel importation. This struggle was waged in a set of legal, organizational and discursive interfaces including the TRIPS ministerial forum, the TRIPS Council, civil society organizations (CSOs) and the global media.

The WTO's dispute settlement system, and national court systems adjudicating IP disputes within the TRIPS framework, emerged as legal interfaces between TNPCs as patent holders and health actors demanding better access to drugs. Courts have to interpret law, which opens up the possibility of mobilizing discursive interfaces about this interpretation and leads to the entrance of a new power vector into the legal 'game'.

CSOs, which have no formal position in the legal conflict, can mobilize public opinion and thus put pressure on actors either not to use the legal option (as in the case of Brazil) or to withdraw from legal action as happened twice in South Africa.[3] Southern governments became increasingly aware that they could have an impact on decision-making within the WTO/TRIPS, and other intergovernmental organizations. This has led to successful efforts to achieve a political redefinition of the legal basis (WTO/TRIPS) and to move the strategy of fighting HIV/AIDS towards a treatment strategy (WHO). Brazil played a central role in both endeavours. In 1996 the Brazilian government declared a policy of free access for all infected people to an ARV therapy. Later, the government and the Brazilian AIDS programme strongly supported a treatment strategy in international forums (PAHO, WHO, cooperation with

CSOs) and defended a broad use of TRIPS safeguards in negotiations on the so-called Doha Declaration (Calcagnotto, 2007).[4]

From 1996 onwards, in close interaction with Brazilian and South African conflicts with TNPCs along legal interfaces, Health Action International (HAI) successfully developed a campaign against the effect of TRIPS in limiting the access of poor people to patented medicines. This can be seen as a starting-point to framing the access conflict in terms of a human rights problem and to developing discursive interfaces with IGOs, TNPCs, political leaders and others on the effects of TRIPS on access to medicines – basically through reports, the internet, lobbying and the mass media. Taking up Long's definition, we can characterize the human rights-based nodal governance system of the access campaign and the system of IPR governance as 'fields of social order, where structural discontinuities [are] based upon differences of normative value and social interest' (1989: 1–2).

The HAI/CSO campaign was supported by MSF, which after receiving the Nobel Peace Prize in 1999 was highly regarded by global public opinion. In November 1999, the MSF Campaign for Access to Essential Medicines was launched. Since then it has assumed the leading role in the coordination of civil society activities in this field and has become an important actor in nodal governance. CSOs intensified pressure on northern states and the pharmaceutical industry by achieving increased media coverage of the access issue and thus influencing public opinion. Furthermore, the Geneva-based South Centre played an important role in strengthening links between CSOs and governments of poor countries.

In cooperation with some southern governments (in particular Brazil) CSOs succeeded in reframing the public dialogue on HIV/AIDS from a focus on prevention to a focus on treatment (Hein, 2007). As a result of this shift in public perception, health-related IGOs as well as IPR-related nodes (IFPMA, US government) had to react. In April 2002, WHO finally added ARVs to its 'Model List of Essential Medicines'. The G7/G8 strategy to use resource-based power to accommodate public demands (and to react to ill-health, which was increasingly seen as a security threat) produces strong interfaces between developed countries and nodes in the field of GHG related to the Millennium Development Goals and, above all, the setting up of the GFATM, while avoiding everything which might call into question the role of IPRs. TNPCs supported differential pricing schemes and the foundation of drug access PPPs (for example, the Accelerating Access Initiative) which can also be interpreted as an indirect transfer of resources (reducing costs to developing countries by forgoing some income). It could be argued that new institutions entered GHG in an attempt to alleviate pressure towards compromises in the IPR field.

Nodal governance institutions linked to TRIPS have offered compromises, as we have seen. The availability of cheap generic products and the increased involvement of southern governments, however, strengthened the access coalition and allowed it to shift its political focus back to the organizational interfaces of intergovernmental organizations with the view of having an impact on international law. Parallel to this process, interfaces between health- and human rights-oriented CSOs, but also the UN human rights system (see General Comment No. 14 on the 'right towards the highest attainable standard of health' by the Committee on Economic, Social and Cultural Rights, 11 August 2000) gained strength. 'Universal access' to medicines (including the need to re-orient R&D towards the needs of 'neglected populations') was increasingly accepted as a norm challenging IPRs as the most important incentive to pharmaceutical research. Although the International Covenant on Economic, Social and Cultural Rights constitutes international law, these rights have been broadly considered as 'non-justiciable', as they 'lack the "absoluteness" that characterizes civil and political rights' (Ruxton and Karim, 2001: 2), which also implies that they would not constitute legal interfaces.

Although much of the CSO campaign was carried out at interfaces unrelated to the WTO, it was focused in significant part on the WTO's ongoing process of TRIPS implementation and interpretation. This culminated in November 2001, when a ministerial meeting of TRIPS signatories issued the Doha Declaration on the TRIPS Agreement and Public Health. The declaration affirmed 'WTO members' right to protect public health and, in particular, to promote access to medicines for all' (Paragraph 4). Following Doha, the TRIPS council took up the issue and defined a set of criteria for parallel importation. These negotiations within the legal interfaces of TRIPS widened the space for using TRIPS flexibilities and reinforced the position of developing countries in negotiations with TNPCs.

Also since about 2001, the US-based Consumer Project on Technology (CpTech) had promoted the concept of a medical R&D treaty, which in 2006, supported by other CSOs and an official proposal by Brazil and Kenya, led to opening negotiations on a Global Framework on Essential Health Research within the WHO. The basic proposal to establish a fund to finance pharmaceutical research independent of market-oriented decisions by private companies was taken up by the WHO-sponsored Commission on Intellectual Property Rights, Innovation and Public Health (CIPIH). The WHO has attempted to take a mediating role in the discursive interfaces between the human rights and the IPR communities. This can be seen as a starting point for shifting the forum for stimulating essential health research from IPR-focused nodes to the WHO. In December 2006, an Inter-Governmental Working Group (IGWG) on Public Health, Innovation and Intellectual Property was established under WHO auspices.

In this situation, acknowledging the pressure they felt from GHG actors and the media (Hein, 2007: 50–2), TNPC lobbyists, including the International Federation of Pharmaceutical Manufacturers and Associations (IFPMA), had to retreat. In response, the private sector resorted again to forum shifting, now towards free trade agreements which were not initially so much in the focus of public debate and thus remained somewhat sheltered from discursive interfaces (Wogart, 2007; Helfer, 2004). Using their powerful system of nodal governance (Drahos, 2004)[5] pharmaceutical companies and the USA continue to employ trade pressures to deter compulsory licensing in a way that to some extent could obviate the concessions reached at Doha (Abbott, 2005). The recent US pressure against Thailand after the issuing of several compulsory licences illustrates the industry's ongoing battle against the use of TRIPS flexibilities.

The processes analysed above cannot be undone. On the one hand, the interfacing between human rights-based CSOs and the IPR system (linked to a broader system of actors interested in global economic integration through free trade) has been related to more general aspects of dealing with the social impacts of globalization. There is an increased awareness of the need to re-balance the relationship between the global economy and global social policies, which has led to a series of protests in cases where corporate interests have openly disregarded the needs of the poor (as in a number of patent-related conflicts). On the other hand, we can observe a reconfiguration of nodes within specific fields of governance, which leads to the question whether the result might be 'an organized entity of interlocking relationships and intentionalities' (Long, 2001: 69) which could lead to an extended superstructural node of global health governance. So far, we can observe a rather loose but intensifying network of discursive interfaces between organizations and/or individual members of these organization in Geneva (Hein, 2007: 60–1).

Thus, the story of access to ARVs offers a rich set of events through which to illustrate the relationship between nodal and interface analyses. The access problem developed around missing institutional links between two fields of global governance which are in fact highly interdependent: IPRs and health, including human rights. In this context, access to ARVs has been improved, but control over this field remains ambiguous. While there have been few changes in legal and decision-making power, the discursive power of advocacy organizations and (some) developing country governments has been strengthened – to a certain degree also because of the increased fear of infectious diseases and the impact of poor health on political instability.

Implications

What can we learn from our analysis of the development of GHG in the field of HIV/AIDS and access to medicines in a perspective on nodal governance and the role of interfaces? Four points seem be important:

1. There has been a considerable change in the global perception of health needs, which has strengthened the position of the human rights-based

governance system. Nevertheless, in order to stabilize the gains made at discursive interfaces the access to medicines issue has to be introduced to the level of organizational interfaces, where international law can be created, modified or authoritatively interpreted, which might finally strengthen the human right to access to essential drugs by creating justiciable law competing with WTO-backed IPR law.

2. Discursive interfaces between global and national CSOs, but also between national governments and international organizations such as the South Centre, have contributed to changing government positions in decision-making bodies (organizational interfaces). This includes an improved capacity of developing countries to defend their positions, for example, in the WTO, but has also changed the positions of donor governments as a result of public pressure.

3. The WHO has linked itself to the discursive interfaces on access to medicines. Important voluntary contributions by some northern countries have helped to strengthen the discursive role of the WHO and to revive its importance as an organizational interface by overcoming deadlocks created by ideologically inflexible voting blocs. Moreover, the SARS epidemic, during which the WHO exercised considerable power through the media, showed the potential impact of discursive interfaces on regulatory questions, and resulted in an expansion of its de jure powers in the new International Health Regulations. By being increasingly open to a large spectrum of stakeholders (based in various systems of nodal governance in global society) and developing flexible forms of accommodating different forms of interfaces, the WHO is changing its character from a conventional intergovernmental organization into a center of nodal governance. In the case of the CIPIH-IGWG process, WHO is using resource-based interfaces (voluntary contributions) to support a discursive process (CIPIH) that has an impact on organizational interfaces (initiatives and voting behaviour in WHA) and might lead to the creation of new international law.

4. The nodal processes around HIV/AIDS have been associated with the deployment of a lot more money for treatment and a smaller increase in funds for prevention through the creation of new resource-based interfaces with the GFATM, PEPFAR, private foundations, in particular the Bill and Melinda Gates Foundation, and PPPs. To some degree this can be interpreted as discursive strategies successfully communicating the seriousness of the situation (including the threat to 'the rich') but it can also be interpreted as an answer to a felt obligation in the context of human rights. Moreover, corporate actors offered resources and compromises in the form of differential pricing as a kind of compensation for defending strong IPRs and preventing modifications of international law which might affect their capacity to use legal interfaces for their interests.[6]

Nodes in the field of access to ARVs, such as the TRIPS Council, the MSF Access Campaign, the WHO Globalization, Trade and Health Team and CIPIH, interface with other nodes in the field of GHG, but hardly at all with local governance structures in the affected areas in poor countries (neglected people). The shortfall of the so-called '3 by 5' initiative[7] is related to the same basic problems – for example, the lack of access to clean water and sanitation, and poverty, which still cause more deaths in the south than HIV/AIDS. It is difficult to reach marginalized groups, and service delivery is difficult where health systems are weak (WHO/UNAIDS/UNICEF, 2007: 9). This links up with the missing interfaces between the nodal structure of global governance and local institutions of 'neglected people'.[8]

Those large CSOs that are integrated into GHG, tend to be: (i) part of a global elite (in spite of advocating for the poor); and (ii) strongly focused on specific health issues rather than on the link between health and the social and economic origins of poverty (in spite of being conscious of this link). It remains to be seen whether the WHO Commission on the Social Determinants of Health can open up some avenues towards overcoming these limitations and support the formation and integration of nodal health governance structures at the local level in poor countries.

In a comprehensive perspective, can we identify a virtuous circuit in the governance of HIV/AIDS? Certainly real participation and mobilization (of people and resources) have increased. GHG has become increasingly open to the participation of new actors, which has mobilized new resources in the form of knowledge, finance and political capital. GHG can now be characterized as a polycentric system of nodal governance and a complex dynamic of interfaces between actors within and across different governance systems. Advocacy by CSOs has given some voice to marginalized people, though many of them are still hardly represented in health policy conflicts and negotiations. Concerning 'implementation' we should ask 'implementation of what?' Certainly, no institution has been in a position fully to implement its specific strategy; we might, however, talk of the implementation of specific results of the self-organization of GHG as, for example, the assurance of TRIPS flexibilities, the development of hybrid institutions in the field of R&D and access to medicines for neglected diseases and the acceleration of a process towards universal treatment.

Thus, the development of nodal GHG has helped to overcome the deadlocks inherent in decision-making processes in international governmental institutions, where different groups of countries frequently block one another by maintaining uncompromising positions or withholding resources. By sidelining international institutions (and governments which represent those powerful interests that have prevailed in national political processes), social groups which have had no chance to be represented by governments have attained access to global political processes and opportunities to form new alliances. The chance to use various forms of power in an expanding field of interfaces allowed actors to move conflicts on specific issues to other institutions of nodal governance systems. This increased the flexibility of GHG in general and in particular enabled a responsiveness to the needs of people who would not have been taken account of in a more traditional government-dominated system.

The strengthened position of developing countries in the interfaces with TNPCs and developed country interests also put the WHO as an intergovernmental organization in a new position; furthermore, the increased salience of health in global politics has considerably increased the WHO's extra-budgetary resources which in turn has increased the organization's flexibility in a situation of stagnant regular budgets. There seems to be a chance that the WHO might regain a still stronger position in a yet more distributed system of nodal governance. The Framework Convention on Tobacco Control represents a bold effort to reclaim its place as a vital Westphalian organizational interface. The WHO has also tried to create superstructural nodes, most recently the Commission on the Social Determinants of Health, but its capacity effectively to integrate and mobilize networks in this way remains uncertain. The Paris Declaration on Aid Effectiveness might help states to reintegrate some of the nodal governance activities in GHG: a number of approaches have been taken towards the coordination of existing and the creation of new GHG activities towards strengthening southern states' capacities to improve national health governance (for example the concept of the 'Three Ones'[9] and the 'Scaling-up for Better Health' initiative[10]). The WHO still constitutes the most important organizational interface with governments in global health politics, and both the International Health Regulations and the Framework Convention on Tobacco Control count as important political successes for the organization.

Conclusion

The description we have offered here may guide the strategies and tactics of the participants in GHG. The WHO remains near the centre of GHG. As the 'official' interface for traditional Westphalian governance, it enjoys some advantages that other richer, politically defter organizations cannot claim. Yet it is now clearly in competition with organizations such as the Bill and Melinda Gates Foundation and the GFATM, and even in exercising its traditional, constitutional function as an interface for states it depends upon its ability to mobilize and coordinate the power of NGOs. The challenge for the WHO is to resolve the tension between its legal identity as a traditional Westphalian institution and its day-to-day need to operate as an interface open to weaker states and civil society. One way of doing that is to link its nodal function as a discursive interface to its capacity as an intergovernmental organization to host negotiating processes to promote further development of international law in the GHG field.

The emergence of hybrid entities such as the GFATM has transformed GHG. States, international organizations and private actors all now perceive advantages in creating new governance entities. New nodes of governance reflect the networked structure of GHG; they have been created to join existing governors and networks in a way that is perceived to be more efficient, in interfaces whose rules are more conducive to achieving the partners' goals. We must also recognize, however, that sometimes new institutions of governance, particularly hybrid institutions, benefit from their ability to escape forms of constraint that have grown up around more traditional public and private institutions. In nodal governance, it is also essential to identify 'missing nodes' where important stakeholders are structurally excluded from the networks and interfaces of GHG. Most of the world's people are poor. Their organizations are generally also poor and need the assistance of wealthier organizations to gain entry into the interfaces of GHG. Increasing the diversity and legitimacy of GHG requires affirmative efforts to open up governance to the poor.

Recognizing a nodal description of GHG highlights fundamental normative issues. Missing nodes and inaccessible interfaces undermine the legitimacy of GHG as a democratic project in the broad sense. A nodal governance description unveils the fact that many powerful governors are not accountable or transparent to the people whose lives are shaped by GHG. Where governance is widely distributed beyond the state, there are democratic deficits even where public governors generally respect, protect and fulfil civil and political rights. The WHO and UNAIDS consistently make efforts to be accessible to NGOs, but their decision-making and accountability structures remain Westphalian. The GFATM has required civil society participation in its CCM device, and sometimes delivers its grants through NGOs, but it is doubtful whether the GFATM has found a robust way to democratize the aid process in a nodal world – very rarely has this kind of NGO participation effectively given a voice to neglected people. The nature of the Gates Foundation's accountability to those whose lives may depend upon its decisions remains unclear.

To achieve a virtuous circle of GHG will, of course, require the political will to do so among the powerful. To the extent that UN organizations and hybrids such as the GFATM are prepared to promote democratic GHG, a number of steps are practicable. First, organizations can be transparent and accountable in their own operations. The GFATM has set a good example in its website, where anyone with a computer can find out a great deal about its fundraising, spending and success in meeting stated goals. Second, they can set a high standard of attention and investment to constituting interfaces accessible to the poorer and weaker actors in GHG. This does not just refer to civil society organizations working at the global level (the superstructural nodes of NGO networks), but also to NGOs and government agencies at the local level. Organizations working in cities, towns and villages are implementers, beneficiaries and potential monitors of the world's aid funding, and including their voices can bring both legitimacy and better information to GHG. Their participation, however, depends largely on the willingness of global actors and donors to open interfaces and fund their participation.

Finally, distributed governance does provide some scope for the relatively poor and weak to influence GHG. Grass-roots NGOs are using nodal strategies to create strategic alliances at the regional, national and international levels. In the HIV/AIDS experience, groups like South Africa's Treatment Action Campaign (TAC) have combined local mobilization with international networking to influence both domestic policy and GHG. With minimal support, such groups concentrate a high degree of technical capacity in one place and deploy it at interfaces where they have a high probability of success. Although comprised of the 'weak', people with a highly stigmatized disease, TAC nonetheless has power drawn from its expertise, its communication and mobilization capacity, and the law. In this way, TAC and other NGOs and weak states can use the nodal weapons of the strong to significant effect (Burris et al., 2007). GHG may be a game that, like other games, rewards the rich more than the poor, but achieving something like a virtuous circle of GHG remains an attainable goal.

Notes

1. This section is based on the results of a research project on 'Global Health Governance' carried out by GIGA between 2004 and 2006, published in Hein et al. (2007); see also Wogart et al. Chapter 7 below.
2. The President's Emergency Plan for AIDS Relief (PEPFAR) was founded by the US government in early 2003 (see below).
3. TNPCs provoked conflicts at the legal interfaces in order to restrict the use of TRIPS safeguards or – in the case of Brazil – to 'censor' national patent laws which in their view were not TRIPS-compliant (local working requirement). These conflicts used the strengthened legal interfaces of the IPR system (through the forum-shifting from WIPO to WTO). The governments of Brazil and South Africa defended the use of TRIPS safeguards and were supported by intensified attacks by CSOs against TNPCs which led (i) to a retreat of pharma corporations and the US government supporting them; and (ii) to a strengthening of CSO networks and the nodal function of MSF as the manager of the access campaign. Whatever the influence of the defenders of strong IPCs within the international trade system they could not prevent the transfer of the conflict to discursive interfaces where global civil society organizations had a much stronger position.
4. The production of ARVs as generics constituted a precondition for access to affordable medicines independent of any price concessions made by TNPCs. Brazil combined the generic production of non-protected drugs with the purchase of additional ingredients from originator firms (after negotiating price reductions), essentially for local production, but Indian manufacturers (for specific transitory clauses of TRIPS India did not have to adjust its patent law before 2005) produced the whole range of first-line ARVs for domestic markets and for export to countries

which were allowed to import these products. Thus, after 2000, cheap ARVs were available on the world market independent of concessions by TNPCs.
5. Drahos points to the overlapping membership of the International Intellectual Property Alliance (IIPA), the Biotechnology Industry Organization, the Business Software Alliance and the Industry Functional Advisory Committee on IPRs for Trade Policy Matters, which advises the US Congress and president (Drahos, 2004: 414).
6. See for example Noehrenberg (2006) who, from the IFPMA perspective, quite clearly links TNPCs' participation in the Accelerated Access Initiative and the defence of IPRs.
7. The target of ARV treatment for 3 million people by 2005 launched by WHO in 2003 was not achieved. By the end of 2005, about 1.3 million people received ARV treatment in low- and middle-income countries (compared to 400,000 in December 2003).
8. See Gould (2005) who stresses that international CSOs are more closely linked to national and transnational elites than to networks of local people.
9. The 'Three Ones' principle introduced by UNAIDS and WHO to achieve the most effective and efficient use of resources and to ensure rapid action and results-based management demanded *one* agreed HIV/AIDS action framework to provide the basis for coordinating the work of all partners; *one* national AIDS coordinating authority, with a broad-based multi-sectoral mandate; and *one* agreed country-level monitoring and evaluation system
10. The 'Scaling-up for Better Health' (IHP+) initiative started in January 2007. Following the example of the 'Education for All – Fast-track Initiative', key international health organizations, governments and private donors are cooperating with the aim of making better use of existing resources, creating more effective mechanisms of accountability and mobilizing additional resources to support national strategic plans for health system development.

References

Abbott, F.M., 'The WTO Medicines Decision: World Pharmaceutical Trade and the Protection of Public Health', *American Journal of International Law*, 99 (2005): 317–58.
Arts, B., M. Noortmann and B. Reinalda (eds), *Non-State Actors in International Relations* (Aldershot: Ashgate, 2001).
Baker, G. and D. Chandler (eds), *Global Civil Society: Contested Futures* (London: Routledge, 2005).
Barnett, M. and R. Duvall (eds), *Power in Global Governance* (Cambridge: Cambridge University Press, 2005)
Bartsch, S., W. Hein and L. Kohlmorgen, 'Interfaces: a Concept for the Analysis of Global Health Governance', in W. Hein, S. Bartsch and L. Kohlmorgen (eds), *Global Health Governance and the Fight against HIV/AIDS* (Basingstoke: Palgrave, 2007), pp. 18–37.
Braithwaite, J., 'Methods of Power for Development: Weapons of the Weak, Weapons of the Strong', *Michigan Journal of International Law*, 26(Fall) (2004): 297–330.
Braithwaite, J., 'Responsive Regulation and Developing Economies', *World Development*, 34(5) (2005): 868–932.
Braithwaite, J. and P. Drahos, *Global Business Regulation* (Cambridge: Cambridge University Press, 2000).

Burris, S., P. Drahos and C. Shearing, 'Nodal Governance', *Australian Journal of Legal Philosophy*, 30 (2005): 30–58.

Burris, S., T. Hancock, V. Lin and A. Herzog, 'Emerging Principles of Healthy Urban Governance: a Background Paper for the Knowledge Network on Urban Settings; WHO Commission on the Social Determinants of Health', World Health Organization Kobe Center, Kobe, 2006.

Burris, S., T. Hancock, V. Lin and A. Herzog, 'Emerging Strategies for Healthy Urban Governance', *Journal of Urban Health*, 84(Suppl. 1) (2007): 154–63.

Burris, S., M. Kempa and C. Shearing, 'Changes in Governance: a Cross-Disciplinary Review of Current Scholarship', *Akron Law Review*, 41(1) (2008): 1–66.

Calcagnotto, G., 'Consensus-Building on Brazilian HIV/AIDS Policy: National and Global Interfaces in Health Governance', in W. Hein, S. Bartsch and L. Kohlmorgen (eds), *Global Health Governance and the Fight against HIV/AIDS* (Basingstoke: Palgrave, 2007), pp.172–201.

Castells, M., 'Materials for an Exploratory Theory of the Network Society', *British Journal of Sociology*, 51(1) (2000): 5–24.

Cohen, J., 'The New World of Global Health', *Science*, 311(13 January) (2006): 162–7.

Dorf, M.C. and C.F. Sabel, 'A Constitution of Democratic Experimentalism', *Columbia Law Review*, 98 (1998): 267–473.

Drahos, P., 'Intellectual Property and Pharmaceutical Markets: a Nodal Governance Approach', *Temple Law Review*, 77 (2004): 401–24.

Dupont, B., 'Security in the Age of Networks', *Policing and Society*, 14(1) (2004): 76–91.

Fidler, D., 'Constitutional Outlines of Public Health's "New World Order"', *Temple Law Review*, 77 (2004): 247–89.

Fung, A., *Empowered Participation: Reinventing Urban Democracy* (Princeton, NJ: Princeton University Press, 2004).

Gostin, L., 'Meeting Basic Survival Needs of the World's Least Healthy People: Toward a Framework Convention on Global Health', *Georgetown Law Journal*, 96 (2) (2008): 331–92.

Gould, J. (ed.), *The New Conditionality: the Politics of Poverty Reduction Strategies* (London: Zed Books, 2005).

Hein, W., 'Global Health Governance and WTO/TRIPS: Conflicts between "Global Market-Creation" and "Global Social Rights"', in W. Hein, S. Bartsch and L. Kohlmorgen (eds), *Global Health Governance and the Fight against HIV/AIDS* (Basingstoke: Palgrave, 2007), pp. 38–66.

Hein, W., S. Bartsch and L. Kohlmorgen (eds), *Global Health Governance and the Fight against HIV/AIDS* (Basingstoke: Palgrave, 2007).

Helfer, L., 'Regime Shifting: the TRIPs Agreement and New Dynamics of International Intellectual Property Lawmaking', *Yale Journal of International Law*, 29 (2004): 1–83.

Hurtig, A.K. and M. San Sebastian, 'The People's Health Movement: What Is It and Should We Care?' *Scandinavian Journal of Public Health*, 33(3) (2005): 236–8.

Joerges, C., I.-J. Sand and G. Teubner, *Transnational Governance and Constitutionalism: International Studies in the Theory of Private Law* (Oxford: Hart Publishing, 2004).

Keohane, R., 'Global Governance and Democratic Accountability', in D. Held and M. Koenig-Archibugi (eds), *Taming Globalization: Frontiers of Governance* (Oxford: Polity Press, 2002), pp. 130–59.

Kooiman, J., *Governing as Governance* (London: Sage, 2003).

Krasner, S., 'Structural Causes and Regime Consequences: Regimes and Intervening Variables', in S. Krasner (ed.), *International Regimes* (Ithaca, NY: Cornell University Press, 1983), pp. 1–21.

Lobel, O., 'The Renew Deal: the Fall of Regulation and the Rise of Governance in Contemporary Legal Thought', *Minnesota Law Review*, 89(November) (2004): 342–471.

Long, N., *Encounters at the Interface* (Wageningen: Wageningen Studies in Sociology, 1989).

Long, N., *Development Sociology: Actor Perspectives* (London: Routledge Chapman & Hall, 2001)

Luhmann, N., 'Globalization or World Society: How to Conceive of Modern Society', *International Review of Sociology – Revue Internationale de Sociologie*, 7(1) (1997): 67–79.

Mayntz, R., 'Governance Theory als fortentwickelte Steuerungstheorie?' in G.F. Schuppert (ed.), *Governance-Forschung. Vergewisserung über Stand und Entwicklungslinien* (Baden-Baden: Nomos, 2005), pp. 11–20.

Noehrenberg, E., 'Report of the Commission on Intellectual Property Rights, Innovation and Public Health: an Industry Perspective', *Bulletin of the World Health Organization*, 84 (5) (2006): 419–20.

Oberthür, S. and T. Gehring (eds), *Institutional Interaction in Global Environmental Governance* (Cambridge, MA: MIT Press, 2006).

Office of the United Nations High Commissioner for Human Rights and UNAIDS, *HIV/AIDS and Human Rights: International Guidelines* (New York and Geneva: United Nations, 1998).

Raab, J. and H.B. Milward, 'Dark Networks as Problems', *Journal of Public Administration Research and Theory*, 13(4) (2003): 413–39.

Rhodes, R.A.W., *Understanding Governance: Policy Networks, Governance, Reflexivity and Accountability* (Buckingham and Philadelphia: Open University Press, 1997).

Rittberger, V. and B. Zangl, *International Organization: Polity, Politics and Policies* (Basingstoke: Palgrave Macmillan, 2006).

Rosenau, J. N., 'Strong Demand, Huge Supply: Governance in an Emerging Epoch', in I. Bache and M. Flinders (eds), *Multi-Level Governance* (Oxford: Oxford University Press, 2004), pp. 31–48.

Ruxton, S. and R. Karim, *Beyond Civil Rights: Developing Economic, Social, and Cultural Rights in the UK* (Oxford: Oxfam, 2001).

Sabel, C., 'Beyond Principal-Agent Governance: Experimentalist Organizations, Learning and Accountability', in E. Engelen and M.S.D. Ho (eds), *De Staat van de Democratie. Democratie voorbij de Staat* (Amsterdam: Amsterdam University Press, 2004), pp. 173–95.

Sell, S. K., *Power and Ideas: the North-South Politics of Intellectual Property and Antitrust* (Albany: State University of New York Press, 1998).

Sell, S. K., *Private Power, Public Law: the Globalization of Intellectual Property Rights* (Cambridge: Cambridge University Press, 2003).

Shearing, C., 'Reflections on the Refusal to Acknowledge Private Governments', in J. Woods and B. Dupont (eds), *Democracy and the Governance of Security* (Cambridge: Cambridge University Press, 2005), pp. 11–32.

Shearing, C. and J. Wood, 'Nodal Governance, Democracy, and the New "Denizens"', *Journal of Law and Society*, 30(3) (2003): 400–19.

Sinden, A., 'The Power of Rights: Imposing Human Rights Duties on Transnational Corporations for Environmental Harms', in D. McBarnet, A. Voiculescu and T. Campbell (eds), *The New Corporate Accountability: Corporate Social Responsibility and the Law* (Cambridge: Cambridge University Press, 2008), pp. 501–27, available at SSRN: http://ssrn.com/abstract=925679 (accessed 4 February 2009).

Slaughter, A.-M., 'The Accountability of Government Networks', *Indiana Journal of Global Legal Studies*, 8 (2001): 347–67.
Slaughter, A.-M., *A New World Order* (Princeton, NJ: Princeton University Press, 2004).
Stokke, O.S., 'The Interplay of International Regimes: Putting Effectiveness Theory to Work', FNI Report 14/2001, The Fridtjof Nansen Institute, Lysaker, 2001.
Teubner, G., 'Societal Constitutionalism: Alternatives to State-Centred Constitutional Theory?' in C. Joerges, I.-J. Sand and G. Teubner (eds), *Transnational Governance and Constitutionalism: International Studies in the Theory of Private Law* (Oxford and Portland, Oregon: Hart Publishing, 2004), pp. 3–28.
Unger, R.M., *What Should Legal Analysis Become* (London and New York: Verso, 1996).
WHO/UNAIDS/UNICEF, 'Towards Universal Access. Scaling-up Priority HIV/AIDS Interventions in the Health Sector', Progress Report, April 2007, WHO, Geneva.
Wogart, J. P., 'From Conflict over Compromise to Cooperation? Big Pharma, the HIV/AIDS Crisis and the Rise of Countervailing Power in the South', in W. Hein, S. Bartsch and L. Kohlmorgen (eds), *Global Health Governance and the Fight against HIV/AIDS* (Basingstoke: Palgrave, 2007), pp. 67–91.
Wood, J., 'Dark Networks, Bright Networks and the Place of the Police', in J. Fleming and J. Wood (eds), *Fighting Crime Together: the Challenges of Policing and Security Networks* (Sydney: University of New South Wales Press, 2006), pp. 246–69.
Wood, J. and C. Shearing, *Imagining Security* (Portland, Oregon: Willan, 2007).
World Bank, 'Acquired Immunodeficiency Syndrome (AIDS): the Bank's Agenda for Action in Africa', Technical Paper, Africa Technical Department, The World Bank, Washington, DC, 1988.
World Bank, *Intensifying Action against HIV/AIDS in Africa: Responding to a Development Crisis* (Washington, DC: The World Bank, Africa Region, 2000).
Young, O. R., 'Institutional Linkages in International Society', *Global Governance*, 2 (1996): 1–23.

5
Governance Norms in Global Health: Key Concepts
Sonja Bartsch, Carmen Huckel Schneider and Lars Kohlmorgen

Norms and theories in global health governance

Global health governance embodies a large number of actors relating to one another in various ways and organized within different formal and informal institutions. Alongside states and intergovernmental organizations such as the World Health Organization (WHO), civil society organizations (CSOs), for-profit corporations and public-private partnerships (PPPs) all claim political space. All in all, the policy field of global health resembles a web of actors, many of whom are closely intertwined. This pluralism of state and non-state actors – and the different governance modes[1] within which they interact – has raised questions about the fairness of current arrangements in terms of access and participation and the potential of such diverse arrangements to achieve desired policy goals. Therefore, standards of governance that all actors – regardless of their governance mode – should uphold are being sought.

A number of normative governance criteria have been raised in current global health governance debates and many of them are applied in other chapters in this book. Examples include the value of underlying approaches, such as evidence-informed policy or primary health-care, or operational standards, such as cost-effectiveness and responsiveness. Within this chapter we concentrate on four overarching standards of governance which encompass a range of governance criteria within broad theoretical frameworks, and argue that it should be an aim of all actors within the global health policy field to achieve effective, legitimate and accountable global health governance, with an even balance of power among the actors. Although these terms – 'effective', 'legitimate', 'accountable', 'balance of power' – are often used within the global health discourse, they still remain, to a large degree, elusive constructs. We aim to present a theoretically founded explication of these terms to enable a better understanding of three things: first, why they are important, second, how they can be theoretically understood and third, how they are to be operationalized as standards of governance.

We do this by drawing on wider debates on global governance particularly from within the discipline of international relations. The *effectiveness* of emerging institutional arrangements marked the starting point of these debates. It was argued that global governance – involving non-state actors contributing to closing gaps in participation and operations – represented a promising approach to effectively regaining the ability to conduct public policy in a globalized world (Reinicke et al., 2000; Kaul et al., 1999; Rittberger et al., 2008).

Questions concerning the normative basis of global governance and the *legitimacy* of the respective governance processes subsequently began to gain greater prominence (see Dahl, 1999; Moravcsik, 2004). On the one hand, it was argued that while governments are legitimized through elections and can be held accountable by mechanisms of democratic control, non-state actors are not subject to checks and balances which fulfil the same functions. On the other hand, proponents of the global governance approach pointed to the fact that participatory (rather than delegative) models and non-hierarchical forms of *accountability* are more appropriate to establishing congruence between those who are affected by a policy and those who make political decisions on the global level (Keohane and Nye, 2001; Zürn, 2004). More recently, the issue of the political influence and power of the different actors who take part in global governance processes have gained attention. Barnett and Duvall (2005) stressed that power relations influence not only the activities of the participating actors but also the effectiveness and legitimacy of global governance processes. Thus, the debate over achieving a fairer *balance of power* was reinvigorated.

Alongside a theoretical explication of these four standards of governance, we will offer various examples of the ways in which organizations within the global health policy field are taking concrete measures to work towards these standards. We do not wish to offer an evaluation of such organizations; they are employed here as examples to illustrate the theoretical constructs that lie behind governance standards. The chapter thus looks at the theoretical debates and the empirical realities with regard to each of the four concepts, concluding with suggestions for concrete measures that would contribute to improving standards of governance in global health.

Effectiveness

As many organizations of global governance are focused on specific problems or problem areas, finding solutions to specific policy issues can be considered of foremost importance. Conceptualizing and mapping effectiveness is, therefore, an important tool that can assist the policymaking process. For example, the effectiveness of one organizational approach rather than another is one criterion on which actors might base their decision of whether or not to engage with a global institution. Also, because policymakers are meant to seek ways to become more effective, identifying certain qualities that promote or hinder effectiveness can optimize problem-solving. The WHO and the Global Fund to Fight AIDS, TB and Malaria (GFATM) present exemplary cases. The dual role of the WHO incorporates measuring and reporting accurately on the effectiveness of various public health efforts worldwide as well as promoting its own strategic health issues. GFATM, with its more narrow focus, needs to know if certain programmes within countries are working and whether its funding modalities are effective or not. The same could be said for the World Bank and the projects and programmes it supports in the health sector. Effectiveness is, therefore, an important standard for global health governance and adequate monitoring and evaluation activities are crucial to improving policymaking processes.

Assessing effectiveness

Assessing effectiveness is a complex task. Increasingly, institutions of global governance must address problems of a complex long-term nature for which definitive solutions either do not exist or are, at least in the near to mid-term, unlikely. Organizations such as the WHO, the World Bank and the GFATM work towards the alleviation of health problems that will most certainly span decades. Furthermore various actors work concurrently with different mandates, strategies and interests. Identifying effectiveness, therefore, faces two main theoretical problems. First, how to identify effectiveness when the overall aim is not yet achieved, that is, how to identify whether new and/or ongoing problem-solving strategies are working when an ex post assessment is not possible; and second, how to trace any results back to any one particular rule, action or organization.

In order to move past this problem, it is helpful to recognize that problem-solving and the provision of public goods encompass different phases. The attainment of interim goals in each of these phases has been conceptualized as different *dimensions* of effectiveness, three of which – outputs, outcomes and impacts – have been identified as representing significant stages of the problem-solving process (Easton, 1965; Underdal, 2004; Young and Levy, 1999). The measures of these three dimensions are summarized in Table 5.1.

The output dimension of effectiveness refers to the early stages of problem-solving, entailing the norms, rules and actions agreed upon by the parties involved that are set in motion by an organization or network. The action and results that stem from this initial output are outcomes and impacts. Outcomes refer to changes in behaviour in response to the initial rules and actions. Impacts refer to effects on the problems at hand. First impacts (procedural indicators of success) can be distinguished from final impacts (the solution of the problem, or the production of a final public good) (Underdal, 2004).

A few illustrative examples of outputs, outcomes and impacts from GFATM can help demonstrate how these dimensions manifest themselves in global

Table 5.1 Dimensions of effectiveness

Dimension	Measures	Examples from GFATM
Output	Agreed upon norms, rules and actions for addressing a problem	Guidelines for Establishing Country Coordinating Mechanisms
Outcome	Changes in behaviour in accordance with agreed norms, rules and actions	Integration of new actors Mobilization of new resources Distribution of medicines
Impact: effects on the problems at hand		
First impacts	Procedural indicators of success	Increased number of people receiving ART treatment
	Production of a public good	A functioning primary health-care system
Final impacts	Dissolution of the problem	Increased life expectancy Reduced malaria incidence rates

health governance. Outputs may be concrete, such as the Guidelines for Establishing Country Coordinating Mechanisms. Through these guidelines outcomes may be achieved in that the participation of new actors (and the mobilization of their resources) is facilitated, and states, community groups and other actors are empowered to take concrete action such as making financial investments, carrying out education campaigns or providing anti-retroviral drug treatments. Early impacts can include initial indicators of success, such as increased treatment rates; final impacts would include achievements such as decreases in infection rates.

By looking for indicators in each of these three dimensions, policymakers can make a more systematic assessment of the effectiveness of various global health governance efforts in global governance. If impacts cannot be measured or used as a suitable level of judgement, outputs and outcomes can provide us with intervals at which to measure effectiveness.

What influences effectiveness?

A theoretical mapping of effectiveness is also important for policymakers searching for those qualities that contribute to greater effectiveness and those that hinder it. Here, particular attention is directed towards three issues that affect outputs, outcomes and impacts: access to resources, the nature of the interplay between different institutions and the involvement of non-state actors in global health governance.

Both material and non-material resources are required for global health governance. Resources such as access to policy-relevant information and modes of negotiation are deployed during agenda-setting, debating, drafting and decision-making. Implementation requires resources, such as access to field technologies, logistics, and the knowledge and means required for monitoring and seeking or obtaining compliance (Rittberger et al., 2008: 40). Ensuring adequate (or identifying inadequate) resources during each stage of the policymaking processes is an important step for ensuring effectiveness.

Various institutions with different objectives, resources and membership structures interact in global governance processes. This phenomenon, which consists of 'situations when the development, operation, effectiveness or broad consequences of one institution are significantly affected by the rules and programs of another', is referred to as 'institutional interplay' (Loewen, 2006: 11; see also Young, 2002). Institutional interplay – either intentionally or unintentionally – can occur at the 'interfaces' between institutions on the same political level, for example between the WHO, the World Bank, GFATM and UNAIDS, or between institutions at different political levels, for example, the WHO, states and local CSO-networks (see Hein et al., Chapter 4). Interaction can also affect outputs, outcomes and impacts at any stage of the policymaking process (Bartsch et al., 2007; Gehring and Oberthuer, 2003). The results of the institutional interplay can be either positive (supportive to problem-solving) or negative (obstructive to problem-solving), depending on factors such as power, interests and institutional settings. While institutional competition, normative discord and duplication of work can lead to disruption and thus a reduced effectiveness of global governance processes, exchange of information, joint planning and coordination of activities at the various stages of the policy cycle can contribute to synergistic effects in global policymaking and increased effectiveness (Stokke, 2001).

The increasing involvement of non-state actors in policymaking processes is a third factor to consider when discussing effectiveness. On the one hand, non-state actors have the potential to be a positive influence on problem-solving through the introduction of additional resources and their contributions to the norm-building process. They have comparative advantages and specific material and non-material resources that they can bring into the policy process (Keohane and Nye, 2001; Reinicke et al., 2000). Foundations (such as the Bill and Melinda Gates or Rockefeller foundations) and CSOs (such as MSF or Oxfam) provide examples of organizations that contribute financial resources as well as policy and management experience. Their inclusion in policymaking processes is also relevant where voluntary compliance with norms and rules is crucial for the effectiveness of policies (Börzel and Risse, 2005; Zürn and Joerges, 2005). Participation can increase a sense of ownership and thus a desire to ensure success. On the other hand, however, a significant participation of non-state actors has the potential to decrease the effectiveness of global health governance if it contributes to a further fragmentation of efforts or an overlap of mandates or if its remit conflicts with other aims (Dahl, 1994). Consider, for example, the situation in many developing countries, where – besides the World Bank and bilateral development agencies – hundreds of non-state actors are active in the fight against HIV/AIDS, each with their own agendas, approaches and reporting requirements. International organizations – being interconnected in UNAIDS – and donor agencies responded to these increasing coordination problems with the 'Three Ones' policy (Sidibé et al., 2006). These are principles for coordination and alignment at the country level that aim at one agreed HIV/AIDS action framework providing the basis for coordinating the work of all involved organizations, one national HIV/AIDS coordinating authority, and one agreed country-level monitoring and evaluation system. Whereas from a political science perspective, initiatives such as the Three Ones point in the right direction, its success in fostering alignment and coordination has yet to be proven. Early evaluations show that there is a 'patchy progress towards the Three Ones' and that many countries 'still deal with multiple donors, projects, processes and procedures' (Attawell and Dickinson, 2007: 39). Research on this topic is complex and needs to be comprehensive, taking into account the work of international organizations, donor agencies and the coordination efforts in each country to gain a clear picture of the progress made towards attaining specific goals.

In sum, the level of effectiveness is an important yardstick for global health governance. In examining what contributes to effectiveness it is important to distinguish different facets of global governance and to consider resources, relationships and actors and the way in which each affects the achievement of outputs, outcomes and impacts. Each actor and governance mode differs in terms of its outputs, outcomes and impacts and in the avenues that are open to it to change the determinants of effectiveness. The conceptualization of effectiveness discussed above offers insights into how to assess and improve on effectiveness by posing the following systematic questions: are sufficient outputs, outcomes and impacts being produced? Has access to resources at all stages of the governance process been ensured? Is institutional interplay managed in a way that supports the attainment of the goals set? What are the different roles of state and non-state actors and how is the specific potential of non-state actors used?

Assessing the overall effectiveness of any one organization is an extremely difficult endeavour. The process for assessing effectiveness described above is therefore most fruitful when applied to specific projects or undertaken by looking at a specific organizational aim. The two main cases (the WHO and GFATM) we use in this chapter provide excellent examples of highly complex organizations that undertake wide ranges of activities working towards various aims. This is especially the case with regards to the WHO, which undertakes a large scope of activities, widespread both geographically and in terms of policy focus. Assessing the overall effectiveness of the WHO therefore requires breaking down its activities, aims and mandates into manageable units, and posing the above questions with regard to each one. For example, it might be possible to look specifically at the outputs, outcomes and impacts of the WHO's campaign to eradicate polio, or the effectiveness of the revised International Health Regulations. In each of these cases resources had to be ensured, institutional interplay required management and non-state actors were utilized in different ways.

Legitimacy

Effectiveness is of central importance for policymakers seeking criteria for distinguishing between policy options and answers to questions regarding the achievement of health aims. However, care should be taken in adopting a too-narrow view of global health governance as simply a collection of instruments for solving specific problems. Global health governance not only tackles existing problems in a reactive way, but provides an order through which political life on the global level, not only in health but also in related areas, is organized. Long-term sustainable and acceptable processes and practices are required for stable global governance, and cumbersome yet robust structures that show limited effectiveness in the short term may safeguard against irresponsible actions in the future or unbalanced power relationships between actors in the long term. Therefore, a thorough understanding of what legitimacy entails and how it can be maintained are important for global health governance.

The significance of legitimacy

Possibly the greatest difference between governance of the state and governance beyond the state (for example, global health governance) is the absence of the monopoly of force applied within a given territory. Ultimately, it is this monopoly of force that gives the state the power to enforce its rules.

In contrast, in global health governance, compliance with rules cannot be enforced. Instead, requests, proposals, recommendations and agreements prescribe (or proscribe) certain behaviour for managing relations between actors working towards a solution to a given public health problem or providing a public good. For example, the WHO's normative work comprises the proposal of standards and policy recommendations for execution by health services (among others), while GFATM solicits funds from states and private donors on a voluntary basis.

For some, the voluntary nature of global health governance and the possibility to 'exit' any agreements suggest that institutions of global health governance are not powerful enough to require legitimation (Hurrell, 2005). It is, however, precisely because there are no mechanisms of force, that institutions in the global health policy field have a particularly urgent need to maintain legitimacy; without it, expectations of compliance are unstable and arbitrary. Thus, legitimacy is desirable from both a normative point of view and a practical one.

This need for legitimacy follows the logic of reasons for compliance with rules. A rule addressee may accept and follow the decisions of a rule-maker: first, because of incentives or coercion, such as financial incentives, threat of physical force or material sanctions; second, because of positive outcomes, such as when the rules clearly coincide with one's own interests; or third, because the rule is seen as legitimate, or stemming from a legitimate source, and therefore ought be followed, regardless of material advantages or disadvantages (Hurd, 1999: 379; see also Kratochwil and Ruggie, 1986). Global health must be seen as a realm in which interests and preferences are frequently unclear, disputed, and change over time – for example, as a result of conflicting priorities with other issue-areas or the dynamic nature of global health in terms of policy options – and although resource-rich institutions are able to use rewards and sanctions to encourage compliance, for example through performance-based funding, ultimately compliance with rules is voluntary. This is particularly the case when resource-rich actors are presented with options for engagement in global health governance, for example, bilateral or multilateral engagement. For acceptance of, and compliance with, the 'rules' that they lay out, actors such as GFATM and the WHO therefore rely (for the most part) on the belief in the legitimacy of their rules, or a perception on behalf of their relevant audiences that they are the rightful organization to make such rules (Hurd, 1999).

Conceptualizing legitimacy: ruletakers and rulemakers

Within the global health policy field, policymakers can find themselves at different times in the position of either ruletakers (addressees) or rulemakers. For example, the GFATM might respond to demands from civil society groups for more transparent decision-making processes, but it might also draw up policies prescribing certain behaviour from others (for example, it might set specific reporting standards on funded activities). In both instances an organization has to be clear of its own values and beliefs concerning good rules and rulemaking, as well as willing to adjust its rules and rulemaking procedures to the shared values of others. Depending on the position in which a policymaker finds itself, there are two basic ways to approach legitimacy (see also Steffek, 2003: 253).

The first is to take a *normative-assessment approach*, which is used when policymakers find themselves in the position of ruletakers and want to determine whether a certain rule should be followed or not (for example, whether they should fund a certain organization, or whether they should follow recommendations to adopt a certain health promotion strategy). This approach to legitimacy entails looking at a rule and its origins and adjudicating on its acceptability.

The second approach to rulemaking is an *empirical or strategic* one, in which policymakers seek to determine the values and beliefs (principles and wishes) that exist among the broader community and apply them to the adjustment or justification of their own rules and rulemaking procedures. The difference between this and the previous approach is the assumption that normative values cannot be determined by some overarching universalism, but rather exist within the community itself, and that these values need to be established through the discovery of empirical evidence. This is not an easy task as, in essence, the values, beliefs and therefore the perceptions, of ruletakers are neither fixed nor clearly discernable. Nevertheless, this does not make it any less important for policymakers to attempt to align their own rulemaking processes with the standards of their wider community.

For either approach, it is useful to differentiate between various dimensions of legitimacy. Generally there are three dimensions, each of which entails different substantive measures on which the legitimacy of a rule and its rulemaking institution might be judged: namely inputs, throughputs and outputs, as summarized in Table 5.2 (Scharpf, 1999; Zürn, 1998).

Table 5.2 Dimensions of legitimacy

Dimension	Substantive measures	Examples from WHO	Examples from GFATM
Inputs	Access to participation	Member states participate formally through the World Health Assembly	Five constituencies (donor and recipient governments, CSOs, the private sector and affected communities) each have voting rights at board meetings
Throughputs	Safeguards against abuses of power: • Resources to participate • Transparency • Decision-making rules	• Different levels of involvement of non-state actors • Restricted access to some documents • One country, one vote; majority decision	• Support of CSOs • Open access to most documents • Donor/recipient voting groups; consensus
Outputs	Problem-solving competence and congruence of effects and expectations	Technical norms; technical support	Financing

The first category, *inputs*, refers to who should be involved in rulemaking and who they represent. The most commonly cited source is that of democratic representation or delegation (Easton and Dennis, 1980: 35–46). However, at the global level, this is considered problematic because of the complexities of building a just 'world state' (for example, the many degrees of separation between citizens and global representatives) and because many states themselves are not democratic (Junne, 2001: 195; Zürn, 2004). Therefore, input legitimacy on the global level has come to entail standards of representation linked to a cosmopolitan participatory democracy or deliberative democracy (Held, 1995; Habermas, 1996). An institution with a high level of input legitimacy allows for the participation of a wide array of interests through different channels, such as states, CSOs or other representatives. For some, however, this perception is still considered problematic, and there are those who maintain that sovereign states must remain the central pillar of legitimized international governance.

Throughput legitimacy refers to those elements of the decision-making process that safeguard against abuses of power and ensure fair and just solutions in the context of a variety of interests. Three elements are considered vital for throughput legitimacy: fair access to decision-making in terms of the resources required to participate (distance of travel, technology, language); transparency in decision-making and everyday operations (allowing criticism and reflection); and appropriate rules of decision-making, whether through debate and consensus-building or a system of voting among the participants (Habermas, 1996).

Finally, *output* legitimacy refers to the standards of the organization's problem-solving capacity and congruence between the effects of the rulemaking institution and the expectations and needs of the wider community (especially rule addressees). This is closely tied in with the elements of effectiveness and it indeed helps to look at the outputs, outcomes and impacts as described above. The crucial difference however, is the extent to which the outputs, outcomes and impacts of the organization meet with, and address, what are perceived as the real deficits or needs of those affected by the rules (the level of responsiveness) and the extent to which outputs are based on evidence of need and scientific evidence that the applied strategies have a high potential to solve problems.

If we look at the WHO and GFATM (see Table 5.2) it becomes clear that different types of organizations – a state-based international organization, on the one hand, and an inclusive public-private partnership, on the other – differ in the ways that these three dimensions of legitimacy are manifested. In terms of inputs, the WHO is legitimized through the near universal membership of sovereign states in its governing body, the World Health Assembly, acting as delegates. Its output legitimacy is, to a large extent, derived from the strong scientific base of many of its working programmes, which increases problem-solving capacity. The legitimating inputs of GFATM follow principles of intergovernmentalism combined with participation and access along the lines of cosmopolitan participatory democracy, involving a number of different constituencies represented through state and non-state actors. Its legitimating outputs are to a large extent determined by its ability to demonstrate positive effects in terms of its primary aims. Of course both organizations have additional input elements. GFATM – despite its partnership structure – derives a considerable part of its input legitimacy from the high number of its members who represent sovereign states and act as leaders of delegations of geographically defined groups of states. The WHO engages with civil society and private actors both at the global level, for example by granting consultative status to CSOs, and at the national level, by working through ministries of health. In terms of throughputs, GFATM has taken a number of steps to increase its legitimacy, for example, through publishing large amounts of material, introducing a partnership forum and online discussions and thus enabling public access to internal documents. At the WHO, the extent to which throughput elements of legitimacy have been incorporated into work programmes varies considerably. Some departments have transparent decision-making structures and encourage participation from outside actors, for example through consultation rounds.

Legitimacy is an important standard for global health governance but one that is notoriously difficult to maintain, especially considering differences of opinion concerning which inputs are valid and which are not. Still, maintaining legitimacy though close contact with all stakeholders, willingness to learn from the expectations of others and to match inputs, outputs and throughputs to those expectations is the standard of legitimacy to be striven for.

Accountability

Accountability is a vital theoretical concept for dealing with the various legitimacy problems of global governance. Broadly defined, accountability refers to a relationship 'in which an individual, group or other entity makes demands on an agent to report on his or her activities, and has the ability to impose costs on the agent' (Keohane, 2002: 12). Establishing mechanisms to hold the various global health governance actors accountable is important for two reasons.

First, the activities of the different actors depend on the authorization through, and the support of, their respective members and/or stakeholders. In order to ensure that support – and enhance the input-legitimacy of the actor's own policies – mechanisms of *internal accountability* need to be put in place. Second, the interests of groups outside the respective organizations – those who are affected by the activities without being able to participate in the decision-making processes – need to be taken into account. Creating *external accountability* is more difficult, but normatively may be even more important than internal accountability.

Internal accountability

Different types of organizations vary in terms of their functions, membership, resources, governance structures and accountability relationships. For example, governments are accountable to the citizens who authorize them through elections, companies are accountable to the shareholders who provide them with financial resources, and international organizations have to justify their activities to their member states and to their donors. CSOs and PPPs have both an upward accountability to their donors and a downward accountability to their members, stakeholders and beneficiaries. These multiple accountability relationships can be observed clearly, for example, in product development partnerships such as the Medicines for Malaria Venture or the Aeras Global TB Vaccine Foundation, which receive considerable sums from the Bill and Melinda Gates Foundation while also being accountable to the various scientific organizations that participate in the research and development process, the CSOs that support them, and the potential users of newly developed products.

Some general principles for the creation of internal accountability apply to all of the above-mentioned actors (although to different degrees). Grant and Keohane (2005: 36) highlight four common mechanisms. The first is *hierarchical accountability* which is created through 'superiors [that] can remove subordinates from office, constrain their tasks and room for discretion, and adjust their financial compensation'. *Supervisory accountability* refers to relations between organizations where one collectivity is authorized to act as a principal with respect to specified agents. It applies, for example, to the relationship between government and legislature, between a decision-making board of a PPP and a (non-profit) organization, for example GFATM board members and the secretariat, or between an international organization and its member states, for example the World Bank. A third mechanism is *fiscal accountability*, which describes 'mechanisms through which funding agencies can demand reports from, and ultimately sanction, agencies that are recipients of funding' (Keohane, 2002: 16). *Legal accountability* refers to the requirement of the actors to obey national and international law, to follow formal rules and to be prepared to justify their actions either in courts or in quasi-judicial arenas such as the World Trade Organization Dispute Settlement Mechanism.

To establish and sustain internal accountability and enhance mutual learning processes two requirements must be met. The first is *transparency*. The availability of information is a necessary condition for the ability of a principal to hold a power-wielder to account. This includes information on the purposes and goals of the organization, on the selection of members, on voting rules, on sources and use of funding, as well as on performance and evaluation criteria. Information asymmetries need to be tackled, as the quantity and quality of information are crucial for the principals' potential to impose accountability. For example, it is important that all members of the GFATM board have full access to information on the workings of the fund and time to process this information. The same applies for representatives of states attending the World Health Assembly or of member states and organizations of the Programme Coordinating Board of UNAIDS. In order to achieve the desired results, however, a second condition must also be met: the ability to impose *sanctions*. As 'the right to hold people to account is meaningless without the capacity and resources, political and financial, to exercise this right effectively' (Newell and Bellour, 2002: 7), power relationships become crucial. If the principal has no or only limited ability to impose costs on the agent, the effectiveness of the different accountability mechanisms will suffer. Costs can be of a financial nature (for example, economic sanctions), but can also take other forms (for example, cancellation of membership, mobilization of the public, exposure and embarrassment).

External accountability

While in the case of internal accountability only members of the respective organizations are entitled to act as principals, the notion of external accountability goes one step further and refers to those groups who are affected by the activities of the different actors without being included in decision-making structures – that is, all stakeholders.

The question then becomes: through which mechanisms can external accountability be created? Grant and Keohane (2005) emphasize two ways: *peer accountability* (applicable when agents are answerable to others working on similar levels) and *public reputational accountability* (applicable when a negative reputation among a wider audience can seriously damage the ability to exercise activities). Let us take a look at various types of actors and the ways that external accountability can be achieved.

With regard to states it is important to distinguish between different types. Weak states that depend to a considerable degree on foreign aid and/or foreign investment can relatively easily be held to account by external actors – provided that the information required to assess their activities is available. The case is more difficult when it comes to powerful states. In order to enhance their external accountability it is crucial for policymakers to develop an understanding of the 'intermestic' (simultaneously domestic and international) nature of policymaking and interdependence with other actors. Integration into multilateral organizations and a further political institutionalization at global level, as well as the inclusion of non-state actors in decision-making processes are essential to making powerful states more responsible for the consequences of their activities (see also Keohane, 2002; Risse, 2006).

International organizations are subject to a number of demands from actors outside their institutional structures. They can be judged mainly on the basis of three criteria. Do they serve the purposes for which they were established, that is, do they effectively fulfil their respective mandates? Do they have standards regarding benefits and harms, that is, do they follow the core principles of 'do-no-harm' and 'assist-and-protect'? Do they include affected groups in their decision-making processes? Often these criteria interfere with other mechanisms of accountability, and divergent interests among stakeholders, leading to the situation in which 'external accountability claims based on the impact of these organizations compete with internal accountability claims, largely by governments, based on authorisation and support' (Keohane, 2002: 20). For example, in the case of the WHO, internal accountability towards its member states interferes with measures to enhance external accountability, such as greater inclusion of CSOs.

The same problem can be found – to an even larger degree – with regard to transnational corporations (see Buse and Naylor, Chapter 9 below). Private for-profit actors are first and foremost oriented towards maximizing their individual benefits, which makes the creation of external accountability a difficult task. However, if mechanisms can be established that negatively affect the performance and the economic gains of for-profit actors if they do not comply with specific standards, a shift from the narrow shareholder towards a broader stakeholder perspective can be stimulated. Many companies now highlight their corporate social responsibility so as to be less susceptible to criticism and potential sanctions as CSO campaigns can seriously damage the reputation of a company and affect the behaviour of both consumers and investors. The 'Access to Essential Medicines' campaign is a telling example (see McCoy and Hilson, Chapter 10).

External accountability is of particular importance to CSOs and PPPs. This is related to the fact that they are often created specifically to advocate the interests of those groups who are affected by their activities and the activities of the other actors in global governance. They can, therefore, claim that accountability is quasi-inseparable from their primary function. Many CSOs and global PPPs also have specific accountability mechanisms in place, including certification requirements, reporting and auditing requirements or independent evaluations. Yet these organizations can suffer from the tensions of being simultaneously accountable to their donors and to their stakeholders or their different constituencies – groups that do not necessarily hold similar expectations.

There is much room for improvement in accountability standards in the global health policy field. Transparency, access to information and public awareness can play a greater role in assuring accountability and giving those with little sanctioning power greater leverage to hold various actors accountable.

Balance of power

Power is one of the most important facets of the political sphere. Most concepts of power in political science refer to Max Weber's (1968: 52) broad definition of power as 'the probability that one actor within a social relationship will be in a position to carry out his own will despite resistance'. Following Weber, authority, rule or dominance can be understood as depersonalized, institutionalized (in a sense of regulated by law) and often legitimized forms of power (for example, as employed in or by a government or an administration). Yet, *power* is unspecific in how it functions, often not institutionalized, and can be attributed to personal and interorganizational relationships as well as to structures. While power appears in institutions, its forms of exertion are not necessarily formalized or constitutionally institutionalized, but also consist of informal ways of influencing behaviour. Such an understanding of power provides the opportunity to assess the capabilities of different actors to exert influence on politics, even if some of the actors (such as CSOs and other non-state actors) are not institutionally in a position to do so.

If we take a look at the state of global health, it becomes apparent that those living in political and physical environments that correspond with poor health often have the least resources at their disposal to influence others, demand effects or, importantly, resist the will of others. For many, access to state institutions is limited and representation on the global level even more so. At the same time, certain wealthy states and private actors with vast resources can invest considerably in exercising power on the global level.

Therefore, one of the most important aspects of good global health governance is achieving a greater *balance of power* between the various actors, including those with the material capacity to contribute to problem solving and, importantly, those who are most affected by public health policy (or a lack thereof). A better understanding of the concept of power and the various modes through which power can be exercised – independently of material wealth – demonstrates how it is possible to empower those that have the greatest stake in global health policy. For this we draw on international relations theory for insights.

Concepts of power

Each of the three main traditional 'schools' of international relations, realist, neo-Marxist and liberal-institutionalist, treat power differently. In the tradition of realism, international politics is seen as nation-state centred and anarchical (Morgenthau, 1973). Sovereign states are the main actors, and they act rationally and in their own self-interests. These self-interests – expressed in the goals of achieving maximum wealth for their own country and security in relations with other states – are the drivers of international politics. Non-state actors are given a lower ontological status and are therefore not recognized as vital for power interactions (Waltz, 1979). According to this school of thought, ill-health in developing countries and the transborder spread of infectious diseases are perceived as a potential threat to national and international security. It is suggested that this is a central reason for the onset and dynamics of global health governance. Thus the main incentives to expand and intensify the activities to fight infectious diseases and to strengthen the health situation in developing countries derive from the self-interests of industrialized countries and from security interests (Ostergard, 2002; Fidler, 2004). Industrialized states remain the most powerful actors in global health governance, when measured in terms of their ability to impose their will.

Neo-Marxist approaches emanate from social structures and struggles for power in modern societies between different social forces (such as social classes and the governments and organizations in international politics shaped accordingly). The current international economic and political order constitutes structural power (such as the capitalist world market) that affects all activities and constrains the capabilities of weak actors to pursue their goals and influence politics. In neo-Gramscian approaches power is closely related to hegemony, understood as the dominance of one group over others, with or without the threat of force (Cox, 1987; Gill, 1990). Although coercion is important for the development and maintenance of hegemony, hegemonic political power is the result of intellectual, ideological, moral and cultural leadership. In a hegemonic situation, a dominant political practice appears naturalized and without alternative, leading the powerless to obey voluntarily. For instance, neo-liberal concepts and strategies had a hegemonic status in the 1980s and 1990s with the structural adjustment policies of the IMF and the World Bank affecting both fiscal and health policies. Structural adjustment programmes often comprised cuts in public spending and privatization as a means of macroeconomic stabilization and affected fragile attempts to develop primary health-care systems in poor countries. Although there was some resistance in developing countries and by CSOs, for a time these concepts seemed to offer the only alternative – thus shaping the power relations of health politics.

Liberal and institutionalist approaches add in the importance of international institutions, cooperation and the idea that every state is part of an interdependent international system. Since the 1990s, scholars favouring these approaches have included non-state actors in their analyses and thus have assigned greater importance to transnational structures and processes of global politics. Robert Keohane and Joseph R. Nye deal in particular with 'hard and soft power' (1998: 86). Hard power is 'the ability to get others to do what they otherwise would not do through threats or rewards' and includes both coercion (for example, military threats) and forms of coaxing (for example, economic incentives). Soft power is 'the ability to get desired outcomes because others want what you want'. It alludes to the ability to reach objectives through attracting other actors to one's own goals, policies, ideas, culture and economic practices. Keohane and Nye argue that exerting soft power can increase the legitimacy of actions taken by powerful actors. For instance, the US government's commitment to global health governance and a will to cooperate could increase its acceptance and legitimacy as leading actor in other policy areas.

Power in global governance

If we combine some of the elements of the concepts of power we can state that power has both a structural and an actor-specific dimension. Focusing on the actors and their capabilities, characteristics and positions in economic and political structures it is possible to differentiate between four types of power in global governance (see Arts, 2003; Bartsch et al., 2007).

Discursive power

Discursive power relates to the ability to frame and influence discourses. Discursive power is exercised by participating in global debates as to which strategies and policies are most appropriate for global health. If actors can increase the number of avenues through which they participate in global health discourses and the intensity with which they participate, they gain discursive power. An actor that is frequently cited in the media and frequently invited to key meetings plays a part in determining which global health issues appear to be most pressing and which approaches to address these issues are most appropriate. These actors successfully 'frame' the respective discourse. For example, CSOs have come to hold discursive power in the conflicts over access to medicines and patents and intellectual property rights. Since the late 1990s, CSOs have been advocating and campaigning for greater access to ARVs for the poor who are living with HIV/AIDS in campaigns such as 'Access to Essential Medicines', and they framed the debate on intellectual property rights, patents and medicines as an issue of equitable access to medicines and of fighting poverty related diseases. Research shows that CSOs had a major influence on the reduction of prices of ARVs, on TRIPS negotiations inside the WTO, and on treatment in the fight against HIV/AIDS (Bartsch and Kohlmorgen, 2007; Hein, 2007).

Decision-making power

Decision-making power refers to the ability to be involved in decision-making and in formal norm-setting. CSOs traditionally have low decision-making power as they (and other non-state actors) are not involved in most of the decision-making bodies of international institutions and national governments. While in the global governance system, states provide the central pillar for legitimizing intergovernmental organizations, with the establishment of GFATM and also with increasing participatory elements in the WHO and UNAIDS, the decision-making power of non-state actors in global health governance has grown slightly.

Legal/regulatory power

This corresponds to the ability to exert power according to legal structures and laws and the ability to make rules. State actors have legal/regulatory power as state institutions remain the formally legitimized structures of politics and as governments and international organizations remain the main actors in norm and rule-setting. The WHO is, at least formally, the central norm-setting body in the global health realm and thus holds a considerable degree of regulatory power (although it depends to a large extent on the voluntary compliance of its member states and other actors in the health arena).

Resource-based power

Resource-based power reflects the availability of material resources (money, funding), non-material resources (knowledge, information) and an actor's ability to disburse them. Through providing finance, the governments of industrialized countries and the World Bank have power and influence over global health issues and national health policies in developing countries. Private actors, such as pharmaceutical companies and private foundations with large amounts of material resources, are also powerful in global health governance. The Bill and Melinda Gates Foundation, with grants for global health initiatives and programmes of approximately US$900,000 million per annum[2] and its large endowment, has more resource-based power in global health issues than the WHO. Yet, the WHO still has at its disposal another type of resource-based power – one based on knowledge resources. For example, the WHO provides countries with the knowledge and information required to prioritize and carry out certain evidence-based policies. This also provides a means of shaping agendas and political strategies.

If we look at the development of global health governance since the end of the Second World War, we can observe shifts in the balance of power. Where decision-making power was previously in the hands of state actors, we can now observe some tendencies towards a wider dispersal among non-state actors, as the example of global health partnerships attests (see Buse and Harmer, Chapter 12). Resource-based power has always been crucial in global health, and resource-rich actors remain at the centre of power relations. However, in a globalized, networked and computerized world, non-material resources such as knowledge and information have gained greater importance. Discursive power now plays a much larger role, as political campaigns can be conducted around the globe and media attention can be mobilized through the use of new information technologies. Thus, even actors with relatively few material resources at their disposal can exercise certain types of power if they are successful in framing discourses and managing knowledge. Regulatory power at the global level still remains relatively weak, but the strengthening of the WHO through, for example, the International Health Regulations and the Framework Convention on Tobacco Control, shows that international organizations have an important role to play and that further power shifts in the global health policy field are likely.

Conclusions

In order to improve the current structures and processes of global health governance it is necessary to address the power and accountability relationships between the various actors in global health and to introduce mechanisms that support more effective and legitimate policymaking. Several concrete measures for improved global health governance emerge from an understanding of these concepts. Many of them have already been accepted and are emerging as standard practice in some institutions. Still, a broader adoption of these principles is desirable to ensure sustainability, equity and goal achievement in global health governance.

First, honest and open recognition of the disparities in access to material and non-material resources is required, and assistance in balancing these disparities must be provided. Actors with fewer resources at their disposal often have trouble finding the time, money and personnel to travel long distances, work through all necessary information and develop strategies to participate at an equal level in global health policymaking institutions. More support needs to be provided for actors in these situations, for example by following the UNAIDS policy on fulfilling 'Greater Involvement of People Living with HIV' (GIPA) (UNAIDS, 2007). GIPA proposes that the communities of people living with HIV could be empowered through, for example, easier and cheaper access to information through the internet; through strengthening their ability to shape discourses and influence agenda-setting, for example through short management courses; and via financial support enabling their participation in formal decision-making processes in institutionalized settings. Furthermore, actors with few material resources and little decision-making and regulatory power can exert some pressure on governments and intergovernmental organizations by framing debates and discourses on health issues both at the national and global levels. This can increase their political influence and cause a shift in existing power relations.

Second, policymakers' understanding of the desires and expectations of their stakeholders must be strengthened. Discursive power is crucial to achieving policy shifts to support the development of goals which are more strongly focused on perceived needs and equity considerations. Developing more participatory modes for decision-making, implementation and monitoring would assist in creating legitimate and, therefore, robust and sustainable governance structures with higher levels of compliance. It would also increase the level of congruence between those who are affected by a policy and those who make the political decisions. More comprehensive collection and publication of data on the opinions, desires and policy positions of all stakeholders with regards to global health policy would improve the situation considerably. This can partly be achieved through the establishment of community and/or stakeholder forums, such as the Global Fund forums[3] or the various discussion lists of the Health and Development Network.[4]

Third, there should be an increased focus on differentiated goals of global health governance, broken down into outputs, outcomes and impacts, to assist in determining where the possible causes of reduced effectiveness lie. Some organizations, such as GFATM, already do this in part, referring to interim targets and impact goals. Yet, more specific identification of when, and where, rules and agreements (outputs) are not – or are only reluctantly – accepted and where behavioural changes (outcomes) are lacking is necessary if the root causes of limited impact are to be identified. More systematic evaluations of the various organizations of global health governance and clear criteria for measuring effectiveness in its various dimensions need to be developed.

Fourth, better coordination between various actors, organizations and their roles would help to reduce problems arising when the operations of one institution are impaired by the rules and activities of another. One recent example is the case of overlapping functions in the WHO prequalification project and US Federal Drug Administration (FDA) drug approval. The WHO, as the leading authority on global health, is increasing its normative activities in this regard, acting as an interface manager and more forcibly voicing its policy preferences. This is particularly important when health priorities are impaired by institutions from other issue areas, such as trade (see Helble et al., Chapter 8 below).

Fifth, external accountability needs to be increased, especially among powerful states, international organizations and for-profit actors. This can be achieved, at least partly, through stronger collective definitions of what is considered desirable behaviour, and agreement on the types of behaviour that should be sanctioned and on actors' particular responsibilities. A minimum acceptable level of external accountability would involve transparency and reporting of the activities of actors within institutional settings, opening them to public scrutiny. Ways to hold power-wielders accountable that do not rely on material resources need to be devised and could include reputation, club membership and networking. Advocacy networks and the media play a crucial role in this context.

This chapter has addressed four key standards for good global health governance – effectiveness, legitimacy, accountability and balance of power – and discussed both their theoretical content and their practical importance for the global health policy field. Policymakers, health experts and researchers, in both their strategic and evaluating roles, need to strive to achieve all of these standards. This means looking beneath some of the more benign interpretations of global governance – as being naturally cooperative and progressive – and addressing both the positive and negative realities related to each of these constructs.

Notes

1. Governance modes refer to the various ways in which actors are assigned roles in policymaking processes and how these roles are organized. It is possible to distinguish between four basic governance modes: (i) state governance, for example, through intergovernmental organizations; (ii) private governance through private actors and associations, such as the Global Business Coalition on HIV/AIDS, Tuberculosis and Malaria; (iii) hybrid governance comprising cooperative action between states/international organizations, the private sector and/or civil society, for example, public-private partnerships; and (iv) civil society governance such as the health projects of Médecins Sans Frontières (MSF).
2. See http://www.gatesfoundation. org/nr/public/media/annualreports/annualreport 06/AR2006GrantsPaid.html, accessed 12 December 2008.
3. http://myglobalfund.org/forums/Default.aspx?lang=/en, accessed 12 December 2008.
4. http://www.hdnet.org/v2/home/, accessed 12 December 2008.

References

Arts, B., 'Non-State Actors in Global Governance – Three Faces of Power', *Preprints of the Max Planck Institute for Research on Collective Goods*, 74 (2003).
Attawell, K. and C. Dickinson, 'An Independent Assessment of Progress on the Implementation of the Global Task Team Recommendations in Support of National AIDS Responses', HLSP Institute, London, 2007.
Barnett, M. and R. Duvall, 'Power in Global Governance', in M. Barnett and R. Duvall (eds), *Power in Global Governance* (Cambridge: Cambridge University Press, 2005), pp. 1–32.
Bartsch, S. and L. Kohlmorgen, 'The Role of Civil Society Organizations in Global Health Governance', in W. Hein, S. Bartsch and L. Kohlmorgen (eds), *Global Health Governance and the Fight against HIV/AIDS* (Basingstoke: Palgrave Macmillan, 2007), pp. 92–118.
Bartsch, S., W. Hein and L. Kohlmorgen, 'Interfaces: a Concept for the Analysis of Global Health Governance', in W. Hein, S. Bartsch and L. Kohlmorgen (eds), *Global Health Governance and the Fight against HIV/AIDS* (Basingstoke: Palgrave Macmillan, 2007), pp. 18–37.
Börzel, T.A. and T. Risse, 'Public-Private Partnerships. Effective and Legitimate Tools of International Governance?' in E. Grande and L.W. Pauly (eds), *Complex Sovereignty: Reconstituting Political Authority in the Twenty-First Century* (Toronto: University of Toronto Press, 2005), pp. 195–216.
Cox, R.W., *Power, Production, and World Order* (New York: Columbia University Press, 1987).

Dahl, R.A., 'A Democratic Dilemma: System Effectiveness versus Citizen Participation', *Political Science Quarterly*, 109(1) (1994): 23–34.
Dahl, R.A., 'Can International Organizations be Democratic? A Skeptic's View', in I. Shapiro and C. Hacker-Gordon (eds), *Democracy's Edges* (Cambridge: Cambridge University Press, 1999), pp. 19–36.
Easton, D. and J. Dennis, *Children in the Political System: Origins of Political Legitimacy* (Chicago: University of Chicago Press, 1980).
Fidler, D., *SARS, Governance and the Globalization of Disease* (Basingstoke: Palgrave, 2004).
Gehring, T. and S. Oberthuer, 'Investigating Institutional Interaction: Toward a Systematic Analysis', paper prepared for the 2003 ISA Convention, Portland, 26 February–1 March 2003.
Gill, S., *American Hegemony and the Trilateral Commission* (Cambridge: Cambridge University Press, 1990).
Grant, R.W. and R.O. Keohane, 'Accountability and Abuses of Power in World Politics', *American Political Science Review*, 99(1) (2005): 29–43.
Habermas, J., *Between Facts and Norms*, 2nd edition (Cambridge: MIT Press, 1996).
Hein, W., 'Global Health Governance and WTO/TRIPS: Conflicts between "Global Market-Creation" and "Global Social Rights"', in W. Hein, S. Bartsch and L. Kohlmorgen (eds), *Global Health Governance and the Fight against HIV/AIDS* (Basingstoke: Palgrave Macmillan, 2007), pp. 38–66.
Held, D., *Democracy and the Global Order: from the Modern State to Cosmopolitan Governance* (Stanford, CA: Stanford University Press, 1995).
Hurd, I., 'Legitimacy and Authority in International Politics', *International Organisation*, 53(2) (1999): 379–408.
Hurrell, A., 'Legitimacy and the Use of Force', *Review of International Studies*, 31(Special Issue) (2005): 15–32.
Junne, G.C.A., 'International Organizations in a Period of Globalization: New (problems of) Legitimacy', in J.M. Coicaud and V. Heiskanen (eds), *The Legitimacy of International Organisations* (Tokyo: United Nations University Press, 2001), pp. 189–220.
Kaul, I., I. Grunberg and M.A. Stern, *Global Public Goods: International Cooperation in the 21st Century* (New York: Oxford University Press, 1999).
Keohane, R.O., 'Political Accountability', paper presented at the conference on Delegation to International Organizations, Park City, Utah, 3–4 May 2002.
Keohane, R.O., 'Global Governance and Democratic Accountability', in D. Held and M. Koenig-Archibugi (eds), *Taming Globalization: Frontiers of Governance* (Cambridge: Polity Press, 2003), pp. 130–57.
Keohane, R.O. and J.S. Nye, 'Power and Interdependence in the Information Age', *Foreign Affairs*, 77(5) (1998): 81–94.
Keohane, R.O. and J.S. Nye, 'Democracy, Accountability and Global Governance', KSG Working Paper 01(4), 2001.
Kratochwil, F. and J.G. Ruggie, 'International Organization: a State of the Art on an Art of the State', *International Organization*, 40(4) (1986): 753–75.
Loewen, H., 'Towards a Dynamic Model of the Interplay between International Institutions', GIGA Working Paper 17, 2006.
Moravcsik, A., 'Is There a 'Democratic Deficit in World Politics? A Framework for Analysis', *Government and Opposition*, 39(2) (2004): 336–63.
Morgenthau, H.J., *Politics among Nations: the Struggle for Power and Peace* (New York: Knopf, 1973).

Newell, P. and S. Bellour, 'Mapping Accountability: Origins, Contexts and Implications for Development', IDS Working Paper 168, 2002.
Ostergard, R.L., 'Politics in the Hot Zone: AIDS and National Security in Africa', *Third World Quarterly*, 23(2) (2002): 333–50.
Reinicke, W., F. Deng, T. Benner and J. M. Witte, *Critical Choices: the United Nations, Networks, and the Future of Global Governance* (Ottawa: IDRC Books, 2000).
Risse, T., 'Transnational Governance and Legitimacy', in A. Benz and Y. Papadopoulos (eds), *Governance and Democracy: Comparing National, European, and International Experiences* (London: Routledge, 2006), pp. 179–99.
Rittberger, V., C. Huckel, L. Rieth and M. Zimmer, 'Inclusive Global Institutions for a Global Political Economy', in V. Rittberger and M. Nettesheim (eds), *Authority in the Global Political Economy* (London: Palgrave Macmillan, 2008), pp. 13–54.
Scharpf, F.W., *Governing in Europe: Effective and Democratic?* (Oxford: Oxford University Press, 1999).
Sidibé, M., I. Ramiah and K. Buse, 'Alignment, Harmonisation, and Accountability in HIV/AIDS', *Lancet*, 368 (2006): 1853–54.
Steffek, J., 'The Legitimation of International Governance: a Discourse Approach', *European Journal of International Relations*, 9(2) (2003): 249–75.
Stokke, O.S., 'The Interplay of International Regimes: Putting Effectiveness Theory to Work', *FNI Report*, 14 (2001).
UNAIDS, 'The Greater Involvement of People Living with HIV(GIPA)', UNAIDS Policy Brief, March 2007, http://data.unaids.org/pub/BriefingNote/2007/JC1299_Policy_Brief_GIPA.pdf (accessed 20 January 2008).
Underdal, A., 'Methodological Challenges in the Study of Regime Effectiveness', in A. Underdal and O.R. Young (eds), *Regime Consequences: Methodological Challenges and Research Strategies* (Dordrecht: Kluwer Academic, 2004), pp. 27–48.
Waltz, K. N., *Theory of International Politics* (Reading: Longman, 1979).
Weber, M., *Economy and Society*, ed. Guenther Roth and Claus Wittich (New York: Bedminster Press, 1968).
Young, O.R., *The Institutional Dimensions of Environmental Change: Fit, Interplay, and Scale* (Cambridge, MA: MIT Press, 2002).
Young, O. R. and M. A. Levy, 'The Effectiveness of International Environmental Regimes', in O.R. Young (ed.), *The Effectiveness of International Environmental Regimes: Causal Connections and Behavioral Pathways* (Cambridge, MA: MIT Press, 1999), pp. 1–32.
Zürn, M., *Regieren jenseits des Nationalstaats* (Frankfurt/Main: Suhrkamp, 1998).
Zürn, M., 'Global Governance and Legitimacy Problems', *Government and Opposition*, 39(2) (2004): 260–87.
Zürn, M. and C. Joerges (eds), *Law and Governance in Postnational Europe: Compliance beyond the Nation-State* (Cambridge: Cambridge University Press, 2005).

6
Global Health Governance and Global Public Goods

Richard D. Smith

Introduction

Globalization is a much used, and abused, term that encapsulates many different phenomena peculiar to the late twentieth and early twenty-first centuries. Essentially, however, it refers to continual advances in travel and telecommunications that have facilitated a greater mixing of people, customs and cultures, and more rapid cross-border flows of goods and services, people and capital, ideas and information. For some this heralds increasing standards of living for all. For others it brings greater exploitation of poor countries and the destruction of indigenous cultures. Whatever one's view, though, what is clear is that this is a process that is continuing apace, and that will have significant effects on health and health-care (Smith, 2008).

The most fundamental implication, of course, is that one can no longer view a nation's health, or evaluate national interventions and policies, in isolation from other nations. This is becoming increasingly evident, as global health issues have been pushed to the forefront of national and international agendas (Smith, 2006a: 650). Once the domain of health ministers and departments, global health issues are now regular front-page news, especially the delivery of basic health needs and the provision of security from widespread outbreaks of infectious disease (with concerns over avian influenza providing a topical example). Yet, the greater interdependence of nations presents challenges to national health sovereignty and security, heightening the need to develop a robust system of global health governance (Smith and MacKellar, 2007).

Currently, most institutions and systems are designed around dealing with domestic (national) organizations, issues and disputes. Increasingly globalization in health and health-care will generate cross-national issues and disputes and it is neither clear how these will be resolved nor, critically, how they will be financed. How do current governance systems mobilize the contributions of civil society, networks and a diverse group of systemically different countries and international institutions on issues such as the Millenium Development Goals, possible pandemic threats such as avian influenza, and access to essential medicines? How, and how well, have civil society organizations, networks and other groupings contributed to global health governance? What system of global health governance is most efficient?

It is with these questions in mind that this chapter begins to explore the financing context of global health governance. It does this from the perspective of global public goods, which offers a framework for analysis when considering the who, how, where, when and why of international finance. This chapter is structured as follows. In the next section, an overview of the way in which global health governance and global public goods are defined and used in this chapter is provided. A consideration of the sources and mechanisms of financing global health governance suggested by the global public goods framework follows, and the final section concludes with policy recommendations arising from this discussion.

Defining global health governance and global public goods

Defining global public goods

All goods (a term which includes both commodities and services) are defined within economics according to where they lie along two axes. One axis measures rivalry in consumption, which refers to whether the good may be consumed by more than one consumer equally. The other axis measures excludability, which refers to whether the producer may prevent the consumption of the good. We are most used to pure private goods, such as a loaf of bread, that are diminished by use (rival in consumption), and where one may readily be excluded from consuming them. Pure public goods are the opposite, where they are not diminished by use (are non-rival in consumption) and if the good is produced it is freely available to all (hence non-excludable). The armed forces or clean air are often cited as examples of pure public goods. Lying between these are a range of 'impure' goods, which are characterized by varying degrees of rivalry and excludability (Cornes and Sandler, 1996). In this sense, 'health' is a private good, as are the majority of goods and services used to produce health (Woodward and Smith, 2003).

The closer a good is to a pure public good the less likely it is that the market (the interplay of demand and supply through the price mechanism) will result in the optimal provision of the good because: (i) less rivalry means that there is less incentive to purchase the good for oneself as it is easily shared; and (ii) less excludability means that the price the producer requires is less able to be enforced. In the case of pure public goods, the state usually intervenes, either by producing the good directly (the traditional approach) or arranging for its production by a private firm (outsourcing). Police protection, national security and artistic ensembles constitute examples of public goods. Within health, a classic example of a global public good for health is infectious disease control, where the reduction in disease prevalence in country A has a benefit for countries B, C and D as well. This is especially true where eradication is feasible, such as polio, and for diseases that are highly transmissible, whether by human carriers (such as severe acute respiratory syndrome), by trade in products (such as bovine spongiform encephalopathy), or by animal vectors (such as avian influenza) (Smith et al., 2004: 271).

The problem comes with those goods that are quite clearly public at the global level, such as greenhouse gas emission control. In this case we might define a global public good as 'a good which it is rational, from the perspective of a group of nations collectively, to produce for universal consumption, and for which it is irrational to exclude an individual nation from consuming, irrespective of whether that nation contributes to its financing' (Woodward and Smith, 2003). The core issue is thus how to ensure collective action in the absence of a global government that could directly produce or organize the production of the good (Sandler, 1998: 221). As we are dealing with global collective action, we are clearly now within the realm of global governance, as outlined below.

Defining global health governance

In this chapter governance is taken to refer to the actions and means adopted by societies to promote *collective action* and deliver *collective solutions* in the pursuit of common goals. Central to this is the establishment of institutions, legislation, rules, norms, principles and decision-making procedures that bring order and structure to this collective action. One critical element of this is the financing of these institutions and so on, another is the results of the legislation, rules and so on developed to achieve the collective solutions.

Typically, of course, we are governed by nation-states and other less formal means. Increasingly, however, nation-states are being seen as less relevant for a wide range of issues, for a number of reasons associated with globalization (Smith and Lee, forthcoming 2009). Interest has thus focused more on global governance, which refers to the processes and institutions by which governments *and non-government* organizations take action across national boundaries to address issues that span these boundaries. Global health governance then concerns the ways in which societies, both within and beyond national borders, structure their responses in order to act collectively on health challenges.

This conceptualization poses particular problems within health as health governance has very largely (compared with most other sectors) been synonymous with national government. Further, governance has been characterized as within states (vertical governance) and between states (horizontal governance). For example, communicable disease represents both an endogenous (domestic) threat, with the objective to reduce disease threats *within* states (vertical governance), and an exogenous threat, with the objective to reduce traffic *between* states (horizontal governance). In this latter (horizontal) respect governments have taken (multilateral, regional, bilateral or unilateral) international action (Lee and Fidler, 2007: 215).

However, globalization challenges these (vertical and horizontal) governance structures precisely because they are based on the conduct of the nation-state. With the rise of faster transport and communications, and associated increases in the movement of people and goods, supra-state governance structures have emerged, and continue to do so (see Berridge et al., Chapter 2, and Walt et al., Chapter 3) (Smith et al., 2007). Such supra-state structures include, for example, regional trading arrangements, such as the European Union, North American Free Trade Association or the Association of South East Asian Nations. Although ostensibly legal frameworks for resolving constraints on free trade, these are also highly political organizations. There have also been more deliberate moves to look to more international systems for governance, contributing to the development of organizations such as the United Nations (and associated sub-organizations, such as the United Nations Development Programme, United Nations Environment Programme and United Nations Conference on Trade and Development), the International Monetary Fund, the World Bank, the World Health Organization and the World Trade Organization.

In more recent years, a particularly important feature of globalization has been the increased importance of cross-national non-governmental organizations, especially multinational corporations. Indeed, it has been mooted that the nation-state is now largely irrelevant on the global stage, and it is in these other forms of organization that the power – political as well as economic – now lies (Smith and Lee, forthcoming 2009). As indicated elsewhere, health has historically escaped this process to a large extent, as it is a predominantly service-oriented sector (Smith, 2006b). However, over the last decade trade in services has begun to rise exponentially, and other health issues, such as communicable disease control and outbreaks, have come to the fore (see Helble et al., Chapter 8). It is, therefore, prescient to be considering how global governance may apply to health at this point, before substantial growth in this sector occurs. It is also worth noting that many of these organizations are increasingly taking international action for reasons that are ostensibly internal to them (for example, business reorganization), or because they otherwise benefit (exporting or importing, cultural and educational exchanges). It is also the case that they often forge alliances in order to influence governments or other organizations in how they address issues of the global commons (such as the environment, health and intellectual property) (see Buse and Naylor, Chapter 9).

Globalization has thus challenged existing horizontal structures of international governance (governance between nation-states) with the need to consider global governance (governance between nation-states, intergovernmental organizations *and* non-state actors, such as non-governmental organizations, multinational corporations and civil society). It is the addition of these non-state actors that fundamentally changes governance structures as it challenges the state-centric strategies; but this also complicates the financing situation for such governance structures. For instance, the processes and institutions by which these governments and non-governmental organizations take action – that is the processes and institutions of international or global governance – can be formal (for example, treaties and trade agreements organized under the World Trade Organization) or informal (conventions, norms). Yet, since the responsibility for health remains predominantly national, this generates a potential mismatch – or even conflict – between global health problems and current institutions and mechanisms to deal with them. Considering the structure of financing for governance is thus both critical and complex.

From the economics perspective, this discussion points to the global public goods concept for three main reasons (Woodward and Smith, 2003). First, global health governance is concerned, by definition, with collective action, which is precisely what the global public goods concept is concerned with securing; how best to ensure collective action at the international level. Second, the global public goods concept is concerned with securing this collective action through cooperation between state and non-state actors. Third, the global public goods concept explicitly recognizes the spillover effects between health and non-health sectors, such as trade or the environment, and seeks to structure the global response accordingly. This is illustrated by the Framework Convention on Tobacco Control, where the limitations of national and international governance, structured around nation-states and intergovernmental organizations, provided the impetus to its development.

Summary

The production of global public goods is much more complex than the production of national public goods. National public goods can be organized – financed and/or produced – under the aegis of a national government and, hence, national governance. In the case of emerging global public goods there is no obvious body to undertake this finance/production. Thus, there is a need to develop a process for determining which global public goods to provide (or prioritize), how to provide them, how much to provide and, critically, how, where, when and by whom they are to be financed. Thus, the financing of global public goods is a key element of global health governance: the creation of relevant institutional forms, incentive structures and production pathways capable of mobilizing and/or allocating sufficient resources to achieve a system of global health governance. It is to these points that the chapter now turns.

Financing global health governance: sources and mechanisms

Sources of financing

As we have seen, at the centre of global health governance and global public goods is the collective action problem. Fundamental to collective action is a consideration of the major players and their agendas, and the dynamics of international cooperation. This is of considerable importance as not only will these players be involved in the financing of global public goods, but between them they will determine the structure of global health governance and set the agenda for which global public goods will be financed. *Publicness* is generally not an inherent characteristic of the good but a matter of policy choice and *globalness*, as a special dimension of *publicness*, may also depend on policy choices.[1]

Consider, for example, global public-private partnerships, of which there are currently estimated to be over 400[2] (from just 35 in 1990) spending some US$1 billion annually (Widdus and White, 2004; Cohen, 2006: 162; Okie, 2006: 1084). These are not only changing the financing landscape of global health (as indicated below), but also the way in which priorities are set. For instance, a mapping exercise of these partnerships reveals that while the majority are focused on communicable diseases, few target health systems development or other areas representing considerable disability-adjusted life years losses, including maternal health (for example, obstructed labour, unsafe abortion), depressive and other neuropsychiatric disorders, alcohol dependence, motor vehicle injuries, cancer prevention and treatment and nutritional disorders (Buse, 2004a). Moreover, most partnerships are product-oriented, place more emphasis on treatment than on prevention, and very few aim to challenge the structural and societal determinants of ill-health. This is arguably the case because both private and public sectors tend to pick the easier targets, but also because addressing issues such as non-communicable diseases might threaten commercial interests – although innovative partnerships might, for example, be forged with companies in the healthy food and lifestyle industries (Buse and Harmer, Chapter 12, and Buse and Naylor, Chapter 9).

Major decision-makers in the financing of GPG include: (i) national governments, as potential beneficiaries, sources of funding (internally and externally) and providers; (ii) international agencies (including philanthropic foundations and non-governmental organizations), as forums for consensus-building and collective decision-making, coordinators, promoters and channels of government support, and supporters of control mechanisms and regulatory frameworks; and (iii) pharmaceutical and other commercial companies, as developers and suppliers of relevant medical technologies, and as political players at the national and international levels (Woodward and Smith, 2003).

However, the problem is that these players' agendas (their preferences or priorities) do not necessarily coincide with each other, or with public health priorities. For example, it is unlikely that each national agenda will give equal priority to communicable disease control, and companies' agendas will inevitably differ from those of governments and international agencies. The more divergent these agendas are, the greater is the potential for free-riding (that is failure to contribute), among other constraints to solving collective problems. Impediments to international cooperation, and the role of international bodies in facilitating it, are therefore central to consideration of global health governance.

A good illustration of this is provided by comments by Kickbusch (2001: 153a) on the Bill and Melinda Gates Foundation, where she states that:

> Global health challenges are no longer the exception they are the rule. An ad hoc response system run on good will and philanthropic largesse like [the Bill and Melinda Gates Foundation] can only be an intermediary step. Already the law of unintended consequences is starting to have its effect. Newly established global disease investment funds, run from office suites in New York, Washington, Geneva and Brussels are set to fundraise, compete and conquer, each seeking contributions in the billions of dollars from the same sources for 'their' disease.

What is public and what is global depends as much on choice as it does on anything intrinsic to the good or service in question. It is unfair to single out the Bill and Melinda Gates Foundation, but this is a classic case where the foundation – especially as it is so well resourced – supports global health development in areas of *their choice* (vaccine development and maternal and child health), but with massive ripple effects elsewhere. The rise of wealth in private hands has perhaps panicked us into searching for new financing mechanisms to harness it, but in doing so perhaps we have taken our eye off the ball in terms of what these finances are for and whether they are funding the 'right' things.

The value of the global public goods concept in this respect is in highlighting the importance of assessing where specific health issues are on different players' agendas, why particular issues feature highly and the relevant costs and benefits. Resolving collective action problems requires a clear understanding of the nature, scale and timing of costs and benefits to different countries and other parties, a good understanding of the problem in question *and* proactive efforts to reconcile different interests and priorities in its resolution. Thus, for example, to ensure informed decision-making, it may be preferable to extend the decision-making process, to reach an initial agreement in principle with full agreement following only after a period of intensive technical and economic analysis. This requires international forums that are legitimate, credible and effective in decision-making, and in which national public interests are effectively and proportionally represented. A markedly unequal distribution of power may limit the commitment of some countries (and other actors) to decisions taken, undermining global health governance.

A limit to global collective action, and hence to global health governance, is the ability of countries (and other actors) to pay according to the proportion of benefits received. This impedes effective global collective action by undermining the political will to cooperate and limiting effective participation in international action. Even the creation of a legal duty does not ensure compliance, as this depends on having adequate resources to fulfil such obligations (Smith et al., 2003a). Further, where countries with inadequate resources do participate in global programmes, financial and human resources may be diverted from other essential activities, with possible adverse effects on health. The opportunity cost of these resources is far greater in developing than developed countries, creating tensions in securing global cooperation and reducing the net health benefits. Circumventing this problem requires that financial and other contributions reflect each country's ability to contribute, as well as its potential benefits. In practice, this means that financing needs to come predominantly from the developed world (Smith et al., 2003b).

Contributing to the production of global health governance may mean that resources (whether domestic or foreign) are spent on activities that do not accord with national priorities, in at least some countries. This issue is at its most acute, for example, in the latter stages of a disease eradication programme. The polio eradication initiative's estimated external financial needs – excluding volunteer time and governments' contributions to control efforts in their own countries – were US$370 million in 2001–02 (Aylward et al., 2003). Based on an incidence rate of 537 cases, this implies a cost of around $700,000 per case. Reallocating this money to more immediate health priorities could improve health outcomes in the short term, although these benefits might be outweighed in the long term by the major (and permanent) costs (health and financial) from the resulting failure of the eradication effort; even accounting for the cost of continuing vaccination in the case of non-eradication, variations in discount rates, and the most plausible future scenarios to achieve eradication. Diverting existing development assistance to finance global health governance could also generate negative effects on health elsewhere, and these opportunity costs would need to be explicitly assessed. Clearly, much of this analysis depends upon the time-frame for assessing benefits. In the case of eradication, the benefits are infinite, but even in areas of control they may run to many years in the future, meaning that the willingness to forgo benefits now is a critical issue.

The main contribution of the global public goods framework is to show that supporting international efforts and other countries' efforts is not a question of aid, but a self-interested investment in domestic health in which the primary objective is to improve the health of one's own nation. This suggests that national health budgets in donor countries are a more appropriate source of funding for global public goods, leaving existing aid monies unaffected, and thus increasing total funding to developing countries rather than merely reallocating it between uses (Smith et al., 2003b).

Another possible source of finance for global public goods is the non-government sector. Non-governmental organizations play an important role in global health governance, particularly as health service providers. In this capacity, they are likely to fund their activities largely from their own resources. However, few non-governmental organizations have sufficient resources to provide significant financing for many of the activities required. Private foundations and philanthropic trusts may be a more feasible funding source, as in the case of Rotary International's financial support for the polio eradication initiative (Aylward et al., 2003). However, the relatively limited resources available overall from such institutions (compared with developed country governments) means that their main role is in catalyzing larger contributions from public sector institutions.

The commercial sector may also be a possible source of financing in some areas, principally through 'in-kind' contributions, such as donation of vaccines or pharmaceuticals. In other cases, however, they may have little incentive. However, in the current political climate, it is likely that the private sector would be looked to for collaboration in the development of new therapies and in the case of infectious diseases such as HIV, through a variety of workplace and non-workplace programmes (Davis et al., 2007). In the latter case, specific incentives for research and development may be required, including alterations to patent regimes, purchase funds, advance purchase commitments and/or public-private partnership in investment.

Finally, one must bear in mind that the ultimate source of finance will be from those programmes that have had their funding withdrawn. For instance, there is some evidence that international assistance for the production of global public goods may reduce assistance for the production of non-global public goods by around 25 per cent (that is, the average bilateral donor allocation of US$1 to the production of global public goods entails a reduction in non-global public good assistance of US$0.25) (Reisen et al., 2004). Similarly, the availability of new philanthropic funds for medical research has been found to crowd out funding from government agencies (Cohen, 2006).

Financing mechanisms

With advancing globalization, openness and the need for collective action to address common problems, there is a new finance emerging, characterized by a blurring and porosity of the borders between public and private and domestic and foreign, creating a free-flowing pool of numerous possible combinations of all these sources of finance. This requires institutions: that is, mechanisms for collecting and distributing finances. New public finance, as it has been coined, is thus more complex than traditional governmental tax and spend, and among the complexities are the multifarious means for channelling resources from these various actors under various regulatory and monitoring structures and institutions (Kaul and Conceição, 2006).

There are numerous possible mechanisms for collecting the finance for global public goods. Of the more traditional, voluntary contributions are the most straightforward option, but are particularly prone to the free-rider problem – as demonstrated by the contributions thus far to the Global Fund to Fight AIDS, Tuberculosis and Malaria – since each country has an incentive to minimize its contribution (Smith and MacKellar, 2007). More formal coordinated contributions, negotiated or determined by an agreed formula, are commonly used to fund international organizations, such as the World Health Organization. While limiting the free-rider problem, each country has an incentive to negotiate the lowest possible contribution for itself (or the formula that will produce this result). Attempting to sidestep this problem by rewarding contributions with influence (in relationship to posts or voting) skews the balance of power towards the richest countries (as with, for example, the International Monetary Fund and the World Bank); but without such incentives (or effective sanctions), countries have little incentive to pay their contributions in full (as with US contributions to the United Nations generally or more particularly to what it sees as not in its interests, for example, UNFPA). Global taxes, although theoretically the most efficient means for financing global public goods, face substantial opposition, limiting the prospects of securing funding from this source for the foreseeable future. More 'market'-based systems have been advocated, but as the US withdrawal from the carbon-trading system proposed in the Kyoto Agreement demonstrates, without effective enforcement mechanisms the free-rider problem remains. More recently, the constructive use of debt has been suggested, allowing the world to consume global public goods now and pay for them later. For certain high-risk diseases and the poverty that they perpetuate, debt (and hence loans) might make good sense. Buying time might also allow those countries who are not presently able to help pay for global public goods to do so in the future when their economies are more productive (Sagasti and Bezanson, 2001).

However, the global nature of the problem and the nature of global health governance mean that voluntary – or even coordinated – contributions cannot be relied upon to generate sufficient revenues in many cases. It is, therefore, likely that some form of market-based and/or global tax system will be most suitable. In this respect, while there are various less traditional, or more innovative, financing mechanisms available, such as airline travel taxes or a global lottery, progress in their development and implementation has been slow (Stansfield et al., 2002). In the health field especially, advance purchase commitments represent the most obvious advance (Lob-Levyt and Affolder, 2006: 885). Here donors commit to future purchases of new therapies or other interventions if the research and development is successful in conforming to the donor's requirements. Although a welcome innovation, this, and other such mechanisms, remain focused on mobilizing resources from established and familiar international donor agencies.

Similarly, the poverty reduction strategy process, from which the Millenium Development Goals emerged, is intended to encourage countries to adopt a long-term vision (Devaradjan et al., 2002; World Bank, 2003). The process is designed to be country-driven, results-oriented and participatory, including civil society and industry (Christiansen and Hovland, 2003). The process is also designed to make explicit the linkages between fiscal resource allocation decisions and poverty reduction through establishing medium-term expenditure frameworks (Roberts, 2003). Again, progress in these areas has not matched the rhetoric.

Among other innovative finance mechanisms, perhaps the most recognizable include guarantees issued by aid agencies to reduce the risk to investors, thus lowering the cost of capital and stimulating greater flows into developing countries; securitization of future flow receivables in hard currency; GDP-indexed bonds, which link payments on state debt to the issuing country's rate of economic growth, acting as automatic stabilizers on government resources, reducing the need for drastic spending cuts when growth is slow and restraining excessive spending when growth is high; macro-markets, which enable the trading of securities linked to aggregated (hence macro) income, such as GDP of a single or of multiple countries, or components of GDP such as the income of specific occupational groups (such markets would allow public and private actors to insure against volatility in these income streams by buying securities that offset severe swings); and international pollution permit trading, which allows countries where reductions are costly to pollute more by purchasing permits from those countries where reductions are less costly, thus keeping overall emissions within defined targets but allowing this reduction to be produced most efficiently on the global scale (Kaul and Conceição, 2006).

Indeed, a cost-benefit analysis of these specific innovative finance mechanisms suggests that there is much to be gained (through the increased efficiency with which these mechanisms allocate resources) as they together present a net benefit (net present value) of some US$7 trillion over 10 years, or US$360 billion annually. This benefit is split almost equally between developed and developing countries, but with the cost impact considerably skewed; with developed countries having a one-off cost of around US$6 billion, but developing countries a one-off cost of around US$23 billion and a recurrent annual cost of around US$20 billion (Kaul and Conceição, 2006).

Why this explosion of new finance mechanisms? First, the new actors – the sources of finance referred to above – often come from the business world, bringing with them a set of financial skills and expectations. This new entrepreneurial aid environment has led to competition in how finance can be sourced and channelled. For instance, much of the focus now is on results-oriented payment systems. Second, these new mechanisms may entail market incentives, such that commercial opportunities may be exploited as a part of the mechanism of obtaining and channelling funding. For instance, the Medicines for Malaria Venture provides not just support for private research and product development, but also grants industry patent rights on the intellectual property developed with its support. Third, developments in technology often reduce the cost of, or make feasible, specific mechanisms for collecting and distributing funds, such as the international emission permits market. Although it is not clear which of these mechanisms may turn out to be a fad and which may become a fixture, it is clear that the finance landscape will be forever changed. This will pose a challenge and create an opportunity for global public goods provision and global health governance.

Conclusions

The continuing process of globalization entails ever-greater interdependence. Interdependence is better organized through cooperation than through competition or by being left to chance. Considering the development and process of financing for global health governance that is required for this cooperative interdependence through the global public goods lens highlights several issues.

First, it is evident that public-private partnering will be required in financing. Global public goods are public in consumption as well as in production, including their financing. This means that many actors are involved, and adequate financing involves fostering a sufficient allocation of both private and public money. Second, the production path of health-related global public goods often includes national and international building blocks, and hence requires resource allocations to be disbursed at the national and the international level (but, of course, budgeted for at the national level). In the case of low-income countries, the national budget allocations could be financed from national revenue and/or private finance as well as from foreign aid that would augment scarce public revenues. Third, the incentives must be appropriate to ensure that international cooperation works. International cooperation – whether it consists of the provision of national-level building blocks or the joint provision of international ones – has mostly to happen voluntarily. This implies that it is of critical importance to get the incentives to cooperate right. This poses a challenge, given that policy priorities/preferences tend to differ between countries, international organizations, population groups and others. However, in an interdependent, globalizing world, national (self-)interest can often best be served by promoting an enhanced provision of a desired global public good, even if this means having to make compensatory transfer payments. Fourth, since global public goods provision is a multi-actor process in most instances, involving firms, individual countries/governments/households/and other entities such as civil society organizations, incentives to cooperate may have to be tailor-made for each actor group Finally, there is unlikely to be 'taxation without representation'. The willingness to pay of actors towards a system of global health governance for global public goods production is linked to their participation in determining what the goods should be, how they should be provided and at what net benefit and cost to whom.

What then should be done? There are three core recommendations for policy following from this analysis. First, at the national level there needs to be a move towards a firmer consensus on the role of the state as an intermediary between external and domestic policy demands. It is essential that nations gain a common understanding of what role the state is to play in the twenty-first century if it is to exercise appropriate sovereignty. Further, national governments, in collaboration with other actors, would do well to support research in the many new finance mechanisms that are being developed and proposed. This may well lead in turn to revisions to domestic financial management and organization.

Second, at the international level there is much that may be undertaken. For instance, the systematic re-engineering of intergovernmental organizations to incorporate the representation of non-state actors or the use of business-planning techniques. If such organizations are to be central to the development, operation and finance of global health governance there needs to be an understanding of their role vis-à-vis other global actors. International organizations should also lead on the evaluation and adoption of innovative financing for international cooperation. Such organizations have tended to mobilize resources on the basis of a very broad business plan, but the new public-private partnerships in particular have encouraged greater specificity in what is produced and the development of financing mechanisms that are structured accordingly.

Third, the recognition that in such a new and fast-paced global environment there needs to be a closer interaction between policymaking and research. In some cases the concepts, frameworks and mechanisms developed by academics may influence reality, but equally reality is required to drive and evaluate these developments.

National governments clearly continue to have an important role in health governance. But with the globalization of markets and the increased mobility of factors of production and consumers, there are other powers at work within the realm of global health governance. The analysis presented in this chapter suggests that significant determinants of the structure of global health governance will be sources and mechanisms of finance for global public goods.

Notes

1. The publicness, and to a degree the globalness, of many goods is not an intrinsic characteristic, but one determined by technology and/or a policy decision that they should be provided as if they were public goods, usually because they have significant externality effects. Much of health-care comes under the latter criteria

as being provided as if it were a public good for reasons predominantly concerned with an ethical stance and/or infectious disease and other health externality effects (Woodward and Smith, 2003).
2. Although Buse and Harmer (Chapter 12 below) argue that if a public-private partnership is defined by the representation of both public and private for-profit actors on decision-making bodies, one finds far fewer of this organizational form in practice than otherwise estimated.

References

Aylward, B., A. Acharya, S. England, M. Agocs and J. Linkins, 'Polio Eradication', in R.D. Smith, R. Beaglehole, D. Woodward and N. Drager (eds), *Global Public Goods for Health: a Health Economic and Public Health Perspective* (Oxford: Oxford University Press, 2003), chapter 2.
Buse, K., *Global Health Partnerships: Mapping a Shifting Terrain* (London: DFID Health Resource Centre, 2004a).
Buse, K. 'Governing Public-Private Infectious Disease Partnerships', *Brown Journal of World Affairs*, 10 (2004b): 225–42.
Christiansen, K. and I. Hovland, 'The PRSP Initiative: Multilateral Policy Change and the Role of Research', Overseas Development Institute Working Paper 216, Overseas Development Institute, London, 2003.
Cohen, J., 'The New World of Global Health', *Science*, 311 (2006) 162–7.
Cornes, R. and T. Sandler, *The Theory of Externalities, Public Goods, and Club Goods* (Cambridge: Cambridge University Press, 1996).
Davis, M., F. Samuels and K. Buse, 'AIDS and the Private Sector: the Case of South Africa', Overseas Development Institute Briefing Paper 30, Overseas Development Institute, London, 2007.
Devaradjan, S., M. Miller and E. Swanson, 'Goals for Development: History, Prospects, and Costs', World Bank Policy Research Working Paper No. 2819, World Bank, Washington, DC, 2002.
Kaul, I. and P. Conceição, *The New Public Finance: Responding to Global Challenges* (New York: Oxford University Press, 2006).
Kickbusch, I., 'A Note to Bill Gates', *Journal of Epidemiology and Community Health*, 55 (2001): 153a–154a.
Lee, K. and D. Fidler, 'Avian and Pandemic Influenza: Progress and Problems for Global Health Governance', *Global Public Health*, 2 (2007): 215–34.
Lob-Levyt, J. and R. Affolder, 'Innovative Financing for Human Development', *Lancet*, 367 (2006): 885–7.
Okie, S., 'Global Health – the Gates-Buffet Effect', *New England Journal of Medicine*, 355 (2006): 1084–8.
Reisen, H., M. Soto and T. Weithoener, 'Financing Global and Regional Public Goods through ODA: Analysis and Evidence from the OECD Creditor System', OECD Development Centre Working Paper No. 232, OECD Development Centre, Paris, 2004.
Roberts, J., 'Poverty Reduction Outcomes in Education and Health Public Expenditure and Aid', Overseas Development Institute Working Paper 210, Overseas Development Institute, London, 2003.
Sagasti, F. and K. Bezanson, 'Financing and Providing Global Public Goods. Development Financing 2000 Study', Swedish Ministry for Foreign Affairs, Stockholm, 2001.
Sandler, T., 'Global and Regional Public Goods: a Prognosis for Collective Action', *Fiscal Studies*, 19 (1998): 221–47.

Smith, R.D., 'Trade and Public Health: Facing the Challenges of Globalization', *Journal of Epidemiology and Community Health*, 60 (2006a): 650–1.
Smith, R.D., *Trade in Health Services: Current Challenges and Future Prospects of Globalisation*, in A.M. Jones (ed), *Elgar Companion to Health Economics* (Cheltenham, UK and Northampton, MA: Edward Elgar, 2006b), chapter 16.
Smith, R.D., 'Globalization: the Key Challenge Facing Health Economics in the 21st Century', *Health Economics*, 17 (2008): 1–3.
Smith, R.D. and K. Lee, 'Economic Power and Global Health Governance: Who's in Control?' in A. Kay and O. Williams (eds), *The Crisis of Global Health Governance: Challenges, Institutions and Political Economy* (Basingstoke: Palgrave, forthcoming 2009).
Smith, R.D. and L. MacKellar, 'Global Public Goods and the Global Health Agenda: Problems, Priorities and Potential', *Globalization and Health*, 3(9) (2007), http://www.globalizationandhealth.com/content/3/1/9, accessed 22 February 2008.
Smith, R.D., R. Beaglehole, D. Woodward and N. Drager (eds), *Global Public Goods for Health: a Health Economic and Public Health Perspective* (Oxford: Oxford University Press, 2003a).
Smith, R.D., R. Beaglehole, D. Woodward and N. Drager, 'Global Public Goods for Health: from Theory to Policy', in R.D. Smith, R. Beaglehole, D. Woodward and N. Drager (eds), *Global Public Goods for Health: a Health Economic and Public Health Perspective* (Oxford: Oxford University Press, 2003b), chapter 14.
Smith, R.D., D. Woodward, A. Acharya, R. Beaglehole and N. Drager, 'Communicable Disease Control: a "Global Public Good" Perspective', *Health Policy and Planning*, 19 (2004): 271–8.
Smith, R.D., C. Blouin, N. Drager and D.P. Fidler, 'Trade in Health Services and the GATS', in A. Mattoo, R.M. Stern and G. Zanini (eds), *A Handbook of International Trade in Services* (Oxford, Oxford University Press, 2007), chapter 11.
Stansfield, S.K., M. Harper, G. Lamb and J. Lob-Levyt, 'Innovative Financing of International Public Goods for Health', Committee for Macroeconomics and Health Working Paper No. WG2:22, World Health Organization, Geneva, 2002.
Widdus, R. and K. White, *Combating Diseases Associated with Poverty: Financing Strategies for Product Development and the Potential Role of Public-Private Partnerships*, the Initiative on Public-Private Partnerships in Health (Geneva: World Health Organization, 2004).
Woodward, D. and R.D. Smith, 'Global Public Goods for Health: Concepts and Issues', in R.D. Smith, R. Beaglehole, D. Woodward and N. Drager (eds), *Global Public Goods for Health: a Health Economic and Public Health Perspective* (Oxford: Oxford University Press, 2003), chapter 1.
World Bank, 'Achieving the MDGs and Related Outcomes: a Framework for Monitoring Policies and Actions', background paper prepared for the 13 April 2003 meeting of the Development Committee, World Bank, Washington, DC, 2003.

Key readings

Kaul, I., I. Grunberg and M.A. Stern, *Global Public Goods: International Cooperation in the 21st Century* (New York: Oxford University Press, 1999).
Kaul, I., P. Conceição, K. Le Goulven and R. Mendoza, *Providing Global Public Goods: Managing Globalization* (New York: Oxford University Press, 2003).
Kaul, I. and P. Conceição (2006).
Smith, R.D., R. Beaglehole, D. Woodward and N. Drager (2003a).

7
AIDS and Access to Medicines: Brazil, South Africa and Global Health Governance

Jan Peter Wogart, Gilberto Calcagnotto, Wolfgang Hein and Christian von Soest

Introduction

During the 1990s the number of people dying of HIV/AIDS in developing countries grew rapidly. Effective medicines that could work to turn the pandemic into a chronic, but not necessarily deadly, disease were increasingly available, yet remained too expensive for the vast majority of affected people in developing countries. As a result of the enforcement of intellectual property rights (IPRs), transnational pharmaceutical companies (TNPCs) were in a position to charge high prices for innovative medicines; in the case of AIDS, these were antiretroviral medicines (ARVs). The Agreement on Trade Related Intellectual Property Rights (TRIPS), introduced with the establishment of the World Trade Organization (WTO) in 1995, demanded the adjustment of IPR rules in developing countries to high international standards. Thus, there were ever higher barriers to the production of cheap generic versions of ARVs (and the trade in generics) in developing countries.[1]

The conflicts around access to ARVs and to essential medicines for the poor in general have assumed a multidimensional character, involving – in addition to groups of countries defending and opposing strict IPRs – a large number of civil society organizations (CSOs) networked through the Médecins sans Frontières (MSF) access campaign.[2] Utilizing a variety of means, such as the production or import of generics (where transitory regulations in the TRIPS Agreement allowed) but also concessions from pharmaceutical companies, developing countries succeeded in having the prices of ARVs significantly lowered (Hein, 2007: 56). At the same time, developing countries have been able to reach international agreements to clarify the right to use TRIPS safeguards, such as compulsory licences[3] and parallel importation,[4] in order to 'protect public health', thus decreasing the risk of trade conflicts related to stringent patent rights protection.

Trade conflicts epitomize the changing character of international relations over the last 20 years. Relations between state actors have been increasingly challenged through a densification of global social relations in which private actors (CSOs as well as corporations) have a growing impact on the course of events. States remain important in particular as they conclude binding international agreements, provide the hardware of public health-care (Fidler, 2007) and continue to play a crucial role in pursuing strategies to deal with health issues. Therefore, approaching the issue of access to ARVs by analysing the interaction between public and private actors in global politics as well as in two important developing countries will help us to move towards a better understanding of how health problems are tackled in a globalizing society.

We understand global health governance (GHG), as 'the totality of collective regulations to deal with international and transnational interdependence problems in health' (Bartsch and Kohlmorgen, 2005: 64). These regulations are the results of conflictive and cooperative processes and the starting points for new conflicts about specific health policies (such as providing universal access to ARVs). These processes imply 'interfaces' between actors with conflicting perceptions, values and interests resulting from the systemic contexts in which they operate. 'Interfaces' (following Long, 1989) are defined as 'socio-political spaces of recurrent interactions of collective actors in the handling of transnational and international affairs' (Bartsch et al., 2007: 30). An analytical differentiation is made between four major types of interfaces closely related to different types of power, that is, legal, resource-based, organizational and discursive power (ibid.) That differentiation helps to highlight the change in the relative importance of different means of interaction in shaping financial and economic, institutional, political and social aspects of national and global health governance.

The first part of this chapter focuses on conflicts around the issue of the TRIPS Agreement and access to medicines related to intellectual property rights, involving the interests of TNPCs and their impact on government policies in the developed countries. The second part examines the different types of interfaces that drove conflicts and compromises between national health governance (NHG) and GHG in the context of the global fight against HIV/AIDS, focusing on the examples of Brazil and South Africa. Power relationships between the developed and developing countries and the nature of interfaces are explored in some detail.

We maintain that NHG in Brazil and South Africa has played a crucial role in the ways in which global challenges have been taken up and opportunities to influence GHG have been realized. Their socio-political settings allowed both countries to pursue different objectives in fighting HIV/AIDS and interacting at the global level. By doing so, they have changed both their own approaches to NHG and the way GHG was evolving, with correspondingly different results.

Recurrent interactions between major GHG actors have manifested themselves in different ways according to the types of interfaces involved. While closely interconnected, it is asserted here that discursive interfaces and their worldwide repercussions were more important in shaping the conflicts around access to treatment for HIV/AIDS patients than the seemingly powerful resource-based interfaces, and that the emerging legal and organizational interfaces reflect that constellation. Both findings should have significant policy implications for present and future global governance in the health sector and beyond.

Internationalizing intellectual property rights

The process of globalization has been accompanied by increased pressure to base the integration of global markets on international law. The interest of the technologically advanced industrialized countries in strengthening international rules on intellectual property rights (IPRs) has to be seen in the context of protecting IPRs related to advances in computer and information technology, biotechnology and the patentability of life organisms. Besides a further deepening of GATT in the WTO context, including a strengthening of dispute settlement mechanisms, industrialized countries introduced other agreements which have affected GHG both directly and indirectly. They include the General Agreement on Trade in Services (GATS), the Agreement on Sanitary and Phytosanitary Measures (SPS) and the TRIPS Agreement and are totally new types of agreements compared to the old GATT, although internationalizing and institutionalizing IPRs have a venerable tradition, dating back into the nineteenth century.[5]

With the establishment of the World Intellectual Property Organization (WIPO) in 1967, international protection of intellectual property rights reached a new level of institutionalization. Even then, many of the developed countries were not members, and it took another 20 to 30 years before such major industrialized countries as Canada, Austria, Spain, Switzerland and Norway adopted strong patent protection that reflected the rules and regulations elaborated by WIPO in an international setting. As membership grew, WIPO's one country-one vote rule led to stalemates. Furthermore, WIPO did not have any strong mechanism to enforce compliance. Therefore, the USA and other developed countries with strong interests in the protection of IPRs looked for an agreement to submit IPRs to the WTO for an enforcement and dispute settlement system much stronger than that provided within GATT (Sell, 2000). Within the context of that institutional setting it was possible to put pressure on the more advanced developing countries, which were known not only to copy and reverse-engineer innovations, but had also been successful in exporting those more sophisticated products all over the world. In the field of medicines, growing competition from international generic producers, which circumvented the strict patent laws of the USA and other OECD countries, was increasingly perceived to hurt the sales of patented drugs, both at home and abroad (Sell, 2003: 104–11).

Moving the focus of the implemention of international IPR rules from WIPO to TRIPS represented the first round of 'forum shifting' in this field, that is, it represented an attempt to shift the main thrust of the fight for an international agreement to a different international organization or forum in the hope of securing particular objectives (Drahos, 2002; Sell and Prakash, 2004). The same strategy was also used by pharmaceutical companies and US negotiators in bilateral trade agreements. Early agreements, such as the North American Free Trade Agreement, were negotiated either before or at the same time as TRIPS. The majority were signed in the late 1990s and the move continued during the first five years of the twenty-first century. All of them contained rigid IPR stipulations excluding TRIPS flexibilities for pharmaceuticals. These so-called 'TRIPS-plus' agreements became rallying points of opposition to the trade agreements in the respective countries. Even respected free-trade advocate Jagdish Bhagwati described the WTO's intellectual property protection as a tax that most poor countries pay on their use of knowledge, 'constituting an unrequited transfer to the rich producing countries' (Sexton, 2001: 10).

In the second half of the 1990s, however, CSOs used discursive interfaces to win public support and to increase pressure on TNPCs and developed countries to improve access to essential medicines, in particular ARVs. Public support also proved decisive in preventing TNPCs from making full use of their strong legal and resource-based positions. In 1997 (and again in 2001), the Pharmaceutical Manufacturer's Association of South Africa went to court to fight against a law that allows domestic production of generics, but on both occasions withdrew under the pressure of global public opinion and CSO action. Negotiations with Brazil on ARVs (delivery and licences) in 2001 led to steep price reductions, despite calls for the United States Trade Representative to take legal action at the WTO (see below). As a consequence of these conflicts, CSOs and developing countries, led by Brazil, took the initiative to press for a clarification of the right to use TRIPS flexibilities in the pursuit of public health. This led to the Doha Ministerial Declaration on the TRIPS Agreement and Public Health in November of 2001.

In the Doha Declaration, ministers 'affirm that the (TRIPS) Agreement can and should be interpreted and implemented in a manner supportive of WTO members' right to protect public health and, in particular, to promote access to medicines for all'. Behind that decision was the rapid spread of AIDS in developing countries, which provided the base for an unanimous global decision at the beginning of the twenty-first century. It was another two years, however, before an agreement was reached on the issue defined in paragraph 6 of the Doha Declaration allowing countries that needed to import low-cost generic medicines to issue compulsory licences for generic production in a foreign country.[6]

WTO members finally approved these changes to Article 31 of the TRIPS Agreement in December 2005.[7] After ten years of existence, this was the first time that a core WTO agreement was amended. To what extent the Doha Declaration and the TRIPS amendment will facilitate compulsory licensing to improve access to medicines remains to be seen. Until 2008, only a few developing countries, among them Malaysia, Indonesia, Thailand, Brazil, Ghana, Zambia and Mozambique, have used compulsory licensing and only Rwanda used the new mechanism introduced in Article 31. Officials in smaller and poorer countries have not issued compulsory licences, either because there were too many cumbersome regulations and/or the research-oriented TNPCs were willing to provide low-cost versions of their patented products.[8]

In the meantime, the deadline for the least developed countries (LDCs) to enact and implement patent and other intellectual property rights has been postponed to 2016. The developing countries' increasing involvement in the international negotiating process of matters touching on health governance has been a constant feature of the long negotiation process of the 'amended' TRIPS Agreement. While we will revert to that process in the context of the two countries' legal and organizational interfaces, it can already be stated that the amendment of the TRIPS Agreement provided an example of a paradigm shift of international negotiations not only in that the 'voices of the poor' were heard but also in legislating accordingly.

TNPCs, the TRIPS Agreement and AIDS

TNPCs, IPRs and access to medicines: 1994–2008

The interactions between TNPCs and the other major actors in the global and national health arena have been analysed in a number of publications (for example, Sell, 2000, 2003; Drahos, 2002; Hein, 2007). Figure 7.1 summarizes the timeline of events related to IPRs and access to essential medicines between 1994 and 2006.[9] What is unique in the case of ARVs and HIV/AIDS is that the TNPCs were not only the major actors in the fight with government officials of the developing countries over prices of ARVs, but were also responsible for the introduction and negotiations of the TRIPS Agreement and TRIPS-plus in the US bilateral treaties, although those were officially governmental interactions. Their involvement demonstrated not only that TNPCs have vast financial power, but that they have also become increasingly involved in decision-making and formal GHG norm-setting.[10]

As a consequence, TNPCs found themselves engaged in a number of interfaces. These included legal interfaces, as in the encounters with the South African government in the country's courts and the drafting of the TRIPS legislation and its discussion with the US Trade Representative, as well as organizational and discursive interfaces. The fight over drug pricing with Brazil's government and NGOs, and discussions with public and private partners and opponents – both through their major associations on the national and international level, the Pharmaceutical Research and Manufacturers of America (PhRMA) and the International Federation of Pharmaceutical Manufacturers and Associations (IFPMA) and via top executives of the major

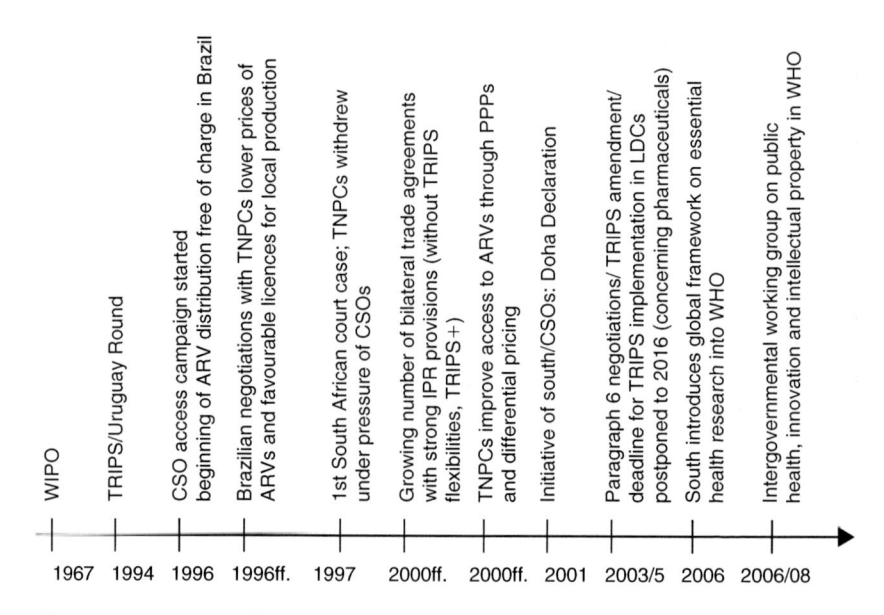

Figure 7.1 Timeline of decisions and conflicts around IPRs and access to medicines

Timeline entries (1967 → 2006/08):
- 1967: WIPO
- 1994: TRIPS/Uruguay Round
- 1996: CSO access campaign started beginning of ARV distribution free of charge in Brazil
- 1996ff.: Brazilian negotiations with TNPCs lower prices of ARVs and favourable licences for local production
- 1997: 1st South African court case; TNPCs withdrew under pressure of CSOs
- 2000ff.: Growing number of bilateral trade agreements with strong IPR provisions (without TRIPS flexibilities, TRIPS+)
- 2000ff.: TNPCs improve access to ARVs through PPPs and differential pricing
- 2001: Initiative of south/CSOs: Doha Declaration
- 2003/5: Paragraph 6 negotiations/ TRIPS amendment/ deadline for TRIPS implementation in LDCs postponed to 2016 (concerning pharmaceuticals)
- 2006: South introduces global framework on essential health research into WHO
- 2006/08: Intergovernmental working group on public health, innovation and intellectual property in WHO

companies – were important discursive events. TNPCs also used resource-based interfaces, employing their vast financial resources on all fronts. Most encounters effectively combined two or three types of interfaces. Too great an emphasis on legal interfaces at the beginning of the discourse on access to medicine in poor countries did not produce the hoped-for results for TNPCs, as they admitted quite openly afterwards.[11]

TNPC strategies and the responses from developing countries

Pharmaceutical industry analysts have long used game theory in developing their strategic advice to management. In deciding between alternative research projects, which not only face a significant risk of failure but also the possibility of strong competition even after many years of successful R&D, management is well advised to use this approach to help them choose which projects to sponsor and which to drop or delay. In the case of internationalizing IPRs, the TNPCs chose the regime-shifting strategy, which they considered secure since it had the backing of the US government. Initially the strategy did seem to work well, when the shift of a new legal and enforceable base for IPRs from WIPO to WTO was accomplished without major opposition.

By simultaneously pressing for the internationalization of IPRs at WIPO, into which the US government introduced the Sustained Patent Treaty (SPT), attaining a successful introduction and legislation of the TRIPS Agreement at WTO, and insisting on even tougher IPR regulations (TRIPS-plus) in various

AIDS and Access to Medicines 143

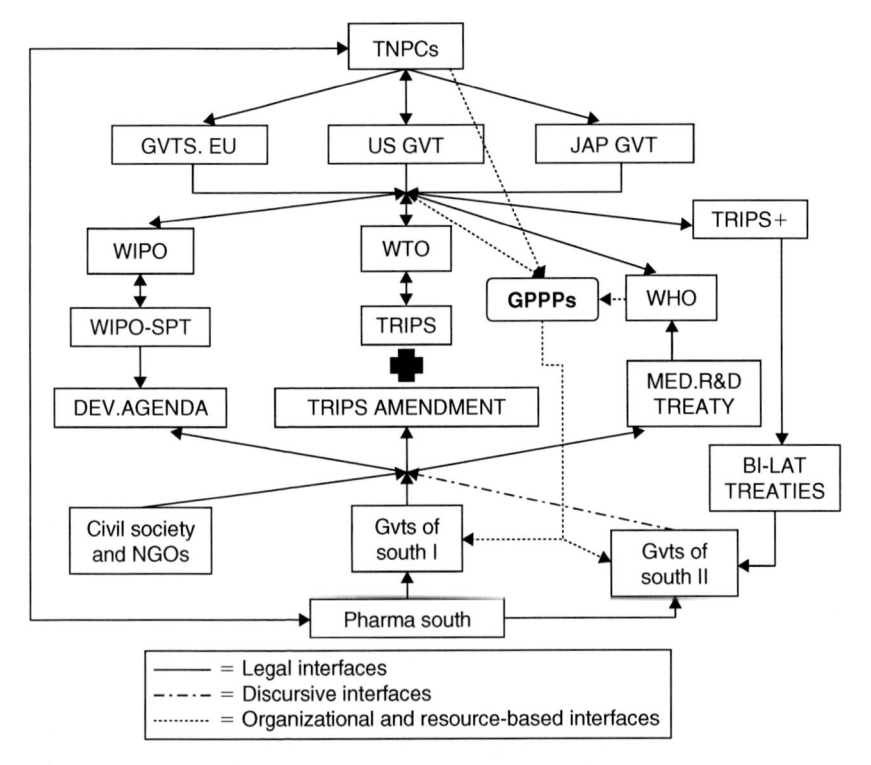

Figure 7.2 North versus south interfacing in an emerging GHG

Notes: Gvts of south I are the emerging economies, such as Argentina, Brazil, South Africa, India, China and Thailand. Equally, Pharma south stands for the pharmaceutical industries in those countries. Gvts of south II are the smaller and mostly poorer developing countries, including most of the Sub-Saharan nations as well as small Latin American nations, such as Guatemala and Haiti. TNPCs: Transnational pharmaceutical companies. GPPPs: Global public-private partnerships.
Source: Hein et al. (2007, figure 3.5).

bilateral treaties, governments of developed countries in general and the US Trade Representative in particular followed the script designed and proposed by the high-tech TNCs, among which the TNPCs played a crucial role.[12]

Success on the national front encouraged Brazil and the NGOs to play an increasingly active and demanding role in the international global health arena, not only along legal interfaces, but also by mobilizing discursive ones. The outcomes were realized in two initiatives at WIPO and WHO. In 2004, under the leadership of Argentina, Brazil and Kenya, developing countries pushed negotiations for a 'Development Agenda' in WIPO and a medical R&D treaty in WHO, hoping to provoke further discussion of the value and the optimum timing of IPR legislation in developing countries (WIPO, 2005) (Figure 7.2).

By also using the strategy of forum shifting, the developing countries countered the initiatives of the developed countries with an increasing number of initiatives of their own, transferring the spotlight of global health issues from the WTO to the WHO, where it would seem to belong. The scenario depicted in Figure 7.2 brings together the multiple interfaces between the major actors in the contemporary health arena. From the early discussions regarding TNPCs' interactions with governments of the north in pressing for internationalizing IPRs and the response from the developing countries to fight for an amendment of the TRIPS Agreement and to introduce new initiatives at WHO (and WIPO), it has become clear that WHO and WTO/TRIPS as major pillars of the global health architecture are in a period of significant change. While neither the TNPCs nor the NGOs are members of those pillars, their actions and interactions have played a major role in events within the WHO and the World Bank, WIPO and WTO, the last two of which would have seemed unlikely candidates for wide-ranging discussions and decisions concerning global health issues in the twenty-first century.

Mutually reinforcing interfaces in confronting AIDS

Resource-based and discursive interfaces: provoking different responses in Brazil and South Africa

Brazil and South Africa have faced major HIV/AIDS crises, with 'important aspects of the epidemic following a similar pattern in both countries' (Gauri and Lieberman, 2004: 2). While experts predicted a major expansion of the disease in both countries in the mid-1980s, Brazil has been able to keep the prevalence rate at less than 1 per cent of its population (UNAIDS, 2004: 202). The 660,000 estimated cases of HIV-infected people in Brazil contrast with the estimated 5.54 million HIV-infected South Africans, who constitute close to 11 per cent of the country's population (Doherty and Colvin, 2004: 196). Table 7.1 summarizes the major similarities and differences in the two countries concerning their readiness to fight HIV/AIDS.

With national incomes reaching similar levels and public health expenditures taking a similar share of public expenditures, the governments of both Brazil and South Africa were equipped with a similar resource base to fight the disease, notwithstanding Brazil's greater external foreign debt exposure. In short, on economic and social grounds South Africa would have seemed to be at least in a similar if not better position to fight the HIV/AIDS pandemic than Brazil, and yet the opposite occurred. While the Brazilian government rolled out ARVs free of charge in 1996 (AZT as early as 1991), South Africa only began to do so in 2003, and even then reluctantly. Startling differences in behaviour can also be observed concerning the relationships of actors in each country with GHG representatives.

Table 7.1 Brazil's and South Africa's fight against HIV/AIDS: similarities and differences

Item	Brazil	South Africa
Trajectory	HIV-infected people 1992: about 770,000 or prevalence rate <1%	HIV-infected people 1990: <1%
	HIV prevalence 2006: 0.61% (620,000 HIV-infected people)	HIV prevalence 2006: 11% (5.54 million HIV-infected people)
Per capita income	US$3000 (2006)	US$3630 (2004)
Income distribution	Seriously unequal (Gini index was 59.3 for 2005)	Seriously unequal (Gini index was 57.8 for 2005)
Public health expenditures	7.3% of federal budget with additional state and municipal spending	11.5% of total public budget
ARV distribution free of charge (year of beginning)	Free of charge: since 1988: DST-medication, since 1991: AZT since 1996: ARV	Since April 2002: legal entitlement for HIV-positive mothers (Nevirapine), since November 2003: ARV rollout for all citizens through public health system
HIV/AIDS policy at federal level (year of beginning)	Since 1985: National HIV/AIDS Programme	Since 1994: National AIDS Plan

Note: Shaded areas indicate major divergences between Brazil and South Africa.

The Brazilian response to AIDS emerged from the demands of civil society groups and developed through active collaboration between the local government of São Paulo and NGOs and through support from within the official health system, first at state levels and then – with a delay of three years – at the federal level. The civil society organizations had been the most critical opponents of federal government health policies in the 1980s and early 1990s and of governmental reluctance to formulate a comprehensive national HIV/AIDS programme. In the early years of the epidemic, NGOs and some local governments constituted the major protagonists of prevention and care (Galvão, 1994: 341–52).[13] They also drew heavily on resources from abroad by interfacing with global actors through the internet and at international AIDS conferences.

Lack of money in the Brazilian public health system (aggravated by the debt crisis) resulted in an increasing gap between rapidly growing demands for AIDS treatment and scarce financial resources in the late 1980s and early 1990s. A 1989 estimate revealed direct treatment costs for each AIDS patient to be about US$15,670 per year, with total costs of US$3.5 billion for all known AIDS patients, giving them an average survival time of six months (Medici, 1994: 328). One of the arguments behind the government willingness to provide free treatment for AIDS patients was that treatment was expected to have both a care and a preventative effect.[14]

The prevention versus treatment debate became a significant issue between the Brazilian government and the World Bank during loan negotiations after 1992. With the reorganization of the National AIDS Programme in the Ministry of Health, there was a concerted effort on all sides (governmental programmes at every level, NGOs, universities) to work together in seeking to formulate a national response to the epidemic. This collaborative spirit was reinforced and solidified during the process of elaborating a proposal for the first World Bank AIDS Project (1994–98), at which traditional rivalries and territorial disputes were set aside in favour of cooperation in fighting the disease.[15] While the Bank did not finance treatment directly, the national component of the funds did and the Bank funds going to the NGOs did too, one way or another. Together with the AIDS II (1998–2003) and the following AIDS III project, the Bank provided US$435 million, supplemented by government contributions of US$325 million. There was a special emphasis on prevention services, epidemiological surveillance, capacity-building and the improvement of the quality of life for people living with HIV/AIDS (World Bank, 2005: 26–7).

Disbursements by the Bank were followed by a dramatic expansion of both federal government programme expenditures for the treatment of HIV/AIDS and sexually transmitted diseases (STDs) and purchases of ARVs and other drugs. It helped to finance capacity-building and the creation of facilities at state and municipal levels and prevention projects by CSOs, thus consolidating one component of the overall Brazilian STD and HIV/AIDS Programme, BHAP.[16]

The Bank agreed that programme resources should be used for both prevention and treatment. This would not have been possible without the intense use of discursive interfaces in the form of a strong and skilful argumentation related to the country's awakening democratic spirit and a willingness to cooperate articulated by national government and NGOs such as the Brazilian Interdisciplinary AIDS Association (ABIA) and others. These civil society organizations helped to restrict the World Bank's influence to an almost exclusively resource-transfer character, and consequently the Brazilian government could maintain its comprehensive prevention and treatment approach (Parker et al., 2001: 110; Calcagnotto, 2007: 193). In short, Brazil jointly used resource-based and discursive interfaces, both within the country and internationally.

Other external donors have supported HIV/AIDS programmes in Brazil, but their financial contributions are small in comparison. The discursive interfacing reached crisis proportions in some cases and led, for instance, in 2005 and 2006 to the refusal of US$40 million USAID money because of the USAID insistence on the 'ABC' approach ('Abstinence, Be faithful, and Condoms', in this order of priority), which the Brazilian authorities rejected, especially as it related to sex-workers and abstinence. But while there may have been dissent along discursive interfaces, there was still cooperation along resource-based interfaces between BHAP and USAID continued in other STD/HIV related activities.[17] Particularly in the foundation period (1985–92), Brazilian CSOs working on HIV/AIDS made significant use of sources from abroad, such as the Ford Foundation, Misereor and Brot für die Welt, and they worked actively along discursive interfaces with international CSOs (Galvão, 2000: 87).

The financial and discursive interfaces have also been intense between the Brazilian business sector, government and civil society. As part of the BHAP the Brazilian National AIDS Council has not only been active in supporting workplace programmes it has also exerted an important global diffusion function in disseminating best practices of those programmes on the shop floor. In this context, multinational business and private foundations began to view NGOs and labour unions as partners fighting HIV/AIDS (Terto, 1997: 154).

South Africa's encounter with the HIV/AIDS challenge was – on the governmental level – neither influenced by financial contributions nor by discursive interfaces with global actors for a considerable time. According to Schneider and Gilson (1999: 266) total international aid to the health sector was just over 1 per cent of the South African annual government health budget in the period 1994 until 1999. As a middle-income country with relatively low external debt,[18] South Africa was not willing to rely on conditional donor aid. Throughout the 1990s, the ANC government thus refused external offers of financial or technical assistance, which it did not consider would fit into its policy framework, particularly with respect to treating HIV/AIDS.

This combative approach came into the open in 2002, when the ANC government blocked the disbursement of US$72 million granted by the Global Fund to Fight AIDS, Tuberculosis and Malaria (GFATM) to the Enhancing Care Initiative of the province of KwaZulu-Natal. GFATM's HIV/AIDS programme included – among other things – the financing of schemes to reduce the risk of mother-to-child transmission (PMTCT) of the virus and to provide antiretroviral treatment to infected persons (Pawinski and Lalloo, 2002). Despite the fact that the South African National AIDS Council had not been functioning at that time, the Minister of Health argued that only the national government could apply to the GFATM (Weinel, 2005: 45). It took another two years before the funds were transferred to KwaZulu-Natal's Enhancing Care Initiative.

Other official inflows of foreign financial support against HIV/AIDS were accepted by the national government only in 2004, more than a decade after Brazil initiated its large programme requesting external assistance. The US President's Emergency Fund for AIDS Relief (PEPFAR) provided US$221.5 million in 2004/5 for treatment, prevention, care of orphans and palliative care (United States Global AIDS Coordinator, 2005: 115). As stated by the US embassy in South Africa, 60 per cent of the funds have been allocated to the South African government and 40 per cent to civil society organizations working in the field of HIV/AIDS (United States, 2006). With it the ANC-government integrated PEPFAR funds into its changed strategies to fight HIV/AIDS.

In contrast to the government's approach of stressing autonomy, many South African civil society actors have been partially or fully funded by external actors, such as aid agencies, international organizations or private foundations. Most prominent has been the Treatment Action Campaign (TAC), founded in December 1998, that has quickly emerged as the most vocal civil society actor in the area of South Africa's HIV/AIDS policy. Almost the entire organization's 23.5 million rand budget for the financial year ending in February 2005 came from foreign donors (TAC, 2005: 19; Mbali, 2005: 22–3).

Similarly to the lack of official resource transfers, discursive interfaces have been hampered by internal conflicts in South Africa and international misunderstandings. Global actors operating in the country have only gradually been able to shape discourses on HIV/AIDS in general and on antiretroviral treatment in particular. In contradiction to government positions, they were able to demonstrate that antiretroviral treatment of HIV/AIDS is an effective and feasible option for the country. Nevertheless, it was difficult to overcome the South African policymakers' unwillingness to engage in a dialogue on treatment of HIV/AIDS (von Soest and Weinel, 2007).

One of the most prominent HIV/AIDS antiretroviral projects emerged in the Western Cape, the only province which, besides KwaZulu-Natal, had not been governed by the ANC until 2004. In January 1999, with the support of the Western Cape provincial government, MSF started an ARV-based programme to reduce the risk of mother-to-child transmission in Khayelitsha, a large township in Cape Town (Médecins Sans Frontières, 2003: 14). In May 2001, the organization established the first public sector service to provide antiretroviral treatment to people living with HIV/AIDS in South Africa. Although the national government disapproved this action, the political constellation in the Western Cape Province permitted the engagement of MSF. The Khayelitsha project set a publicly visible example that ARVs can be successfully administered even in the setting of a poor township. This is reflected in the 2003 report of TAC (2003), a close ally of MSF.

While public-private partnerships developed in Brazil in order to prevent and treat AIDS in business and industry, the private sector was on its own in South Africa. Without entering into the discussion whether businesses' reaction has been adequate to the magnitude of the HIV/AIDS problem, it can safely be said that the highly publicized workplace programmes of such important enterprises as the Anglo-American mining company, the parastatal power utility Eskom and the multinational car manufacturers DaimlerChrysler, BMW and Volkswagen had – beyond a very specific impact within the firms' employees and their families – a demonstration effect on South Africa's HIV/AIDS policy (Marais, 2000: 30; Butler, 2005: 11).

Civil society was less constrained in South Africa than companies and interacted intensively both at the national and international levels. TAC actively forged networks with international non-governmental organizations (INGOs) and international organizations which have had significant impacts on GHG. In cooperation with its partners, TAC organized international protests supporting South Africa's government in the court case brought by the Pharmaceutical Manufacturers' Association challenging the Medicines and Related Substances Amendment Act (Gumede, 2005: 157). INGOs later also conducted solidarity protests during TAC's civil disobedience campaign against the government, which included demonstrations in front of South African embassies around the world (Mbali, 2005: 36).[19]

Legal and organizational interfaces: disputes with repercussions on the global level

Legal interfaces broaden or narrow the access of people to public health systems. The legal recognition of universal access to health as 'a right of all and a duty of the State' by the 1988 Brazilian Constitution (Republic of Brazil 1988, Article 196, see Senado Federal, 2003: 119) served as an important base for negotiations with the World Bank, since the constitutional recognition implies the right of all citizens to health-care, including treatment (Parker et al., 2001: 110). On the global level, Brazil's fight for a human right to access antiretroviral treatment succeeded with the April 2001 Resolution of the UN Commission on Human Rights dealing with the 'Access to medication in the context of pandemics such as HIV/AIDS'.[20] Brazil had lobbied intensively for this resolution, beginning with the efforts to put free technology transfer and ARV price reduction on the international agenda. Brazilian representatives obtained the inclusion of the issue of ARV treatment and generics on the agenda of several international and multilateral organizations, such as the Okinawa G8 Summit in July 2000, the Executive Committee of WHO in January 2001, the UNHCR in February 2001 and the UNAIDS board in April/May 2001. As a consequence, the ground was prepared for the great battle against the 2001 complaint by the USA to the WTO against Brazil's patent law, as well as for the Doha Declaration in November 2001 (Teixeira, 2005: 13–14).

The legal battle between Brazil and the United States over pharmaceutical patent rights had strong repercussions for both GHG and NHG. The

US pharmaceutical association, PhRMA, started to lobby against the Brazilian patent law, which excluded medical products from patent protection, as early as 1988 (Marques, 2002: 43; Tachinardi, 1993: 67). Only after the application of harsh commercial sanctions in 1990 through punitive customs duties on selected Brazilian exports (Silva, 2005: 131) did the Brazilian government issue a revised patent law in 1996, which included the protection of pharmaceutical products.

However, the 1996 Brazilian patent law still limited the scope of pharmaceutical patent rights. Paragraph 68 forced TNPCs to produce their drugs locally within three years of patent approval, non-compliance allowing the government to issue compulsory licences. The United States filed a complaint on this paragraph with the WTO in 2001 (Galvão, 2002: 216; Marques, 2002: 44, 46). The dispute was only resolved when Brazil restricted compulsory licensing to cases of a national health emergency. On 25 June 2001, the United States withdrew its complaint. In turn, Brazil agreed to notify the US government in advance if it found it necessary to issue a compulsory licence. This solution was a response to open pressure from NGOs, simultaneously articulated through discursive interfaces in the USA and Brazil (Cepaluni, 2005: 80–1; Ashraf, 2001: 2112; Galvão, 2002: 215–16; Wogart and Calcagnotto, 2006: 95–6).

In summary, the United States was not able to utilize legal interfaces to strengthen the position of TNPCs, which would have blocked Brazil's policies of providing universal access to treatment, producing generic ARVs, and of negotiating prices for patented drugs – policies which have been referred to as the 'Brazilian model' for AIDS treatment. In May 2007, Brazil issued its first compulsory licence for an ARV. Under its terms, Brazil imports generic Efavirenz from drug companies other than the patent holder Merck (Nunn et al., 2007: 12–13).

In South Africa as well, legal interfaces have been the site of significant confrontations. The country came into the international spotlight when the Pharmaceutical Manufacturers' Association of South Africa (PMA), backed by PhRMA, sued the South African government for violating their IPRs before South Africa's High Court in 1997.[21] The lawsuit, which was based on the legal provisions of the TRIPS Agreement, was supported by the United States government, which threatened to impose trade restrictions on South Africa (Lanoszka, 2003: 191–2). Its target was the Medicines and Related Substances Control Amendment Act, signed by President Mandela in December 1997, which gave the South African Minister of Health the power to allow both compulsory licensing and the parallel importation of patented medicines in general and of antiretroviral drugs in particular (Kühl, 2002: 76). Responding to intense national and international public pressure and with only a slim chance of winning the case, the 39 TNPCs represented by the PMA backed down in late 1998 (Weissman, 2001).

In January 2001 the lawsuit was reinstated. The chances for victory by the pharmaceutical manufacturers had considerably improved, because South Africa was now obliged fully to comply with the requirements of the TRIPS Agreement (Kühl, 2002: 76). The TNPCs maintained that the case was not directed against South Africa's efforts to seek price reductions for antiretroviral medicine. However, that was exactly the impression that AIDS activists and NGOs in South Africa and around the world tried to create. Internationally-recognized NGOs such as Médecins Sans Frontières, Oxfam, CPtech and ACT-UP pressured TNPCs to withdraw the case. Even the Bush administration refrained from openly supporting the pharmaceutical industry (Weissman, 2001). Demonstrations were organized in South Africa, but also in front of several TNPCs' headquarters in Europe and North America. The pharmaceutical industry, fearing another public relations nightmare, withdrew the lawsuit in mid-April 2001 (Lanoszka, 2003: 192) and agreed to 'a settlement almost on the government of South Africa's terms. The only concession made by the government was to comply with decisions made by the World Trade Organization on TRIPS Agreement' (Kühl, 2002: 78).[22]

On balance, legal interfaces have thus been an important focus for the interaction of South African actors at the global level. The case strengthened the South African government's argument against the TNPCs and augmented the international pressure to reduce the prices for antiretroviral drugs. In the use of legal interfaces, the strategies of the Brazilian and South African governments have shown close similarities. Both governments fought against TNPCs as the parties responsible for high ARV prices and promoted the human right to access to essential medicines. According to Gauri and Lieberman (2004: 27), Brazil and South Africa 'have styled themselves as emboldened leaders of the developing countries in this regard'.

Closely related to legal interfaces are organizational interfaces, which act as crucial indicators for the degree of cooperation between the national and the global level of health governance. Once more, while Brazilian policymakers had made extensive use of opportunities for cooperation even before the threat of AIDS required some degree of organizational interface, South African organizational links had been much more restrained, an attitude which tended towards isolationism during the AIDS crisis in the 1990s.

Since the 1970s, the WHO has developed multiple initiatives with Brazilian health authorities and academic institutions through its regional representative, the Pan American Health Organization (PAHO). These joint activities laid the conceptual basis for the reform of the Brazilian health system in the 1980s and 1990s. That in turn shaped the Brazilian BHAP (Lima, 2002: 92–3; Fontes, 1999: 113–14). The UNAIDS Theme Group on HIV/AIDS, established in Brazil in 1997, includes seven UN System Agencies and in its 'expanded group' also two federal ministries (health/BHAP and foreign affairs), three international organizations (FAO, ILO and UNIFEM), two bilateral donor organizations (GTZ and USAID), the global NGO, Family Health International, and two representatives from civil society (UNAIDS, 2001: 3). With this multilateral composition, the Theme Group was able to articulate the activities of international organizations in the country with national actors and so to mobilize organizational and, since 2001, also programmatic support for the Brazilian HIV/AIDS policy. According to the former director of BHAP, Paulo Teixeira, the UNAIDS Theme Group in Brazil brought 'positive synergic effects' at federal, state and municipal levels of government,[23] mainly through support for implementation of the 'Three Ones' principles: one national AIDS coordinating authority, one AIDS action framework and one country-level monitoring and evaluation system. It has decisively influenced the organization of the Brazilian HIV/AIDS prevention campaigns, for instance through motivating local mayors to participate actively and to inform their communities about the epidemic during the Red Ribbon Campaign.[24]

Brazilian actors also effectively used organizational interfaces to influence GHG. In 2004, Brazil's representative was unanimously elected vice-president of the UNAIDS Programme Coordinating Board and in 2005 he assumed the presidency of the body (CNAIDS, 2004). This increased Brazil's impact at the global level and exemplifies the government's general policy of actively working on HIV/AIDS in international organizations. There is also evidence that Brazil's civil society exerted some influence on GHG. ABIA, for instance, was actively involved in the Fifth International AIDS Conference in Montreal in 1989 (Galvão, 2000: 87). On that occasion, the International Council of AIDS Service Organizations (ICASO) was established, with the main aim of strengthening the global response of civil society organizations. Acting as the ICASO Secretariat for Latin America, ABIA also spearheaded the creation of the Latin American and Caribbean Council of AIDS Service Organizations as a further organizational interface (Galvão, 2000: 87).[25]

Although the South African government has rarely engaged in organizational interfaces concerning the treatment of HIV/AIDS, there have been several organizational interfaces in the prevention area. One of those has been the LoveLife public-private partnership on HIV prevention. Co-financed by the US-based Kaiser Family Foundation and other donors as well as the South African government, which provided 34 per cent of the overall budget, LoveLife also received substantial resources from the GFATM. Running South Africa's biggest HIV/AIDS prevention programme for teenagers, it designed accessible and youth-friendly clinics and social marketing campaigns and sponsored various events.[26] LoveLife enjoys a cordial and collaborative relationship with the government and even has the minister of health on its advisory board. In short, it acted as a 'government service-provider' (Mbali, 2005: 18).

There is also some evidence that experts from the Clinton Foundation were involved in the Joint Health and Treasury Task Team that was set up to investigate the feasibility and the costs of universal access to treatment of HIV/AIDS in South Africa in 2002 (Ijumba et al., 2004: 333). The US foundation was thus linked to the national level through an organizational interface. Yet, although the Clinton Foundation was – on the global level – very influential in reducing prices for antiretroviral drugs, their experts were later denied further access to South African institution, with the government stopping any further cooperation with the foundation.[27]

Table 7.2 provides a synopsis of the comparison between the Brazilian and the South African cases, focusing on the different types of interfaces involved. Resource-based interfaces regarding material (service and financial) exchanges turned out to be powerful as expected and favoured the early development of the Brazilian treatment programme. The intensive links between resource-based and discursive interfaces, however, are highly important for explaining the role of Brazil as a forerunner in the access politics of developing countries and as a state ally of the CSOs' access campaign.

Conclusions

The examination of the fight against AIDS and the confrontation over ARV prices between Brazilian and South African government representatives – supported by local and global civil society groups – and the TNPCs and governments of industrialized countries reveal a number of points that could be important for future policy decisions. First, the seemingly all-powerful transnational corporations were forced to negotiate and retreat vis-à-vis two developing countries in view of a global health crisis. While the importance of the NGOs' involvement is undeniable and has been cited here and elsewhere, the emergence of strong national health governance in Brazil and the successful opposition of both Brazil and South Africa to a narrow TNPC-oriented interpretation of the TRIPS Agreement, were crucial examples for other developing countries looking to defend their own interests in GHG in a more self-conscious way. The role of CSOs in Brazil and their successful stance against the South African government points to the strength of global civil society in the case of health issues and to the fact that conflicts on access to medicines are not fought along ideologically hardened north-south lines alone.

Second, these accomplishments were achieved through the artful use of different interfaces, the combination of which made the change possible. Important as it was as a first step, defending presumed 'national interest' along legal interfaces – as the Brazil and South African governments did – was a necessary but insufficient condition to have an impact on the rules and regulations governing access to medicines; that was accomplished by using opportunities and reacting to challenges along resource-based, organizational and especially discursive interfaces in the multi-level global polity. As a

Table 7.2 Fighting HIV/AIDS: major interfaces of Brazilian and South African NHG

Interfaces	Brazil	South Africa
Resource-based	Civil society and public health sector substantially supported by global institutions and NGOs since 1980s.	Civil society supported by global institutions and NGOs since 1980s, but decisively only since 1990s.
	Heavy reliance on foreign financing for public health in 1980s and 1990s (debt crisis; public health free of charge), including state and federal HIV/AIDS programmes (since 1983).	Government's health budget not constrained by high indebtedness. Significant global financing for government programmes only since 2000, treatment programmes since 2003.
Discursive	Since the 1980s, civil society's human rights discourse for integrated prevention-treatment approach (dialogue between national and global NGOs and all levels of government).	Since the 1980s civil society's human rights discourse for an integrated prevention-treatment approach has been developed through dialogue between national and global NGOs.
	Early responsiveness of states (since 1983) and (since 1985) progressively federal governments (except 1990–92) to CSO pressure for the integrated prevention-treatment approach	Late (i.e., 2003) responsiveness of most provincial governments and of national government to civil society's pressure for integrated prevention-treatment approach.
Legal	Constitutional provisions (1988) of universalistic public health system as foundations for the Brazilian HIV/AIDS Program BHAP.	Application (by national government) of the 'Medicines and Related Substances Control Amendment Act' of December 1997 (allowing compulsory licensing and parallel importation of patented drugs, based on TRIPS) against TNPCs' lawsuit of 1998/ 2001.
	Government resists US pressures against patent policy (since late 1980s) and presses TNPCs on pricing of ARVs in Brazil (2001–07) based on Act 9313/November 1996 for ARV distribution free of charge and Patent Act No. 9279/14.5.1996 allowing compulsory licensing in certain cases.	Explicit government commitment to comply with WTO rules as compromise in legal conflict with TNPC (2001). Despite its provisions, Act has not been used for compulsory licensing and parallel importation of drugs.

Organizational	Brazilian government fought successfully for recognition of AIDS treatment as a human right at UNCHR and WHO (2001).	Government fighting for using TRIPS flexibilities in WTO/Doha negotiations 2001 together with Brazil and 50 other developing countries.
	Spearheaded fight of developing countries to use TRIPS flexibilities (WTO/Doha negotiations 2001) and generally to facilitate compulsory licensing and parallel imports of essential medicines.	
	Cooperation with WHO since 1970 about health reform and the unified public health system, but dissent about HIV/AIDS-treatment approach since the 1980s.	Little organizational cooperation by South African government concerning treatment of HIV/AIDS, at least up to 2003.
	Cooperation (government/NGOs) with UNAIDS-Theme Group in prevention campaigns since 1997.	Refusal of national government to cooperate with Clinton Foundation for universal access to HIV/AIDS-treatment after preliminary studies in 2002.
	Intense use of global organizational channels by government to influence UNAIDS approach to HIV/AIDS-treatment.	Organizational interface was hardly used by government to influence global level.
	Active participation of Brazilian NGOs in developing international and Latin-American cooperation between HIV/AIDSNGOs.	PPP cooperation until recently only concerning HIV/AIDS-prevention (e.g. LoveLife).

Note: Shaded areas indicate major divergences between Brazil and South Africa.

consequence, future developments in NHG and GHG will depend on policy-makers using the multiplicity of interfaces in order to achieve comprehensive solutions in global health issues.

Third, while it is impossible entirely to separate the various interfaces during the conflict on TRIPS and access to medicines, each played a prominent part in the multiple negotiations between 1995 and 2008. The TRIPS Agreement, the legal interfaces in the South African courts, the Doha Declaration and the TRIPS Amendment played a crucial role in supporting Brazil's legal battles and claims of the right to access low-cost medicines. The increasing global involvement in the fight against HIV/AIDS permitted Brazil to engage fully in a number of organizational interfaces, which helped not only Brazil but other emerging economies as well to find ways of defending their interests in the field of TRIPS and health and ensuring that the defenders of strong IPRs reconsider their positions concerning global health issues. Resource-based interfaces played a different role in each country. Once the Brazilian federal government had determined to make the fight against the pandemic a top priority, it was in a position to negotiate the terms of cooperation with major financial donors and creditors. In contrast, South Africa's financial independence and the government's stance in respect to treatment of HIV/AIDS led to an independent determination of health policies, at a high price for sufferers of the disease. Successes at the negotiating tables have been strongly supported by discursive power, which was first and foremost used successfully by civil society at all levels, but in which government representatives and the TNPCs increasingly also engaged. The number of papers and reports issued by the industry's national and international associations, some of them written by international think-tanks, signalled an increased willingness of the pharmaceutical industry to enter into discursive interfaces on a quasi-academic level.

Fourth, the rapid response of the TNPCs moves the argument into a new round of confrontation that will challenge the participants to engage further in multiple interfaces. 'Forum shifting' by major developed countries away from the multilateral stage and the increased attention to bilateral trade treaties containing TRIPs-plus clauses has been answered by developing countries introducing a 'Development Agenda' into WIPO and proposing a 'Global Framework on Essential Health Research and Development' in the World Health Assembly in May 2006. This, in turn, led to the establishment of an Intergovernmental Working Group on Public Health, Innovation and Intellectual Property aiming at an international agreement on these questions.

This new round of negotiations on the funding of health research and the evolving norm of 'universal access to essential medicines' points to new institutional forms of GHG. Certainly, intergovernmental agreements continue to play an important role for establishing binding rules. Nevertheless, state actors are also becoming part of a more open field of global politics in which various types of non-state actors (CSOs, TNCs, GPPPs, philanthropic foundations) are strengthening their position and creating a complex field of interfaces. Private companies and CSOs are now playing a more open role in pushing for legal agreements, for amendments or authoritative interpretations of existing rules, as has been demonstrated for the conflicts around the TRIPS Agreement. In some GHG institutions, such as GFATM and in GPPPs, private actors have voting rights and play an important role as experts, as well as strong lobbyists for their own interests.

Eventually, a new and enlarged set of legal norms should emerge from the organizational, financial and discursive interfaces described above. That in itself should simplify and clarify the role of the various actors in the changing field of global health. As we have seen, the first steps in that direction have already been taken and are waiting to be supplemented and coordinated by further agreements for the emergence of an improved GHG.

Notes

1. This process was smoothed to some degree by TRIPS Article 65 which allows different transitory periods for developing countries.
2. The role of global civil society in this conflict is analysed in more detail in Chapter 4 above by Hein, Burris and Shearing; see also Sell and Prakash (2004) and Hein et al. (2007).
3. Under WTO rules, a compulsory licence allows governments to produce or to grant a third-party authority to produce a drug without consent of the patent holder in cases of national public health emergency, among other limited circumstances (see, http://www.wto.org/english/tratop_e/trips_e/public_health_faq_e.htm, accessed 12 December 2008). The TRIPS Agreement, as confirmed by the Doha Declaration and adopted on 14 November 2001, affirms governments' rights to use the agreement's flexibilities or may grant compulsory licences in order to avoid any reticence the governments may feel (see, http://www.wto.org/English/tratop_e/dda_e/dohaexplained_e.htm#trips, accessed 12 December 2008).
4. 'Parallel importation refers to the imports of goods purchased in a foreign market by an independent third party and later resold in the domestic market where much lower prices compete with the prices charged by authorized distributors' (Kühl, 2002: 18).
5. After the Paris Convention for the Protection of Industrial Property (1883), and the Berne Convention for the Protection of Literary and Artistic Works (1887), a common international secretariat was established in 1893. During the first half of the twentieth century, the political and economic upheavals of the two world wars and the economic problems associated with them did not allow any further institutionalization until 1967, when the Stockholm Convention Establishing the World Intellectual Property Organization (WIPO) was signed.
6. The 2003 Decision actually took the form of a waiver related to the obligations of member states under Articles 31f and 31h of TRIPS. To soothe the fear of TNPCs and their governments in the developed countries, the General Council's chairperson underlined the fact that the 'system that will be established by the Decision should

be used in good faith to protect public health and, without prejudice to paragraph 6 of the Decision, not be an instrument to pursue industrial or commercial policy objectives' (WTO, 2003). For a detailed legal interpretation and a discussion on the relationship between the Decision and the Amendment see, South Centre and CIEL (2005).
7. As in 2003, the compromise in 2005 was reached as a hopeful overture to the WTO trade negotiations, which followed suit.
8. On compulsory licensing, see http://www.cptech.org/ip/health/cl/recent-examples.html (accessed 7 July 2008). Companies such as GSK and Merck either used different packing and/or bottling or embossed tablets for their HIV/AIDS medication with a different number from the same pills sold in rich countries.
9. For the conflict between Brazil and the TNPCs see Wogart and Calcagnotto (2006). For the discussion on the TRIPS Agreement see Wogart (2007) and Hein (2007).
10. For a discussion of the direct involvement of the TNPCs in national and global politics, see Sell (2000) and Jawara and Kwa (2003).
11. *The Economist*, 'Prescription for Change', 16 June 2005.
12. For an extensive discussion of the TNPCs' role in drafting the TRIPS Agreement, see Sell (2000).
13. This changed with the new orientation of the Brazilian Sexually Transmitted Diseases and HIV/AIDS Programme (BHAP) in 1992, which provided a wide range of prevention and care services. The development of a network of NGOs since then has mainly been financed by the federal government, which has channelled funds towards them from World Bank projects.
14. 'The promise of treatment gave an incentive for more at-risk individuals to be tested and gave doctors an incentive to report AIDS cases, thus improving surveillance and prevention programs' (Berkman et al., 2005: 1170). The implementation of BHAP in 2001 needed an investment of US$232 million, but was estimated to result in total savings of US$1.1 billion (thanks to the reduction of hospitalization and other costs).
15. The Minister of Health, José Serra (1998–2002), has maintained somewhat dryly in an interview: 'The Bank's participation was positive for it obliged us to do something well organized to make an efficient management and accounting effort' (see Biehl, 2004: p. 111).
16. The relevance of this qualitative contribution is reflected in the prevention component for which the Bank lent US$253 million in 1994–2003. In 2000, purchases of ARV drugs by the federal government alone amounted to US$290 million, 69 per cent of total federal spending on AIDS that year (World Bank, 2005: 28). It would have been difficult for the Brazilian government to maintain its level of expenditure if the World Bank had not have covered the prevention component so substantially.
17. 'Nota Técnica do Programa Nacional de DST e AIDS' in: http://www.aids.gov.br/main.asp?View={E77B47C8-3436-41E0-AC19-E1B215447EB9} of 13 March 2006 (accessed 1 August 2008), and http://www.reduc.org.br/news.php?recid=125 of 3 April 2006 (accessed 1 August 2008); also: http://brazil.usaid.gov/noticiaINT.php?id=90, from 10 December 2007 (accessed 1 August 2008).
18. In 1996, shortly after the democratic transition, South Africa's total external debt amounted to US$23.6 billion (World Bank, 1998: 249), against a total debt of US$83.3 billion for Brazil (mid- and long-term debt; Central Bank of Brazil, 1983: 93).

19. In its campaign tactics, TAC has learnt from the US-based NGO AIDS Coalition to Unleash Power (ACT-UP) (Schneider, 2001: 18). This provides further evidence of the strong interaction between NGO actors from the national and the global level through discursive interfaces.
20. The resolution was passed by a 52-0 vote with only one abstention (Galvão, 2002: 219). One month later, the WHO World Health Assembly, following a Brazilian proposal, also confirmed 'the right to health and that the progressive realisation of that right in the context of HIV/AIDS involves access to treatment' (ISHR, 2001).
21. Extensive documentation of the case can be found on the web page of the American NGO CPTech, http://www.cptech.org/ip/health/sa/ (accessed 7 July 2008).
22. As a consequence the Medicines and Related Substances Control Amendment Act from 1997 remained largely unchanged. While the Doha Declaration explicitly permits countries to issue compulsory licences in case of national health emergencies, the government rejected proposals from civil society to declare the HIV/AIDS epidemic a national emergency (Gauri and Lieberman, 2004: 26).
23. Interview with Paulo Teixeira, former General Coordinator of BHAP (2000–03) and Director of the HIV/AIDS Department of WHO (2003–04), 24 August 2004.
24. Interview with Luciano Milhomem, Media and Partnership Consultant of UNAIDS-Brazil, 15 September 2004.
25. In Galvão (2000), further examples of Brazilian NGOs entering into organizational interfaces can be found.
26. Interview with John O'Connor, Managing Director of LoveLife, 11 May 2005.
27. Information given by a respondent who requested anonymity.

References

Ashraf, H., 'USA and Brazil End Dispute over Essential Drugs', *Lancet*, 357 (2001): 2112.
Baer, W. and C. Paiva, 'Brasiliens inflationäre Erblast und der Plano Real', in G. Calcagnotto and B. Fritz (eds), *Inflation und Stabilisierung in Brasilien. Probleme einer Gesellschaft im Wandel* (Hamburg: Schriftenreihe des Instituts für Iberoamerika-Kunde, 1996), pp. 66–93.
Bartsch, S. and L. Kohlmorgen, 'Nichtregierungsorganisationen als Akteure der Global Health Governance – Interaktion zwischen Kooperation und Konflikt', in J. Betz and W. Hein (eds), *Neues Jahrbuch Dritte Welt 2005. Zivilgesellschaft* (Wiesbaden: VS Verlag, 2005), pp. 57–87.
Bartsch, S., W. Hein and L. Kohlmorgen, 'Interfaces: a Concept for the Analysis of Global Health Governance', in W. Hein, S. Bartsch and L. Kohlmorgen (eds), *Global Health Governance and the Fight against HIV/AIDS* (Basingstoke: Palgrave Macmillan, 2007), pp. 18–37.
Berkman, A., J. Garcia, M. Muñoz-Laboy, V. Paiva and R. Parker, 'A Critical Analysis of the Brazilian Response to HIV/AIDS: Lessons Learned for Controlling and Mitigating the Epidemic in Developing Countries', *American Journal of Public Health*, 95(7) (2005): 1162–72.
Biehl, J.G., 'The Activist State: Global Pharmaceuticals, AIDS, and Citizenship in Brazil', *Social Text*, 22(3) (2004): 105–32.
Calcagnotto, G., 'Consensus-Building on Brazilian HIV/AIDS Policy: National and Global Interfaces in Health Governance', in W. Hein, S. Bartsch and L. Kohlmorgen

(eds), *Global Health Governance and the Fight against HIV/AIDS* (Basingstoke: Palgrave Macmillan, 2007), pp. 172–201.

Central Bank of Brazil, *Annual Report 1982* (Brasília: Central Bank of Brazil, 1983).

Cepaluni, G., 'Regimes Internacionais e o Contencioso das Patentes para Medicamentos: Estratégias para Países em Desenvolvimento', *Contexto Internacional*, 27(1) (2005): 51–99.

CNAIDS, Protocol, 20 June 2004, 71st Session (Brasília: Comissão Nacional de AIDS (CNAIDS), 2004), www.aids.gov.br/final/parcerias/atas.asp (accessed 10 February 2006).

Doherty, T. and M. Colvin, 'HIV/AIDS', in P. Ijumba, C. Day and A. Ntuli (eds), *South African Health Review 2003/2004* (Durban: Health System Trust, 2004), pp. 191–211, www.hst.org.za/uploads/files/SAHR2003_04_1.pdf (accessed 7 July 2008).

Drahos, P., 'Negotiating Intellectual Property Rights: Between Coercion and Dialogue', in P. Drahos and R. Mayne (eds), *Global Intellectual Property Rights: Knowledge, Access and Development* (Basingstoke: Palgrave, 2002), pp. 161–82.

Fidler, D., 'Architecture amidst Anarchy: Global Health's Quest for Governance', *Global Health Governance*, 1(1) (2007): 1–17.

Fontes, M. B., 'Interfaces entre as políticas internacionais e nacionais de AIDS', in R. Parker, J. Galvão and M.S. Bessa (eds), *Saúde, Desenvolvimento e Política. Respostas frente à AIDS no Brasil* (Rio de Janeiro: ABIA Editora 34, 1999), pp. 91–122.

Galvão, J., 'AIDS e Ativismo: O Surgimento e a Construção de Novas Formas de Solidariedade', in R. Parker, C. Bastos, J. Galvão and J. S. Pedrosa (eds), *A AIDS no Brasil (1982–1992)*, ABIA/IMS-UERJ (Rio de Janeiro: University of Rio de Janeiro, 1994), pp. 341–52.

Galvão, J., *AIDS no Brasil. A agenda de construção de uma epidemia* (Rio de Janeiro: ABIA Editora 34, 2000).

Galvão, J., 'A política brasileira de distribuição e produção de medicamentos anti-retrovirais: privilégio ou direito?', *Cadernos Saúde Pública*, 18 (1) (2002): 212–19.

Gauri, V. and E.S. Lieberman (2004), *AIDS and the State: the Politics of Government Responses to the Epidemic in Brazil and South Africa*, http://comparativepolitics.stanford.edu/Papers2004-05/Liebermanv2.440dJan17.pdf (accessed 7 July 2008).

Gumede, W.M., *Thabo Mbeki and the Battle for the Soul of the ANC* (Cape Town: Zebra Press, 2005).

Hein, W., 'Global Health Governance and WTO/TRIPS: Conflicts between "Global Market-Creation" and "Global Social Rights"', in W. Hein, S. Bartsch and L. Kohlmorgen (eds), *Global Health Governance and the Fight against HIV/AIDS* (Basingstoke: Palgrave Macmillan, 2007), pp. 38–66.

Hein, W., S. Bartsch and L. Kohlmorgen (eds), *Global Health Governance and the Fight against HIV/AIDS* (Basingstoke: Palgrave Macmillan, 2007).

Ijumba, P., C. Day and A. Ntuli, 'Access to Antiretroviral Therapy', in P. Ijumba, C. Day and A. Ntuli (eds), *South African Health Review 2003/2004* (Durban: Health System Trust, 2004), pp. 319–38, www.hst.org.za/uploads/files/SAHR2003_04_1.pdf (accessed 7 July 2008).

ISHR, *54th World Health Assembly (Geneva 14–22 May 2001)* (Geneva: International Service on Human Rights (ISHR), World Health Organization (WHO), 2001).

Jawara, P. and A. Kwa, *Behind the Scenes at the WTO: the Real World of International Trade Negotiations* (London: Zed Books, 2003).

Kühl, H. (2002) *TRIPS and AIDS in South Africa: New Actors in International Relations – Weighing Patents, Pills and Patients* (Los Angeles: Occidental College, 2002).

Lanoszka, A., 'The Global Politics of Intellectual Property Rights and Pharmaceutical Drug Policies in Developing Countries', *International Political Science Review*, 24 (2) (2003): 181–97.
Lima, N.T., 'O Brasil e a Organização Pan-Americana da Saúde: Uma História em Três Dimensões', in J. Finkelman (ed.), *Caminhos da Saúde Pública no Brasil* (Rio de Janeiro: Fiocruz 2002), pp. 23–116.
Long, N., *Encounters at the Interface* (Wageningen: Wageningen Studies in Sociology, 1989).
Mail & Guardian (2005a), 'Is LoveLife Making them Love Life?', *Mail & Guardian*, 24 August 2005, www.mg.co.za/articlePage.aspx?area=/insight/insight__comment_ and_analysis/&articleId=248887 (accessed 7 July 2008).
Mail & Guardian (2005b), 'Major LoveLife Funder Pulls the Plug', *Mail & Guardian*, 21 December 2005, www.mg.co.za/article/2005-12-21-major-lovelife-funder-pulls-the-plug (accessed 7 July 2008).
Marais, H., *To the Edge: AIDS Review 2000* (Pretoria: Centre for the Study of AIDS, University of Pretoria, 2000).
Marques, M.B., *Acessibilidade aos medicamentos. O desafio de vincular ciência, tecnologia, inovação e saúde no Brasil* (Brasília: Centro de Gestão e Estudos Estratégicos, 2002).
Mbali, M., 'The Treatment Action Campaign's Strategies to Government AIDS Policy in South Africa', research paper commissioned by the Global Health Governance Project of the German Overseas Institute, Hamburg, 2005.
Médecins Sans Frontières, 'Providing HIV Services Including Antiretroviral Therapy at Primary Health Care Clinics in Resource-Poor Settings: the Experience from Khayelitsha', Activity Report (2003), http://www.hst.org.za/uploads/files/khayelitsha03.pdf (accessed 7 July 2008).
Medici, A., 'Impactos Socioeconômicos da AIDS', in R. Parker, C. Bastos, J. Galvão and J.S. Pedrosa (eds) (1994), *A AIDS no Brasil (1982–1992)*, ABIA/IMS-UERJ (Rio de Janeiro: University of Rio de Janeiro, 1994), pp. 325–9.
Nunn, A. S., E. M. Fonseca, F. I. Bastos, S. Gruskin and J. A. Salomon, 'Evolution of Antiretroviral Drug Costs in Brazil in the Context of Free and Universal Access to AIDS Treatment', *Public Library of Science Medicine*, 4(11) (2007): e305.
R. Parker, C. Bastos, J. Galvão and J.S. Pedrosa (eds) (1994), *A AIDS no Brasil (1982–1992)*, ABIA/IMS-UERJ (Rio de Janeiro: University of Rio de Janeiro, 1994).
Parker, R., R.A. de Mattos and V. Terto Jr, 'As estratégias do Banco Mundial e a resposta à AIDS no Brasil 2001', in F. Barros (ed.), *As estratégias dos bancos multilaterais para o Brasil (2000–2003)* (Brasília: Rede Brasil sobre Instituições Financeiras Multilaterais, 2001), pp. 107–30.
Pawinski, R. and U. Lalloo, 'Throwing a Lifeboat to the Titanic: the Global Fund and HIV in South Africa and KwaZulu-Natal', *Aids Analysis Africa*, 2002, http://wwwc.redribbon.co.za/learn/user_page.asp?page_number=2985&prev_page=2938 (accessed 7 July 2008).
Schneider, H., 'A Struggle for Symbolic Power', *Siyaya Magazine*, 8 (winter): 18–21.
Schneider, H. and L. Gilson, 'Small Fish in a Big Pond? External Aid and the Health Sector in South Africa', *Health Policy and Planning*, 14 (3) (1999): 264–72.
Sell, S., 'Structures, Agents and Institutions: Private Corporate Power and the Globalization of Intellectual Property Rights', in R.A. Higgott, G. Underhill and A. Bieler (eds), *Non-State Actors in the Global System* (London: Routledge, 2000), pp. 91–106.
Sell, S., *Private Power, Public Law: the Globalization of Intellectual Property Rights* (Cambridge: Cambridge University Press, 2003).

Sell, S. and A. Prakash, 'Using Ideas Strategically: the Contest between Business and NGO Networks in Intellectual Property Rights', *International Studies Quarterly*, 48 (2004): 143–75.

Senado Federal, *Constituição da República Federativa do Brasil* (Brasília: Subsecretaria de Edições Técnicas, 2003).

Sexton, S., 'Trading Health Care Away? GATS, Public Services and Privatization' (Sturminster Newton: The Corner House Briefing 23, 2001), www.thecornerhouse. org.uk/pdf/briefing/23gats.pdf (accessed 24 June 2006).

Silva, A.G. da, 'Poder Inteligente – a questão do HIV/AIDS na Política Externa Brasileira', *Contexto Internacional*, 27 (1) (2005): 127–58.

South Centre and Center for International Environmental Law, *Intellectual Property Update*, Fourth Quarter, 2005.

Tachinardi, M.H., *A Guerra das Patentes: O Conflito Brasil X EUA sobre Propriedade Intelectual* (Rio de Janeiro: Paz e Terra, 1993).

Teixeira, P., 'Interfaces Horizontais e Verticais do Programa Nacional de AIDS, com Destaque para as Interfaces Nacional-Global, unpublished manuscript (report for this case study).

Terto Jr, V., 'A AIDS e o Local de Trabalho no Brasil', in R. Parker (ed.), *Políticas, Instituições e AIDS. Enfrentando a Epidemia no Brasil* (Rio de Janeiro: Zahar/ABIA, 1997), pp. 135–75.

Treatment Action Campaign (TAC), Report for January 2002–February 2003 (Cape Town, 2003), www.tac.org.za/Documents/report02to03.pdf (accessed 7 July 2007).

Treatment Action Campaign (TAC), Annual Report, 1 March 2004–28 February 2005, Draft (Cape Town, 2005), http://www.tac.org.za/DraftAnnual2004.pdf (accessed 7 July 2008).

UNAIDS, *Integrated Plan of the UNAIDS Theme Group to support the National Response on STD/HIV/AIDS. Brazil* (Brasília: Joint United Nations Programme on HIV/AIDS (UNAIDS) Brazil, 2001), http://www.br.undp.org/hiv/UNAIDS%20Brazil%20Integrated%20Plan. pdf (accessed 7 July 2008).

UNAIDS, *2004 Report on the Global AIDS Epidemic: 4th Global Report* (Geneva: UNAIDS).

United States, Frequently Asked Questions PEPFAR. Web page United States Embassy South Africa (Pretoria: United States Embassy South Africa, 2006), http://usembassy. state.gov/posts/sf2/wwwhquestions.html (accessed 7 February 2006) .

United States Global AIDS Coordinator, *Engendering Bold Leadership: the President's Emergency Plan for AIDS Relief. First Annual Report to Congress* (Washington, DC: United States Global AIDS Coordinator, 2005).

Von Soest, C. and M. Weinel, 'The Treatment Controversy: Global Health Governance and South Africa's Fight against HIV/AIDS', in W. Hein, S. Bartsch and L. Kohlmorgen (eds), *Global Health Governance and the Fight against HIV/AIDS* (Basingstoke: Palgrave Macmillan, 2007), pp. 202–25.

Weinel, M., 'AIDS Policy in South Africa: Between Denial and Action', Working Paper, German Overseas Institute, Hamburg, 2005.

Weissman, R., 'AIDS and Developing Countries: Facilitating Access to Essential Medicines', *Foreign Policy in Focus*, 6 (6) March (2001).

Wogart, J.P., 'From Conflict over Compromise to Cooperation? Big Pharma, the HIV/AIDS Crisis and the Rise of Countervailing Power in the South', in W. Hein, S. Bartsch and L. Kohlmorgen (eds), *Global Health Governance and the Fight against HIV/AIDS* (Basingstoke: Palgrave Macmillan, 2007), pp. 67–91.

Wogart, J.P. and G. Calcagnotto, 'Brazil's Fight against AIDS and its Implications for Global Health Governance', *Healthcare Quarterly*, 9 (1) (2006): 90–103.

World Bank, *World Development Indicators 1998* (Washington, DC: World Bank, 1998).
World Bank, 'Evaluation of the World Bank's Assistance in Responding to the AIDS Epidemic: Brazil Case Study by Chris Beyrer, Varun Gauri and Denise Vaillancourt', World Bank, Washington, DC, 2005.
World International Property Organization (WIPO), 'Information on WIPO's Development Cooperation Activities (January 2001–2005)', WIPO, Geneva, 2005.
World Trade Organization, 'TRIPS and Pharmaceutical Patents', WTO Fact Sheet, WTO, Geneva, 2003.

8
International Trade and Health: Loose Governance Arrangements across Sectors

Matthias Helble, Emily Mok, Benedikte Dal, Nusaraporn Kessomboon and Nick Drager

Introduction

The outbreak of Severe Acute Respiratory Syndrome (SARS) in late 2003 aroused considerable international attention. It was feared that SARS might develop into a global pandemic comparable to the 'Spanish' influenza which cost millions of lives around the world in the early twentieth century. However, thanks to major efforts by governments and the international community, the spread of the disease was contained and the death toll was limited to a comparatively small number. As SARS is transmitted through droplets, the sectors in which face-to-face interaction is common, such as tourism or trading activities, witnessed the strongest contraction. The disruptions of international trade led to severe economic losses throughout South-East Asia. Yet, from a health perspective, limiting the economic interactions between countries was useful since it helped to stem the spread of the disease (World Bank, 2007).

The SARS outbreak provides a telling example of how closely the trade and health sectors are intertwined. These interlinkages can be complex and the flow of causation can run in either direction. The emergence of new diseases can affect the trade performance of countries. Yet, the trade regime may also influence public health outcomes. For example, a more open trade regime might increase exposure to infectious disease, and at the same time make health products more readily available.

Despite these close links, rules and institutional arrangements *across* the health and trade sectors have only emerged very recently. Over the past century, however, we have witnessed considerable developments in governance arrangements *within* each sector. On the trade side, a dense net of bilateral and regional trade agreements covered Europe before the First World War. The collapse of world trade in the interwar period revealed the fragility of this architecture. It was only with the conclusion of the General Agreement on Tariffs and Trade (GATT) in 1947 that the international trading system was put on a more solid base. Chapters 2 and 3 above (Berridge et al. and Walt et al.) describe the ways in which rules and institutions have developed to govern international health concerns.

As international socio-economic and political integration has gained pace, the possible areas of conflict or cooperation between the trade and health sectors have also increased. As a reaction to this development, new governance arrangements spanning both sectors have emerged over the past two decades. The purpose of this chapter is to give an overview of these cross-sectoral arrangements and to consider challenges and potential solutions to the current system.

In our view, governance arrangements are defined by rules and institutions. The first section below reviews the key international rules governing the collaboration between the trade and health sectors. Next, we illustrate how the rules have been translated into an institutional design at the international, regional and national levels. The penultimate section analyses emerging trends that might challenge the current loose governance arrangements. Finally, we summarize the key lessons learned and advance several policy recommendations to achieve policy coherence between trade and health.

Rules spanning the trade and health sectors

One of the main drivers of globalization has been the opening of countries to international trade in goods and services. Over the past two decades, a large number of countries have liberalized their trade regimes, and today a dense net of bilateral, regional and multilateral trade agreements spans the globe. The World Trade Organization (WTO) has emerged as a key pillar of the international trade system. Since its inception in 1995, the WTO has achieved almost universal membership offering a rule-based system that covers trade in goods, services and intellectual property rights. Being aware of the possible linkages between trade and health, several WTO agreements contain provisions that are related to health.

Key WTO agreements related to health

Among the various WTO agreements related to health, the Agreement on Trade-Related Aspects of Intellectual Property Rights (TRIPS) has attracted the most attention due to its pivotal role in access to medicines. TRIPS establishes minimum standards for the protection and enforcement of intellectual property rights such as pharmaceutical patents. The TRIPS agreement, however, also provides governments with certain flexibilities when applying patent protection. One such flexibility is the use of compulsory licensing, which enables a government to allow a third party or government agency to produce a patented product or process without the patent owner's consent, but by paying an adequate remuneration to the owner.

Despite the existence of these flexibilities, there was disagreement about the conditions under which they could be applied. The Doha Declaration on the TRIPS Agreement and Public Health sought to clarify the TRIPS provisions by emphasizing 'WTO members' right to protect public health and, in particular, to promote access to medicines for all' (WTO, 2001). Furthermore, the Doha Declaration identified the need for a solution for WTO members with limited manufacturing capacity. This issue was eventually addressed in August 2003 through the creation of a waiver that allows third countries with manufacturing capacity to produce the medicines on behalf of the countries that cannot (WTO, 2003a).

While TRIPS can be seen as representing an effort to find a balance between the sometimes conflicting considerations of patent protection to promote innovation and patent protection that limits access to medicines, it is the implementation of TRIPS and its interpretation that determines that balance. In the future, TRIPS will also need to address emerging health issues such as biotechnology, traditional knowledge and information technology.

As the service sector became the largest sector in many economies and more easily deliverable across borders, in 1995 WTO members agreed on a general framework for multilateral trade liberalization in services, the General Agreement on Trade in Services (GATS). Under GATS, WTO members need to fulfil certain obligations, some of which are conditional on their liberalization commitments and others which are unconditional. However, these obligations do not apply if members need to take measures to protect human, animal or plant life or health (Art. XIV GATS). As of the time of writing, in early 2008, WTO members have only made relatively limited trade liberalization commitments under GATS and, therefore, services liberalization is likely to be an important theme of future trade negotiations.

Under GATS, WTO members can choose which service sector and mode[1] they wish to open to international trade. The liberalization of health services may have important impacts on the health system of a country. For example, medical travel (Mode 2 under GATS) might generate considerable revenues for the receiving country, while drawing critical resources away from local patients (Blouin et al., 2006). Overall, GATS provides a framework for trade liberalization in services with a discretionary policy space for member countries to take into account health risks and opportunities.

The agreements on Technical Barriers to Trade (TBT) and the Application of Sanitary and Phytosanitary Measures (SPS) both aim at ensuring that regulations, standards, testing and certification procedures do not create unnecessary obstacles to trade. Both agreements give WTO members the right to set standards that they consider appropriate and hence to restrict trade, as long as the underlying objectives are legitimate. The TBT agreements allow member states to impose standards in order to protect, for example, animal or plant life or health. The SPS contains specific rules in order to ensure food safety and the protection of human life from plant- or animal-borne diseases. Both agreements encourage WTO members to follow international standards when applying measures. However, governments can also develop their own requirements (in the case of SPS they need to be scientifically justified). If other WTO members consider that the measures are overly trade restrictive, and in the case of SPS that they are not supported by sufficient scientific evidence, the case may be contested.[2]

Health-related TBT measures have been widely used by WTO member countries and form the largest part of all TBT measures notified each year to the WTO secretariat. Examples of such notification include regulations on blood and related products or on magnets in toys (WTO, 2008). SPS measures are used less frequently and cover, for example, measures such as microbiological standards for foodstuffs. The SPS agreement identifies the joint FAO/WHO Codex Alimentarius as one of the relevant standard-setting bodies for SPS measures.

Both agreements represent international governance arrangements that span the health and trade sectors. It is important to note that in both agreements, public health concerns are taken into account. In the SPS, the work of the WTO and FAO/WHO have been mutually beneficial to the health and trade sectors of member states. For example, adopting international food standards helps governments to take effective measures to protect public health. At the same time, international standards minimize unnecessary trade costs and, therefore, promote international food trade. Common interests have thus facilitated collaboration and yielded fruitful results for both sectors.

WHO agreements related to trade

This section presents two international health rules with trade linkages, namely the new International Health Regulations (IHR) and the Framework Convention on Tobacco Control (FCTC). Both agreements represent international health rules that span trade and health sectors, and raise questions on governance arrangement across sectors (Fidler, 2002).

As the international, economic and social context in which the first International Health Regulations were adopted in 1969 had changed dramatically, WHO member states agreed on a revision process, which began in 1995. It was not, however, until the SARS outbreak in 2003 that substantial progress on the revised IHR was made. The handling of the SARS outbreak highlighted several weaknesses of the 1969 IHR. For example, WHO members adopted unduly restrictive travel and trade measures (Abdullah, 2007). The new IHR (WHO, 2005) were adopted by consensus by WHO members in May 2005.

The new IHR set forth an integrated framework whereby public health objectives are interconnected with international norms and agreements on trade, human rights, environmental protection and security. One of the main objectives of the new IHR is to provide an adequate public health response to the international spread of disease (Article 2). International trade might be affected by these policy measures and, consequently, WHO and its members are requested 'to avoid unnecessary interference with international traffic and trade' (WHO, 2005). This can be achieved by identifying, in real time, the appropriate public health measures for the assessed risk. WHO's experts may provide guidance in assessing and controlling the respective public health risks. During a public health emergency of international concern, WHO may also directly recommend the application of time-limited measures affecting international travel and trade.

In 1998, WHO launched the Tobacco-Free Initiative in response to the globalization of the tobacco epidemic. The initiative led to the adoption of the Framework Convention on Tobacco Control in 2003 (WHO, 2003). The FCTC constitutes the first legally-binding international health treaty and, therefore, represents a paradigm shift in the development of a regulatory strategy to address global health problems. The preamble to the FCTC gives priority to the right to protect public health and thus provides opportunities for tobacco control in the face of potential trade challenges.

Institutions and cooperation across sectors

In this chapter we use a rather narrow definition of institutions as formal or informal organizations that are established for a specific objective (in contrast to understanding them as rules of the game as is the norm in political science and sociology, for example). Institutions can include actors from the public and/or private sector and they can be active on the local, national, regional or international level. Institutions are necessary to translate rules into policy action. In our case, the rules established at the international level concerning trade and health need to be implemented at the national or regional level. This task is generally assumed by public institutions. The primary goal for implementation is to achieve policy coherence, by which we mean a balanced outcome between trade and health objectives.

Institutions are not formed only to react to international rule-setting, but also to influence it. In many cases, public institutions have the legitimacy to provide support or directly participate in international negotiations on rules. Private institutions typically follow the negotiations and try to lobby and inform decision-makers. The role of institutions in the trade and health nexus is therefore twofold: to participate in rule-setting and to implement the agreed upon rules.

The purpose of this section is to present the major institutions that have emerged at international, regional and national policy levels to address issues spanning the trade and health sectors. It then focuses on the role of non-governmental organizations.

International institutions across sectors

The WHO works to achieve greater coherence between trade and health policy so that international trade and trade rules maximize health benefits and minimize health risks, especially for poor and vulnerable populations. The focus of WHO's work in this area is to strengthen capacities within ministries of health to enable them to work effectively with their colleagues in the ministries of trade, commerce and finance in efforts to shape and manage the trade policy environment for improved health outcomes.

In 2006, WHO member states adopted a resolution on international trade and health.[3] Recognizing the increased demand for information about the implications of international trade and trade agreements for health and health policy at the national, regional and global levels, the resolution urged member states to promote dialogue and to consider the linkages between international trade and health. The overall objective of the resolution is to create a constructive interactive relationship across sectors, engaging in multi-stakeholder dialogue, and to generate coherent trade and health policies.

WHO's work on trade and health can be divided into three main tasks. First, performing analysis and research to better inform policy decisions, negotiations, dispute settlement and agenda-setting. Second, creating tools and training materials to build capacity in member states to fully understand the public health implications of multilateral trade agreements. Third, promoting policy coherence across the WHO on trade and health issues and developing global strategic partnerships to ensure that public health concerns are addressed in trade policy and trade rules.

These functions are carried out across a number of WHO departments, with staff at all levels, coordinated by an internal technical working group on globalization, trade and health. The group aims to ensure that the WHO achieves coherence in its policies and programmes related to globalization, trade and health, with particular reference to multilateral trade agreements and public health (see also Box 8.1).

Given the linkages between the aforementioned WTO agreements and health, the WTO and WHO have been collaborating through a range of formal and informal activities at global and national levels. Collaborative work includes research and analysis generation, training courses, tool development, high level policy consultations, informal consultations, governance meetings, regional and national meetings and country missions.

While there is no formal agreement between the WTO and WHO on trade and health, the two organizations participate in each other's formal meetings as 'observers'. Currently, WHO holds observer status in WTO Ministerial Conferences and the SPS and TBT Committees and ad hoc observer status in the TRIPS and GATS Councils. The WTO possesses observer status at the World Health Assembly (WHA) as well as various WHO technical

> **Box 8.1 Diagnostic tool and companion workbook in trade and health**
>
> In response to WHA resolution 59.26 on International Trade and Health, WHO is working with WTO, the World Bank, WIPO, UNCTAD, international experts and trade and health policymakers from ten countries to develop a diagnostic tool and workbook on trade and health (Blouin et al. 2009). The use of the diagnostic tool and workbook will enable policymakers to develop national policies and strategies related to trade and health and to identify their capacity-building needs in this area. In recent years, there has been a substantial increase in the amount of external resources provided to developing countries for capacity-building in trade. This increase in 'aid for trade' presents an opportunity to support countries to develop capacity on trade and health. The national assessments on trade and health, which are based on the diagnostic tool, will be used to structure the requests for capacity-building to existing and new funding mechanisms. The diagnostic tool and workbook will also assist countries in preparing positions for trade and health-related bilateral and multilateral negotiations as well as current multilateral global health diplomacy issues that have trade related issues – such as the Intergovernmental Working Group on Public Health, Innovation and Intellectual Property and the Intergovernmental Meeting on Avian and Pandemic Influenza Virus Sharing and Access to Vaccines.

meetings – such as the Framework Convention on Tobacco Control deliberations. As observers, the organizations are permitted to attend discussions that are of direct interest to them and to provide expert advice on matters related to their respective areas. For example, WHO's observance at the WTO's SPS meetings has given WHO the opportunity to comment on the human health risks of mad cow disease (bovine spongiform encephalopathy) and the health effects of genetically-modified organisms in food (WTO and WHO, 2002).

Overall, the institutional arrangements between the two organizations have two aims. On the one hand, through collaboration they seek to better understand and influence the international trade and health agendas. On the other hand, they aim to enable countries to promote trade and health policy coherence through the development and dissemination of the knowledge base, tools and training.

Regional institutions

Policy coherence at the regional level has become increasingly important with the recent growth in regionally-based free trade agreements (FTAs).

These agreements are often negotiated under regional trade organizations and involve trade rules which differ from WTO rules. Many developing countries join regional organizations because of the potential for economic growth through trade and cooperation with neighbours. At the same time, developed countries and trading entities (such as the USA and the EU) may seek to engage with these regional organizations as a means of participating in trade with developing regions. In this section, the case study of the Association of South-East Asian Nations (ASEAN) helps to illustrate how policy coherence between health and trade is being achieved at the regional level.

ASEAN is a regional organization seeking economic growth through cooperation in areas such as trade, investment and intellectual property.[4] Trade and health have traditionally been of high importance for ASEAN member states. For example, the Philippines and Indonesia are two of the world's largest exporters of health-care workers. Several other member states, including Malaysia, Singapore and Thailand, have been growing as destinations for medical travel.

In 1995, the growing importance of trade in services, including health services, in South-East Asia was recognized through the creation of the ASEAN Framework Agreement on Services (AFAS). The AFAS was formulated as an effort towards the freer flow of trade services in the region. Its objectives include the enhancement of regional cooperation in services, the elimination of restrictions for regional trade in services, and the expansion in the scope of the liberalization of trade in services beyond GATS.[5] Though the AFAS applies the GATS framework as a minimum requirement, it differs from GATS in certain respects. For example, AFAS pushes for commitments beyond GATS, the so-called GATS-Plus principle. The new commitments can be made to all ASEAN countries including to non-WTO members. Under AFAS liberalization, commitments are made on a bilateral basis and thus two or more ASEAN countries can agree deeper services sector integration between themselves. The principle that concessions do not need to be extended to all ASEAN members is known as 'ASEAN Minus X' formula. Others can join at a later stage whenever they are willing (ASEAN, 2008).

Another recent development in ASEAN cooperation on trade in services includes the Mutual Recognition Arrangements (MRA) which facilitate the movement of professional services providers within the ASEAN region (Philavong, 2008). For example, MRA on nursing services have been concluded that aim at strengthening professional capabilities by promoting the flow of relevant information and exchange of expertise, experience and best practices (ASEAN, 2007a).

The ASEAN Sectoral Integration Protocol for Health Care is an example of attempts by ASEAN to enable the progressive and systematic regional integration of the health-care sector (ASEAN, 2007b). It is a roadmap for regional liberalization that covers, among other things, tariff elimination, non-tariff measures, rules of origin, customs procedures, standards, logistics services, outsourcing, trade in services and the movement of professionals (ASEAN, 2007c).

The AFAS negotiation process helps to illustrate how policy coherence is achieved within ASEAN. Negotiations took place under the Coordinating Committee on Services, which reports to the ASEAN economic ministers and is charged with trade in services policies. These negotiations were conducted in rounds, whereby each round produced packages of commitments for each ASEAN country in the agreed economic sector and mode of supply. During the third round of negotiations, a new sectoral working group for health-care services was created by the Coordinating Committee on Services following a decision by the ASEAN leadership to include health-care as one of the eleven ASEAN priorities for integration.

Though the governments of ASEAN member states have initiated the AFAS and other related agreements on trade in health services, few commitments have been made to date (Philavong, 2008). ASEAN governments face the challenge of designing mutually supportive trade and health policies that can deliver optimal outcomes in both fields. As several ASEAN member states are undertaking reforms of their health system in general, the idea of achieving policy coherence should be an integral part of the reform efforts.

Institutional design at the national level

Using the cases of Thailand and Malaysia, this section discusses which institutions have emerged on the national level to comply with international rules on trade and health.

Thailand: joined-up and bottom-up trade–health policy development

As Thailand was becoming increasingly engaged in bilateral, regional and multilateral trade negotiations, the Thai government decided to put in place a sophisticated structure to deal with trade and health issues simultaneously. In December 2003, the prime minister appointed the Committee of International Trade Policy, drawing its membership from different ministries. Although the Ministry of Public Health (MOPH) is not a member, it plays a key role for all trade negotiations involving the health sector, since it is the focal point for all health sector-related negotiations. Therefore, for all issues related to health, the MOPH participates in committee meetings and prepares the country's positions (Pachanee and Wibulpolprasert, 2006).

In order to further strengthen its role in international trade negotiations, the MOPH established a Committee on Trade in Health and Social Services in 2004. The objective of this committee is to develop positions for all trade negotiations on health services by assessing the possible implications of trade liberalization policies on the health sector. It is composed of representatives from the MOPH, but also from other related public and private organizations including the Ministry of Commerce, the Health System Research Institute, the Private Hospitals' Association, and other professional bodies. In addition to this formal set-up, the MOPH provides support in various fields. For example, it collaborates with the Department of Export Promotion in an effort to improve the marketing of health services (Pachanee and Wibulpolprasert, 2004).

Thailand has further developed a sophisticated institutional structure to ensure the involvement of public and private stakeholders in policy formulation. The basic idea of this bottom-up approach is that all interested stakeholders are consulted at the local, regional and national levels. The exact set-up can vary from topic to topic, but generally, all interested groups meet first at the local level to elaborate policy proposals. Participants in the local meetings come from NGOs, academia and government offices, as well as the private sector. Together they try to find consensus around a common position. The agreed proposals are then submitted to a regional health assembly at which key local-level stakeholders are present. The regional assembly gathers the propositions from the local meetings and tries to formulate another common, consensus-based position. Finally, the National Health Assembly collects all regional positions and discusses them at an annual meeting. At the end of the meeting, the assembly adopts non-binding policy recommendations for the respective authorities. Typically, the proposals urge local, regional or national authorities to take action or request further research by academic institutions. The whole process of policy formulation can take over a year. In general, participation is open to all interested parties.

This institutional structure was first employed in 2003 and in 2004, trade and health issues were included on the agenda. Agenda items included the mechanism and process of trade negotiation, the protection of intellectual property rights, the protection of knowledge on Thai traditional medicine and the liberalization of trade in health services. Since then, the National Health Assembly has passed numerous policy recommendations concerning health and trade. For example, it proposed that negotiations for liberalization on medicines and health services should be carried out under multilateral rather than bilateral agreements, and that the country should aim at self-reliance on drugs and health as provided in the Thai constitution (Health System Reform Office, 2006).

Malaysia: policy arrangements in medicines and tobacco

The Malaysian government has consistently promoted an open trade regime, negotiating trade deals at the bilateral, regional and multilateral levels. Conflicts between trade and health policy first became apparent at the end of the 1990s. Malaysia was facing a mounting challenge from HIV/AIDS and the Ministry of Health was eager to improve access to appropriate medicines, in particular antiretroviral medicines (ARVs). As a first step, the Ministry of Health requested price reductions from pharmaceutical companies. As the negotiations did not yield the expected results, the Ministry of Health organized an expert meeting on parallel importing and compulsory licensing to inform relevant government agencies on the topic. Following this meeting, the Malaysian government decided to promote the local production of HIV medicines which were not patented in Malaysia. In addition, the government prepared to make use of the Malaysian Patent Act of 1983 which allows for compulsory licensing as well as parallel imports (Thani, 2005).

These activities, however, encountered strong opposition not only from the pharmaceutical industry, but also from several Malaysian ministries which feared a decline in foreign investment. The Malaysian government was, nevertheless, able to push through the authorization of drug imports and issued an import licence to a local company. In 2004, the Ministry of Health began negotiations with a foreign company on the import of HIV medicines. As a result of these efforts, drug prices dropped significantly and more patients could be treated. Eventually, the patent holding companies became more cooperative and lowered their prices (Thani, 2005).

The Malaysian government took a similar approach to achieving policy coherence when dealing with tobacco control (Thani, 2005). Having ratified the FCTC, the Malaysian government was determined to curb tobacco consumption in the country. At the same time, it was aware of possible negative effects on local tobacco growers who depended heavily on sales in the domestic market. As a first step, the Ministry of Health organized meetings with researchers, WHO experts and NGOs in order to evaluate the possible impacts of anti-tobacco measures. As a first policy measure, the government decided to impose progressive rises in sales tax on cigarettes. At the same time, it commissioned the Ministry of Agriculture and Agro-Based Industries and the Ministry of Plantation Industries and Commodities to provide support for tobacco farmers, primarily by helping them to switch to alternative crops. Nonetheless, the government faced severe resistance from the tobacco industry. The government finally agreed to extend certain deadlines and to delay the implementation of several anti-tobacco measures. These concessions were strongly condemned by NGOs and civil society. It became apparent that in achieving policy coherence a delicate balance of interests needed to be struck. The Malaysian government made considerable efforts to include all stakeholders in the discussion and eventually reached a consensus between the conflicting interests.

Achieving policy coherence between the trade and health sectors at the national level is a complex undertaking. On many issues the sectoral interests collide rather than coincide. It is up to the government to weigh the different interests and to reach a compromise. Formal set-ups to tackle this task seem to yield the most promising outcomes, as the case of Thailand suggests. Ad hoc arrangements have the benefit of being able to react flexibly to emerging problems, although they might not be sufficient to achieve a sustainable compromise.

Non-governmental institutions and cooperation

Non-state actors, particularly civil society organizations (CSOs), play a critical role in influencing international trade and health policy coherence. Not only have CSOs served as a driving force behind the creation of international trade and health agreements (for example, TRIPS and FCTC), they have also played an active role during the implementation of these rules. In this section, we consider the different roles of CSOs within the current loose governance arrangement for trade and health. The term 'civil society', as McCoy and Hilson (Chapter 10 below) note, is often used loosely as a broad catch-all term for non-state, public actors. They also note that definitions of CSOs usually do not include business actors; however, in some cases, corporate organizations have been included. For the purposes of this section, we use the term CSOs to include industry-related NGOs (for example, the International Federation of Pharmaceutical Manufacturers Associations), but we exclude for-profit corporations.

Informal CSO involvement in international trade and health traditionally started at the national level. Prior to the emergence of the WTO, CSOs would principally lobby or protest to their state governments on trade issues. In the case of industry-related CSOs, this often involved requests for foreign policy interventions involving trade watchlists and sanctions. Another national level means of influence for CSOs is a seat on trade advisory committees. It has been noted, however, that seats usually went to industry NGOs rather than health NGOs in the USA (Gerhardsen, 2005). This has prompted calls in the past few years for more balanced representation between the interest groups (US House Committee on Ways and Means, 2006).

With the rise of the WTO and other trade agreements, CSOs seized new informal avenues to influence international trade and health. The emergence of transnational coalitions of CSOs has allowed interest groups to lobby their countries at the domestic or regional level in hopes of achieving greater impact in international negotiations. As Buse and Naylor (Chapter 9) observe, the US Intellectual Property Committee (IPC) formed a international alliance that urged Canadian, Japanese and European corporations to lobby their respective countries for the inclusion of IP in the Uruguay Round negotiations. Eventually, the IPC's draft proposal for TRIPS was passed almost in its entirety (Sell, 2003).

CSOs have also gained a few formal avenues for participation within intergovernmental organizations. At the WTO, an acknowledged but contentious procedure is the submission of *amicus curiae* briefs by non-parties (for example, CSOs) to the panel or Appellate Body. Under panel proceedings, the panel may seek advice from any relevant source and it may also determine whether or not it wants to accept unsolicited briefs. Under Appellate Body procedures, if an appellate or appellee attaches a brief with their submission (that is, as an exhibit), the Appellate Body must consider the brief. Unsolicited briefs may still be submitted to the Appellate Body, but the Appellate Body may decide not to consider them. According to the WTO, none of the unsolicited *amicus curiae* briefs submitted have been considered by the Appellate Body (WTO, 2003b). Other avenues for CSO involvement at the WTO include participation in informal WTO symposia (CONGO, 2006).

At WHO, a formal means of CSO participation is acceptance into 'official relations'. This status confers several rights to CSOs, including designation of a non-voting representative to WHO meetings (as well as to committees and conferences), access to non-confidential documents and director-general approved information, and submission of memorandums to the Director-General (CONGO, 2006). CSO entry into WHO official relations starts with 'mutually benefiting acts' and builds towards an informal, long-term relationship (CONGO, 2006). The Executive Board ultimately decides whether or not to grant 'official relations' status to the CSO. In the past, the process of obtaining official relations status has been criticized as long, bureaucratic, demanding and formal (WHO, 2002). WHO is addressing these concerns through the application of a special fast-track process to permit greater CSO participation in selected meetings. The fast-track procedure has been used in recent major WHO meetings, such as the sessions for the Framework Convention on Tobacco Control and the Intergovernmental Working Group (IGWG) for Public Health, Innovation and Intellectual Property (WHO, 2002; WHO, 2007).

While CSOs have made significant strides in asserting their influence in international trade and health policy, they continue to press for greater international participation and it appears that they will play an increasingly important role in the future. The diverse forms of CSOs that fall within this broad categorization bring a mix of industry and public health interests to the table. In the earlier cases of CSO involvement, it seems that health-related CSOs had arrived too late. This is illustrated by the case of industry dominance in the formulation of TRIPS, as well as the findings of unbalanced CSO involvement on trade advisory committees. Health-related CSOs, however, are attempting to catch up, as demonstrated by the proactive role they have been taking at recent international discussions, such as the IGWG for Public Health, Innovation and Intellectual Property and the Intergovernmental Meeting (IGM) on virus sharing.

Trends and challenges for global governance in trade and health

New trends in international trade and health are challenging the current governance arrangements described in the previous section. Among the many new developments, we have selected four that we consider as particularly important, namely the power shift in international negotiations, bilateralism and regionalism, migration of health workers and trade and healthy diets. In order to cope with these challenges and to ensure policy coherence, a new governance arrangement is needed.

Power shift in international negotiations on trade and health

Over the past decade, the balance of power in international negotiations on trade and health has shifted markedly. Developing countries, especially the largest ones, have been able to make their voices better heard in international negotiations. Prior to the start of the Doha Development Round in 2001, developing countries, which by then constituted the overwhelming majority of WTO members, repeatedly stated their disenchantment with the outcomes of the previous round. They not only felt left out of major liberalization gains, but also faced problems implementing the previously signed WTO agreements. In Doha, WTO members therefore agreed that the focus of the new round should be on the needs and interests of developing countries. A strong emphasis on development was new in the history of GATT/WTO and raised hopes and expectations.

From the beginning of the multilateral negotiations, several coalitions of developing countries formed in order to break the traditional domination of the trade talks by the EU and USA. At the ministerial conference in Cancun in 2003, a new group of 20 (G20) developing countries[6] emerged and became one of the key players for the subsequent negotiations. Under the leadership of Brazil, China, India and South Africa, the G20 pushed for a liberalization of the agricultural market, in particular for an ending of EU and US subsidy systems. The EU and the USA decided to integrate the G20 more fully into the negotiations, especially on agriculture, and set up an informal group of five interested parties (EU, USA, Australia, Brazil and India).

This new level of attention raised the confidence of other developing countries. Soon afterwards, a group of 33 (G33), including some of the G20 countries, was created with the aim of achieving better protection for their domestic markets. Finally, a group of 90 (G90) developing countries from Africa, the Caribbean and the Pacific region joined forces in an effort to block the inclusion of certain issues on the negotiation agenda. In 2005, at the ministerial meeting in Hong Kong, all three groups were able to come together around a common declaration that reiterated the call for a stronger consideration of developing countries' interests and for a liberalization of the agricultural sector in developed countries. Even though similar declarations were made during previous rounds, the power shift towards developing countries was evident. Developing countries are now coming very well prepared to the negotiating table and are willing to defend their positions regardless of their economic levels.

The shift towards a new power balance in international negotiations was also felt in the health sector. Within WHO, developing countries are trying harder than ever to shape the agenda. The following serves to illustrate the apparent power shift in international health relations. In May 2006, WHO member states agreed to establish an Intergovernmental Working Group on Public Health, Innovation and Intellectual Property. The purpose of the IGWG is to prepare a global strategy and plan of action, addressing particularly the diseases affecting developing countries. Even in the first two sessions of the IGWG at the end of 2006 and 2007, it was evident that developing countries were eager to take on new responsibilities. For example, during the second session in November 2007, both the Brazilian and Mexican delegations outnumbered the US delegation.

Another expression of the new confidence of developing countries involved Indonesia's refusal, towards the end of 2007, to share avian influenza virus samples with the WHO. Their argument was that any resulting vaccine that would be produced commercially would be offered at excessive prices for developing countries. Indonesia's refusal was supported by other developing countries in the region. To address this situation, a meeting entitled 'High Level Meeting on Responsible Practices for Sharing Avian Influenza Vaccines and Resulting Benefits' was organized in February 2007, and resulted in a joint statement, in which the Indonesian government expressed its willingness to resume sharing of influenza viruses with the WHO. However, the virus sharing was made dependent on action by the WHO and countries to improve access to resulting influenza vaccines. At the time of writing (December 2008), negotiations are still ongoing and have not yet produced an agreement.

In summary, we observe a power shift in international negotiations on trade and health issues towards developing countries. The ministerial meetings in Cancun and Hong Kong were major events that demonstrated the rebalancing of power and this trend has gained momentum since. Developing countries are better informed and thus find themselves able to raise their voice more effectively. However, having an increasing number of active players in the arena of international negotiations requires an increasingly sophisticated approach to diplomacy in order to bring the different views and interests together.

Bilateral and regional free trade agreements (FTAs)

Despite the recent power shift towards developing countries within multilateral forums, developed countries have pursued other avenues to preserve their hegemonic status and maintain control over trade issues through a series of bilateral and regional FTAs. These agreements serve as a means through which developed countries can push for trade measures that they could not achieve in negotiations under the WTO. For the USA, this includes the promotion of stronger intellectual property protections than those under TRIPS. The EU, on the other hand, had not sought stronger IP protections until recently. Developing countries also see legitimate economic and political reasons for joining these FTAs. Economically, FTAs hold the attractive promise of new or greater preferential access to the markets of their trade counterparts.

The Central America[7]-Dominican Republic FTA (CAFTA-DR) provides an example of an American attempt to promote stronger IP protection than is included in the TRIPS agreement, such as longer duration of patent protection or broader criteria for patentability. Although the developing countries party to this FTA are not major centres for pharmaceutical production and, hence, IP infringement, it is believed that the USA might use the CAFTA-DR as a blueprint for a future Free Trade Agreement of the Americas (FTAA). Under the FTAA, the TRIPS-Plus ramifications would be more significant (Von Braun et al., 2005).

A second issue is the possible growth in FTAs between developing countries and developed countries as a result of the phenomena known as the 'domino effect' and the 'multiplier effect'. Under the 'domino effect', countries tend to join FTAs as they observe neighbouring countries signing on (Baldwin, 1993). Their motives are fear of possible negative repercussions arising from non-membership or the observation of other countries benefiting. The 'multiplier effect' suggests that, as a result of TRIPS Art. 4 (most favoured nations principal) any concession granted to one member must also be granted to other members. This includes concessions made under regional and/or bilateral FTAs (after the TRIPS agreement entered into force in 1995). Hence, the CAFTA-DR countries could be expected to extend IP concessions to other countries such as those of the European Union. Von Braun et al. (2005: 30) argue that this means that the FTA could establish a 'new minimum floor of IP obligations given to all WTO members without formality'.

Given recent EU FTA negotiations, the EU may not be waiting for the multiplier effect to take hold. It has been observed that recent EU policy is making a significant shift towards more stringent IP protections in its FTA proposal to the Caribbean Forum of African, Caribbean and Pacific States (CARIFORUM) (Santa Cruz, 2007). Previously, FTAs with the EU only included IP provisions that reinforced multilateral IP conventions (such as TRIPS). The inclusion of TRIPS-Plus measures in the EU-CARIFORUM FTA is starting to raise concerns among developing countries, especially those that have been considering entering into a regional FTA with the EU, such as countries from the African, Caribbean and Pacific (ACP) region, the Andean region, the Central American region, and the Association of South-East Asian Nations.

As the multilateral trade negotiations under the Doha Development Agenda are stalled, it will become an increasing challenge for governments, especially those lacking economic weight, to negotiate fair trade agreements and to protect their health.

Migration of health-care workers

The rapid expansion of the health sector in developed and developing countries often outstrips the supply of qualified health-care workers. Today, more than 11 per cent of nurses and 18 per cent of doctors in OECD countries are foreign born (OECD, 2008).[8] The OECD (2008) reports that since 2000 migration flows of health professionals have increased, with major impacts on the health systems of several developing countries. The migration of health-care workers between countries is often motivated by higher incomes abroad, but might also be caused by shortages or oversupplies in certain health subsectors. In this case, the flows of health-care workers between countries can help mitigate market failures. One might also observe migration of health-care workers within countries. Booming economic centres are likely to offer better job opportunities than stagnating rural areas.

Flows of health-care workers at the national, regional and international levels are often closely intertwined and subject to complex dynamics. When deciding on policy measures, the appropriate mix between possible benefits and risks needs to be achieved. The outflow of health workers may have the positive effect on their country of origin of increased foreign exchange earnings and reduced unemployment. Yet their loss might contribute to shortages of medical professionals, further undermining an already difficult situation. Whatever policy is applied, the overall objective should be to improve access to and affordability of health-related services.

At the international level, the migration of health-care workers is covered under Mode 4 of GATS, as explained above. At present, few market access commitments have been made by WTO members in the health sector. The health sector remains highly regulated in many countries and the recognition of relevant qualifications between countries is as yet very limited. GATS does not contain obligations to open markets and it recognizes the right of WTO members to regulate their services in order to meet national policy objectives (Adlung and Carzaniga, 2002).

When designing an appropriate policy approach to health workforce issues, one needs to consider that market access commitments in sectors other than trade can have a substantial effect on the migration of health-care workers. For example, Thailand's liberalization of financial markets in the 1990s led to an influx of foreign capital which was partly invested in private hospitals. The increased demand for medical doctors was met by a severe internal brain drain from the rural areas to the cities (Wibulpolprasert, 2003). To manage the flows of health-care workers therefore requires inter-sectoral collaboration involving a multitude of stakeholders. In 2007, the World Health Assembly (resolution WHA 57.19) requested the Director-General to prepare a code of practice on the international recruitment of health personnel, in consultation with member states and all relevant partners. In response, the Secretariat has prepared a draft code of practice for presentation to the Executive Board in January 2009.

Trade and healthy diets

Diet-related diseases, such as obesity, cardiovascular disease, hypertension and strokes, have become a major cause of disability and premature death in low- and middle-income countries (see Stuckler et al. in Chapter 13 below). Dietary patterns are determined by a panoply of cultural, social and economic factors. In the following, we briefly outline the links between the trade and investment regime of a country and dietary patterns and illustrate a possible role for cross-sectoral policy arrangements.

Over the last two decades, many countries have liberalized their trade and investment regimes. In the food sector, the consequences have been considerable: international trade in foodstuffs has increased substantially, transnational food companies have invested heavily in new production facilities across the globe, and international supermarket chains have rapidly expanded their distribution networks, in particular in developing countries.

The liberalization of trade and investment schemes has had positive effects on the availability of food within many countries. The food on offer has often become less expensive, more diverse and increasingly safe. However, liberalization can also negatively impact dietary patterns. The new price structure can provide incentives for an increased consumption of unhealthy food. This is the case if the demand, for example, shifts away from fresh produce to processed food, which is typically more energy-dense and contains excessive levels of sugar, salt and fat. Trade and investment liberalization can also profoundly change the food supply chain. International supermarket chains tend to prefer to collaborate with large-scale producers and international food companies, with detrimental effects on small-scale farmers. At the same time, supermarkets often displace small stores and encourage bulk purchases (Hawkes, 2005).

The liberalization dynamics are complex and, once again, the trade and health sectors need to work hand in hand to ensure favourable policy outcomes. Trade liberalization can help provide a more diverse and healthy diet. However, flanking policy measures from other sectors, in particular from the health sector, are necessary to ensure that this objective is achieved in practice. The need for a wider policy approach has been recognized by WHO member countries. In 2004, the World Health Assembly adopted the Global Strategy on Diet, Physical Activity and Health, which called for multi-sectoral policies at the national, regional and global levels. In 2006, 53 countries in the European region signed the European charter on obesity which also puts emphasis on inter-sectoral and international partnerships.

The topic of food labelling illustrates how health policy instruments, which are also relevant for trade, can be used to influence consumers' dietary patterns. Food labelling enables consumers to make better-informed and more health conscious choices when shopping for food.[9] In Canada, since December 2007, all food companies that sell prepackaged foods need to comply with an ambitious labelling law. The cost for compliance by the private sector is estimated to amount to between CAN$260–400 million. Health Canada expects, however, that better nutritional labelling could save the country around CAN$5 billion over the next 20 years, as dietary improvements lead to lower costs for the treatment of many non-communicable diseases (Health Canada, 2008).

Summary and policy recommendations

Summary

This chapter has described the governance arrangements that exist within and between the trade and health sectors. The chapter first described the key multilateral trade rules which might impact health systems, namely the TRIPS, GATS, TBT and SPS agreements. We then explored possible linkages between the IHR, FCTC and international trade. Overall, we found that, in general, public health concerns enjoy priority over trade concerns. However, how far this policy outcome materializes depends on the institutional design.

We next analysed institutions that span the two sectors at the international, regional and national levels. The WHO collaborates closely with the WTO internationally, including through joint research, training and country missions. Regional collaboration that reaches across both policy concerns is relatively new. The ASEAN example illustrated that while important institutional steps to ensure policy coherence have been taken, much work remains to be done. At the national level, several countries have put in place institutional structures to deal with trade and health concerns simultaneously. The case of Thailand shows that a multitude of stakeholders can be integrated into the policymaking process. We find that non-state actors have built up different transnational institutions that are successful in influencing policy outcomes in the arena of trade and health. At the same time, the WHO and the WTO have both given civil society more opportunity to express their views and preferences.

Overall, we conclude that the institutional arrangements between the trade and health sectors are assuming different forms and becoming increasingly influential. Nonetheless, we consider the existing governance arrangements to be loose, as in most cases they have emerged on an ad hoc basis and still lack consolidation and institutionalization. In recent years, we have, however, observed a more proactive approach.

Such a proactive approach is urgently needed to cope with new challenges that require a rethinking of the current system. One of the most remarkable trends is the shift of power towards developing countries in international negotiations. Another determining movement is the growing number of bilateral and regional free trade agreements. The increasing flow of healthcare workers towards developed countries constitutes another threat to the current system. The governance arrangements between the trade and health sectors need to accommodate these new forces and identify appropriate responses and adaptations.

Policy recommendations

Past experience suggests that it is possible to identify several elements that favour a coherent policy outcome between health and trade. Below we formulate four policy recommendations that we believe are critical to balancing conflicting interests and to achieving policy coherence.

First, the precondition to improving the trade-health policy nexus is a sound understanding of the interplay between the sectors. The dynamics of trade liberalization are complex and need to be very well understood before taking any policy action. Research needs to be undertaken for each country individually since the links between trade and health often differ substantially from one country to another. The diagnostic tool (described in Box 8.1) could become an essential instrument to conduct this type of study. The research should be conducted in a transparent manner and the results should be made publicly available in order to increase societal awareness.

Second, before deciding any policy that affects both sectors, an open and inclusive dialogue should be held with all concerned stakeholders. The objective should be to reach a broad consensus on the measures to be taken. The discussions should take a bottom-up approach. The efforts to engage in an ongoing dialogue with all stakeholders has been described in the literature as 'deliberative policy'. The case of the National Health Assembly in Thailand provides an example of an attempt to put this deliberative policy approach into practice in the trade-health domain

Third, a policy approach can only be implemented successfully under reliable leadership. Ministries of public health are often comparatively weak and lacking in resources. In order to assume leadership that will result in policy coherence, substantial resources are needed and the government must grant the respective policy space. Leadership is not only needed to negotiate the necessary consensus, it is also required to implement agreed policies. As we have seen in the case of Malaysia, governments can encounter substantial resistance during the implementation phase.

Fourth, the institutional links and cooperation between the trade and health sectors can still be further strengthened at all levels. The diagnostic tool and companion workbook (see Box 8.1) constitute an important step in increasing the understanding of the linkages, which ultimately will help in building stronger institutional relationships. This tool needs to be rolled out more widely. For this to happen, trade and health need to achieve the same sort of public profile currently afforded to disease-specific programmes and health finance and delivery issues.

Notes

1. GATS distinguishes four modes of services according to the nature of delivery. Mode 1 is defined as cross-border supply of services, such as telemedicine or telediagnosis. If a service is consumed abroad, as in the case of patients who are treated in a

foreign country, it belongs to Mode 2. Mode 3 covers the commercial presence of a service supplier abroad, for example a company runs a hospital in a foreign country. Finally, Mode 4 applies to the presence of persons abroad, such as health professionals working in countries other than their country of origin.
2. For example, in 2002 the USA requested dispute settlement consultation with Japan. Japan had imposed restrictions on imported US apples to protect Japanese plants from disease. In 2003, the Appellate Body ruled that the measures were 'without sufficient scientific evidence' (WTO, 2003c) and Japan had to withdraw them.
3. Resolution WHA 59.26 at http://www.who.int/gb/ebwha/pdf_files/WHA59/A59_R26-en.pdf (accessed 23 January 2008).
4. ASEAN was established in 1967 and is comprised of ten member states. For more information see http://www.aseansec.org/64.htm (accessed 23 January 2008).
5. For the non-WTO members of ASEAN, their commitments need to be no less favourable than the commitments granted on the most favoured nation principle.
6. For more information about the G20 and its members see http://www.g-20.mre.gov.br/ (accessed 16 January 2008).
7. Central American countries include Costa Rica, El Salvador, Guatemala, Honduras and Nicaragua.
8. Outside OECD countries.
9. According to several surveys conducted or supported by the Center for Food Safety and Applied Nutrition of the US Food and Drug Administration, see http://vm.cfsan.fda.gov/~lrd/ab-label.html (accessed 16 January 2008).

References

Abdullah, A.S., 'International Health Regulations (2005)', *Regional Health Forum*, 11(1) (2007): 10–16.

Adlung, R. and A. Carzaniga, 'Health Services and the General Agreement on Trade in Services', in N. Drager and C. Vieira (eds), *Trade Health Services: Global, Regional and Country Perspectives* (Washington, DC: Pan American Health Organization, 2002), pp. 13–33.

Association of Southeast Asian Nations (ASEAN), ASEAN Mutual Recognition Arrangement on Nursing Services, 2007a, http://www.aseansec.org/19210.htm (accessed 7 February 2008).

ASEAN, ASEAN Sectoral Integration Protocol for Healthcare, 2007b, http://www.aseansec.org/16713.htm (accessed 7 February 2008).

ASEAN, Appendix I: Roadmap for Integration of Healthcare Sector, 2007c, http://www.aseansec.org/16716.htm (accessed 7 February 2008).

ASEAN, Services, 2008, http://www.aseansec.org/6626.htm (accessed 7 February 2008).

Baldwin, R., 'A Domino Theory of Regionalism', National Bureau of Economic Research Working Paper, 4465, 1993.

Blouin, C., N. Drager, and R. Smith (eds), *International Trade in Health Services and the GATS – Current Issues and Debates* (Washington, DC: The World Bank, 2006).

Blouin, C., N. Drager and R. Smith (eds), *Trade and Health Diagnostic Tool and Workbook* (forthcoming, 2009).

CONGO NGO Participation Arrangements at the UN and in Other Agencies of the UN System, The Conference of NGOs in Consultative Relationship with the United Nations, Geneva, Switzerland, March 2006.

Fidler, D., 'Health Governance: Overview of the Role of International Law in Protecting and Promoting Global Public Health', World Health Organization, Geneva, and London School of Hygiene and Tropical Medicine, 2002.

Gerhardsen, T., 'Public Health Groups Sue US Government for Lack of Consultation', 2005, http://www.ip-watch.org/weblog/wp-trackback.php?p=181 (accessed 1 November 2007).

Hawkes, C., 'The Role of Foreign Direct Investment in the Nutrition Transition', *Public Health Nutrition*, 8(4) (2005): 357–65.

Health Canada, 'Food Labeling', http://www.hc-sc.gc.ca/fn-an/label-etiquet/index_e.html (accessed 11 February 2008).

Health System Reform Office, 'What we do at the Health System Reform Office', http://www.hsro.or.th/en/documents/What_is_HealthSystem_Reform.pdf (accessed 11 February 2008).

Organization for Economic Cooperation and Development, *International Migration Outlook*, 2007 edition (Paris: OECD, 2008).

Pachanee, C. and S. Wibulpolprasert, 'The Motivations, Progress and Possible Implications of Liberalization of Trade in Health Services in the ASEAN Context', Ministry of Public Health, Thailand, 2006, www.aaahrh.org/conf2006/s291006/AAAH%20-%20Chaaim%20-2029%20October %202006.ppt (accessed 11 February 2008).

Philavong, B., 'ASEAN Cooperation on Trade in Health Services', unpublished paper presented at the Prince Mahidol Award Conference, Bangkok, Thailand, 30 January–1 February 2008.

Santa Cruz, S.M., 'Intellectual Property Provisions in European Union Trade Agreements: Implications for Developing Countries', International Centre for Trade and Sustainable Development (ICTSD) Programme on IPRs and Sustainable Development, Issue Paper No. 20, June 2007.

Sell, S., *Private Power, Public Law: the Globalization of Intellectual Property Rights* (Cambridge: Cambridge University Press, 2003).

Thani, N.N., 'The Malaysian Experience', unpublished paper presented at the Workshop and Handbook for Practitioners on Trade and Health, Montreal, Canada, 6–7 October 2005.

U.S. House Committee on Ways and Means, 'Statement of Center for Policy Analysis on Trade and Health', San Francisco, California, 2006, http://waysandmeans.house.gov/hearings.asp?formmode=printfriendly&id=4731 (accessed 1 November 2007).

Von Braun, J., P. Roffe and D. Vivas-Eugui, 'Public Health Policy and the New Generation of Regional and Bilateral Trade Agreements', unpublished paper presented at a workshop at McGill University, Montreal Conference, Montreal, Canada, 5–7 October 2005.

Wibulpolprasert, S., 'International Trade and Migration of Health Care Workers: Thailand's Experience', in A. Mattoo and A. Carzaniga (eds), *Moving People to Deliver Services* (Washington, DC: World Bank and Oxford University Press, 2003), pp. 171–7.

World Bank, 'Economic Impact of Avian Flu Global Program for Avian Influenza and Human Pandemic', http://go.worldbank.org/DTHZZF6XS0 (accessed 1 November 2007).

World Health Organization, 'WHO's Interactions with Civil Society and Nongovernmental Organizations', Civil Society Initiative Review Report, 2002, WHO/CSI/2002/WP6.

World Health Organization, 'Framework Convention on Tobacco Control', 2003, http://www.who.int/tobacco/framework/WHO_FCTC_english.pdf (accessed 23 January 2008).

World Health Organization, 'International Health Regulations', 2005, http://www.who.int/csr/ihr/en/ (accessed 22 January 2008).

World Health Organization, EB120(3), 120th Session of the Executive Board Decision and List of Resolutions, 2007, EB120/DIV/3, http://www.who.int/gb/ebwha/pdf_files/EB120/B120_DIV3-en.pdf (accessed 22 January 2007).

World Trade Organization, 'Declaration on the TRIPS Agreement and Public Health', 2002, WT/MIN(01)/DEC/W/2.

World Trade Organization, Implementation of Paragraph 6 of the Doha Declaration on the TRIPS Agreement and Public Health, WT/L/540 and Corr.1, 2003a.

World Trade Organization, Participation in Dispute Settlement Proceedings. Dispute Settlement System Training Module, 2003b, http://www.wto.org/english/tratop_e/dispu_e/disp_settlement_cbt_e/c9s3p1_e.htm (accessed 1 November 2007).

World Trade Organization, Report of the Appellate Body Japan – Measures Affecting the Importation of Apples, Appellate Body, Doc. WT/DS245/AB/R, Geneva, Switzerland, 2003c.

World Trade Organization, Notifications Issued during the Month of January 2008, Note by the Secretariat, G/TBT/GEN/N/85, Geneva, Switzerland, 27 February 2008.

WTO/WHO, WTO Agreements and Public Health: a Joint Study by the WHO and the WTO Secretariat, 2002, http://www.wto.org/english/res_e/booksp_e/who_wto_e.pdf (accessed 26 February 2008).

9
Commercial Health Governance
Kent Buse and Chris Naylor

Introduction and overview

Commercial organizations have long played a role in the health sector. Firms have had a significant direct impact on health through the development, manufacture and sale of their products, from cigarettes to pharmaceuticals, therapeutic and diagnostic equipment, and indirectly through their employment or environmental practices. Most countries have some mix of public and private health-care providers and in some countries the private sector is the leading provider. Moreover, the commercial sector plays an active part in health policymaking through its influence over legislative and regulatory processes at the international and national levels. Indeed, the commercial sector cannot be ignored when it comes to thinking about illness, health-care or health governance.

The advent of globalization has amplified the impact of the commercial sector on health in a number of ways. It has extended the reach and scale of global firms and industries, increased the concentration of ownership in specific industries, changed the ways in which goods and services are produced, marketed and sold, and in some situations altered the balance of power between public and commercial sectors. Consequently, the development of policies and programmes on any health issue increasingly requires that attention be paid to understanding and shaping the activities of the commercial sector.

This chapter provides an introduction to the relationship between the commercial sector and global health governance (GHG). It begins by defining the commercial sector and categorizing the range of commercial entities with an interest in or impact on global health. The chapter goes on to describe the commercial sector's involvement in GHG. In particular, it differentiates between three prominent approaches: (i) establishing private systems of global health governance; (ii) influencing public governance; and (iii) co-regulation with the public sector. Examples of each of these approaches are provided alongside a discussion of their strengths and limitations and the debates that they often provoke. The final section offers recommendations for advancing public health aims in the context of commercial health governance.

Defining the commercial sector

It is common to distinguish between public and private actors. Public refers to state, governmental and intergovernmental organizations, whereas private is a residual category of all remaining organizations and entities. Amongst private actors, a further distinction can be drawn between the commercial sector and civil society. 'Civil society' provides a banner for a diverse range of actors characterized by their voluntary and non-commercial nature (see McCoy and Hilson, Chapter 10 below). In contrast, the commercial sector is characterized by its market-orientation. Profit, or a return on investment, is the central defining feature of the commercial sector.

The commercial sector can, however, also be conceived as including a range of organizations that are not-for-profit in their legal status, but established to support a commercial firm or industry. These include business federations, professional organizations and informal networks of commercial actors. This approach to conceptualizing the commercial sector corresponds with that employed by the UN, for whom the commercial sector includes 'members of the business community ... and their representatives (who may act through not-for-profit organizations, such as chambers of commerce or philanthropic foundations)' (UN, 2000). Further muddying the conceptual landscape is the growth of hybrid-type organizations, such as public-private partnerships, which are often either legally incorporated as non-profits or housed within public sector organizations, but which are governed by a collective of public and commercial organizations.

The key point is that although for-profit organizations form the core of the commercial sector, consideration of the role of the commercial sector in GHG requires a wider purview to include those bodies that are non-profit but which serve corporate ends. If this approach is adopted, a diverse range of commercial and commercially-oriented organizations and networks with an interest in global health emerges. Table 9.1 presents a typology of such actors.

Why a concern with the commercial sector in global health governance?

There has been a great deal of debate and, indeed, acrimony over the respective roles of the state, civil society and the commercial sector as the three main spheres of global social organization. Later in this chapter, we demonstrate

Table 9.1 Commercial sector actors with an interest in or impact on global health governance

For-profit organizations	• Multi- and transnational corporations with an interest in or impact on health e.g. Pfizer, Coca Cola • Global cartels in the health sector e.g. of pharmaceutical producers
Not-for-profit organizations	• International business associations, e.g. International Chamber of Commerce, World Economic Forum • Associations of privately employed professionals with an interest in global health, e.g. International Private Practitioners Association • Non-profit, philanthropic organizations, e.g. the Bill and Melinda Gates Foundation • Issue-specific, industry funded think-tanks, foundations and institutes with interests in global health, e.g. the Global Business Coalition on HIV/AIDS • Patient groups established by firms to advance industry interests, e.g. International Alliance of Patients' Organizations, Global Alliance of Mental Illness Advocacy • Institutionalized, industry-established scientific networks with an interest in health issues, e.g. the International Life Sciences Institute • Standardizing associations which cover health related domains and are subject to high levels of industry influence, e.g. the International Organization for Standardization (ISO)
Informal groups and networks	• Loose issue-oriented networks with an interest in global health, e.g. ARISE (Associates for Research into the Science of Enjoyment) • More tightly integrated private policy and regulatory communities, e.g. the Intellectual Property Committee, PharmaMarketing Network

that the involvement of the commercial sector in global health governance has had both beneficial and detrimental consequences for global public health. The general view taken, however, is that the commercial sector is and ought to be involved in GHG. This section provides arguments supporting this and also supporting the view that state-centric analysis of GHG is simply inadequate to grappling with what is happening as the world becomes increasingly interdependent.

The commercial sector is too large to ignore in most policy fields, including health. In a world where the majority of the one hundred largest economies are corporations rather than states, private corporate standards and rules cannot be deemed inconsequential. Furthermore, it is not just the size of the commercial sector that makes it powerful, but also the degree of transnational organization. Global corporations have been described as 'the first secular institutions run by men (and a handful of women) who think and plan on a global scale' (Barnet and Cavanaugh, 1994). The global scale and interconnectedness of many commercial actors enables them to contribute significantly to GHG.

There has been a global shift in the health sector to a more private-friendly environment since the 1990s.[1] Globalization has a cognitive dimension, and the values and policy responses of political leaders across many countries have converged towards greater involvement of the commercial sector in health-care funding and provision (Lee et al., 2002). Large, commercially-oriented trusts and foundations such as the Bill and Melinda Gates Foundation have grown in importance. The Gates Foundation, for example, donated US$0.9 billion to global health programmes in 2006, placing it on a similar scale to the World Health Organization, whose total programme budget for 2006–07 was $3.3 billion. The emergence of such foundations has also led to the unprecedented involvement of other commercial sector actors, such as management consultancy firms McKinsey and Company and KPMG, in global public health programmes. Moreover, in 2005 the commercial sector funded 51 per cent of global health research, with 41 per cent coming from the public sector and the remaining 8 per cent coming from the private not-for-profit sector (Global Forum for Health Research, 2008). A study by the International Finance Corporation suggests that about half of all health services in sub-Saharan Africa are provided by the commercial sector, with private growth predicted to outpace public sector growth over the next decade (IFC, 2007). The report argues that whilst the dominance of for-profit provision can pose problems for access, the private sector remains the only option in many areas, and hence the best strategy to improve health infrastructures is not hostility towards the private sector but rather constructive engagement and integration with public systems, including through improved regulatory oversight.

The commercial sector has particular strengths that can be utilized to improve global health outcomes and governance. It has a comparative advantage, and in some domains an outright monopoly, in terms of skills and knowledge and manufacturing, distribution, and marketing capability. These assets are highly attractive contributions as the commercial sector is generally 'ahead of the curve' in relation to new technologies. Consequently, some argue that the vast resources of the commercial sector can, should be, and increasingly are being harnessed to support GHG.

The prominent role of the commercial sector in influencing various cross-border and transborder flows provides a further reason for engaging the sector in GHG. These flows include human migration but also movements of goods, information, pathogens and environmental pollution. The capacity of governments to manage these currents and their health consequences is limited, even when acting collectively through intergovernmental organizations.

The question increasingly arises as to how to involve the commercial sector in governing cross-border flows in such a way that it can contribute positively to public health goals. In sum, globalization demands responses that go beyond the classical, state-centric public health model and involve the commercial sector.

Commercial actors have a variety of reasons for engaging in health governance. As firms become increasingly global, they have an increasing need for global rules governing their transactions wherever they operate. These rules serve to minimize uncertainty and lower transaction costs associated with information gathering, negotiation and enforcement. Firms may also have a direct interest in population health in areas in which they operate – witness their engagement in AIDS programmes in sub-Saharan Africa (Davis et al., 2007). It is therefore not surprising that firms increasingly govern health issues, at times alongside public authorities and at others on their own.

Where commercial and public interests intersect, commercial governance may prove more effective and efficient than comparable public efforts at GHG, and may alleviate the need for public sector governance, thereby reducing public outlays. In other cases private governance may be ineffective or have negative consequences for health outcomes (examples are provided in the next section). The disparate trajectories of commercial health governance have led to heated debate and polarized views with calls for scrutiny of emerging mechanisms of private sector governance. What is now required is consideration of the circumstances under which private health governance is appropriate and how to go about identifying when additional safeguards to protect public health are warranted.

The manner of commercial sector involvement in global health governance

This section provides a conceptual framework for classifying the involvement of the commercial sector in GHG. It identifies three main types of governance where the commercial sector plays an important role: self-regulation, influence on public regulation and co-regulation (see Figure 9.1). These three forms of involvement occur at the national and global levels. They might be related to profit or public interests. The benefits and threats associated with each are examined in turn.

Self-regulation through private rules and standards

Self-regulation concerns efforts by private companies to set and enforce their own rules for operating within a specific domain. For example, rules governing how to design, categorize, produce and handle particular goods and services may be adopted by individual companies, industries or commerce

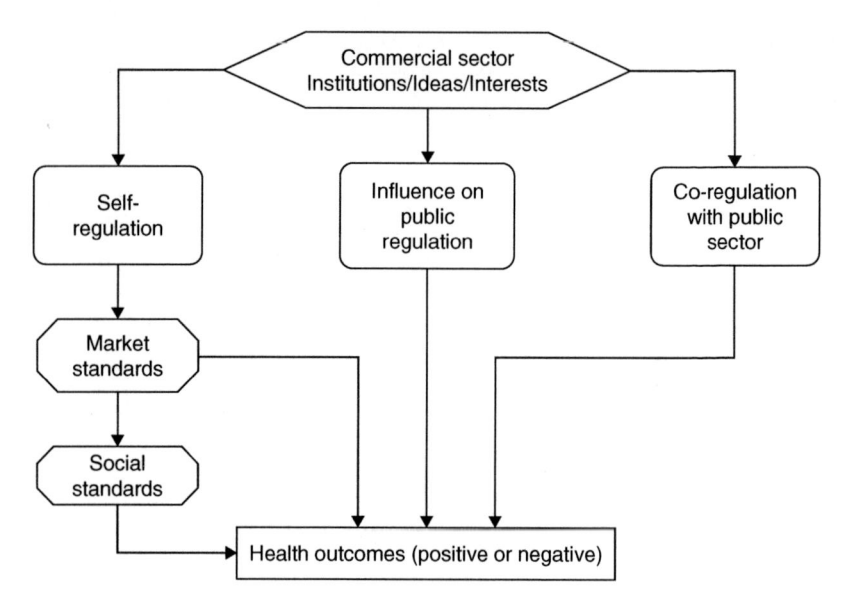

Figure 9.1 Commercial governance pathways

more widely. Equally, such efforts might involve defining rules for relationships between manufacturers in the same industry or between manufacturers, distributors, employees and consumers. These rules, regulations and norms are enforced by entities within the market itself (for example, the International Chamber of Commerce, ICC) and are often neither monitored by nor subject to public verification.

For our purposes, it is possible to distinguish between two principal types of self-regulation. On the one hand are those efforts that attempt to regulate what might be termed 'market standards' and, on the other hand, regulation of 'social standards'. In the case of market standards, the overriding purpose is to facilitate commerce, for example by reducing transaction costs, increasing compatibility between components or processes, or increasing confidence in a product. Nonetheless, many market standards have social impacts. For example, global private market standards have been developed in the area of electronic health informatics through the work of the Global Information Infrastructure Commission (GIIC), a confederation of CEOs of firms that develop and operate information technology infrastructures. As early as 1996, the GIIC published a paper on health-care and telemedicine (GIIC, 1996) covering areas such as:

- Clinical information systems allowing patient records to be accessed electronically

- Remote consultation through telemedicine
- Administrative information systems allowing electronic data interchange
- Personal health information systems targeting patients directly

The paper recommended further development of global rules and vocabulary across all of these areas to facilitate the emergence of global markets for the health information industry. The GIIC provides a good example of a nascent process to establish self-regulation of market standards which will have important implications for health-care.

Global private market standards have been established when industry perceives the need for them either as a result of weak or non-existent public regulation or fear of (inter)governmental action. A major empirical analysis of private standards concluded that 'it is more common for globalization of law (with teeth) to follow globalization of a new standard of business practice than for globalization of a new standard of business practice to follow after a new law demands it' (Braithwaite and Drahos, 1999).

Self-regulation in relation to *social standards* consists of voluntary efforts by business and industry to adopt and observe specific practices on the basis of public or social concern rather than in consideration of the functioning of the market per se. Social standards self-regulation by the commercial sector is generally undertaken in response to:

- Concerns raised by consumers
- Shareholder activism
- The threat of impending (potentially more onerous) public regulation
- The understanding that it may provide a competitive advantage to firms upholding the standards

Below we describe and critique two prominent modes of self regulation of social standards – corporate social responsibility and codes of conduct.

Corporate social responsibility

Corporate social responsibility (CSR) is an umbrella term for a range of self-regulatory initiatives and industry-promoted measures which are intended to improve the practices of firms and industries so that they operate in a responsible manner in so far as their social and environmental impacts are concerned. Among others, there are now a plethora of social reporting (for example, SOCRATES), social investment (for example, FTSE4Good Index) and corporate citizenship initiatives (such as drug donation programmes).

Multinational firms operating in low- and middle-income countries (LMIC) are increasingly involved in the provision of health-care for their workforces. In some cases this is not limited to employees but also extends to others in their families and communities, and to people working in the firm's supply chain. For example in South Africa, firms such as Anglo Coal, Virgin Group, Mercedes-Benz and TNT have been involved in HIV initiatives which target not just employees but the firms wider 'sphere of influence' (Davis et al., 2007). These examples represent a very literal form of CSR where in the absence of adequate public infrastructure or engagement (as in the case of the HIV/AIDS policies of the South African government), firms take direct responsibility for some needs within the communities in which they operate and/or the supply chains on which they depend. Nonetheless, there must always be a business case behind such initiatives, the ultimate motive being enlightened self-interest. Evidence suggests that in some high-income settings investment in employee health pays an average threefold return where there is no adequate public health insurance, by raising productivity and reducing absenteeism and staff turnover (Goetzel et al., 2005). Comparable figures do not appear to be publicly available for LMIC contexts. Firms may also have reputation-based reasons for adopting socially responsible practices.

Codes of conduct

Voluntary codes of conduct are perhaps the most visible form of self-regulation of social standards. These cover a wide variety of corporate practices that have significant impact on health, including workplace and occupational health and safety, minimum age of work, product safety, responsible marketing, protection of the environment and human rights.

In the late 1990s, codes of conduct were rapidly multiplying and 'competing for the hearts and minds of consumers and corporate managers alike' (Pearson and Seyfang, 2001: 56). Most transnational and multinational firms as well as whole industry sectors have developed their own codes, many of which are global in reach. For example, all company members of the International Federation of Pharmaceutical Manufacturers and Associations (IFPMA) are required to adhere to the federation's Code of Pharmaceutical Marketing Practices. Similarly, membership of the World Self-Medication Industry requires that trade associations abide by a set of conditions and standards among which is the development of voluntary codes of advertising governing marketing of non-prescription medicines directly to consumers.

Codes of conduct have been popular with business because, in addition to serving social purposes, they have the potential to serve important business functions. Codes may improve profitability in any of the following ways:

- Responding to concerns of consumers and thereby increasing sales
- Responding to the demands of civil society groups and thus staving off product boycotts

- Responding to concerns of investors and shareholders, thereby gaining increased investment
- Differentiating the firm from competitors which do not participate in the code and thereby increasing sales
- Decreasing costs to business associated with poor employee health
- Staving off or delaying statutory regulation

From a social perspective, voluntary codes can have a number of benefits over statutory regulation. First, they may bring new groups of stakeholders into the regulatory process. For example, casual and temporary labourers, often women, have participated in developing workplace codes of conduct whereas they had not typically been represented in comparable processes conducted by the International Labour Organization. Second, voluntary codes may generate better compliance than intergovernmental and national regulation, where enforcement may be ineffective. Third, voluntary codes are obviously less costly to the public sector than statutory regulation. There are, however, reasons to remain sceptical of the ability of voluntary codes adequately to govern many global health concerns.

The academic Prakash Sethi reviewed a large number of voluntary corporate codes and concluded that 'corporate codes of conduct are treated with disdain and largely dismissed by knowledgeable and influential opinion leaders among various stakeholder groups, as well as by outside analysts and the public-at-large' (Sethi, 1999). Sethi argues that such scepticism arises because:

- Codes tend to enunciate general principles as opposed to specific standards (that is, quantifiable and measurable indicators)
- Codes tend to focus on the concerns of Western consumers (for example, child labour, or pesticide residue on organic fruit) as opposed to the concerns of employees (for example, the right to collective bargaining, pesticide exposure)
- Codes are rarely linked to internal reward structures, operating procedures, or corporate culture
- Companies typically do not make public the process by which they seek to comply with the code and the findings related to the code
- Reporting of code implementation is often not subject to external scrutiny

An analysis of voluntary codes of pharmaceutical marketing practices, including the IFPMA code referred to above, concluded that they lack transparency and public accountability because consumers are not involved in monitoring and enforcement, they omit major areas of concern and they lack timely and effective sanctions (Lexchin and Kawachi, 1996). Similarly, a former executive director of the WHO argues that self-regulation in the case of tobacco manufacturing and smoke-free policies 'failed miserably' (Yach, 2004: 7).

A further problematic aspect of voluntary codes is their 'aspirational' nature – whereby they often represent company 'commitment' to stakeholders to undertake certain actions. Undertaking voluntarily to uphold a particular principle is qualitatively distinct from being held accountable under law to ensuring specific rights, for example, of those affected by company operations. As a consequence, such patchwork self-regulation results in 'enclave' social policy governing only select issues and specific groups of workers. Some fear that these self-regulatory efforts will erode societal commitment to universal rights and entitlements.

In summary, an increasing number of self-regulatory mechanisms are being adopted by the business community as evolving forms of global health governance. Self-regulation is of two varieties: market and social. While both types may facilitate improved global health they may also both have negative consequences. In light of the potential problems with private self-regulation, governance in many domains has remained under the purview of public regulation. Yet as the following section demonstrates, for the commercial sector many of these domains are considered too important to leave to governments and intergovernmental organizations.

Commercial sector involvement in global public health governance

Where the commercial sector is not in a position to self-regulate, firms will often seek to influence any relevant public statutory regulation that might impact on their profitability. They may do so directly by lobbying or indirectly through the use of a range of front organizations. Industry may draft legislation and policy documents or may use the media and other communications channels to appeal to the public to support pro-industry regulation. Table 9.2 presents some of the tactics used at the global level.

Two case studies are provided in Boxes 9.1 and 9.2 to illustrate the range of tactics adopted by the commercial sector to imprint its interests on global 'public' governance, and the implications that this is likely to have for public health.

Whilst the literature is scant, it is apparent that industry is active in the realm of influencing public sector regulation that has the potential to impinge on its bottom line. With increasing awareness of these strategies, the public sector (as well as civil society and consumer groups) is in a better position to develop policies and guidelines to protect against conflicts of interest, undue influence, and conferring unfair advantages to certain segments of the market so as to protect and promote health.

Table 9.2 Tactics used by industry to influence public global health governance

Tactic	Example
Using ostensibly independent front organizations, e.g. research institutes, trade associations	International Life Sciences Institute – dominated by the food, alcohol, tobacco, pharmaceutical and chemical industries (James, 2002)
Acting via industry-established or controlled 'patient' groups	Global Alliance of Mental Illness Advocacy Networks – created by pharmaceutical company Bristol-Meyers Squibb (Herxheimer, 2003)
Manipulating scientific research	Suppression of disappointing efficacy trial results for Synthroid by pharmaceutical company Boots (Rampton and Stauber, 2001)
Proactive use and manipulation of mass media	Planned organization of televised child health event to distract media attention from World Conference on Tobacco or Health (Zeltner et al., 2000)
Direct lobbying	Lobbying governments of low-income countries and UN agencies (e.g. FAO) to resist WHO's tobacco control programmes (Zeltner et al., 2000)
Drafting and promoting alternative policy	Proposing a voluntary code as an alternative to EC-level regulation of tobacco advertising (Neuman et al., 2002)
Discrediting opponents	Paying academics to question the 'mission and mandate' of the WHO (Zeltner et al., 2000)
Using litigation or public appeal	Planned use of European Court of Justice to challenge EC tobacco advertising legislation (Neuman et al., 2002)

Co-regulation

Co-regulation presents a third way between traditional public regulation and private self-regulation. It has arisen, in large part, because of the inadequacies of public and private regulation operating alone. As argued above, public statutory arrangements have been seen as wanting in an era of globalization as state and intergovernmental capacity for regulation lags behind technological advances made by industry, suffers from jurisdictional constraints (national law does not apply in global space), and is perceived by some on the right of the ideological spectrum as too costly. At the same time, private self-regulation alone is recognized as not always in the public interest. Hence a case remains for some external public control over self-regulation. Co-regulation may be viewed as public sector involvement in business self-regulation, or as concerted attempts to involve non-state actors in public governance. Others have called it 'distributive governance' in that all concerned actors cooperate to shape norms, develop sanctions for transgression, and

Box 9.1   The commercial sector and the 'public' TRIPS Agreement

Firms from the chemicals, information, entertainment and pharmaceutical industries were actively involved in the creation of the World Trade Organization (WTO) rules governing intellectual property rights – the Trade Related Aspects of Intellectual Property (TRIPS) Agreement. Recognizing that weak intellectual property protection beyond the USA resulted in what was perceived as 'piracy' and a significant threat to returns on investment in research and development, the CEOs of 12 US-based transnational corporations established the Intellectual Property Committee (IPC) in 1986 (Sell, 2003). By linking inadequate global protection of IPR to US balance of payment deficits, the IPC was able to win the support of the US government for its aims. The IPC then encouraged commercial allies in Canada, Japan and Europe to lobby their governments to support efforts to include IP protection in the Uruguay trade negotiations. In the interim, the IPC hired a trade lawyer to draft an international treaty governing IP. The industry report was adopted by the US administration and served as the negotiating document in Uruguay – illustrating the power of the commercial sector to propose 'public' governance instruments. The IPC was also able to position one of its key members, the CEO of Pfizer, as an adviser to the American delegation to the Uruguay trade negotiations. Although the governments of India and Brazil attempted to stall negotiations and drop IPR from the round, economic sanctions imposed by the US administration as well as technical arguments elaborated by industry lawyers eventually undermined their opposition. As a result, agreement on TRIPS was reached. According to the industry consultant who drafted the treaty, the 'IPC got 95% of what it wanted' (Jaques Gorlin, quoted in Sell, 2003: 115).

The TRIPS Agreement has the status of international law. The WTO has responsibility to oversee the implementation of the agreement and has, by international legal standards, a particularly powerful enforcement mechanism. Industry has remained active in the implementation stage. For example, in 2007, Abbott Laboratories threatened to withdraw all new medicines from Thailand after the Thai government used allowances in the agreement for compulsory licensing, through which in certain circumstances countries may force a patent holder to grant permission to manufacture their product (Cawthorne et al., 2007; also Wogart et al., Chapter 7 above).

This case study provides an example of relatively direct participation of industry in global health governance. Indeed given the level of commercial involvement, TRIPS could be viewed as a privatization of norm-making capacities that are subsequently enacted in the public domain.

> The involvement of industry in successfully governing the intellectual property regime from behind the scenes is likely to have profound implications for health. Critics point to the restrictions that are placed on the use of generic drugs and the inevitable increase in the price of pharmaceutical products as well as the barriers to innovation that patenting entails (Orsi et al., 2007).

condition actors' acceptance of appropriate conduct (Detomasi, 2002). Like private and public governance, these arrangements may be formal or informal.

Co-regulation represents a bargain between public authorities and the private sector. The public and private actors negotiate on an agreed set of policy or regulatory objectives that are often results-oriented (that is, an emphasis is placed on outputs or outcomes). Subsequently, the private sector takes responsibility for implementation of the provisions. Monitoring compliance might remain a public responsibility or might lie with the commercial participants, or it could be contracted out to a third party – sometimes an interested NGO-cum-watchdog. Co-regulatory initiatives often involve a mixture of public, private and civil society organizations.

The advent of co-regulation is relatively new, and the majority of formal experimentation with it has been at the national and regional levels. For example, the European Union is experimenting with co-regulation with respect to the internet, journalism and e-commerce. There is also increasing interest in co-regulation in low- and middle-income countries. For example, governments in Latin America and Asia have experimented with co-regulatory instruments in the field of environmental management (Hanks, 2002). In Indonesia, the government responded to stubbornly poor compliance with public environmental regulation by introducing the much-lauded Programme for Pollution Control, Evaluation and Rating (PROPER) in 1995. Under this, participating firms submit bi-monthly emissions figures to a public agency, which only investigates when figures appear anomalous. Firms are then rated according to whether they have met, failed to meet, or exceeded standards. These ratings are publicly disclosed, providing a reputation-based incentive for firms to meet or exceed public standards. An initial evaluation suggested the scheme was more effective than formal regulation in promoting compliance and reducing emissions (Afsah et al., 2000).

At the global level, the global public-private health partnerships (GHPs) that have become such a prominent feature in the global health architecture over the last ten years can be seen as a form of co-regulation, in that they represent an attempt to develop systems of transnational governance in

> **Box 9.2 The tobacco industry and public governance**
>
> Internal documents released by the tobacco industry as a result of litigation against companies in the USA revealed ongoing efforts by the industry to influence public governance. One of the most ambitious attempts involved an effort to build a covert global network of scientific and medical consultants referred to as the 'International ETS [Environmental Tobacco Smoke] Consultant Program' or 'Project Whitecoat' (Barnoya and Glantz, 2002; Drope and Chapman, 2001; Muggli et al., 2001). Consultants were to act as conduits for the industry message on the issue of environmental tobacco smoke (or 'passive smoking'), whilst keeping their relationship with the industry concealed. The programme was constructed by law firm Covington and Burling at the behest of Philip Morris International and British American Tobacco, and had arms in the USA, South America, Europe and Asia. Consultants were used at the national level to lobby governments and testify in regulatory hearings, and to infiltrate international agencies such as the WHO International Agency for Research on Cancer (Muggli et al., 2001).
>
> An enquiry into tobacco industry influence in WHO revealed that an elaborate, well-financed and usually invisible global effort had been undertaken by the tobacco industry 'to reduce budgets for the scientific and policy activities carried out by WHO, to pit other UN agencies against WHO, to convince developing countries that WHO's tobacco control programme was a "first world" agenda carried out at the expense of the developing world, to distort the results of important scientific studies, and to discredit WHO as an institution' (Zeltner et al., 2000). Tobacco companies, their law firms and public relations agencies hid evidence, subverted facts, and used ostensibly independent experts, NGO-front organizations and the media to influence the debate on tobacco. The enquiry concluded that industry subversion of WHO tobacco control activities resulted in 'significant harm'.
>
> Other documented attempts by the tobacco industry to influence public governance at the global level include the following:
>
> - Attempts to exert influence on FAO/WHO food and nutrition policies by positioning ostensibly independent experts on various regulatory committees; establishing transnational monitoring systems to give early warnings of potential regulatory changes which industry could lobby against; and funding sympathetic libertarian think-tanks and academics to promote anti-regulatory ideology (Hirschhorn, 2002).
> - Manipulation of potential international allies on the issue of environmental tobacco smoke, for example the International Hotel and Restaurant Association, which has consultative status with the United

> Nations, the Organization for Economic Cooperation and Development, and other international organizations (Dearlove et al., 2002).
> - Covert use of surrogate bodies to attempt to influence international technical standards. For example, lobbying via Multinational Business Services Inc. against the inclusion of a code for damage caused by environmental tobacco smoke in the WHO International Classification of Diseases (Cook et al., 2005).

which both public and private sectors have a voice in decision-making and in which funding is often provided on the basis of results achieved (see Buse and Harmer, Chapter 12 below).[2] Critics, however, question what sort of improvements in representation occur through GHPs. Certainly, civil society and the private sector have seats in the governing bodies of the Global Fund to Fight AIDS, TB and Malaria, in the GAVI Alliance and other GHPs, but these are often biased towards the north and the policy elite. Moreover, the extent to which GHPs distort priorities and undermine health systems is the subject of both research and controversy (see Buse and Harmer, Chapter 12). A further example of co-regulation at the global level is provided by the ICC-UN Global Compact (see Box 9.3).

Conclusions

Lee and Goodman (2002: 98) argue that in the new, pluralized world of global health governance, private sector actors should be seen as more than just interest groups seeking to influence formal, state-focused processes. The commercial sector is increasingly 'part of the decision-making structure formerly reserved for state actors'. Fitting with this analysis, there is a global trend towards placing an increased emphasis on self-regulation and co-regulation, in place of formal statutory regulation. This approach has both benefits and costs. Minogue (2001) argues that institutional trust between the regulator and the regulated is a critical determinant of success:

> The benefits of corporate governance [self- and co-regulation] are clear: flexibility, the capacity to utilize appropriate expertise, responsiveness to changing conditions, and lower institutional complexity. Equally clear are the costs: potential for abuse and bias, lack of transparency, and an orientation to private rather than public interest. Whether benefits outweigh costs, however, depends upon the existence of trust ... Regulators must be seen as competent, reasonable, and credible [by the targets of regulation] while at the same time trusting regulatory targets to exercise self-restraint and to accept public interest values. Trust is therefore a two-way process.

Box 9.3 The ICC-UN Global Compact

The ICC-UN Global Compact is an initiative to promote responsible corporate practice which may be viewed as a form of co-regulation. The initiative comprises a network of over 3600 companies, six UN agencies, and labour and civil society organizations. It is governed by a multi-stakeholder board which has been touted as the first UN advisory body with both public and private sector representation (although it should be noted that the International Labour Organization has long had a tripartite board). Compact participants engage in policy dialogue, learning activities and projects to achieve two objectives: (i) to mainstream ten social and environmental principles into business activities so as to advance responsible corporate behaviour; and (ii) to catalyze commercial sector action in support of broader UN goals. For example, members have used the convening power of the compact to develop policy recommendations on how to improve the fight against HIV/AIDS by improving workplace HIV/AIDS policies among member companies (Global Compact, n.d.). Members are asked to publish illustrative examples on the ways in which they are enacting the principles of the compact through concrete business practices annually on their websites.

The compact's literature stresses that the arrangement is not a regulatory one. It induces corporate change by relying on public accountability and the enlightened self-interest of members. Others view such networked, horizontal, non-hierarchical and learning-based approaches as non-conventional forms of regulation. Such approaches, it is argued, will become increasingly prevalent in a globalizing world (Ruggie, 2001).

The compact has, however, been highly controversial. Critics are concerned that the initiative will enable firms to engage in 'bluewash' – improving their corporate image through association with the UN. After the launch of the compact, civil society organizations led by CorpWatch and including Greenpeace, Amnesty International and ActionAid formed the 'Alliance for a Corporate-Free UN' to oppose the initiative. The alliance, now dismantled, produced a series of exposés of prominent corporate members who continued to violate compact principles while at the same time publicizing their membership. Examples included Unilever, which was found discharging mercury into the groundwater in India (Jayaraman, 2001), and Aventis, whose genetically modified corn approved only for animal consumption was found in human food (Flora, 2001).

Critics have also pointed to a potentially more damaging aspect of the compact. By driving a wedge between moderate and more radical civil society groups, the compact may undermine efforts to bring about international legally-binding regulation, and in the process erode democratic decision-making and accountability within society. The perspective taken on the compact by Greenpeace is that 'voluntary action, though welcome, can never be a substitute for much-needed government regulation' (Daniel Mittler, quoted in Capdevila, 2007). In response to calls for a legally enforceable equivalent to the compact, ICC President Adnan Kassar added what he called an important proviso to ICC's support of the compact: 'There must be no suggestion of hedging the Global Compact with formal prescriptive rules. We would resist any tendency for this to happen' (ICC, 2000). In short, the Global Compact demonstrates both tensions over the degree of public sector involvement that the commercial sector is willing to tolerate within co-regulatory arrangements, and broader tensions over the appropriate relationship between the private sector and the UN.

Whether the necessary trust can exist depends both on the context and on the nature of the industry in question. Minogue suggests that many developing countries are 'low-trust' societies with little tradition of collaboration between the public and private sectors. There may also be less scope for benign corporate governance where there is a risk to health deriving from the commercial product itself (as opposed to the production process, or by-products). For example, Saloojee and Dagli (2000) argue that the tobacco industry has a track record of using involvement with public governance solely as a means of perverting it.

The various forms of commercial governance – from self-regulated market standards at one extreme, through self-regulated social standards and co-regulation to formal public regulation – each have the potential to affect public health in beneficial or harmful ways. The public health community should attempt to engage with each stream of regulation to improve health impacts. Where efforts at one level of regulation fail, the goal should be to shift governance to the next level, increasing the degree of public involvement (see Figure 9.2).

In the case of self-regulated market standards, public health practitioners need to be aware of mechanisms that impact upon their sphere of health concern, and attempt to influence the development of such standards so that they promote and protect public health. This is likely to prove to be a challenging endeavour given that market standards evolve quickly, and the networks and organizations that produce them may be reluctant to involve other players. Where external pressure does not compel commercial actors to address health impacts effectively, public health groups should attempt to shift governance from the realm of self-regulation to co-regulation, whereby civil society and the state have some say in how issues are governed.

Many self-regulated social standards have proven controversial; some as a result of their poor design and management (for example, codes of conduct

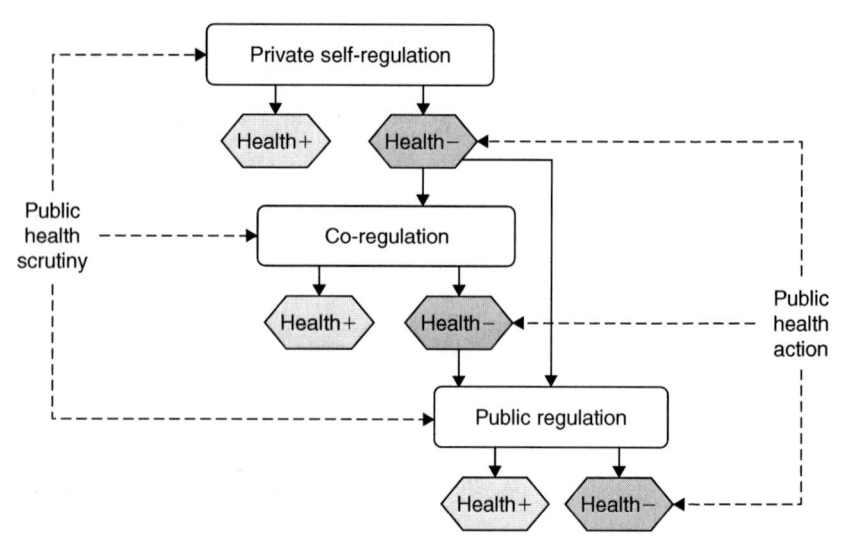

Figure 9.2 A framework for public health involvement

without internal rewards or external scrutiny) and some as a result of their negative impact on statutory regulation (for example, pre-empting public regulation and diluting impetus for public action). A pragmatic response to these criticisms may entail: (i) fostering public and civil sector involvement in the development of voluntary social standards regulation so as to ensure that they balance market incentives with safeguards such as credible third-party watchdogs; and (ii) simultaneously continuing to develop and implement public regulation where it is warranted. In effect, the idea is again to move these instruments away from self-regulation to some form of co-regulation. As noted above, this may prove difficult as private actors may resist public involvement. While the threat of public regulation might provide industry with an incentive to reconsider the health impacts of these private arrangements, attempts to develop incentives that will benefit compliant firms may present a more credible and productive approach. For critics, such a strategy is overly sanguine in that it fails to acknowledge the threat of voluntary initiatives to statutory processes. However, empirical work suggests that statutory regulation tends to build on voluntary initiatives, rather than being undermined by them (Braithwaite and Drahos, 1999).

If those predicting that the co-regulation model will become more widespread are correct, there may be considerable opportunities for increased public and civil sector involvement in what are currently private, self-regulatory mechanisms. However, the model also poses threats. The public health community needs to ensure that co-regulation is not exploited by industry as a softer alternative in situations where legally-binding public regulation would be more appropriate. Similarly, it should not become a means by which firms can improve their public image whilst making negligible changes to their practices. Co-regulatory mechanisms need to be transparent and accountable, and should contain carefully-designed incentive structures to encourage compliance.

In the case of public regulation, the public health community should aim to counter commercial sector efforts to influence decision-making within the intergovernmental system in ways detrimental to public health. Recent revelations about the extent of these efforts and the tactics used suggest that defensive action ought to be taken. Multilateral organizations are already putting in place policies and procedures to protect themselves from pernicious influence. What remains to be seen is how effective such measures will prove to be; further research is needed here. In addition to taking defensive measures, public health advocates may also consider how the strategies currently used by the commercial sector to influence public governance can in turn be adopted by the public health community to foster health goals. These include the highly proactive use of the media and deployment of scientific research, and the formation of transnational strategic alliances. There is an important role for global advocacy coalitions through which like-minded public and civil society actors (for example, Global Health Watch) can monitor the influence of the commercial sector over public governance processes, promote transparency and accountability, and identify those areas where public governance fails to lead to improved health outcomes.

It is worth re-emphasizing that the purpose of a commercial organization is to generate profits for its owners or shareholders. Whilst in some cases a clear business case can be made for commercial organizations to be involved in global health governance in ways beneficial to public health, in others, trade-offs between profit and health will inevitably arise. Where they do, there are good grounds, from a public health perspective, for some form of co-regulation or public sector regulation. The key challenge faced by the public health community, nationally, regionally and globally, is to match the appropriate forms of regulation with the diversity of activities of the commercial sector, in ways that best protect and promote public health.

Notes

1. Here we refer to the commercial sector, see McCoy and Hilson (Chapter 10) for a discussion of civil society organizations.
2. It goes without saying that co-regulation obtains solely to the areas where partners agree to the same rules of the game and that this often represents fairly narrow policy space (for example, agreement that the GAVI Alliance should only finance auto-destruct syringes).

References

Afsah, S., A. Blackman and D. Ratunanda, 'How do Public Disclosure Pollution Control Programs Work? Evidence from Indonesia', Resources for the Future, Washington, DC, 2000, http://www.rff.org/documents/RFF-DP-00-44.pdf (accessed 26 May 2008).

Barnet, R.J. and J. Cavanaugh, *Global Dreams: Imperial Corporations and the New World Order* (New York: Touchstones, 1994).

Barnoya, J. and S. Glantz, 'Tobacco Industry Success in Preventing Regulation of Secondhand Smoke in Latin America: the "Latin Project"', *Tobacco Control*, 11(4) (2002): 305–14.

Braithwaite, J. and P. Drahos, 'Ratchetting Up and Driving Down Global Regulatory Standards', *Development*, 42(4) (1999): 109–14.

Capdevila, G., 'UN: Global Compact with Business "Lacks Teeth" – NGOs', CorpWatch, 2007, http://www.corpwatch.org/article.php?id=14549 (accessed 26 May 2008).

Cawthorne, P., N. Ford, D. Wilson, K. Kijtiwatchakul and V. Purahong, 'Access to Drugs: the Case of Abbott in Thailand', *Lancet Infectious Diseases*, 7(6) (2007): 373–4.

Cook, D.M., E.K. Tong, S.A. Glantz and L.A Bero, 'The Power of Paperwork: How Philip Morris Neutralized the Medical Code for Secondhand Smoke', *Health Affairs*, 24(4) (2005): 994–1004.

Davis, M., F. Samuels and K. Buse, 'AIDS and the Private Sector: the Case of South Africa', Overseas Development Institute, London, 2007, http://www.odi.org.uk/Publications/briefing/bp_hiv_privatesector_nov07.pdf (accessed 26 May 2008).

Dearlove, J.V., S.A. Bialous and S.A. Glantz, 'Tobacco Industry Manipulation of the Hospitality Industry to Maintain Smoking in Public Places', *Tobacco Control*, 11 (2002): 94–104.

Detomasi, D., 'International Institutions and the Case of Corporate Governance: Towards a Distributive Framework?' *Global Governance*, 8(4) (2002): 421–42.

Drope, J. and S. Chapman, 'Tobacco Industry Efforts at Discrediting Scientific Knowledge of Environmental Tobacco Smoke: a Review of Internal Industry Documents', *Journal of Epidemiology and Community Health*, 55(8) (2001): 588–94.

Flora, G., 'Aventis: Global Compact Violator', CorpWatch, 2001, http://www.corpwatch.org/article.php?id=621 (accessed 26 May 2008).

Global Compact, 'HIV/AIDS: Everybody's Business', Global Compact, n.d., http://www.globalcompact.org/docs/news_events/8.1/HIV_AIDS.pdf (accessed 26 May 2008).

Global Information Infrastructure Commission, *Healthcare and Telemedicine* (GIIC, 1996).

Goetzel, R.Z., R.J. Ozminkowski, C.M. Baase and G.M. Billotti, 'Estimating the Return-on-Investment from Changes in Employee Health Risks on the Dow Chemical Company's Health Care Costs', *Journal of Occupational and Environmental Medicine*, 47 (2005): 759–68.

Global Forum for Health Research (GFHR), 'Monitoring Financial Flows for Health Research 2008: Prioritizing Research for Health Equity' (GFHR, 2008), http://www.globalforumhealth.org/Site/002__What%20we%20do/005__Publications/004__Resource%20flows.php (accessed 7 December 2008).

Hanks, J., 'A Role for Negotiated Environmental Agreements in Developing Countries?' in P. ten Brink (ed.), *Voluntary Environmental Agreements: Process, Practice and Future Use* (Sheffield: Greenleaf Publishing, 2002), pp. 159–75.

Herxheimer, A., 'Relationships between the Pharmaceutical Industry and Patients' Organizations', *British Medical Journal*, 26 (2003): 1208–10.

Hirschhorn, N., 'How the Tobacco and Food Industries and their Allies Tried to Exert Undue Influence over FAO/WHO Food and Nutrition Policies', unpublished report, WHO, New Haven, Connecticut, 2002.

International Chamber of Commerce (ICC), 'Business Supports Kofi Annan's Global Compact – But Rejects "Prescriptive Rules"', ICC Press Release, ICC, Budapest, 4 May 2000.

International Finance Corporation (IFC), 'The Business of Health in Africa. Partnering with the Private Sector to Improve People's Lives', IFC, 2007, http://www.ifc.org/ifcext/healthinafrica.nsf/AttachmentsByTitle/IFC_HealthinAfrica_Final/$FILE/IFC_HealthinAfrica_Final.pdf (accessed 26 May 2008).

James, J.E., 'Third-Party Threats to Research Integrity in Public-Private Partnerships', *Addiction*, 97 (2002): 1251–5.

Jayaraman, N., 'Unilever's Mercury Fever', CorpWatch, 2001, http://www.corpwatch.org/article.php?id=624 (accessed 26 May 2008).

Lee, K. and H. Goodman, 'Global Policy Networks: the Propagation of Health Care Financing Reform since the 1980s', in K. Lee, K. Buse and S. Fustukian (eds), *Health Policy in a Globalising World* (Cambridge: Cambridge University Press, 2002), pp. 97–119.

Lee, K., S. Fustukian and K. Buse, 'An Introduction to Global Health Policy', in K. Lee, K. Buse and S. Fustukian (eds), *Health Policy in a Globalising World* (Cambridge: Cambridge University Press, 2002), pp. 3–17.

Lexchin, J. and I. Kawachi, 'Voluntary Codes of Pharmaceutical Marketing: Controlling Promotion or Licensing Deception?' in P. Davis (ed.), *Contested Ground: Public Purpose and Private Interest in the Regulation of Prescription Drugs* (New York: Oxford University Press 1996), pp. 221–35.

Minogue, M., 'Governance-Based Analysis of Regulation', Centre on Regulation and Competition, Manchester, 2001, http://ageconsearch.umn.edu/handle/30590 (accessed 26 May 2008).

Muggli, M.E., J.L. Forster, R.D. Hurt and J.L. Repace, 'The Smoke You Don't See: Uncovering Tobacco Industry Scientific Strategies Aimed against Environmental Tobacco Smoke Policies', *American Journal of Public Health*, 91(9) (2001): 1419–23.

Neuman, M., A. Bitton and S. Glantz, 'Tobacco Industry Strategies for Influencing European Community Tobacco Advertising Legislation', *Lancet*, 359 (2002): 1323–30.

Orsi, F., C. D'Almeida, L. Hasenclever, M. Camara, P. Tigre and B. Coriat, 'TRIPS Post-2005 and Access to New Antiretroviral Treatments in Southern Countries: Issues and Challenges', *AIDS*, 21 (15) (2007): 1997–2003.

Pearson, R. and G. Seyfang, 'New Hope or False Dawn? Voluntary Codes of Conduct, Labour Regulation and Social Policy in a Globalising World', *Global Social Policy*, 1(1) (2001): 49–78.

Rampton, S. and J. Stauber, *Trust Us, We're Experts: How Industry Manipulates Science and Gambles with Your Future* (New York: Tarcher/Putnam, 2001).

Ruggie, J.G., 'global_governance.net: the Global Compact as a Learning Network', *Global Governance*, 7(4) (2001): 371–8.

Saloojee, Y. and E. Dagli, 'Tobacco Industry Tactics for Resisting Public Policy on Health', *Bulletin of the World Health Organization*, 78(8) (2000): 902–10.

Sell, S., *Private Power, Public Law: the Globalization of Intellectual Property* (Cambridge: Cambridge University Press, 2003).

Sethi, P.S., 'Codes of Conduct for Multinational Corporations: an Idea Whose Time Has Come', *Business and Society Review*, 104(3) (1999): 225–41.

UN General Assembly, 'Comments by the Administrative Committee on Coordination on the Report of the Joint Inspection Unit entitled "Private sector involvement and cooperation with the United Nations system"', UN, 2000, http://www.un.org/ga/54/doc/A54700a1.pdf (accessed 26 May 2008)

Yach, D., 'Politics and Health', *Development*, 47(2) (2004): 5–10.

Zeltner, T., D.A. Kessler, A. Martiny and F. Randera, 'Tobacco Company Strategies to Undermine Tobacco Control activities at the World Health Organization', report of the Committee of Experts on Tobacco Industry Documents, WHO, Geneva, 2000.

10
Civil Society, its Organizations, and Global Health Governance

David McCoy and Margaret Hilson

Introduction

The past few decades have seen an explosion in the number of civil society organizations (CSOs). The first registered international non-governmental organization (NGO), the Anti-Slavery Society, was formed in 1839 (UNDP, 2002). Although the task of counting the number of civil society organizations (CSOs) is difficult because of data limitations and the problem of what should be taken into account, according to Anheier et al. (2001), the number of *international* NGOs increased from 1083 in 1914 to approximately 37,000 in 2000, with nearly a fifth forming after 1990. An analysis by Sikkink and Smith (2002), which focused only on international NGOs concerned with promoting social change (that is, excluding NGOs focused on delivering services), concluded that the number of such organizations had risen from about a hundred in the 1950s to about 700 in the 1990s.

The value and worth of civil society (CS) actors in catalyzing social progress has been well documented. The anti-slavery movement, female emancipation, the civil rights movement and the partial cancellation of unfair 'third world debt' are examples of social progress that have been spearheaded by CS actors, often dragging reluctant or unconcerned governments and businesses along behind them.

Because globalization has increased the importance of global or supranational actors and institutions, many CS organizations and campaigns are now themselves international or transnational in nature. Easier international travel and new information and communication technologies have facilitated the development of global CS constituencies that cut across national identities and physical distance. One outcome of this is that national movements and campaigns can more easily become internationalized. For example, the South African fight against apartheid became a worldwide consumer, sports and cultural boycott against the South African regime. According to the 2002 Human Development Report, 'it is plausible to posit the emergence of "global civil society" as a constituency of networks committed to attaining global justice on a range of issues' (UNDP, 2002: 106).

This chapter discusses civil society in relation to the governance of health at the global level. It is structured in two parts. The first part consists of a broad discussion about what we mean by CS engaging with or acting upon global health governance (GHG). Global health governance is loosely defined as the structures, systems, rules and processes at the global level for: (i) making decisions about health policy and priority-setting; (ii) financing and implementing global health initiatives, programmes and plans; and (iii) ensuring appropriate and effective systems of accountability. We describe the meaning and heterogeneity of civil society organizations, how they relate to institutions with a GHG function, and their interactions with each other and other actors such as governments and business. The second part consists of a more detailed discussion about the engagement by CSOs with the World Health Organization (WHO) and with the governance structures and systems that exist for the WHO.

Civil society and GHG: introductory issues

Civil society is a broad and loose concept, often described as a sphere of society that is separate from the state and the market. CSOs are in turn usually described as being distinct from government and state institutions, and from businesses or corporations. The World Health Organization, for example, describes civil society as 'a sphere separate from both the state and market' and notes that CSOs are typically understood as being *non-state* and *not-for-profit* (WHO, 2002).

While most authors agree that CSOs function outside the state's official apparatus (Scholte, 1999; Edwards, 2000; UNDP, 1997), some organizations, including UNAIDS and the UN Commission on Global Governance, view businesses as a part of 'civil society'. We believe that the differences between profit and non-profit organizations are significant enough to justify the more common practice of distinguishing CSOs from businesses. However, three points need to be made about the tripartite system which distinguishes between governmental, business and civil society actors. First, there is no 'global government'. Second, CSOs are themselves an extremely diverse group of actors. And third, the distinction between CSOs, state institutions and businesses is not always clear or valid.

In the absence of a 'global government', governance at the widest level takes the form of a loose and unstructured configuration of multiple structures and systems. The closest thing to a government at the global level is the United Nations (UN), which performs global governance functions mainly through authority delegated by national governments.

The UN system is vast. According to the official website locator for the UN System of Organizations, there are 112 distinct UN entities with overlapping mandates and functions. It includes organizations such as the WHO, UNICEF and UNFPA with explicit global health mandates, as well as organizations like UN-HABITAT, UNDP, the World Bank and the International Monetary Fund (IMF) whose core responsibilities have a more indirect impact on health (for example, by setting international laws and regulations on intellectual property or trade) or which cover the underlying determinants of health (for example, macroeconomic and development policy).

Interestingly, the different organizations of the UN system have different governance structures and arrangements. For example, the WHO is governed by an assembly of all UN member states with equal voting power. The World Bank is governed through a system that gives greater voting power to certain high-income countries. UNAIDS is guided by a 'Programme Coordinating Board' consisting of representatives from 22 governments, the UNAIDS co-sponsors (consisting of other UN agencies including the WHO, UNICEF and the World Bank), and five NGO representatives. The International Labour Organization has a tripartite arrangement with allocated seats on its governance body and executive structures for governments, employers and workers.

In addition to the UN system, there are other intergovernmental organizations (IGOs) to consider. For example, the G8 has a substantial global health agenda of its own, which many NGOs seek to influence. The Organization for Economic Cooperation and Development (OECD) and the Bank for International Settlements (BIS) are two other examples of non-UN IGOs whose actions have either a direct or indirect impact on health.

Civil society's engagement with GHG therefore needs to cover a wide set of IGOs. While this is challenging enough for civil society, two other sets of actors need to be considered, especially in the health sector: global health partnerships (GHPs) and private foundations.

GHPs are a relatively new feature of the global health landscape and often consist of governments, UN bodies, businesses and CSOs working together through a secretariat (Buse and Walt, 2000). Examples include the Global Fund to Fight AIDS, TB and Malaria (Global Fund), the GAVI Alliance, and Roll Back Malaria (RBM).

These form part of a wider public-private partnerships paradigm that has been promoted as a solution to the perceived failings of intergovernmental cooperation, whilst harnessing CS energy and business acumen to support more nuanced and effective policymaking and more effective and efficient delivery of global programmes (Kaul, 2006; Utting, 2000). They are part of what is called 'complex multilateralism' (O'Brien, 1997), which describes a system of governance which involves formal state-based institutions (national and multilateral) as well as the private sector and civil society. According to Nelson and Zadek (2000: 7), 'traditional power hierarchies are being replaced by a more complex, multi-relational balance of power, where citizens and companies are playing an active role in shaping socio-economic change and addressing problems that were previously the sole responsibility of government'.

As a result, the UN's recognition of a role for CS has been accentuated. Arguments in favour of more CSO involvement in global governance have emerged in part from pro-democracy movements working to allow citizens from across the world to 'have voice, input and political representation in international affairs, in parallel with and independently of their own governments' (Archibugi and Held, 1995: 13). Globalization and the growth in number and influence of transnational CS constituencies across a range of policy spheres have also encouraged thinking about the incorporation of CSOs into the workings of the UN. In 1998, Kofi Annan, then UN Secretary General, called for 'new approaches, attitudes, methods and responses' towards relations with civil society (UN, 1998).

In the health sector, GHPs raise a number of issues relevant to CS and GHG. One is that the global health landscape has become populated with ever more global institutions for CSOs to engage with and influence, presenting them with substantial logistical and financial challenges. Poor coordination and the dissipation of roles and responsibilities across so many different actors also obscure lines of authority and accountability within the GHG architecture, presenting another challenge for CS.

Yet, the emergence of GHPs also appears to have opened up the space for more direct CS participation in GHG. In one overview of 23 GHPs, out of a total of 298 board seats, 23 per cent and 5 per cent were occupied by academic and NGO representatives respectively (Buse and Harmer, 2007). The Global Fund has three out of 20 voting member seats allocated to NGOs on its board of governors (one for a developed country NGO, one for a developing country NGO and one for 'communities affected by the diseases'). While traditionally, CSOs have played an advocacy and/or watchdog role with respect to global health institutions, they now operate from within the formal structures of global health institutions, thereby strengthening the opportunity for CS actors to set policy and determine practice.

However, the overall impact of all this on GHG needs to be questioned. First of all, we need to consider if (and how) the voice of CS has changed as a result of being included or co-opted into the formal structures and systems of governance. Second, we need to consider the accompanying increase in the influence of big business (see Buse and Naylor in the previous chapter). In the analysis of 23 selected GHPs mentioned earlier, 23 per cent of all governing board seats were occupied by the private (corporate) sector (Buse and Harmer, 2007), and it has been argued that the public-private partnership paradigm has shifted the balance of power and influence between governments, CS and the corporate sector in favour of the corporate sector (Richter, 2003). According to the Transnational Research and Action Centre, 'new partnerships are leading down a slippery slope toward the partial privatization and commercialization of the UN system itself' (TRAC, 2000).

Linked to the new GHPs is another set of actors – private foundations. Foundations have helped to shape international health policy for several decades and have usually been viewed as one of several CS actors (see Owen et al., Chapter 11 below). However, the emergence of the Bill and Melinda Gates Foundation as a major funder of global health initiatives and institutions requires us to view it as an institution that 'governs' as much as another type of CSO (Global Health Watch, 2008a).

The total amount of cash paid out by the Gates Foundation for all its grants in 2007 was US$2.012 billion, of which US$1.22 billion (60.6 per cent) was spent on global health (Bill and Melinda Gates Foundation, 2007). Its grantees include most of the major GHPs, the World Health Organization (WHO), international health departments in major universities, such as Harvard and Johns Hopkins, global health policy think-tanks, such as the Centre for Global Development, NGOs, such as Action Aid, and public advocacy campaigns, such as the One Campaign in the United States (Global Health Watch, 2008a). It also has close links to the pharmaceutical corporate sector. The Gates Foundation's influence is thus far-reaching. In addition, it is not a passive funder – it has an active and assertive secretariat. The foundation thus highlights the need to differentiate between different types of CSOs in relation to their role and power with regards to GHG.

Indeed there are many different types of CSO, including formal or professionalized NGOs, universities and research organizations and think-tanks, professional associations and trade unions, faith-based organizations, consumer groups and organized social or peoples movements. Furthermore, CSOs reflect the wide political and economic disparities that define global CS more broadly, allowing a relatively small number of big NGOs, mostly based in Europe and North America, to dominate CS presence within and around global health institutions.

International NGOs (INGOs) such as Care International, Save the Children, Oxfam, World Vision and the International Planned Parenthood Federation are large, well staffed and well funded.[1] Many are so large and institutionalized that they have adopted corporate-type identities, structures and practices, competing with each other for funding, brand recognition and influence. Compared to NGOs from the south, northern-based NGOs have easier and less costly access to most global institutions, as well as greater opportunity to influence the powerful national governments with disproportionate influence over global governance institutions.[2]

The majority of the 2.7 billion people living on less than US$2 per day are thus hugely dependent on either relatively weak low-income country governments or on large northern-based international NGOs to act and speak on their behalf at the global level. The professionalized and well-funded corporate structures of many large international NGOs increasingly cut a sharp contrast with the living conditions and social movements of the global poor, raising questions about legitimacy and the commercialization of aid, poverty relief and global health.

It is also important to recognize that the distinction between CSOs, government and business can be false. CSOs can be established and funded to act as organs of both government and the corporate sector. For example, pharmaceutical companies fund consumer and treatment advocacy groups to lobby governments on their behalf (Ball et al., 2006; Marshall and Aldhous, 2006).

NGOs can also become overdependent on government aid funding. According to Stefano Prato of the Society for International Development, as a result of growing dependency on government grants, NGOs in the United States are increasingly being co-opted into supporting governmental policies and agendas (Prato, 2006). Even GHPs have helped establish CSOs to advocate on their behalf. For example, the Global Fund has helped create and support 'Friends of the GF' organizations in the United States, Europe and Africa.

CSOs that raise funding predominantly from broad-based membership subscriptions or public fundraising campaigns may have greater legitimacy in representing themselves as CSOs. Trade unions or professional associations also have claims of legitimacy, albeit from a narrower base. In contrast, funding from corporate donations, philanthropic foundations or government grants threatens to dilute legitimacy and weaken independence. In some instances, organizations effectively end up as contractors working for governments or other funding agencies, rather than as independent CSOs. The creation and funding of CSOs by both big business and governments has led some observers to distinguish PINGOs (public-interest NGOs), from BINGOs (business-interest NGOs) and GONGOs (government-organized NGOs).

The issue of legitimacy raises the question of how the aspirations, needs and voices of the poor and marginalized global majority are represented by CSOs, particularly by the large and influential international NGOs. How is the poor health, poverty and lack of access to health-care of the poor explained and understood? What solutions are offered and what actions are taken on their behalf? These questions reveal ideological, political and policy differences in the way CSOs interpret global health problems and choose to engage with GHG.

Sparke (forthcoming) distinguishes between and discusses three broad-brush economic discourses that relate to GHG, noting the context of a globalization that has shrunk the policy space of nation-states and curtailed social citizenship rights. These are 'market fundamentalism', 'market foster-care' and 'market failure'.

The first discourse represents the neo-liberal market fundamentalism that has undermined political citizenship through the corporatization of the public sphere, the marketization of service sectors and the monetization of politics. Sparke argues that this discourse calls for GHG to improve the health of the poor by furthering economic integration and liberalization, and by advocating market-based and private sector solutions to meet the expressed demand for health care by the poor.

The market foster-care discourse is described as a partial response to the deficiencies and shortcomings of market fundamentalism and calls for poor regions and populations to be served with critical health interventions that might enable them to function and participate more effectively within the current global economic system. Sparke argues that this approach has led to a well-meaning and ethical approach to the alleviation of suffering and to a 'verticalization' of health governance with targeted biomedical programmes as a practical means of lifting people out of 'poverty traps'.

The market failure discourse emphasizes the political and economic inequalities that underlie poor health, including their historical antecedents. Rather than highlighting 'natural' causes of poverty and poor health, it analyses how and why social inequalities are generated and reproduced by socio-economic and political forces (Navarro, 2002), or by what Farmer (2005) calls 'structural violence'. The appropriate response is for global health advocates to push for the ameliorating interventions of market foster-care, but also for a re-ordering of the global political economy.

Alternatively, Scholte (1999) describes three positions that can be adopted according to the prevailing order: 'conformists' uphold and reinforce existing norms, 'reformists' wish to correct flaws in existing regimes while leaving underlying social structures intact, and 'radicals' seek a comprehensive transformation of the social order. Whether CS actors seek to conform, reform or radically transform may be a question of tactics, or may reflect fundamental differences in politics and ideology. Some CSOs that conform to the existing political and economic order could be considered closer to northern governments and multinational corporations than they are to CSOs that seek radical change.

CSO differences may also be exhibited by different health policy orientations. For example, there are different views about the relative roles of hierarchies and markets within health-care organizations, or about the balance between vertical, disease-based approaches to health improvement and a 'horizontal' health systems approach (see Walt et al., Chapter 3 above). Many NGOs are not impartial to the outcomes of the debates and discussions that emanate from these policy tensions.

Crucially, differences in political and policy orientation are important in determining the ways in which CSOs with a pro-health and pro-development agenda might be able to engage with GHG, depending on the extent to which they agree with or support the dominant views of global health institutions. Five ways in which CSOs might engage with or impact upon GHG are as follows.

First, CSOs might participate within or alongside the decision-making structures of GHG institutions; they do this by advising or making recommendations to the governance or management structures of global institutions, often through formally constituted advisory or technical committees. Global health institutions may also consult informally with CSOs, perhaps drawing on the expertise and knowledge of academic institutions to inform their decision-making. And as described earlier, many GHPs have taken CS participation in governance a step further by incorporating CSOs into decision-making structures.[3]

Second, CSOs can influence global health institutions by lobbying and campaigning 'from the outside'. By operating outside the formal governance and management structures of global health institutions, they have greater freedom to express their views and opinions and are not burdened with the responsibility for achieving consensus with other actors. They are also freer to criticize, embarrass or shame global health institutions when required. An important part of effective lobbying and campaigning is the generation of knowledge and evidence, highlighting an important role for universities and research organizations.

Third, CSOs can influence GHG by improving the accountability of global health institutions through monitoring and evaluating their actions and policies, playing a watchdog role. The information generated may then feed into lobbying and campaigning activities. Global Health Watch, for example, publishes an 'alternative world health report' that includes an evaluation of the actions and policies of a number of global health institutions.[4] Social Watch, an international network informed by national citizens' groups, monitors the fulfilment of internationally agreed commitments on poverty eradication and equality. Aidspan, an NGO which provides a regular news service about the Global Fund, also comments on its performance. The Bretton Woods Project in the United Kingdom monitors and critiques the IMF and World Bank through a social justice lens. Medical journals such as the *Lancet* and the *British Medical Journal* also play a GHG role by explaining and reporting on global health matters, such as developments in global health financing and intellectual property rules affecting medicines.

Fourth, CSOs can engage with GHG by supporting fairer intergovernmental negotiations. Because the technical, political and economic capacity of developing country delegations within IGOs and other international forums is weak, CSOs can play an important role in providing support and technical assistance. For example, the expertise of the Third World Network has been used by some developing country governments to support their delegations at WTO negotiations. More recently, the Third World Network has provided legal and technical support to the Indonesian government during intergovernmental negotiations over the sharing of avian influenza viral material.

Finally, CSOs might engage with GHG by opposing or resisting global institutions. As described earlier, much progressive social change in the past has emerged from confrontational modes of action, including the championing of women's rights by the suffragettes in the UK, the civil rights movement in the United States, the street protests in 2000 in Cochabamba (Bolivia) to reverse a water privatization deal which threatened access to water for the

Table 10.1 The multiple dimensions and heterogeneity of CSOs

CSO dimensions	
Type	NGOs • Universities and research organizations • Professional associations • Trade unions • Faith-based organizations • Consumer groups and social movements • Private foundations
Base/location	North–south/high-income • Middle-income Low-income
Funding	Government • Private grants • Membership subscriptions
Political economy	Market fundamentalism • Market foster-care • Market failure
Orientation	Conformist • Reformist • Radical
Agenda	Pro-government • Pro-business • Pro-people
Health policy	Verticalist–horizontalist • Pro-market • Pro-hierarchy
Scope	Political economy • Social determinants of health • Health-care services
Mode of action	Participating in GHG • Lobbying and campaigning GHG institutions • Monitoring GHG • Opposing and resisting GHG

poorest households, and the resistance of indigenous communities to the theft or destruction of their ancestral lands. Other examples of opposition to global institutions have included various protests and challenges to the policies and structures of 'unfair globalization' at meetings of the G8, the World Economic Forum and the World Trade Organization.

These modes of action tend to belong to CSOs that oppose and challenge the current global health and development orthodoxy, calling for transformation of the governance architecture rather than conforming to or advocating for incremental reform. In addition, such actions tend not to be directed at global institutions with specific health or development mandates, but at the institutions responsible for setting economic or trade policy, or which have fundamental influence over the structural determinants of health in low-income countries.

Any discussion of the role and influence of CSOs on GHG requires careful navigation through a landscape populated by a diverse range of actors and institutions with different and sometimes overlapping powers, roles and functions. CSOs come in different shapes and sizes; they mirror the social and economic disparities that exist between countries and population groups and they exhibit a wide range of agendas, as well as political and policy views. Some CSOs are incorporated in the governance and management structures of global health institutions; others are significant global health institutions in their own right. The distinction between CSOs, governments and businesses may also be misleading.

CSOs are not a homogeneous group of pro-justice, pro-development or pro-health actors – some may be counterposed to notions of fairness or equitable development. But even within the pro-health and pro-development arena, there are differences between CSOs that may need to be considered when assessing the way in which they engage with GHG. The various dimensions of CSOs (as summarized in Table 10.1) suggest the need for a more nuanced and critical approach to the involvement and analysis of CS in GHG.

The World Health Organization, CSOs and GHG

The World Health Organization is the leading multilateral agency charged with promoting and protecting health at the global level. Although there are many other global health institutions, the WHO is particularly important.

As a specialized agency of the UN and according to its constitution, the WHO is mandated to act as the directing and coordinating authority on international health work. As such, its member states can determine legally-binding international conventions, agreements and regulations with respect to global health matters. Its mandate is broad and comprehensive, in contrast to other global health institutions that focus on specific diseases (for example, the Global Fund and Roll Back Malaria), on specific services or products (for example, GAVI Alliance), or on particular population groups (for example, UNICEF). The WHO can be described as a ministry of health at the global level. Given the degree and extent of globalization, this calls for public interest in and scrutiny of WHO.

The WHO is also important because it represents a progressive and aspirational vision of health and international cooperation as illustrated by the principles governing its constitution (WHO, 2006) and by the 1978 Alma Ata Declaration (WHO/UNICEF, 1978). For example, Article 2 of the Alma Ata Declaration boldly states that 'the existing gross inequality in the health status of the people particularly between developed and developing countries as well as within countries is politically, socially and economically unacceptable', while Article 3 calls for a new international economic order for the purpose of promoting and protecting health. These historic features of WHO are important because they provide a counterbalance to the current neo-liberal, fragmented and selective or verticalized approaches to health that have characterized GHG since the 1980s (Global Health Watch, 2005).

There are many examples of CSOs working with or through WHO structures and systems to achieve progressive change around particular issues. Importantly, CSOs, including the Christian Medical Association of the World Council of Churches, were instrumental in the development of the Alma Ata Declaration (Cueto, 2004). CSOs have also protected and supported the WHO's public health and social justice mission from buckling under pressure or being constrained by corporate and commercial interests. The critical interaction between health advocates from civil society and the WHO is illustrated in relation to medicines, breast-milk substitutes and tobacco (see Boxes 10.1, 10.2 and 10.3).

Box 10.1   The struggle for essential medicines, rational prescribing and affordable prices

The pharmaceutical sector has formed a critical battleground between competing visions of health and between different interest groups. It provides particular insight into the tensions and balance of power between public health advocates and the corporate sector.

In 1978, the Alma Ata Declaration identified the provision of 'essential medicines' as one of the key elements of Primary Health Care (PHC). The WHO's subsequent essential medicines programme was inevitably identified by the pharmaceutical sector as a threat to its core business of selling medicines for as large a profit as possible. Rational prescribing and a regulated market for the supply of medicines were not in their interest. As explained by Laing et al. (2003), CSOs were an important counterbalance to the opposition of the pharmaceutical sector, for example, in lobbying for political support for WHO's work and for implementation of essential medicines policies at the national level. A critical player was Health Action International (HAI) which was formed in 1981 when about 50 NGOs met in Geneva to discuss the WHO's medicines policies.

Since the 1980s, the corporate agenda promoting a liberalized and minimally regulated pharmaceutical sector has held sway over the agenda promoting a rational and cost-effective PHC approach to the use of medicines. In many countries, the sale and use of medicines are largely commercialized and poorly regulated (one result of which is growing antibiotic resistance).

HAI continues to work with and through the WHO. In 2004, for example, it commenced work with the WHO on an initiative to ensure improved education and information for medical and pharmacy students about drug promotion. Although inadequate regulation of prescription, advertising, sale and use of medicines suggests that stronger governance is required at both the global and national levels, the public-private paradigm and the establishment of close working relationships with pharmaceutical companies, coupled with the existence of vocal pharma-funded treatment advocacy groups, has constrained the WHO's ability to push for stronger regulatory frameworks.

At the same time that countries have been struggling to implement effective essential medicines policies and to ensure rational prescribing and use, almost by stealth the research, development and manufacture of medicines became subsumed under the auspices of the WTO and the Agreement on Trade-Related Aspects of Intellectual Property Rights (TRIPS). Rules that ultimately determine the price of medicines were constructed under a trade-related regime which emphasized commercial interests rather than public health or social priorities. A new front in the conflict between public needs and pharmaceutical corporate interests developed, revealing again the interplay between the WHO, governments, the private sector and CSOs in determining the effectiveness of GHG.

A critical juncture occurred in 1997 when South Africa's new Medicines Act, designed to allow parallel importing and compulsory licensing, was challenged by US pharmaceutical companies. Thirty-seven companies sued the South African government whilst the US government put pressure on South Africa to repeal the act. At the same time, pharmaceutical companies were pressing industrialized country governments to oppose a World Health Assembly (WHA) resolution calling for public health to take primacy in pharmaceutical policies.

Adverse publicity eventually forced the drug companies to withdraw their legal action against the South African government and to pay legal bills. And in 2001, governments pledged their agreement to the Doha Declaration, which allowed developing countries to employ a number of flexibilities within the TRIPS Agreement to enable them to safeguard public health needs. CSOs played an instrumental role.

The Treatment Action Campaign and the Aids Law Project, two South African CSOs, supported the South African government and helped dismantle the legal arguments of the pharmaceutical companies. NGOs, such as CPTech, Health Action International and Médecins Sans Frontières, were instrumental in educating developing country government officials about TRIPS and the negative effects of US and EU trade policies, thereby strengthening their ability to negotiate during the Doha round of trade talks. Street-level campaigns and negative media coverage of the large profits being made by drug companies also helped turn public opinion away from the arguments of the pharmaceutical companies.

As with the campaign for rational prescribing and essential medicines, the struggle to promote equitable improvements in health over the commercial interests of pharmaceutical corporations continues. Bureaucratic barriers within the WTO and the threat of economic sanctions prevent many low-income country governments from making use of the Doha Declaration, while new regional and bilateral trade agreements are establishing even more stringent intellectual property standards and weaker regulatory frameworks through what are called TRIP-Plus agreements (see Wogart et al., Chapter 7).

A number of CSOs have also been working to establish a new international treaty for pharmaceutical research and development. This has since been adopted in part in a WHA resolution (59.24) on a 'Global Framework on Essential Health R&D' in 2006. The resolution, initially sponsored by the Brazilian and Kenyan governments, gained momentum within WHO and its member states following lobbying by several NGOs and after a letter was sent to the WHO's director general signed by more than 200 scientists and European parliamentarians (demonstrating again the role of CS actors in buttressing the work and mandate of the WHO). Meanwhile, corporate social responsibility programmes and the funding of think-tanks and NGOs to conduct public campaigns in favour of the existing intellectual property regimes, serves to re-emphasize the point that the key distinction is not so much between CSOs and multinationals, as it is between those supporting the rights and needs of people and those supporting the interests of big business.

The case studies in Boxes 10.1–10.3 illustrate the importance of both the WHO and of CSOs in promoting global health, and the important role of the WHO as a global 'convener' of stakeholders and constituencies. They also illustrate the need for strong and robust approaches to health promotion to overcome powerful vested commercial interests. The governance of the WHO and the ability of its secretariat to hold strong and independent positions on public health, equity and social justice are, not surprisingly, important concerns for many CSOs.

The WHO's primary governing body is the World Health Assembly (WHA), composed of representatives from its 193 member states, which meets once a year. An executive board (EB) consisting of 34 member state representatives meets at least twice a year to give effect to the decisions of the WHA. It also prepares the agenda for the WHA, reviews the proposed programme budget for the WHO, advises on questions of a constitutional and regulatory nature and submits proposals on its own initiative.

In principle, the WHA is governed on the basis of 'one state, one vote'. In practice, most decisions are agreed by consensus and presented as recommendations (that is, resolutions). Moreover, important and key decisions about policy and priority-setting are made elsewhere, such as by the EB and within the secretariat, and by individual member states, especially through their provision of earmarked funding for designated purposes.

In contrast to other global health institutions (for example, UNAIDS and the Global Fund), CSOs do not have any formal representation within WHO's governing structures. However, the WHO does consult and cooperate with various CSOs in carrying out its work; including the active participation of civil society in many technical meetings. Policies and procedures to guide WHO's relations with NGOs are found in four key texts: the WHO Constitution, the Rules of Procedure of the WHA, the Rules of Procedure of the Executive Board (EB) and the 'Principles governing relations between the WHO and NGOs' (WHA Resolution 40.25). Among other things, these

> **Box 10.2 The campaign to protect breastfeeding**
>
> The campaign against the unethical and deadly promotion of breast-milk substitutes by multinational companies also exemplifies the role of CSOs in supporting WHO (and UNICEF) in establishing policies, norms and guidelines that will protect the health of the poor.
>
> The establishment of bottle-feeding cultures is embedded in the history of the development and promotion of industrial 'replacement' products. Since the late nineteenth century, Nestlé, the world's largest producer of infant formulas, has undermined breastfeeding through social marketing campaigns and by co-opting health professionals to promote breast-milk substitutes. Initially, a lack of knowledge about the poor nutritional value of artificial milk and the protective immunological properties of breast-milk created a more accepting environment for artificial feeding. By the 1970s it was estimated that only 20 per cent of Kenyan babies and 6 per cent of Malaysian babies were predominantly breastfed (WABA, 2006).
>
> When it became recognized that artificial feeding was both harmful, and was being promoted in ways that were unethical, a civil society campaign led by the International Baby Food Action Network (IBFAN) successfully enabled WHO and UNICEF to establish the International Code of Marketing of Breast-milk Substitutes. An important role played by CSOs was conducting the scientific research required to measure and describe the harmful effects of infant formula feeding (Chetley, 1986).
>
> Subsequently, a number of additional WHA resolutions have been adopted to help close some of the loopholes in the code that were exploited by the baby food industry. For example, resolutions have been passed to stop the practice of free or low-priced breast-milk substitutes being given to health facilities and to declare that the infant food industry should not be involved in infant nutrition programme implementation.
>
> IBFAN, which now has a presence in over 100 countries, continues to be at the forefront of efforts to protect infant health from commercial interests. Among its ongoing activities are the monitoring of compliance to the International Code of Marketing of Breast-milk Substitutes and subsequent WHA resolutions at the country level, providing public education on the risks of artificial feeding and commercial feeding products, and supporting and providing health worker training for the implementation of the UNICEF/WHO Baby Friendly Hospital Initiative.

documents allow NGOs to enter into 'official relations' with the WHO once they have been accredited, giving them the right to attend the WHA and EB, and to petition the director general to table, at his/her discretion, resolutions and items for discussion at the EB.

Box 10.3   The struggle to contain tobacco consumption

When the tobacco industry shifted its attention to developing countries in response to declining sales in industrialized countries, alarm bells rang for public health advocates across the world. In 1999, the WHA instructed the WHO Secretariat to explore ways to protect developing countries from the public health threat of increasing tobacco consumption.

A technical working group and intergovernmental negotiating body were rapidly established to propose a Framework Convention on Tobacco Control (FCTC). A process, including public hearings, was put in place. NGOs not in official relations with WHO were put through a 'special fast-track' procedure to allow them to participate in the process. After six sessions of the negotiating body, the final text of the FCTC was agreed and adopted by the WHA in 2003.

While the establishment of the FCTC within four years gives the impression of smooth and rapid progress, final agreement was only reached after intense diplomatic manoeuvring, acrimonious negotiations and compromise. The tobacco industry strongly resisted a comprehensive convention and opposed limitations on free trade, smoking bans in public areas that fail to provide smoking areas, and 'shock' images on health warnings. It lobbied receptive governments (particularly the USA, Japan and Germany) to resist making the convention legally binding, a consequence of which is that few of the convention's measures are obligatory (Hammond and Assunta, 2003).

Nonetheless, the establishment of the FCTC is considered a success and one that demonstrates again the role of CSOs in GHG. It was academics, with the support of the American Public Health Association, who proposed the idea that WHO utilize its constitutional authority to develop international law to advance global public health (Roemer et al., 2005). NGOs also played a key role during the formal negotiating sessions by, for example, organizing issue briefings for delegates, discouraging negotiators from embracing 'feel good' measures favoured by the tobacco industry, and meting out a daily 'dirty ashtray award' to shame recalcitrant countries.

More than 180 NGOs from over 70 countries grouped under the umbrella of the Framework Convention Alliance. The World Federation of Public Health Associations (WFPHA), with over 70 national associations as members (half from low- and middle-income countries), gave professional and scientific credibility to the civil society coalition. With the Canadian Public Health Association and the Swiss Society of Preventive Medicine taking the lead, the WFPHA established partnerships with the Centres for Disease Control and Prevention and WHO's Global Tobacco Initiative to mobilize support for the convention.

> Building on expanding global access to the internet, national experiences were exchanged and advocacy strategies shared across borders and languages. By participating in a global campaign, emerging and struggling national public health associations were also accorded scientific and political protection to negotiate with their own governments and to carry out public education campaigns against tobacco products. The national associations of the WFPHA were united as never before, and a number were able to assist their ministries of health to overcome political obstacles within government as a whole to the ratification of the convention.

In January 2008 there were 186 accredited NGOs in official relations with the WHO (2008), but with varying degrees of involvement. According to a study conducted in 2002, an average of 75 NGOs, involving 330 persons, attended meetings of the WHA between 1998 and 2002 and a quarter of accredited NGOs attend EB meetings (Lanord, 2002). However, the true number of CSOs participating at the WHA is larger because some NGOs with official relations status act as umbrella organizations for a those without.

There are a number of perceived deficiencies with the current arrangements for official or formal engagement with WHO by CSOs. First, the procedure for being accredited with official relations status has been described as complicated, bureaucratic and demanding (WHO, 2004; Lanord, 2002). Second, although there is a requirement that CSOs are not commercial or profit-making, there is no requirement for them publicly to declare any connections to businesses (WHO, 2002). Third, once accredited, the potential for CSOs to intervene during the EB and WHA remains limited. For example, although CSOs are permitted to make official statements at these meetings, the latter must be pre-submitted (ostensibly for translation purposes). CSOs are also allowed to submit memoranda, but there is no obligation on the part of the governing bodies to respond formally. Finally, given the cost of travel to and accommodation in Geneva, CS participation is mostly limited to well-resourced NGOs from the north (Lanord, 2002).

In recognition of these deficiencies, and following a review of WHO's relations with NGOs, new guidelines to 'strengthen mutually beneficial relations at global, regional and national levels' between NGOs and WHO were drafted (WHO, 2004). However, the proposed guidelines do not confer significant new powers to accredited CSOs. Furthermore, at the 2004 WHA, consideration of the new guidelines was postponed to give the director general more time to consult all interested parties with a view to reaching consensus on the precise terms of the resolution which would then be resubmitted to the WHA.

However, as illustrated by the earlier case studies, it should be noted that many CSOs contribute to the work of the WHO through informal relations and by taking part in various technical working groups and committees convened by the WHO. An inventory in 2001 revealed that there were 240 NGOs in informal relations with the WHO at headquarters level (Lanord, 2002). Many more NGOs have working relationships with the WHO at regional and country levels.

On the whole, CSOs adopt non-confrontational modes of engagement with the WHO. The organization's mission to improve health is essentially compatible with that of most CSOs concerned with social development and equitable health improvement. However, there are two reasons why CSOs may also need to monitor and challenge the WHO. First, WHO could be influenced by external actors and donors in ways that are regressive. Second, it could find itself constrained by external actors or conditions that inhibit its ability to function effectively.

As far as the first reason is concerned, there are three dangers to consider. The first is that the WHO may be disproportionately influenced by the richer, industrialized countries. The second is undue influence by the corporate sector. The third is that CS engagement itself may be dominated by a small number of elite CSOs.

The threat of WHO being pushed and pulled to serve the political and economic interests of the more powerful member states has been illustrated numerous times by pressure placed on the organization – by the United States in particular – to minimize its work on the impact of trade policy on health (Global Health Watch, 2008b) and weaken its policy recommendations on diet and nutrition (see Stuckler et al., Chapter 13 below).

The danger of undue corporate and commercial influence has become particularly acute following the paradigm shift towards global governance through public-private partnerships (see Buse and Harmer, Chapter 12 below). Two reasons can be hypothesized for the corporate sector wanting to engage with GHG. The first is to protect and expand commercial interests within the health-care sector (for example, by increasing pharmaceutical sales or by expanding market control within health systems). The second is to protect corporate interests from public health regulations that might threaten profit margins. This was the basis for the corporate sector putting pressure on the WHO to water down its clinical and regulatory guidelines on diet and nutrition.

The third danger is that CS engagement with WHO may fail to represent the needs and interests of the poor. As described earlier, many southern-based CSOs lack the capacity or resources to engage with GHG. There is a risk that CS representation may be over concentrated amongst a few northern-based NGOs. There is also a risk that a disproportionate number of these CSOs may mirror the dominant verticalized and disease-based approach to global health, as opposed to a more comprehensive and holistic approach to health and development; or that they may over-represent conservative, non-radical approaches to global health and global governance.

As far as the second reason is concerned, a number of external factors inhibit the WHO in carrying out its mandate. The crowded and poorly coordinated global health landscape, populated with new actors with overlapping mandates and competing interests, challenges and potentially undermines the WHO's authority. Moreover, the funding arrangements for WHO have evolved over the recent past in such a way as to make it more donor-driven.

Because of the three dangers described above, some CSOs see a need both to challenge the WHO and to support it. It needs to be challenged when it opens itself to inappropriate pressure and influence and when it fails to live up to the full breadth of its constitutional mandate and to the principles of the Alma Ata Declaration. Yet it also needs to be supported and strengthened to fulfil its mandate as the leading multilateral agency charged with the equitable promotion of health. One example of a CSO that both challenges and supports the WHO is the People's Health Movement (see Box 10.4).

There are a number of issues for CSOs to consider with regard to the WHO and GHG. First is the adequacy of the WHO's formal governance systems in allowing appropriate and equitable CS participation. The proposed new guidelines on relations with NGOs, which were drafted in 2004, have remained in limbo following the decision to allow time for more consultation. Previous experience shows that CSOs can work with and through the WHO to shape international health policy under existing arrangements – would more formal CS participation on the governance structures of WHO improve global health governance?

The second issue concerns the composition and mix of CSOs that do engage with WHO. To what extent do they represent global civil society? What is the balance between radical and conservative CSOs, or between comprehensive and vertical/selective perspectives? How significant are the perspectives of 'market fundamentalism' or 'market foster-care' compared to 'market failure'? These questions may require further research and analysis if they are to be adequately answered.

A third issue concerns the need for CS to respond to the WHO's own constraints. The WHO needs to be better funded; it needs to be able to ensure complete independence from corporate influence; it needs to be protected from being bullied by its major donors; and it needs to regain some of the public health authority that it has lost to other institutions, including international financial and trade institutions such as the IMF, the World Bank and the World Trade Organization. Although it is possible to debate whether or not these institutions are part of the problem, part of the solution, or even the cause of continued widespread impoverishment and high premature mortality across the world, few would disagree with the assertion that these institutions have failed effectively to help translate an era of unprecedented wealth creation and technological development into sustainable and equitable health improvement. The WHO is usually a target for NGO lobbying and advocacy, but it also needs to be a 'cause' for advocacy.

> **Box 10.4   The People's Health Movement and WHO**
>
> The People's Health Movement (PHM) is a network of CSOs established to promote the vision and principles of the Alma Ata Declaration. It was established following a 'People's Health Assembly' in December 2000 in Bangladesh which was attended by 1454 health professionals and activists from 92 countries. The assembly had been called to protest the world's failure to achieve 'Health for All by the Year 2000'. It was felt that the World Health Assembly was failing to hear the voices of the poor and that the WHO had lost its way.
>
> The WHO itself was conspicuous at the assembly by its absence. It was left to the acting country representative in Bangladesh, three staff members who attended in their personal capacity and a director general emeritus (Dr Halfdan Mahler) to represent WHO. (UNICEF showed even less interest in attending the Assembly and had no representation at all, despite its central role during the Alma Ata Conference.)
>
> However, four months after the assembly, events were organized at the WHO headquarters to allow the discussions of the assembly to be presented and the PHM to express its disappointment over the WHO's lack of interest. This resulted in an invitation to the PHM to present the People's Health Charter (an outcome of the assembly) and the announcement that WHO would establish a 'Civil Society Initiative'.
>
> Since then, the PHM has continued to engage with the WHO. Former director general, Dr Lee Jong-wook, invited the PHM to be the voice of the marginalized and to remind WHO of its need to listen to that voice, stating: 'grassroots movements are enormously important, especially in the health field. These movements bring the views, feelings, and expressions of those who really know. It seems almost hypocritical for WHO people here in Geneva to be talking about poverty – here, as we pay $2 for a cup of coffee, while millions struggle to survive and sustain their families on $1 a day. For this very reason, we urgently need your input. We need to hear the voices of the communities you represent. Some of you may initially have felt powerless. But by uniting your forces, you have reached a critical mass with this People's Health Movement. It is vital for WHO to listen to you and your communities' (People's Health Movement, 2003).

Finally, and cutting across the issues above, how should WHO tackle the underlying social, political and global determinants of ill-health? Since the Alma Ata Declaration, the WHO has retreated from the broader developmental agenda of 'Health for All'. However, in 2008, the Commission on the Social Determinants of Health released its report, highlighting the underlying social and economic factors leading to ill-health and inequalities within and between countries. Many CSOs see the commission as a potential platform from which the WHO could launch stronger measures on the political, economic and social causes of poverty and widening health inequalities.

Conclusions

This chapter makes a number of interconnected points. The first is the need to recognize the importance and diverse roles of CSOs in promoting global health. CSOs have played critical roles in advancing a variety of international health agendas, often helping to overcome indifference or resistance from vested interests. A transnational 'movement' of progressive health professionals can help to promote universal rights to health and health-care. By cutting across national, religious, racial and political boundaries and acting as a global community of health professionals, not only can the concept of global civil society be brought to life, but pressure can be brought upon decision-makers and other levers of power to act towards meeting a global health agenda.

However, the chapter also highlights the fact that the structures and systems of GHG are in themselves issues of concern for CS. There is a need for global health institutions to be effective but also accountable to the public. Presently, the way global health institutions are governed and coordinated leaves much to be desired and requires closer CS attention. In particular, this chapter has highlighted the importance of supporting the WHO's ability to fulfil its constitutional mandate and to live up to its values and principles.

The chapter also points up the contested and complex nature of 'civil society'. In many instances, the boundary between CSOs, businesses and governments is so blurred and porous as to be false. There are many different CS constituencies with conflicting interests and agendas, not to mention different types of CSOs. Assessing the role and modes of action of CSOs within GHG is highly dependent on political and policy perspectives. Implicit in the discussion about the diversity of CSOs is an argument for more empowerment and capacity development of CSOs in the south, for greater representation of voices advocating radical change and for greater attention to be paid to the structural determinants of health.

Notes

1. Save the Children Alliance US and UK spent US$361.2 million and £139.9 million respectively in fiscal year 2007. Care International USA and Oxfam Great Britain spent US$608 and £213.2 respectively in the same year. By contrast, few south-based NGOs have significant spending power, nor a similar global reach to the large INGOs. Perhaps one slight exception is Amref, which has an annual budget of about US$30 million and which carries out a range of projects and activities in eastern and southern Africa. It also has offices in Austria, Canada, Denmark, France,

Germany, Holland, Italy, Monaco, Spain, Sweden, the UK and the USA that focus on fundraising and some advocacy.
2. The dominance of English as the language of international communication provides a further advantage to certain NGOs. The north-south imbalance between NGOs is mirrored elsewhere. US and European university-based departments of international health can be bigger and better resourced than the entire medical and population health faculties of universities in low-income countries.
3. CSOs can also support more operational GHG functions. For example, the ability and willingness of research institutions from across the world to work together helped WHO come up with a standardized case definition and diagnostic test for Severe Acute Respiratory Syndrome which in turn helped prevent the further spread of the disease. The Global Outbreak Alert and Response Network, a collaboration of various institutions from across the world, provides a platform for ongoing CSO support and involvement.
4. The first report included chapters on WHO, UNICEF and the World Bank, while the second includes chapters on the Gates Foundation, WHO, the World Bank and the Global Fund.

References

Anheier, H., M. Glasius and M. Kaldor, 'Introducing Global Society', in H. Anheier, M. Glasius and M. Kaldor (eds), *Global Civil Society* (New York: Oxford University Press, 2001), pp. 3–22.

Archibugi, D. and D. Held, 'Introduction', in D. Archibugi and D. Held (eds), *Cosmopolitan Democracy* (Cambridge: Polity Press, 1995).

Ball, D.E., K. Tisocki and A. Herxheimer, 'Advertising and Disclosure of Funding on Patient Organisation Websites: a Cross-sectional Survey', *BMC Public Health*, 6 (2006): 201.

Bill and Melinda Gates Foundation, Annual Report 2007, http://www.gatesfoundation.org/nr/public/media/annualreports/annualreport07/AR2007/GrantsPaid.html (accessed 13 February 2009).

Buse, K. and A. Harmer, 'Seven Habits of Highly Effective Public-Private Health Partnerships: Practice and Potential', *Social Science and Medicine*, 64(2) (2007): 259–71.

Buse, K. and G. Walt, 'Global Public-Private Partnerships: Part II – What are the Health Issues for Global Governance?' *Bulletin of the World Health Organization*, 78(5) (2000): 699–709.

Chetley, A., *The Politics of Baby Food: a Successful Challenge to International Marketing Strategy* (New York: St Martin's Press, 1986).

Commission on the Social Determinants of Health, *Closing the Gap in a Generation: Health Equity through Action on the Social Determinants of Health* (Geneva: World Health Organization, 2008),

Cueto, M., 'The ORIGINS of Primary Health Care and SELECTIVE Primary Health Care', *American Journal of Public Health*, 94(11) (2004): 1864–74.

Edwards, M., 'Civil Society and Global Governance', paper presented at 'On the Threshold – the United Nations and Global Governance in the New Millennium', 19–21 January 2000, United Nations University, Tokyo, http://www.unu.edu/millennium/edwards.pdf (accessed 4 July 2008).

Farmer, P., *Pathologies of Power: Health, Human Rights, and the New War on the Poor* (Berkeley: University of California Press, 2005).

Global Health Watch, 'The World Health Organisation', in *Global Health Watch, 2005–2006* (London: Zed Books, 2005).
Global Health Watch, 'The Gates Foundation', in D. McCoy, D. Sanders and A. Ntuli (eds), *Global Health Watch 2* (London: Zed Books, 2008a).
Global Health Watch, 'United States Foreign Assistance and Health Related Interventions', in D. McCoy, D. Sanders and A. Ntuli (eds), *Global Health Watch 2* (London: Zed Books, 2008b).
Hammond, R. and M. Assunta, 'The Framework Convention on Tobacco Control: Promising Start, Uncertain Future', *Tobacco Control*, 12 (2003): 241–2.
Kaul, I., 'Exploring the Space between Markets and States: Global Public-Private Partnerships', in I. Kaul and P. Conceição (eds), *The New Public Finance: Responding to Global Challenges* (New York: Oxford University Press, 2006), pp. 91–140.
Laing, R., B. Waning, A. Gray, N. Ford and E. Hoen, '25 Years of the WHO Essential Medicines Lists: Progress and Challenges', *Lancet*, 361 (2003): 1723–29.
Lanord, C., 'A Study of WHO's Official Relations System with NGOs', WHO, Geneva, CSI/2002/WP4, 2002, http://www.who.int/civilsociety/documents/en/study.pdf (accessed 4 July 2008)
Marshall, J. and P. Aldhous, 'Patient Groups Swallowing the Best Advice?', *New Scientist*, 28 (2006): 19–22.
Navarro, V., 'Introduction', in V. Navarro (ed.), *The Political Economy of Social Inequalities: Consequences for Health and Quality of Life* (Amityville: Baywood Publishing Company, 2002), pp. 1–9.
Nelson, J. and S. Zadek, *Partnership Alchemy: New Social Partnerships in Europe* (Copenhagen: The Copenhagen Centre, 2000).
O'Brien, R., 'Complex Multilateralism: the Global Economic Institutions and Global Social Movements Nexus', paper presented at conference on 'Non-State Actors and Authority in the Global System', University of Warwick, 1 November 1997.
People's Health Movement, Notes of meeting between PHM and Dr J.W. Lee, 2003.
Prato, S., 'Funding NGOs: Making Good the Democratic Deficit. Interview with Stefano Prato', *International Development*, 49 (2) (2006): 11–14.
Richter, J., '"We the Peoples" or "We the Corporations"? Critical Reflections on UN-business "partnerships"', IBFAN-GIFA, Geneva, 2003, http://www.ibfan.org/site2005/abm/paginas/articles/arch_art/393-1.pdf (accessed 4 July 2008).
Roemer, R., A. Taylor and J. Lariviere, 'Origins of the WHO Framework Convention on Tobacco Control', *American Journal of Public Health*, 95(6) (2005): 936–8.
Scholte, J.A., 'Global Civil Society: Changing the World?' CSGR Working Paper no. 31, Centre for the Study of Globalisation and Regionalisation, University of Warwick, May 1999, http://www2.warwick.ac.uk/fac/soc/csgr/research/workingpapers/1999/wp3199.pdf (accessed 4 July 2008).
Sikkink, K. and J. Smith, 'Infrastructures for Change: Transnational Organizations, 1953–93', in S. Khagram, J. Riker and K. Sikkink (eds), *Restructuring World Politics: Transnational Social Movements, Networks and Norms* (Minneapolis: University of Minnesota Press, 2002), pp. 24–45.
Sparke, M., 'Unpacking Economism and Remapping the Terrain of Global Health', in O. Williams and A. Kay (eds), *Global Health Governance: Crisis, Institutions and Political Economy* (Basingstoke: Palgrave Macmillan, forthcoming), see http://faculty.washington.edu/sparke/GH.pdf (accessed 15 December 2008).
Transnational Resource and Action Center, 'Tangled up in Blue: Corporate Partnerships at the United Nations', TRAC, 2000, http://s3.amazonaws.com/corpwatch.org/downloads/tangled.pdf (accessed 4 July 2008).

United Nations, 'Arrangements and Practices for the Interaction of Non-Governmental Organizations in all Activities of the United Nations System', report of the Secretary-General (Sorenson Report), United Nations, New York, 1998.

United Nations Development Program, 'Governance for Sustainable Human Development', UNDP Policy Document, UNDP, New York, 1997.

United Nations Development Program, 'Deepening Democracy in a Fragmented World', *Human Development Report* (Oxford: Oxford University Press, 2002).

Utting, P., 'UN-Business Partnerships: Whose Agenda Counts?' paper presented at seminar on 'Partnerships for Development or Privatization of the Multilateral System?' organized by the North-South Coalition, Oslo, Norway, December 2000, http://www.unrisd.org/unrisd/website/document.nsf/d2a23ad2d50cb2a280256eb300385855/a687857bd5e36114c1256c3600434b5f/$FILE/utting.pdf (accessed 4 July 2008).

WHO, Constitution of the World Health Organization, 'Basic Documents', forty-fifth edition, Supplement, October 2006, http://www.who.int/governance/eb/who_constitution_en.pdf (accessed 4 July 2008).

WHO/Unicef, 'Declaration of Alma Ata', drafted at the International Conference on Primary Health Care, 1978, WHO, http://www.who.int/hpr/NPH/docs/declaration_almaata.pdf (accessed 4 July 2008).

World Alliance for Breastfeeding Action (WABA), 'Gender, Child Survival and HIV/AIDS: from Evidence to Policy', Joint Statement from the conference at York University, Toronto, Canada, 2006, http://www.waba.org.my/hiv/conference2006.html (accessed 4 July 2008).

World Health Organization, 'WHO's Interactions with Civil Society and Nongovernmental Organizations', WHO, Geneva, CSI/2002/WP6, 2002.

World Health Organization, 'Policy for Relations with NGOs', note by Director-General, World Health Assembly document, A57/32, Provisional Agenda Item 21, Geneva, 2004, http://www.who.int/gb/ebwha/pdffiles/WHA 57/A5732-en.pdf (accessed 4 July 2008).

11
The Role of Foundations in Global Governance for Health

John Wyn Owen, Graham Lister and Sally Stansfield

Introduction

The *Financial Times* reported on 28 June 2006 that 'there was a mood of reverence in the New York Public library as the world's two wealthiest men met to announce a landmark development in charitable giving'. At that moment, Warren Buffett's donation of shares worth US$31 billion nearly doubled the resources of the Bill and Melinda Gates Foundation. Furthermore, Bill Gates pledged to add another US$50 billion to what was already the largest endowment in history. Much of this money will be spent on health, poverty alleviation and increasing access to technology in developing countries.

The Gates and Buffett endowment is of course still less in total than the annual amount of official development assistance provided by governments (directly or through official bodies such as the World Bank and the World Health Organization), which amounted to US$106 billion in 2005 for all sectors. Foundations, however, have greater freedom than official aid channels to pursue innovative solutions to development issues, they can address areas neglected by governments and mobilize civil society and business partners to achieve long-term aims free of short-term political pressures. For these reasons foundations are increasingly important players in the changing landscape of global governance.

This chapter examines the past, present and potential role of foundations in global governance, an area largely overlooked until recent publicity highlighted the role of private philanthropy in addressing global challenges. It will examine the characteristics of foundations and the ways in which they are responding to global challenges. Drawing largely on the experience of European foundations, it will discuss policy issues for the future role of foundations and global governance and finally examine responses to global health issues as an example of the potential for foundation partnership action.

Global governance

Rosenau's (1995) conception of global governance as a system of rules, norms and decision-making structures and organizations which brings order to cooperation with transnational repercussions is a useful starting point for examining the role of foundations in the global arena. In the past, the international system was founded on the written and unwritten assumptions of international relations between states formalized in the 1944 Bretton Woods and San Francisco agreements, which established the institutional and financial framework for the rise of global governance.

In a globalizing world, states are not the only actors in global governance; the concept must now apply to intergovernmental organizations and less formal associations of nation-states (such as the G8), multinational companies, non-governmental organizations (NGOs), civil society movements including foundations and others who cooperate across national borders. It is also apparent that regional organizations of states, such as the European Union and the African Union (including the New Partnership for Africa's Development), are an increasingly important focus for the development of policy in relation to global issues. There are now many different organizations and interfaces between them that are relevant to global governance and different rules and assumptions may apply in each context.

In a 2005 report from the Directorate General for Research, the European Union (European Commission, DGR, 2005) claimed that foundations have a unique role in modern society as private entities serving public goals. The growing importance of foundations must be understood in the context of social and political change in a world in which the state is no longer the only guardian of the public interest. Foundations, the report argues, have an increasingly crucial role in promoting public benefit and global public goods. This EU perspective is reflected in the view expressed in a US Council on Foundations report of 2005 which states that 'international charitable work fills critical gaps in the global socioeconomic infrastructure ... Without international charity more people in the world would live in poverty ... The Rockefeller Foundation, for example, was established in 1913 with a mandate "to promote the well-being of mankind throughout the world"' (2005: 2). The Rockefeller Foundation played a key role in the establishment of the League of Nations Health Organization – the forerunner to the World Health Organization – as well as in the establishment of European schools of public health (see Berridge et al., Chapter 2 above).

In the past, foundations usually acted independently of governments, often in partnership with other organizations, to run or fund projects and stimulate national or international collaboration. A number of foundations are increasingly focused on what goes on beyond their national boundaries, with partnerships and work programmes having global and regional remits.

In Europe we can see the emergence of a more global role for foundations: for example, in the Netherlands 31 per cent of foundations are active at the international level and in Belgium 13 per cent of foundations' expenditure is abroad. The emergence of the European Foundation Centre's (EFC) 'Europe in the World Initiative' offers further evidence of the internationalization of the work of foundations.[1] This campaign was launched in 2004 to mobilize leadership, collaboration and partnership in European foundations for global development.

Increasingly governments are recognizing the importance of the foundation sector and civil society groups. Foundations find they have better access for advocacy and may sometimes be 'contracted' to provide services or may be welcomed as funding partners in public-private initiatives. However, public partners and the established institutions of global governance – the UN and intergovernmental organizations – have found it difficult to know how to engage with this sector at international level. Foundations, like other civil society organizations, often represent distinctive points of view, may be perceived to lack the 'democratic legitimacy' to which governments aspire, and might approach issues unconventionally. They can also observe different rules and norms to those established in international diplomacy.

Foundations: a heterogeneous landscape

The expert group established by the EU in 2004 to examine the role of foundations in boosting research and development (R&D) investment (European Commission, 2005) accepted the EFC's use of the term 'foundation' to cover any non-profit entity serving public goals, independent of government and industry, and having its own governing board and source of income (this excludes those NGOs established to serve private sector interests). But the foundation landscape is characterized by a high degree of heterogeneity reflected in variations in organization, governance, operating conditions, legal status, tax treatment and regulation. Before the enlargement of the EU in May 2004, there were estimated to be 200,000 organizations within the 15 EU member states that were identified as foundations; most of these described themselves as national rather than regional or international actors. Nonetheless, there is a growing trend among foundations, both in Europe and in North America, towards activity that transcends the boundaries of the nation-state.

Foundations were characterized in the EU study into four generic categories: (i) independent, (ii) corporate, (iii) government-supported and (iv) community foundations. Definitions of foundations vary: there are legal definitions that reflect common law traditions with emphasis on trusteeship (as in the USA and the UK) or civil law traditions (as in Switzerland and Germany) which make an important distinction between legal entities based on membership (and therefore serving members' common objectives) and those based on assets (with boards interpreting goals established by charter) (Director's Note, 2002). Other definitions focus on the type of founder (private or governmental), purpose (charitable or other), activities (grant-making or operating), revenue (single or multiple sources), asset type (endowment or allocation) and degree of independence from the state, business or family interest.

A conference in Ditchley in Oxfordshire in November 2002 (Director's Note, 2002) examined the role of foundations and the reasons why people gave their time and money to charity. It concluded that there are profound cultural differences between countries in these regards, which underlines the importance of understanding the different perspectives they bring to global governance. It was argued that 'we should celebrate its [the foundation sector's] anarchic tendencies and that in taking risk some efforts were bound to fail and that however irritating to officialdom small advocacy groups were an important element of civil society and more important than simple grant making in building social capital' (Director's Note, 2002). Thus the differences between foundations may be regarded as a source of strength and, as discussed in the next section, a key to their diverse roles in global governance.

The role of foundations in governance

The EU study report (European Commission, 2005) described one role of foundations as that of 'philanthropic venture capitalists'. Their decision-making can be free of political and commercial interests and unbound by cumbersome administrative procedures, enabling them to act freely and flexibly and to add distinctive value by taking risks. As governments are accountable to electorates and for-profit businesses to shareholders, neither the government nor the commercial sector is as well placed as foundations to take a longer-term view or to support unfashionable causes. Foundations' independent thinking and pioneering spirit means they can test bold ideas and provide a source of working capital to foster innovation.

Foundations can decisively influence the nature of public investment in several ways: by demonstrating best practice, by social engineering (creating a political environment conducive to the introduction of novel ideas) or by more direct work in changing the system (supporting knowledge-induced institutional and policy change).

Free of political pressure and the time constraints of political cycles and unencumbered by the need to make a profit, foundations can explore new solutions, transcend disciplines and support orphan areas in R&D. Foundations can facilitate change in public policymaking, exploiting their ability to act as independent brokers to convene meetings with non-traditional stakeholders, which can bring new perspectives to issues of common concern. Furthermore, foundations that raise funds from the public are able to reflect public priorities rather than those mandated by states.

Foundations also have their limitations. For example, foundations created by a historic benefaction may be bound to a mission and goals that lack current relevance, be very much shaped by the dominant perceptions of a particular problem or might reflect the singular priorities of an individual or group. Foundations are also frequently criticized for exhibiting a lack of transparency in decision-making, procedures and governance and a lack of accountability vis-à-vis people affected by their activities.

A study by Anheier and Daly (2005) identified the following as the most common roles for foundations:

- *Complementarity and substitution.* Foundations complement government in many ways: by being involved in what the state does not do, and in filling gaps in areas that have been overlooked by providing financial or other resources. They may also substitute for the state.
- *Preservation of traditions and culture.* Preserving past lessons and achievements likely to be swamped by larger and more pressing contemporary social, cultural and economic forces.
- *Redistribution.* Rooted in early philanthropy, foundations continue to promote the redistribution of (primarily economic) resources from higher to lower income groups.
- *Social change and pluralism.* Many foundations have promoted structural change and a more just society; fostering recognition of new needs and empowerment of the socially excluded, the autonomy of foundations makes them amenable to promoting social experimentation and diversity as well as protecting dissent and civil liberties.
- *Innovation.* Foundations are ideally placed to facilitate innovation, to take potentially controversial risks and invest in philanthropic ventures.

Foundations that are active beyond their national borders face a number of special legal and fiscal barriers. The EU Expert Group claims that, 'at present tax effective charitable giving begins and ends at home'. It arrived at this conclusion because favourable tax treatment of charitable donations only applies to charities located in the country from which the donation is given. In recent years in Europe some foundations have come together to rethink this policy and to promote a more favourable environment for international philanthropy. An EFC EU Committee (2003) has drawn up a model law for public benefit foundations in Europe.

The EFC's 'Europe in the World Initiative' has helped to mobilize and support European foundations and to make their international grant-making more effective by encouraging and supporting coordination, cross-sector collaboration and leveraging of new resources. European foundations are encouraged to work more closely with international organizations, government and business and to identify new partners and funders for global development. The EFC has also established the European Partnership for Global Health (EPGH), which is a member-led network that acts to strengthen the role of European foundations and other partners in global governance and to optimize their contributions to both policy and practice. The EGPH complements the work of the US-based Global Health Council,[2] strengthening the voice of European stakeholders, including foundations.

Policy issues for the future role of foundations in global health governance

There are many ways in which foundations can strengthen their contribution to global governance. They can work at different levels to propose policy options and stimulate international debate, to pave the way for global strategies and support the case for global public goods in all areas of policy.

The most important first step is for foundations to work more closely together in international forums to build synergies in their advocacy and delivery of funding and services relating to global issues. Foundations can combine their strengths at regional level, as the EU has shown, as well as at global level. The Gates, Wellcome and Rockefeller foundations have already worked together with industry and government to create several public private partnerships. This requires loose networks which can provide support and communications without cramping the creative response of foundations to specific needs or blurring their sharp focus on their founding principles.

Second, foundations need to examine their priorities for action on social goals in the context of global needs and globalization. As a third step, foundations should take a leadership role in defining policy options and mobilizing public opinion around global issues by supporting think-tanks, working with the media, convening and building alliances in keeping with their mandates. Fourth, foundations should invest in research and innovation on global issues and their impact on societies, funding knowledge generation and dissemination; they should develop approaches to global challenges, building on their tradition of philanthropy in filling critical gaps in knowledge.

Good practice in the internal governance of foundations

To maintain their positive position, foundations need to emulate best practice in internal governance, ensuring a sound legal framework that will enable them to operate transparently and independently, and, as good partners, to offer a plurality of views. The European Foundation Centre, for example, published a revision in April 2006 (EFC, 2006) of its principles of good practice. These principles include:

- Compliance – foundations must comply with the laws of the state in which they are based and with international and European conventions in which their country of residence is party.

- Governance – foundations must have an identifiable decision-making body whose members and successors should be nominated in accordance with established principles and should act with the highest ethical standards.
- Informed policies – foundations must have a clear set of basic policies and procedures specifying mission, objectives, goals and related programmes and review these on a regular basis
- Stewardship of management and finance – foundations must promote efficient organization whilst ensuring prudent and sustainable management, investment strategies and use of resources.
- Disclosure and communication – foundations must act in a transparent manner.
- Monitoring and evaluation – foundations must organize appropriate monitoring and regular evaluation of their action and programmes.
- Cooperation – foundations must share their know-how and experience with peer organizations and other relevant stakeholders to advance good practice and cooperate to maximize their impact in their respective fields of activity.

While operating in accordance with the donors' intentions, foundations should acknowledge the importance of acting for the public benefit and serving society at large. They should operate with due appreciation and respect of societal norms and should recognize the importance of pluralism and subsidiarity, both nationally and internationally. Increasingly, foundations will also be expected to demonstrate a commitment to transparency, accountability and self-regulation, acknowledging obligations to multiple stakeholders, including public authorities, grantees and global civil society.

The legal framework for the operation of foundations

The role of foundations must be safeguarded with appropriate legislation. Over the last five years, the European Foundation Centre has conducted a comprehensive analysis of the foundation laws in member states and has developed recommendations for a European statute for foundations (EFC, 2006). The primary objective of such a statute should be to provide an efficient policy framework for private investment for the public good across the EU. The European Foundation Statute is designed to facilitate cross-border cooperation, overcome current legal and administrative barriers (for example, operations across borders when assets are held and managed in multiple nations) and provide incentives for best practice in internal governance and operations. 'Foundations' established to provide tax protection for commercial interests or to promote business interests would not be included in the EU or EFC definition of charitable foundations. Stichting Ingka, for example, the world's largest 'charity', was established by the IKEA Group and dedicated to 'innovation in the field of architectural and interior design' (that is, towards the direct commercial interest of the IKEA Group).

It is clear that similar issues apply to foundations in America and other parts of the world. In the USA the legal framework for international grant-making has been given greater prominence since the development of concerns about safeguarding charitable funds from diversion to terrorist uses. The Council of Foundations in the USA has developed principles of international charity. They include the following:

- Charitable organizations must exclusively pursue the purposes for which they were organized and chartered.
- Charitable organizations must comply both with US laws applicable to charities and with the relevant laws of the foreign jurisdictions in which they work.
- Charitable organizations may choose to adopt practices in addition to those required by law that, in their judgement, provide additional confidence.
- The board of directors of each charitable organization must oversee the implementation of the new governance practice.
- Fiscal responsibility is fundamental to international charitable works.
- Each charitable organization must safeguard its relationships with the communities it serves in order to deliver effective programmes. This relationship should be formulated on the local understanding and acceptance of the independence of the charitable organization. The gravest risk to this relationship is the association with a political position, a partisan entity or a particular government's action.

Responding to global challenges through global partnerships

Globalization has exposed new challenges: stark evidence of inequality of wealth and opportunity, the increasing threat of the spread of global disease, and the cultural schisms that add fuel to conflict and terrorism. The current system of global governance remains ill-equipped to address these growing threats. It is already clear that in many parts of the world the Millennium Development Goals cannot be met with current approaches and resources. The capacity of foundations to innovate, create and add value are essential components of a new approach to global governance which better engages all elements of society.

A recent development is the establishment of joint initiatives through public-private partnerships between governments, business and civic society, straddling the conventional divide between state and non-state actors (see Buse and Harmer, Chapter 12). Inge Kaul (2006: 219) claims that 'there has been a rapid growth in the number of public-private partnerships that address global concerns such as climate change, control of communicable disease, and the fight against poverty and hunger'. These partnerships, often centred on a foundation (as Inge Kaul notes, 68 out of 193 such partnerships are centred on foundations), go beyond mere contracting across sectors and entail some joint decision-making and sharing of opportunities and risks. 'Some of these global partnerships ... function as advocates, contributing to international policy dialogue and outreach. Others like the Global Fund are more operational and act on the policy implementation of international cooperation' (2006: 219). Kaul offers three main conclusions. First, global public partnerships come in many forms; second, they are 'here to stay'; and, third, the implications of global public-private partnerships for international cooperation are both far reaching and mixed. These partnerships are designed to be visible, single-focused, results-oriented, innovative and risk-taking. They can do things that larger, more institutionalized intergovernmental organizations find difficult to accomplish (Kaul, 2006: 220).

Partnering is primarily a matter of bringing the interests and aims of different bodies together and of power sharing. Social ventures function primarily as non-profit organizations and rely on donations for financing, often from charitable and philanthropic foundations (Buse and Harmer, 2007). A growing literature has examined why entrepreneurs sometimes prefer non-profit organizations over for-profit enterprises. Inge Kaul explains that the argument is similar to those advanced by Williamson (1985) and others in support of relational contracting for provision of difficult to monitor goods. The impetus to solve seemingly intractable problems comes not from government organizations but from private foundations that have the will and resources to take action. Further, Kaul (2006) examines the dilemma identified by Rosenau of governance without government. Nation-states tend to act internationally as private actors do nationally – in their own national self-interest. Further, as private actors are increasingly acting globally in their own self-interest this has made it more difficult for nation-states to define 'national self-interest'. This creates double jeopardy for many global problems, particularly for the world's poor, who suffer from market failure and international (intergovernmental) cooperation failure. Social venture partnerships oriented towards public service often come in when these failures coincide and threaten to create a global crisis. Frequently they are vehicles for mobilizing contributions from all actors to accelerate constructive solutions.

Partnering examples in global health

Several global health partnerships have been established to overcome 'market failures', that is, to accelerate the development of health technologies for populations too poor to present a compelling opportunity for profit for the pharmaceutical industry. Examples of pro-poor R&D product development partnerships include the International AIDS Vaccine Initiative, the Medicines for Malaria Venture, and the Drugs for Neglected Diseases initiative. The GAVI

Alliance was designed to create greater access to the benefits of immunizations by delivering existing vaccines, thereby enhancing the incentives for the pharmaceutical industry to develop new vaccines to tackle the health problems of the poor.[3]

There are also several global public-private partnerships that mobilize and deliver interventions to control neglected or epidemic disease problems across or within borders. For example, the Onchocerciasis Control Programme, now the African Programme for Onchocerciasis Control, was founded in 1974 to control the spread of river blindness in Africa and was one of the first examples of such public-private partnerships in global health. The International Trachoma Initiative addresses another blinding disease in Africa.[4]

While these partnerships actually deliver interventions in target countries, others are focused primarily at the global level to mobilize support and strengthen policy and technical guidance for implementation. Partnerships have been developed, for example, to accelerate control of malaria, AIDS and tuberculosis. Several newer initiatives, such as the Health Metrics Network and the Global Health Workforce Alliance have been established to improve health by strengthening critical components of the health systems in developing countries instead of using a disease-by-disease approach.[5] These multi-institutional global health partnerships offer an important opportunity to support effective and efficient implementation of health programmes, analysing and documenting experience and sharing lessons learned.

Public-private partnerships have also been established to finance or facilitate market transactions in which developing country governments are the purchaser and private firms the supplier. For example, the GAVI Alliance has used private sector financial expertise to help governments to obtain vaccines at a more affordable price by 'bundling' demand. It has also used capital market mechanisms to raise funds to purchase vaccines and 'advance market commitments' to attract private sector investment in new vaccine products for poor countries by guaranteeing purchase volumes at pre-negotiated prices. The Clinton Foundation[6] has also negotiated differential contracts under which developing countries commit to purchase contracts for drugs and diagnostics. Modelled on this work, UNITAID[7] was founded in September 2006 with leadership from the governments of Brazil and France in order to facilitate the purchase of drugs against HIV/AIDS, malaria and tuberculosis. It is innovatively financed by a levy on airline tickets. The *Financial Times* of 4 July 2006 reported that the UK's Wellcome Trust had recently consulted capital market experts and issued a 30-year bond to raise up to £500 million, increasing its available funding for improving global health.

This recent proliferation of global health partnerships has, however, raised concerns about the aggregate effects of all of these new non-state actors at both the global and field levels. The global health partnerships, which are often constituted legally as foundations or other non-governmental organizations, offer support that may be poorly aligned with country needs and policies (see Buse and Harmer in the next chapter). As noted by Fox (2006), these partnerships often create additional demands and transaction costs that place a burden on 'beneficiary' countries, and may have unclear outcomes and accountability processes.

The recently established International Health Partnership (IHP) seeks to improve the harmonization of these global efforts, aligning them with country plans and increasing the focus on results in strengthening country health systems. Initial signatories to the IHP agreement on 5 September 2007, in addition to numerous bilateral and UN organizations, included global health partnerships such as the GAVI Alliance and the Global Fund to Fight AIDS, TB and Malaria, and the Bill & Melinda Gates Foundation.[8] The IHP and the Health 8 (H8), an informal group of eight health-related organizations working to accelerate the achievement of the health-related Millennium Development Goals, are interesting reflections of the new trend towards the inclusion of global health partnerships and foundations as more formal members of global health governance structures. The H8, in fact, has specifically articulated as an objective that it will 'engage civil society and the private sector – recognizing the dynamic value of public/private consultation'.[9]

Conclusion

This chapter has assessed the past, present and potential roles of foundations in global governance. It was written in recognition of the fact that the world is facing an unprecedented set of global challenges and that the current system for global problem-solving is poorly equipped to deal with them. The chapter has analysed the capabilities of foundations – which until comparatively recent publicity remained an underestimated resource – and the ways in which they create and add value. It has also identified priorities and policy issues that foundations need to address if they are to exploit their comparative advantage at regional and global levels, including: (i) improving internal governance, (ii) developing better legislation and (iii) building broader partnerships. The examples of product development, intervention delivery, policy or advocacy, and financing partnerships for global health, demonstrate the current and potential impact of foundations on global governance issues.

The emergence of foundations and other elements of civil society as partners in global governance complicate and enrich the picture painted by Rosenau of *one* system of rules, norms and decision-making structures in the global governance system. Global partnerships are increasingly being developed to overcome barriers faced by the global public sector. The evidence points to an enduring role for global partnerships, with further growth in their numbers and importance. They represent a transition from intergovernmental cooperation to a multipartite structure drawing in all actors – the state, business and civil society.

The main implications for policy identified in this chapter are for foundations to:

- Examine their current and potential contribution to global governance, including global governance for health
- Extend cooperation and joint working on global issues with other organizations at regional and global levels
- Establish and apply clear definitions, accountability and operating principles for charitable foundations active in global governance
- Press for an appropriate international legislative framework to support the work of foundations with international charitable aims
- Continue to operate as 'charitable venture capitalists' at the forefront of innovation in addressing global health and other issues

In summary, foundations and other leaders of civil society organizations should build collaboration, leveraging their resources when necessary to create new joint ventures, catalyzing new resources or cross-sector collaboration and, above all, encouraging the creation of a forum for all parties to work cooperatively in shaping the future of global governance for health. This approach was given expression in the European Foundation Centre's 2006 publication 'European Perspectives on Global Health: a Policy Glossary' (Kickbusch and Lister, 2006) and, in January 2008, in its partnership with the Global Forum for Health Research and the Geneva Graduate Institute of International Development in the launch of an initiative for a European Council for Global Health which would work to influence policy, research and action for global health. But this is not just a matter for European foundations although they must play their part. This is fundamentally a challenge to our abilities to act together in the places we live, in our political communities and nations, across different countries of the world and through the institutions of global governance. Working with others, foundations can play their part in fulfilling the promise of the benefit of global health for prosperity and security for all.

Notes

1. http://www.efc.be/ (accessed 21 May 2008).
2. http://www.globalhealth.org/ (accessed 10 July 2008).
3. International AIDS Vaccine Initiative (www.iavi.org); the Medicines for Malaria Venture (www.mmv.org); the Drugs for Neglected Diseases initiative (www.dndi.org); the GAVI Alliance (www.gavialliance.org/) (all accessed 4 February 2009).
4. www.trachoma.org/ (accessed 4 February 2009).

5. For control of malaria (www.rbm.who.int/), for AIDS (www.unaids.org/en/, www.aidsaction.org/), and tuberculosis (www.stoptb.org/). Health Metrics Network (see, www.who.int/healthmetrics/en/); Global Health Workforce Alliance (see, www.who.int/workforcealliance/en/) (all accessed 4 February 2009).
6. www.clintonfoundation.org/(accessed 4 February 2009).
7. www.unitaid.eu/(accessed 4 February 2009).
8. On the IHP agreement see, http://www.dfid.gov.uk/news/files/ihp/default.asp (accessed 10 July 2008)
9. Global Campaign for the Health Millennium Goals, Progress Report April 2008: 13, www.norad.no/default.asp?FILE=items/11720/108/Progress%20report.pdf (accessed 10 July 2008).

References

Anheier, H.K. and S. Daly (eds), *The Politics of Foundations: Comparative Perspectives from Europe and Beyond* (London: Routledge, 2005).

Buse, K. and A. Harmer, 'Seven Habits of Highly Effective Global Public-Private Health Partnerships: Practice and Potential', *Social Science and Medicine*, 64(2) (2007): 259–71.

Council on Foundations, *Principles of International Charity – Treasury Guidelines Working Group* (Washington DC: Council on Foundation, 2005).

Director's Note, 'Civil Society: the Role of Philanthropy', Ditchley Foundation 02/13, 2002, http://www.ditchley.co.uk/page/220/philanthropy.htm (accessed 10 July 2008).

European Commission, Directorate General for Research, 'Giving more for Research in Europe – the Role of Foundations and the Non-Profit Sector in Boosting R&D Investment', EUR 21785 EN, European Commission, Brussels, 2005.

EFC, *The Future Priorities for the Action Plan on Modernizing Company Law in the EU*, (Brussels: European Foundation Centre, 2006).

EFC EU Committee, 'Model Law for Public Benefit Foundations in Europe', May 2003, http://www.efc.be/ftp/public/EU/LegalTF/model_law.pdf (accessed 10 July 2008).

Fox, D.M., 'Foundations' Impact on Health Policy', *Health Affairs*, 25(6) (2006): 1724–9.

Kaul, I., 'Exploring the Policy Space between Markets and States: Global Public-Private Partnerships', in I. Kaul and P. Conceição (eds), *The New Public Finance: Responding to Global Challenges* (Oxford: Oxford University Press, 2006), pp. 219–68.

Kickbusch, I. and G. Lister (eds), *European Perspectives on Global Health: a Policy Glossary* (Brussels: European Foundation Centre, 2006).

Rosenau, J., 'Global Governance in the Twenty-First Century', *Global Governance*, 1(1) (1995): 13–43.

Williamson, O., *The Economic Institutions of Capitalism: Firms, Markets, Relational Contracting* (Cambridge: Cambridge University Press, 1985).

12
Global Health Partnerships: the Mosh Pit of Global Health Governance

Kent Buse and Andrew Harmer

Introduction

In his seminal work on global governance, Lawrence Finkelstein wryly observed that 'we say "governance" because we don't really know what to call what is going on' (Finkelstein, 1995: 368). Fortunately, interest in global governance has increased exponentially in the last decade, and a deeper and more precise understanding of the concept has emerged as a result (Dingwerth and Pattberg, 2006). As a conceptual tool for understanding how to respond effectively to the spread of infectious diseases, global governance has attracted considerable attention from academics and policymakers (Weinberg, 2005); and one specific response – global health partnerships (GHPs) – has excited particular attention. The rise of GHPs has been meteoric: in the late 1980s they were a nascent experiment in global health; now they are part of mainstream global health discourse and a dominant model for cooperation in a complex world. GHPs are also controversial, particularly in relation to their governance functions.

This chapter addresses the issue of governance functions of GHPs: what functions do GHPs perform? Are they performed effectively? And how can they be strengthened or reformed? In brief, GHPs have raised the profile of global health on the broader development agenda, they have been the catalyst for innovation in development finance, they have championed new ways of approaching cooperation between public, commercial and civil society sectors and they have pioneered new 'rules of the game' in terms of accountability. But there is room for improvement, and in this chapter we highlight seven areas for reform: stronger commitment to the Paris agenda for aid effectiveness; further improvements in representation of stakeholders; adoption of standard operating procedures across all partnerships; improved GHP oversight; assigning greater value to the 'invisible P' of partnership – people; ensuring that GHPs have adequate resources; and, finally, maintaining 'critical space' for continued assessment of the prevailing partnership paradigm.

We address each of these seven reforms below, but first – and to avoid any 'loose handling' of concepts – we clarify what we mean by GHPs and the concept of global health governance.

Global health partnerships

Public and private actors have collaborated in international health problems since the 1800s (Stern and Markel, 2004), and the idea of 'partnerships' was first mooted in the mid-1940s as a precursor to peace between nations (Mitrany, 1975). The concept of *public-private* partnership, however, and its practical application as a mechanism for resolving health problems, only entered international (subsequently global) health discourse during the mid-1990s. In a very short period of time GHPs have become a dominant mode of interaction between the various national, international, public and private actors involved in global health governance (Box 12.1).

Box 12.1 Key moments in the history of GHPs

- **1992** – Rio Earth Summit and 'Agenda 21' – the public-private partnership approach to sustainable development is formally presented as an innovative alternative to traditional bilateral development arrangements
- **1996** – UN Habitat II Meeting and publication of the OECD DAC report 'Shaping the 21st Century' – the first time that the UN expressed its commitment to public-private partnership as a guiding principle of future action
- **1998** – Gro Harlem Brundtland, incoming Director-General of WHO, embraces partnerships as a guiding principle of her vision for health in the twenty-first century
- **1999** – the Bill and Melinda Gates Foundation established with an interest in global health – particularly technical solutions – and actively incubated many of the GHPs which we study
- **2005** – OECD DAC Paris Declaration on Aid Effectiveness agreed
- **2006** – Follow-ups to DAC High Level Forum (Belgium, February; Tunis, June) agreed GHP-specific guidelines based on the 2005 Paris aid principles
- **2006/07** – Some GHPs take stock of their behaviour through self-assessment concerning aid effectiveness principles
- **2007** – Launch of the International Health Partnership to which a number of GHPs are party

- 2007 – Leadership of GFATM and GAVI Alliance join the Bill and Melinda Gates Foundation and other agencies in the so-called 'H8'[a]

Note: a. H8 = 'Health 8', an informal group of eight health-related organizations – WHO, UNICEF, UNFPA, UNAIDS, GFATM, the GAVI Alliance, Bill and Melinda Gates Foundation and the World Bank – created to stimulate a global sense of urgency for reaching the health-related MDGs.

However, as a unit of analysis, GHPs cause headaches for global health researchers. In addition to the various methodological challenges associated with measuring GHP impact or effectiveness, the researcher must wade through a morass of acronyms, definitions, categories and structures. GHPs are diverse in nature, size and scope; they address different health issues and serve different functions, for example, research and development, technical assistance and health service/system support, advocacy, coordination and finance for various health projects. Consequently, as Caines warns, 'any effort to compare them with the same yardstick has considerable limitations' (Caines, 2005: 6).

Nevertheless, comparison of GHPs is *de rigueur* and so we respond to Caines's warning by narrowing our subset of GHPs to 'relatively institutionalized initiatives, established to address global health problems, in which public and for-profit private sector organizations have a voice in collective decision-making' (Buse and Harmer, 2007: 261), rather than re-visiting the definitional and category debates of earlier studies (Buse and Walt, 2000; Carlson, 2004; Widdus and White, 2004). Applying this definition has a number of advantages: it adds a level of precision to an otherwise unruly melange of initiatives; it makes our sample manageable and more cohesive; and it focuses on the most innovative and controversial feature of GHPs, namely partnership between public and for-profit private sectors.

It also leads to a surprising result. The literature typically cites a figure of 70+ GHPs operating at any one time (McKinsey, 2005; Lorenz, 2007). However, if one looks at the constitution of those partnerships' governing bodies, one finds that very few have representatives from both the public and for-profit sectors – fewer than twenty in fact (Table 12.1). Indeed, it is interesting to note the increasing number of high-profile partnerships that do *not* have public-private representation at board level. For example, the Microbicide Development Programme has sixteen members with voting rights on its management board, all of whom work at academic institutions and/or medical research centres; it has one private sector representative – but by invitation, and without voting rights. The Malaria Vaccine Initiative, which aims to accelerate the development of promising malaria vaccines and ensure their availability and accessibility, is a collaborative programme of the non-government organization PATH; the Drugs for Neglected Diseases initiative (DNDi), the Partnership for Maternal, Newborn and Child Health, and the Global Polio Eradication Initiative are all global partnerships that do not have private sector representation at board level, whilst the Institute for One World Health had, until recently, no public sector representation on its board. These partnerships, and many like them, are more accurately described as Global Health Initiatives rather than public-private partnerships.

At the turn of the century there was considerable excitement and optimism about global health public-private partnerships as a novel form of public and private interaction. Our research, however, draws attention to the sobering fact that there are actually far fewer examples of this mode of cooperation than one might think from reading about partnerships in the global health literature. This misperception about GHPs becomes even more acute when one considers that much of the data that inform policy decisions about partnerships draws on the experiences of the 'big 5' GHPs – the Global Fund to Fight AIDS, TB and Malaria (GFATM), the GAVI Alliance, the International AIDS Vaccine Initiative (IAVI), Roll Back Malaria (RBM) and the Stop TB Partnership (Stop TB). Consequently, when we talk about GHPs, it is important to recognize not just that reports of their public-private nature are widely exaggerated, but also that our knowledge of GHPs is drawn from studies of a surprisingly small data set.

Moreover, our knowledge of GHPs is less robust than might appear at first glance. Despite the torrent of opinion on GHPs, too little of it is based on too little empirical material. Consequently, it is important to determine the provenance and accuracy of data used in GHP assessments. Examples of primary data collection include studies that have conducted comparative assessments of the effects of GHPs on countries' health systems (Brugha et al., 2005; Stillman and Bennet, 2005); assessed resource mobilization and funding practices (Oomman et al., 2007); and evaluated governance structures and processes (EuroHealth Group, 2007; Buse, 2004).

Although primary data are the source for what we know about the effects of GHPs at country level, the quality of country studies that have looked at the effects of GHPs across a range of indicators varies widely. There are several reasons for this. Poor research is one, geography is another: for example, in Malawi – a small country – there is good data on GHP impact on human resources (HR), but poorer quality data are available in other, larger, sub-Saharan countries. Poorly conceived or abstract indicators that do not lend themselves to easy analysis are a third: for example, whilst it is relatively easy to measure HR, it is much harder to assess coordination, alignment or harmonization – or indeed transaction costs – although efforts have been made (Attawel and Dickinson, 2007).

Of course, whilst it is important that funders look more seriously at commissioning research to provide quality data, rather than concentrating

Table 12.1 Representation of key constituencies on 19 GHP boards

Global Health Partnerships (n = 19)	Total board membership (number)	HIC government (donor or other dept) (%)	LMIC government (MOH or other dept) (%)	Int Org (e.g. WB, WHO) (%)	Corporate (%)	NGO or other not-for-profit organization (%)	Foundations (%)	Academic institutions (%)	Other (e.g. GHP secretariat staff) (%)	Female (%)	LMIC (across constituencies) (%)
African Comprehensive HIV/AIDS Partnership	4	0	0	0	1 (25)	0	2 (50)	1 (25)	0	0	25
Alliance for Microbicide Development	5	0	0	0	2 (40)	0	0	2 (40)	1 (20)	2 (40)	0
AERAS, Global TB Vaccine Foundation	13	0	0	0	4 (31)	0	1 (8)	6 (46)	2 (15)	1 (8)	1 (8)
European Malaria Vaccine Initiative	7	0	0	0	4 (57)	1 (14)	0	2 (29)	0	1 (14)	1 (14)
Foundation for Innovative New Diagnostics	5	0	0	1 (20)	3 (60)	0	1 (20)	0	0	0	0
Global Alliance for the Elimination of Lymphatic Filariasis	8	1 (13)	2 (25)	0	0	0	0	4 (50)	1 (13)	2 (25)	4 (50)
GAVI Alliance	19	5 (26)	4 (21)	5 (26)	2 (11)	1 (5)	1 (5)	1 (5)	0	4 (21)	0
Global Alliance for Improved Nutrition	17	2 (12)	2 (12)	2 (12)	7 (41)	1 (6)	2 (12)	1 (6)	0	5 (29)	3 (18)
Global Fund for AIDS, TB, and Malaria	24	8 (33)	7 (29)	3 (13)	2 (8)	3 (13)	1 (4)	0	0	6 (25)	8 (33)
International AIDS Vaccine Initiative	13	0	1 (8)	1 (8)	3 (23)	3 (23)	1 (8)	1 (8)	3 (23)	2 (15)	3 (23)
Institute for One World Health	9	0	0	0	2 (22)	0	3 (33)	1 (11)	3 (33)	3 (33)	0
International Partnership for Microbicides	15	0	0	1 (7)	3 (20)	5 (33)	0	3 (20)	3 (20)	9 (60)	6 (40)
International Trachoma Initiative	9	0	0	0	4 (44)	0	3 (33)	1 (11)	1 (11)	2 (22)	0
Micronutrient Initiative	8	1 (13)	0	5 (63)	2 (25)	0	0	0	0	1 (13)	0
Medicines for Malaria Venture	11	0	2 (18)	1 (9)	4 (36)	1 (9)	2 (18)	1 (9)	1 (9)	2 (18)	3 (27)
Pediatric Dengue Vaccine Initiative	15	1 (7)	1 (7)	2 (13)	3 (20)	0	0	8 (53)	0	3 (20)	6 (40)
Roll Back Malaria	25	3 (12)	9 (36)	6 (24)	0	2 (8)	1 (4)	2 (8)	2 (8)	4 (16)	10 (40)
Stop TB	29	8 (28)	7 (24)	3 (10)	2 (7)	3 (10)	2 (7)	1 (3)	3 (10)	6 (21)	9 (31)
TB Alliance	13	1 (8)	3 (23)	1 (8)	4 (31)	0	2 (15)	1 (8)	1 (8)	2 (15)	3 (23)
Total (number)	249	30	38	30	52	20	22	36	21	55	58
Mean across all partnerships (%)		8	11	11	26	6	11	17	9	21	20
Weighted mean across all partnerships (%)		12	15	12	21	8	9	14	8	22	22

Notes: HIC = High-income country; LMIC = Low-middle income country (Source: World Bank). Data include voting, non-voting, and ex-officio board members. Individuals with 'observer' status are excluded. Source for data – GHP websites (accessed 15/12/2008).

solely on funding quantity, we should not lose sight of the fact that we still need to know more about the impact of GHPs on policymaking processes, on policy dialogue and on priority-setting, and arrangements for providing services and monitoring these. What is most urgently required is a coherent and workable metric that researchers could use to assess GHP performance. We return to this latter recommendation later in this chapter.

Global health governance and GHPs

The concept of global health governance (GHG) attempts to explain, but also respond to, global health issues whose determinants extend 'beyond the capacity of individual countries to address through domestic institutions' (Lee and Collin, 2005: 3). GHPs were established to address various health needs that neither the public nor private sectors had been capable or willing to attend to effectively. But what makes them particularly innovative and interesting is their unique governance arrangement: a cooperative structure that exists without the need for either hierarchical legal authority or the discipline of the market (Buse, 2004). GHPs exhibit a form of networked consultation and decision-making that is more formalized than other networks (see Walt et al., Chapter 3 above).

Research into the governance of GHPs has focused on five core areas: legitimacy, representation and participation, accountability, transparency and effectiveness (Buse, 2004). A partnership is *legitimate* to the extent that its authority is considered valid by those affected by it; *representative* according to the extent and manner through which those affected by the exercise of power are involved in decision-making; *accountable* to the extent that effective mechanisms exist that can render the partnership's executive accountable to its governing body, the governing body accountable to those affected by and participating in the partnership, and the partners accountable to the partnership itself; *transparent* to the extent that information pertinent to decision- and rule-making is freely and readily available to those affected; and *effective* to the extent that partnership goals are met without unacceptable costs being incurred by recipients of partnership aid (Buse, 2004: 4). The analysis of GHPs found variations across and within partnerships against these variables. Yet over the past few years we have witnessed attempts by a number of partnerships to improve governance practices – something that many practitioners saw as a cumbersome distraction from the real issue of delivering results in their earlier incarnations.[1]

In the remaining sections of this chapter, we focus on the fifth core area of governance – the effectiveness of GHPs. These five areas of governance are not discrete elements of 'best practice'; they are linked together. A partnership that lacks legitimacy, perhaps because it is unrepresentative or lacks transparency, may be less effective; and a partnership that is not transparent will struggle to satisfy conditions of accountability, which may again impact negatively on its effectiveness. Consequently, an analysis of how GHPs can become more effective mechanisms of GHG will inevitably draw on analysis of these other core components of governance (Rochlin et al., 2008).

The contribution of GHPs to global health governance

Elsewhere we have written about the remarkable contributions of GHPs to improving health worldwide (Buse and Harmer, 2007). Here we reframe these contributions in terms of the manner in which GHPs have shaped the governance of global health (see Box 12.2). At the heart of governance is the image of steering; so where have GHPs steered global health over the past decade? For one thing, GHPs are arguably responsible – at least in part – for the rise of global health on the international development agenda after languishing so long as a Cinderella issue. They have inspired many to believe that a set of health and development problems is not only tractable (in contrast to poor governance for example) but that they can be solved and should be solved for ethical reasons. It is arguably the case that GHPs have been able to do this in part as a result of the discursive approaches they have adopted (Box 12.3), but also relevant are some of the innovations that they have introduced into the global health arena. Explicit attention and professionalism, for example, has been devoted by GHPs to public relations in a hitherto unprecedented manner. In addition to emotional appeals and advocacy campaigns, efforts have been made to articulate businesslike investment cases so as to appeal to different constituencies – for example the GAVI Health Systems Strengthening Investment Case (GAVI, 2005). As a result, the profile of certain issues and diseases of concern to GHPs was raised in the public conscience as well as among, for example, the leadership of the G8.[2]

Box 12.2 Seven contributions GHPs have made to global health governance

1. Raised the profile of global health on the international development agenda
2. Developed innovative finance mechanisms
3. Encouraged and introduced innovative mechanisms for constituency involvement in decision-making
4. Successfully delivered consensus on key issues
5. Re-oriented health sector priorities
6. Pioneered new 'rules of the game' in terms of results and accountability
7. Established international norms and standards

> **Box 12.3 The functions of discourse within GHPs**
>
> An in-depth analysis of three GHPs found that even across quite different partnerships, a common discursive structure exists that has a number of important causal and constitutive effects on global health policy. Although discourse analysis of GHPs is in is infancy, it offers an innovative methodological approach to understanding how, where and when ideas 'matter' in global health governance (Harmer, 2005). The results of this study suggest that within GHPs, discourse has four distinct 'functions'.
>
> **Cognitive function**
> GHPs are innovative and radical. Consequently, the ideas that frame GHP policy have to be *justified* to the global health 'community'. To facilitate the process of acceptance, discourse performs a series of complementary actions that together form its cognitive function. These actions are:
>
> - Introduce new technical and scientific arguments
> - Depict paradigms and frames of reference that define 'reality' (for example, 'globalization'; 'more for less')
> - Reduce policy complexity through the use of evocative phrases (for example, Stop TB)
> - Appeal to a deeper core of organizing principles and norms (for example, global governance, financing and delivering global public goods)
> - Demonstrate the relevance, applicability, and coherence of the solution proposed by the GHP to the health problem.
>
> **Normative function**
> For the solution proposed by the GHP to be accepted, however, justification is not sufficient; the policy must also be *legitimate*. Here discourse has a normative function which it performs by associating the policy with long-established values. Typically, GHP policy is legitimized by its association with values of equity and fairness (for example, TB Alliance).
>
> **Coordinative function**
> Whereas the cognitive and normative functions of discourse attend to the *ideational* dimensions of the solution to the health problem proposed by the GHP, the coordinative and communicative functions respond to the *interactive* dissemination of the response to the global health community. In order to perform its coordinative function, discourse provides a framework for discussion and deliberation through a common language and vision of the policy.
>
> **Communicative function**
> Finally, discourse performs its communicative function by translating the policy into accessible language for public consumption.

GHPs have also steered a new course when it comes to development finance (see Smith, Chapter 6 above). Innovations include such initiatives as Product-Red, which involves a tie-up between a number of corporations, including American Express, and the GFATM (although it had raised only a rather paltry US$60 million to the end of 2007), and the Global Fund's newly launched 'Corporate Champions Programme', which could take corporate giving to another scale – time will tell (Buse et al., 2008). A GHP is piloting the first use of frontloaded aid through the International Finance Facility (IFF). The IFFIm (the International Finance Facility for Immunization), the first IFF programme launched, aims to raise US$4 billion by 2015 to finance immunization programmes through the GAVI Alliance (IFFIm, 2005). The experience of the R&D partnerships is in large measure directly responsible for the development of the Advance Market Commitment (AMC) to provide a pull factor to industry to invest in market orphans. A staggering US$1.5 billion has been committed to the first AMC for a pneumococcal vaccine, through a partnership in which the GAVI Alliance plays a central management and coordination role (AMC, 2007). In addition, the partnership ethos is evident in UNITAID, which was launched in 2006, as an international effort to levy an airline tax to raise long-term and predictable funds which will be hypothecated for diagnostics and drugs for AIDS, TB and Malaria (UNITAID, 2007). Whether or not the variety of push and pull mechanisms will be successful is a moot point (Grace, 2006), but what we want to stress is that these innovations would likely not have materialized without the interaction between industry, foundations and bilateral donors through GHPs.

Although it is perhaps self-evident, GHPs have introduced new ways of approaching cooperation in the health sector. New constituencies, such as the commercial sector (see Buse and Naylor, Chapter 9) and civil society (see McCoy and Hilson, Chapter 10), have been brought formally into planning processes at the global and national levels through a number of GHP instruments. A variety of formal and informal means through which to consult and hence share power have been devised. New and sophisticated efforts in stakeholder involvement have been developed – particularly by the GFATM (GFATM, 2004) – as have methods to undertake the challenging task of collaborative multi-partner planning and monitoring (this is particularly advanced in the case of the GAVI Alliance). In developing these new approaches to collaboration, new pathways of influence have been introduced by GHPs – the more direct face-to-face relationship between senior UN officials and the private sector constitutes just the most visible of these.

As a result, GHPs have assisted in delivering consensus across a range of contested issues. Through painstaking and often time-consuming deliberations at board level and, perhaps more importantly, in working groups and task teams, in which the Sherpas and technical-level partner members debate and pre-process issues, common policy positions and strategies emerge.

GHPs have been particularly effective in reorienting the priorities of the health sector – the ultimate litmus test of GHG – for better and for worse. Nowhere is this more evident than in the case of financing for HIV, where the concern is that donors' aid is not aligned with government priorities (OECD, 2007). In the case of Rwanda, for example, although the government has identified seven strategic health objectives, total donor funding for the country is heavily earmarked for HIV/AIDS leaving other priorities underfunded and preventing balanced investment in the health system (Republic of Rwanda, 2006: 8). Moreover, in most countries, despite valid concerns raised by health economists (on cost-effectiveness grounds), by health planners (for a variety of reasons), and macroeconomists (due to fiscal space limitations), the allocation to ARVs is out of proportion with the optimum continuum between prevention and care. The impact of the 'success' of AIDS-focused GHPs may not be fully known for some time, but already the effects are felt in relation to the neglect of other disease areas (Shiffman, 2008). GHPs have been particularly effective in re-establishing priorities in low-income countries by working outside established channels of policy dialogue and planning processes, and in particular by making large 'off budget' contributions.

GHPs have pioneered new rules of the game in a number of ways in relation to accountability. They have introduced new approaches to ex ante and ex post conditionality into funding arrangements. Both the GAVI Alliance and the GFATM, for example, set preconditions for funding and then modulate disbursement against performance and results. The partnerships have also experimented with new ways to assess and manage fiduciary risk; relying on private accountancy firms in a way that was not the case even ten years ago. In the case of the GFATM, local fund agents (LFA) are contracted to provide these services. Evaluations of the LFA model present a mixed bag of findings (Kruse and Claussen, 2005; EuroHealth Group, 2007). On the positive side, the LFA model has enabled significant disbursement of funds to grant recipients (US$5.24 billion as of March 2008); it is also adaptable, it allowed the GFATM to 'hit the ground running', and it has encouraged principal recipients (PRs) of GFATM funds to be more conscious of results and accountability. On the negative side, the LFA is itself a parallel monitoring system that is distinct from government and other donors' monitoring processes; and it also employs its own reporting system that imposes significant transaction costs on government (EuroHealth Group, 2007: viii). This creates, as one assessment notes, 'a paradox in which the LFA system seeks to ensure and support PR alignment efforts, even while itself using parallel financial and programme monitoring systems' (ibid.) Moreover, technical review panels, which review country proposals for the Health Metrics Network, GAVI and the GFATM, provide a system of external checks and balances on grant-making, but without a country presence, the reliance of these partnerships on expert panels introduces its own problems (which we return to below). The in-country

Box 12.4 The GFATM Country Coordinating Mechanism: a new system of rule?

The Global Fund to Fight AIDS, TB and Malaria (GFATM) requires that proposals for funding are submitted by a Country Coordinating Mechanism (CCM). CCMs are country-level partnerships that develop and submit grant proposals to the GFATM, monitor their implementation, and coordinate with other donors and domestic programmes. They are intended to be multi-sectoral, and representative of a country's principal stakeholders. The CCM 'model' embodies three core principles: representation, local ownership and harmonization. Over 120 countries have created CCMs.

Arguably, the CCM represents a new system of rule that encourages a country to embrace principles of good governance that go beyond merely ensuring an effective funding proposal. Three forms of power analysis may be employed to explain how such a system might impact on a recipient country.

- *Coercion* – the fund is able to exert coercive power over recipient countries 'by not making them eligible to apply for GFATM funding if they do not establish a CCM' (Abbott, 2008: 38)
- *Agenda-setting* – the guidelines developed by the fund heavily condition issues considered in the grant proposal and hence what the AIDS, TB and malaria communities are *discussing* at the country level
- *Teaching* – an alternative conception of power that embodies constructive insights into the power of actors to 'teach' norms of participation, representation and ownership by communicating them as appropriate and legitimate modes of behaviour. In his pioneering work in this area Abbott, for example, argues: 'the CCM requirement "teaches" the norm of participation, communicating its appropriateness and legitimacy to governments and civil society in applicant countries, and casting it as an international expectation' (Abbott, 2008: 38).

coordination arrangements required by both GAVI and the GFATM also introduce new systems of accountability and new rules of the game (Box 12.4).

Seven recommendations to enable GHPs to contribute to more effective global health governance

Embrace the aid modalities of the Paris agenda

The United Nations reported in 2007 that only one of its eight regional groups was on track to meet all their Millennium Development Goals by 2015 (UN, 2007). Faced with such a gloomy assessment of progress, our first recommendation is that GHPs strengthen their commitment to a set of 'best practice' principles designed to help achieve the health and poverty reduction MDGs (HLF, 2005). Established at a high level forum on the MDGs in Paris in November 2005, these principles were derived from five key areas of aid effectiveness formally expressed in the Paris Declaration on Aid Effectiveness. Additional principles on GHP governance were proposed: GHPs should ensure that their purpose, goals and objectives were clear, procedures were transparent and key documents were made publicly available on the internet (Caines, 2005).

The Paris Declaration committed donors to aligning their assistance with recipient countries' national priorities, providing aid through existing government channels and switching from 'project aid' to 'general budget', 'sector budget' or 'programme' support or engaging in sector-wide approaches. Unfortunately, because GHPs are by design issue-specific and quick results-oriented, they have found it difficult – though not impossible – to embrace the Paris agenda. In 2004, it was reported that the big five GHPs were struggling more than the smaller access partnerships to align and harmonize (Caines and Lush, 2004). The GFATM, for example, continues to struggle to meet its commitments to align (see Box 12.5).

Box 12.5 The GFATM: a mixed response to alignment and harmonization

A review of the GFATM's Country Coordinating Mechanism notes concerns at national level and within the global health community that the GFATM's system of 'rounds' was geared to supporting discrete projects rather than strategic programmes, was undermining coordinated approaches such as SWAps, and was a major source of disharmony for national planning, implementation, monitoring and reporting systems (EuroHealth, 2006: 17). At its sixteenth board meeting in 2007, it was decided that the Fund should accept 'national applications' (that is, national plans as opposed to free-standing applications; GFATM, 2007). This decision could, in theory, improve alignment should CCMs embrace this more liberal interpretation of the Fund's framework document.

In relation to harmonization, the GFATM's local fund agents were criticized both for constituting a parallel system distinct from other government or donor monitoring processes and for the significant transaction costs incurred in their use of a separate fund-specific reporting system (EuroHealth, 2007: viii). Whilst individual country perceptions of the GFATM, in terms of alignment and harmonization, are mixed, the following quote sums up much of the frustration felt by many: 'The way the GF does business flies in the face of donor harmonization and alignment and use of government systems. While other donors try to reduce transaction costs, these aren't a priority for GF' (quoted in EuroHealth, 2006: 67).

Whilst the picture on alignment and harmonization would appear mixed, there are nevertheless signs that GHPs are heading in the right direction. The GFATM's decision to accept what it calls 'Modified Application Process for Supporting Country Programs', or 'National Strategy Applications', is aimed at increasing the use of fund grants to plug identified holes in the national strategy's budget. The GFATM hopes that this will enable further alignment with national systems. Furthermore, a recent study has reported positively on the fund's integration into the Mozambique health SWAp and health common fund – relying on the country's existing financial and auditing controls, and using national reporting and M&E systems (Dickinson et al., 2007). In addition, some country studies, including that of Malawi, reveal progress on alignment (Mtonya and Chizimbi, 2006). Other GHPs are making great strides to improve their alignment and harmonization. The GAVI Alliance, for example, now has a section on its website devoted to harmonization and alignment where it reports target levels of 100 per cent by 2010 for aid flows that are predictable and aligned with country priorities, for avoidance of parallel implementation structures and for use of common procedures.[3]

Ensure even better representation of stakeholders

Our second recommendation is that GHPs should strive towards ensuring a more appropriate and balanced representation of stakeholders in decision-making as a step in the direction of broader participation. In an earlier study of representation in GHPs, which drew on 2005 data, we found that at board level GHPs were unrepresentative of a number of stakeholder groups. From a sample of 23 GHPs we found that constituencies from low- and lower-middle income countries (LMIC) were under-represented on governing bodies, NGOs were least represented, whilst the corporate sector enjoyed relatively high representation (23 per cent) (Buse and Harmer, 2007). We argued that: (i) the high representation of the corporate sector was at odds with its financial contributions; (ii) modest representation of intergovernmental organizations lent weight to the concern that the public sector's influence in global public health may be diminishing; and (iii) skewed representation was not a deliberate move on the part of GHP architects but arose as a consequence of an understandable desire to restrict the size of governing bodies so as to make them manageable while accommodating the demands of funding agencies to have a say in how their resources are spent.

There have been some improvements in the accessibility of data on the composition of the governance teams of GHPs; most of the major GHPs now list their board members by the constituency they represent. Membership of the boards of 19 GHPs in 2008 is presented in Table 12.1 above. A direct comparison of membership of 16 GHPs (selected on the basis of publicly available data) reveals only minor changes in composition between 2005 and 2008 (see Figure 12.1 and Table 12.2). There has been a slight increase in total LMIC

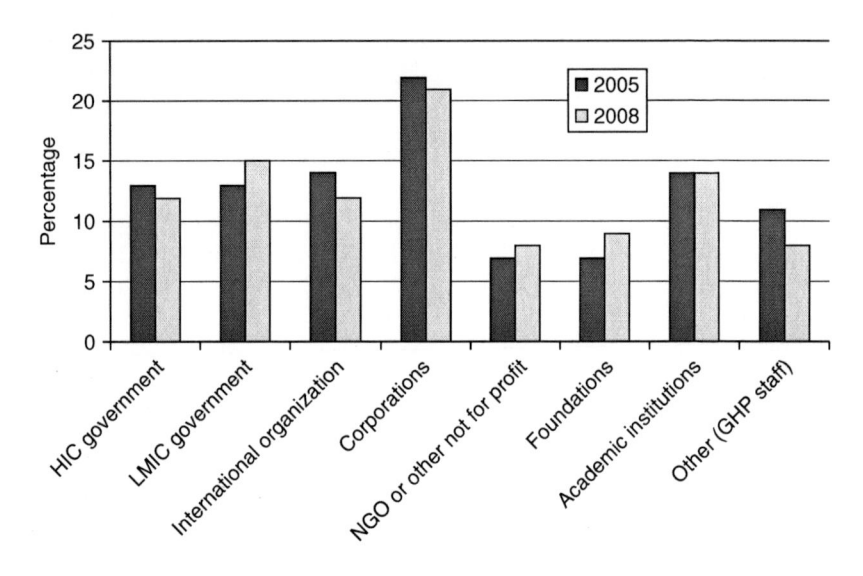

Figure 12.1 Constituency representation within 16 GHPs: 2005 and 2008 compared
Source: Authors.

Table 12.2 Constituency representation within 16 GHPs: 2005 and 2008 compared (percentages in brackets)

	Total number of board members across 16 GHPs	HIC Government	LMIC Government	International organization	Corporations	NGO or other not for profit	Foundations	Academic Institutions	Other (e.g. GHP staff)	Female	LMIC (all)
2005	215	27 (13)	29 (13)	30 (14)	47 (22)	14 (7)	15 (7)	30 (14)	19 (11)	41 (19)	45 (21)
2008	231	29 (12)	36 (15)	29 (12)	47 (21)	20 (8)	21 (9)	30 (14)	19 (8)	51 (22)	54 (23)

Source: Authors.

representation since 2005 (up to 23 per cent of all seats). The corporate sector continues to enjoy good representation as does the persistence of gender disparity: just 22 per cent of board members are female.

Adopt standard operating procedures to improve performance and mutual accountability

GHPs should ensure that their purpose, goals and objectives are clear, and that their procedures are transparent. The business sector has long recognized the importance of structuring partnerships around a set of 'SMART' objectives (that is objectives that are specific, measurable, achievable, realistic and time-bound). In order to be effective, GHPs should embrace a similar approach to objective setting. The Stop TB Partnership has shown the benefit of developing such a strategy through a shared global plan detailing its partners' responsibilities (Caines, 2005). Yet, a study of 74 GHPs revealed that very few articulated objectives in a specific and measurable manner (Buse, 2004).

In addition to having clear objectives, it is also important that partners define their roles and responsibilities more clearly. Clarity of roles and responsibilities pertain at different levels of engagement: between the partners, between a GHP secretariat and the partners and between the GHP's partner and other partners active in a given field (WHO, 2007). Of particular relevance is the need to gain a better understanding of the relationship between the functions and responsibilities of secretariats and the functions and responsibilities of the partners. The result of insufficient clarity has often been sub-optimal working arrangements, performance monitoring and accountability (McKinsey, 2005). In the case of the GFATM, for example, the role of the LFA remains unclear to many CCM members, leading in some cases to false expectations and frustration and in others to the promulgation of a negative image of the fund (EuroHealth, 2007: viii). If GHPs become complacent about the roles and responsibilities of their partners, it will lead inevitably to inadequate performance monitoring, it will undermine accountability and it will impede overall progress of the partnership. Our recommendation is that GHPs should implement strategic, value added and operational business plans with measurable outputs and outcomes, and maintain clearly defined roles for all partners that are developed ex ante and regularly reviewed.

Improve GHP oversight

Our fourth recommendation further develops a central motif of this chapter: the importance of monitoring GHP performance. Elsewhere we have argued for improved systems of management of conflicts of interest[4] and vetting of partners (Buse and Harmer, 2007). Another aspect of oversight concerns performance monitoring. The record is, again, mixed. A recent evaluation of the GFATM, for example, reported that whilst it has improved documentation of the basis for its funding decisions by, among other things, giving an explanation for the performance rating it assigns to its grants, it still lacks the information it needs to manage and oversee LFAs (GAO, 2007). Even though LFAs are the backbone of the fund's risk management strategy – its 'eyes and ears' – the fund at present lacks any systematic assessment of LFA performance: assessment of the LFA is informal and irregular, and the results of the assessment are not systematically documented. In addition, the GFATM does not have a standardized measure of its expectations of LFA performance. To be successfully implemented, such a tool for assessment must be *mandatory*.

The GAVI Alliance, on the other hand, has established METAG (Monitoring and Evaluation Technical Advisory Group) to strengthen and coordinate M&E among its partners.

Value the 'invisible P' of GHPs: people

One of the least well-researched areas of GHP performance concerns the stresses placed on the staff of partnering organizations and of the secretariat they establish to support the partnership. For example, an evaluation of the European Malaria Vaccine Initiative in 2005 noted that 'the secretariat is too small for the expectations of the partnership' (KPMG, 2005). The McKinsey study highlights the extent to which GHPs rely too heavily on in-country development partners to provide technical assistance for GHP-funded programmes. Ostensibly, this is because GHPs are keen to avoid duplication and to be seen as paragons of efficiency; however, with the expanding scale of GHP-funded programmes, country partners' human resources are being stretched. McKinsey quotes one partner in Vietnam reporting: 'We are simply unpaid workers of GHPs like the Global Fund and GAVI. While there is more and more work, our staffing capacity has not been increased at all' (McKinsey, 2005: 21).

Another GHP human resources concern relates to pressures on staff that arise from divided loyalties and inadequate resources for managing partnership collaboration. Divided loyalties are most likely to arise in 'hosted' partnerships where partnership staff loyalty may be split between the host and the partners themselves through the partnership's governing body. In order to alleviate the 'pressure of partnering', staff rules and incentives need to be established; tasks and roles, and therefore expectations, must be clarified so that parent organizations are aware and tolerant of their staff's external efforts; and greater emphasis on consolidated work planning is required (Buse and Harmer, 2007).

Ensure adequate resources for GHPs

While it may appear counter-intuitive to suggest that GHPs, as the well-endowed darlings of the donor community, may be strapped for cash, we contend that if they are to serve as vehicles for GHG, they will need to be realistically resourced. There are three issues that we feel are of some consequence here. First, there is the issue of the purported gap in available financing. As we have reported elsewhere, while there are problems identifying comparable data, in the case of eleven GHPs we found an average 60 per cent deficit between reported needs and donor commitment (Buse and Harmer, 2007).

That funding commitments do not meet the projected financing needs of the GHPs is not surprising in that they establish very ambitious goals in relation to their target diseases. This failure masks the success of the GHPs in establishing these grand targets in the first place, but it also points up a deficit in GHG more generally in that there is a need to establish a more effective system for calculating the financing needs across diseases (and consequently GHPs and other funding mechanisms) and countries and to introduce a mechanism to allocate resources more rationally in response.

This leads to the second issue. The pharmaceutical industry's R&D association IFPMA estimates 'in-kind' donations of the order of US$1.3 billion during the period 2000–06 (IFPMA, 2007). Cash donations were significantly less: for example, US corporate grant-making to AIDS in 2003 was approximately US$70 m (Tanguy, 2005). This represents just 18 per cent of total US philanthropic donations, with the foundations – specifically the Bill and Melinda Gates Foundation – contributing much of the rest.[5] With a few notable exceptions (for example, Merck's US$50 million donation to the African Comprehensive HIV/AIDS Partnership and Pfizer's US$22 million donation to the International Trachoma Initiative), pharmaceutical companies make comparatively small cash donations to GHPs. Companies have their preferred GHPs, but corporate support for the major funding GHPs is poor, with significant corporate cash contributors to the GFATM remaining 'a rather small group' (Tanguy, 2005: 5). Whilst GHPs could undoubtedly do much more to make themselves more attractive investments for corporate philanthropy, one is left wondering whether an industry that boasts annual drug sales in excess of US$200 billion could give more (Angell, 2004).

The third, and equally important, funding issue concerns the provision of adequate financing for GHP secretariats who have to accomplish expensive coordination tasks, with accompanying transaction costs. The McKinsey review comments on the false economy of cutbacks in this area. Some GHPs pass on these costs to partner agencies. Take the GFATM – it advertises itself as a lean machine – but it externalizes the transaction costs to governments and partners. Both GFATM and the GAVI Alliance have been criticized in past assessments for tending to rely too heavily on in-country development partners (particularly WHO, UNFPA and UNICEF but others as well) to finance and provide technical support to develop proposals for GHP grants and support monitoring efforts. In response to the resentment that this perceived exploitation provokes amongst partners, it is heartening to see GHPs, such as the GAVI Alliance, providing funds to governments to source and finance technical support for such tasks.

Reassess the prevailing GHP paradigm

Our final recommendation calls for a critical reassessment of the prevailing GHP paradigm. There are a number of components to this reassessment. First, it is instructive to consider that innovative products are also being produced by non-profit public partnerships as well as by the more ubiquitous public-private model of partnerships. The DNDi's first anti-malarial drug ASAQ, for example, is a once-a-day regimen and is non-patented (DNDi, 2007). Developing drugs that are easy to use and accessible have been elusive goals for many GHPs, and there may be important lessons to learn from DNDi's partnership structure.

Second, a broader reassessment of agencies' relationships to GHPs is required. As we wrote this chapter, work on a number of aspects of GHPs was under way. For example, several agencies (for example, DFID, the World Bank and USAID) were looking at the impact of GHPs on health systems, and how GHPs might strengthen them. But we feel that there needs to be a broader analysis of the how and why of partnership in the sector. At the time of writing, the WHO was engaged in a self-reflective appraisal of its engagement with health partnerships (WHO, 2007) and UNICEF was undertaking a similar exercise. We would encourage other international organizations to take similar stock of their partnering activities – but also that this be linked to wider questions of the role of GHPs in GHG: questions such as the desirability and feasibility of rolling many of the GHPs into one Global Fund for Health.

A third point concerns the potential of the partnership environment to influence or 'steer' partners' behaviour. Should we expect to see demonstrable changes in partners' behaviour as they become exposed to the values of the GHP? Is it enough for pharmaceutical partners simply to grant public-sector researchers access to their libraries of drug compounds, as is the case with many of the product-development GHPs? Or should we expect more? One only has to look at advances that the private sector has made in environmental sustainability to recognize that there *is* flexibility in how multinational companies might perceive their longer-term self-interest. If Interface, one of the largest carpet manufacturing companies in the world, can transform its carpet production model with the aim of becoming 100 per cent sustainable whilst remaining competitive, then perhaps it is time for us to expect pharmaceutical companies to show a similar degree of enlightenment and embrace more fully norms of access and equity – including in the realm of intellectual property rights and pricing. GHPs should be expecting nothing less from their corporate partners.[6]

A final recommendation echoes our earlier calls for partnership architects and proponents to apply the partnership logic to non-communicable diseases and socio-economic health interventions. Regrettably, progress has been slow in both of these areas, although there are a few developments. The Global Health Workforce Alliance, for example, is a new partnership dedicated to identifying and implementing solutions to the health workforce crisis. Hosted by the WHO, the partnership brings together national governments, civil society, finance institutions, workers, international agencies, academic institutions and professional associations to deal with a health systems issue which can serve as a vehicle for all health concerns.[7] Unilever reports on a modest partnership with the World Heart Federation to increase awareness of health disease and its risk factors (Unilever, 2006).

Future development of GHPs

If the international relations 'realists' looked out on the international system in the 1970s and observed a state of anarchy, what would they see in today's world? A great deal more chaos given the proliferation of actors at the global level? Perhaps, and yet the advent of GHPs *has* provided a degree of order in a seemingly disorganized global health arena. Specifically, we have noted seven key areas where GHPs have helped to steer the course of global health governance. GHPs have helped to raise the profile of neglected diseases through a combination of discourse and scientific innovation; championed new development financing strategies; provided new modes of global health cooperation; contributed to considerable consensus in the sector; reoriented the priorities of the global health sector – notably in financing for HIV/AIDS; pioneered new rules of accountability; and established international norms and standards. If global governance is about 'creating the conditions for ordered rule and collective action' (Stoker, 1998: 17–28) then GHPs have laid important foundations.

GHPs have given substance to what, for many, is a notoriously vaporous concept. A decade ago, Finkelstein lamented that global governance 'appears to be virtually anything' (Finkelstein, 1995); now, in the health sector at least, there are development goals, principles of best practice, and norms of appropriate behaviour. It is, however, a nascent framework for GHG, and is deficient in a number of respects. In this chapter we have advanced a number of recommendations that could further serve to improve governance. To reiterate, we urge GHPs to incorporate Paris-inspired principles of best aid practice more fully into their operations; ensure that representation defines constituency management; adopt SOPs to improve performance and mutual accountability; improve oversight; ensure that GHP staff are given sufficient administrative and pastoral support; ensure that GHP secretariats have adequate resources; and continually reassess GHP modes of interaction. This latter point is of particular importance, and we conclude with some thoughts on why developing a *performance metric* should be a priority over the coming years so as to give more order to the prevailing anarchy.

Prospective analysis of the potential problems of GHPs at the turn of the century gave way to evaluations of GHP practice; and whilst evaluations continue, increasing attention is now being given to a range of issues – particularly those related to how GHPs interact with the environments in which they operate. Among these issues, a critical area is the manner in which GHP performance is, and should be, measured. If GHPs are to meet the standards and targets required of them, and donors are to invest effectively and responsibly, then a performance metric is required to guide donors in their investments. The development of tools for measuring GHP performance is still in its infancy but a *useful* tool would need to utilize indicators that are systematic, consistent and broadly applicable across the various categories of

GHPs. Whilst demand for such a metric is evident as national and international donors are beginning to commission analysts to produce frameworks to guide their investments, the development of tools for measuring GHP performance is still in its infancy.

The GFATM has developed a metric to measure its operational performance, grant performance, system effects and impact. The GFATM has also developed an analytical tool for expressing its core performance indicators: the 'Executive Dashboard'. This tool covers mainly financial indicators (resource mobilization, disbursement and grant support, operations management and so on) and not organizational or institutional aspects of fund operations. Kruse and Claussen (2005) suggest that indicators on CCM performance should also be included as key global dashboard information but as yet this reform has not been implemented. Whilst these assessments are appropriate for GHPs which raise and disburse finance, they have only limited application to other non-funding GHPs such as product development and access partnerships where analysis has tended to focus more on indicators of quality (such as the health value of drugs for developing country patients) rather than quantity (Moran et al., 2007).

A review of the literature reveals that missing from the mix is an across-the-board metric that is widely and periodically undertaken along with a development of platforms where the results of the assessments can be discussed by interested parties. Such a metric would help to enhance the performance of partnerships and guide GHP funding agencies in their investment decision-making.

While some might be opposed to the idea that we need more coordinated oversight of the melange of partnership initiatives and their relationships to other developments in the global health sector (fearing that this might inhibit the thousand flowers from blossoming and/or their death by a thousand cuts), GHP evaluations tend to suggest otherwise. Still others might be sceptical of the prospects of bringing increased order through more consistent monitoring and oversight. In our view, while these pessimists may well be right, we hold on to the optimism of those visionaries who dared to believe in the promise of global health partnerships – and were proved, in the main, right.

Notes

1. Personal communications with many partnership practitioners during the period 2000–05.
2. It is arguably the case that GHPs have also induced changes to corporate rules of the game in, among other things, the ways in which corporate entities impact on health. The Global Alliance to Improve Nutrition, for example, has encouraged a range of companies to fortify food consumed by the poor to deal with micronutrient deficiencies (GAIN, 2007).

3. http://www.gavialliance.org/performance/harmonisation/index.php (accessed 18 March 2008).
4. On the question of conflicts of interest see the example of CSO partners of the GFATM in Peru, where CSOs voted to be both implementers of an intervention and be on the CCM deciding which CSOs would get the contracts (Caceres et al., 2007).
5. The Gates Foundation has thus far donated US$350 million to the GFATM alone.
6. http://www.interfacesustainability.com/ (accessed 18 March 2008).
7. http://www.who.int/workforcealliance/en/ (accessed 18 March 2008).

References

Abbott, K., 'Enriching Rational Choice Institutionalism for the Study of International Law', *University of Illinois Law Review*, 3 (2008): 5–46.
AMC, 'Advance Market Commitments for Vaccines', 2007, http://www.vaccineamc.org/about/about_structure.html (accessed 23 February 2008).
Angell, M. (2004), *The Truth about the Drug Companies: How They Deceive Us and What to do about it* (New York: Random House).
Attawell, K. and C. Dickinson, 'An Independent Assessment of Progress on the Implementation of the Global Task Team Recommendations in Support of National AIDS Responses', HLSP, London, 2007.
Brugha, R. et al., 'Global Fund Tracking Study: a Cross-Country Comparative Analysis', final report, RCSI and LSHTM, 2005.
Buse, K., 'Governing Public-Private Infectious Disease Partnerships', *Brown Journal of World Affairs*, 10(2) (2004): 225–42.
Buse, K. and A. Harmer, 'Seven Habits of Highly Effective Global Public-Private Health Partnerships: Practice and Potential', *Social Science and Medicine*, 64 (2) (2007): 259–71.
Buse, K. and G. Walt, 'Global Public-Private Partnerships: Part I – A New Development in Health?' *Bulletin of the World Health Organization*, 78(4) (2000): 549–61.
Buse, K., F. Samuels and M. Pearson, 'Corporate Champions: Doing Good more Effectively', *Lancet*, 371 (2008): 986.
Caceres, C., R. Lopez, J. Pajuelo et al., 'Lessons Learned from the Implementation of GFATM-supported HIV/AIDS Projects in Peru', PPT presentation, GHIN workshop, Dublin, 2007, www.ghinet.org/downloads/Peru.ppt (accessed 24 April 2008).
Caines, K., 'Background Paper: Key Evidence from Major Studies of Global Health Partnerships', report for High Level Forum on the Health MDGs Working Group on Global Health Initiatives and Partnerships, 25–26 April 2005.
Caines, K. and L. Lush, 'Impact of Public-Private Partnerships Addressing Access to Pharmaceuticals in Low and Middle Income Countries: a Synthesis Report from Studies in Botswana, Sri Lanka, Uganda and Zambia', Initiative on Public-Private Partnerships for Health, Geneva, 2004.
Carlson, C., 'Mapping Global Health Partnerships: What They Are, What They Do and Where They Operate', DFID, London, 2004.
Dickinson, C., J. Martinez, D. Whitaker and M. Pearson, 'The Global Fund Operating in a SWAp through a Common Fund: Issues and Lessons from Mozambique', HLSP, London, 2007.
Dingwerth, K. and P. Pattberg, 'Global Governance as a Perspective on World Politics', *Global Governance*, 12(2) (2006): 185–203.

DNDi, 'New, Once-a-Day Fixed-Dose Combination against Malaria Now Available', Press Release, DNDi, 2007, www.dndi.org/pdf_files/press_release_march_1-eng.pdf (accessed 18 March 2008).

EuroHealth Group, 'Assessment of the Proposal Development and Review Process of the Global Fund to Fight AIDS, TB and Malaria: Assessment Report', Denmark: RFP No HQ-GVA -05-010, 2006.

EuroHealth Group, 'The Global Fund to Fight AIDS, Tuberculosis and Malaria: Evaluation of the Local Fund Agent System', Denmark: RFP No. HQ-GVA-06-031, 2007.

Finkelstein, L., 'What is Global Governance?' *Global Governance*, 1 (3) (1995): 367–72.

GAO, 'Global Fund to Fight TB, AIDS and Malaria has Improved its Documentation of Funding but Needs Standardized Oversight Expectation and Assessment', Government Accountability Office: GAO-07-627, 2007.

GAIN, *GAIN Annual Report 2005–2006*, 2007, www.gainhealth.org/system/files/GAIN_AnnualReport0506.pdf (accessed on 23 February 2008).

GAVI, 'Proposal for GAVI to Invest in Health Systems Strengthening (HSS) Support', 2005, www.gavialliance.org/resources/Investment_Case_for_HSS_Nov05.pdf (accessed 25 February 2008).

GFATM, 'Guidelines on the Purpose, Structure, Composition and Funding of CCMs, and Requirements for Grant Eligibility, 9th Board Meeting of the Global Fund', 2004, http://www.who.int/hdp/publications/13d.pdf. Approved at the 16th Board Meeting on 12–13 November 2007 (accessed 25 February 2008).

GFATM, 'Global Fund to Fight AIDS, TB and Malaria. Report of the Policy and Strategy Committee to the 16th Board Meeting', 2007, www.theglobalfund.org/en/files/boardmeeting16/GF-BM16-06_PSC_Report.pdf (accessed 23 February 2008).

Grace, C., 'Developing New Technologies to Address Neglected Diseases: the Role of Product Development Partnerships and Advanced Market Commitments', HLSP, London, 2006.

Harmer, A., 'Understanding the Rise of Health GPPPs: the Role of Discourse and Ideas', PhD thesis, Southampton University, 2005.

HLF, 'High Level Forum on the Health MDGs', 2005, www.hlfhealthmdgs.org/Documents/GlobalHealthPartnerships.pdf (accessed 20 March 2008).

IFFIm, 'IFFm Supporting GAVI', 2005, www.iff-immunisation.org/index.html (accessed 20 March 2008).

IFPMA, 'Updated IFPMA Survey Shows Growing Pharmaceutical Industry Contribution to Improving Developing World Health', http://www.ifpma.org/Documents/NR8477/Release_Partnerships_Survey_02Nov07.pdf (accessed 15 December 2008).

KPMG, 'EMVI Mid-Term Review Report', 2005, www.emvi.org (accessed 19 March 2008).

Kruse, S.E. and K. Claussen, 'Partnerships and Harmonization: Dimensions, Issues and Indicators', in *Measuring the Systems Effects of the Global Fund with a Focus on Additionality, Partnerships and Sustainability: Resource Document* (Geneva: The Global Fund to Fight AIDS, Tuberculosis and Malaria, 2005), chapter 3.

Lee, K. and J. Collin (eds), *Global Change and Health* (Maidenhead: Open University Press, 2005).

Lorenz, N., 'Effectiveness of Global Health Partnerships: Will the Past Repeat Itself?', *Bulletin of the World Health Organization*, 85 (7) (2007): 567–8.

McKinsey & Co, 'Global Health Partnerships: Assessing Country Consequences', Bill and Melinda Gates Foundation, Seattle, 2005.

Mitrany, D., *The Functional Theory of Politics* (London: Martin Robertson and Company, 1975).

Moran, M. et al., 'Neglected Diseases: Doctors can make a Difference', report commissioned by the British Medical Association, with funding from the UK Department for International Development, 2007.

Mtonya, B. and S. Chizimbi, 'Systemwide Effects of the Global Fund in Malawi: Final Report', Abt Associates, Cambridge, 2006.

OECD, 'Aid Effectiveness: Implementing the Paris Principles', in *OECD Development Cooperation Report* (Paris: OECD, 2007), chapter 3.

Oomman, N., M. Bernstein and R. Rosenzweig, 'Following the Funding for HIV/AIDS: a Comparative Analysis of the Funding Practices of PEPFAR, the Global Fund and World Bank MAP in Mozambique, Uganda and Zambia', Center for Global Development, Washington, DC, 2007.

Republic of Rwanda, 'Scaling up to Achieve the Health MDGs in Rwanda', Ministry of Finance and Economic Planning and Ministry of Health, Kigali, 2006.

Rochlin, S., S. Zadek and M. Forstater, *Governing Collaboration: Making Partnerships Accountable for Delivering Development* (London: Accountability, 2008).

Shiffman, J., 'Has Donor Prioritisation of HIV/AIDS Displaced Aid for other Health Issues?' *Health Policy and Planning*, 23 (2) (2008): 95–100.

Stern, A.M. and H. Markel, 'International Efforts to Control Infectious Diseases, 1851 to the Present', *Journal of the American Medical Association*, 292 (2004): 1474–9.

Stillman, K. and S. Bennett, 'Systemwide Effects of the Global Fund: Interim Findings from Three Country Studies' , Abt Associates, Cambridge, 2005.

Stoker, G., 'Governance as Theory: Five Propositions', *International Social Science Journal*, 155 (1998): 17–28.

Tanguy, J. et al., 'Mobilising Additional Resources for the Global Fund: a Planning Guide for the Private Sector', report prepared by the Global Business Coalition on HIV/AIDS / Private Sector Delegation to the Board of The Global Fund to Fight AIDS, Tuberculosis and Malaria.

Unilever (2006) 'Unilever & World Heart Federation Continue Global Partnership to ImproveHeartHealth',2005, http://www.unilever.com/ourcompany/ newsandmedia/ pressreleases/2006/ UnileverandWorldHeartFederationcontinuegloba200641401017. asp (accessed 16 March 2008).

UNITAID, *'What is UNITAID?'* 2007, www.unitaid.eu/ (accessed 24 March 2008).

United Nations, *The Millennium Development Goals Report 2007* (Geneva: United Nations, 2007), www.un.org/millenniumgoals/pdf/mdg2007.pdf (accessed 16 March 2008).

Weinberg, J., 'The Impact of Globalisation on Emerging Infectious Diseases', in K. Lee and J. Collin (eds), *Global Change and Health* (Maidenhead: Open University Press, 2005), chapter 5.

WHO, 'Partnerships: Report by the Secretariat', WHO, Geneva, EB122/19, 2007.

Widdus, R. and K. White, 'Combating Diseases Associated with Poverty: Financing Strategies for Product Development and the Potential Role of Public-Private Partnerships', IPPPH, Geneva, 2004.

13
Governance of Chronic Diseases[1]
David Stuckler, Corinna Hawkes and Derek Yach

Chronic diseases are the leading causes of death and disability worldwide. This chapter evaluates the governance of chronic diseases and their associated risks. A brief overview of the sources of weak global responses to chronic diseases is provided, after which the actions of major players on chronic diseases are mapped. We conclude with some strategies for strengthening chronic disease governance based upon historical precedents of governance interventions.

Global burden of chronic diseases

Each year over 31 million people are estimated to die from just four leading chronic non-communicable diseases – heart disease, common cancers, respiratory diseases and diabetes (Mathers and Loncar, 2006; Stuckler, 2008).[2] Close to half of these deaths are estimated to be premature (WHO, 2005). Nearly 80 per cent occur in low- and middle-income countries, where chronic diseases claim around 80 per cent more lives than all infectious causes put together (Mathers and Loncar, 2006). In 2002, chronic diseases were responsible for 46 per cent of all deaths in developing countries – a figure which will grow to 59 per cent by 2030, or to over 37 million lives a year. In all regions of the world, except sub-Saharan Africa, leading chronic diseases are projected to be the major killers – see Figure 13.1 (Suhrcke et al., 2006; Mathers and Loncar, 2006; Stuckler 2008). For some lower-middle income regions, the original 'Global Burden of Disease' 'pessimistic scenarios' for diabetes (Murray and Lopez, 1996) have now become the 'optimistic scenarios' (Mathers and Loncar, 2006) for the next two decades.

With these foreseeable consequences, and given the potential for prevention, one might expect that key health organizations, such as the World Health Organization and national health ministries, and development institutions that focus on poverty, such as the World Bank and the United Nations Development Programme, would be scaling-up efforts to combat the rising tide of chronic diseases in developing countries, especially in light of recent

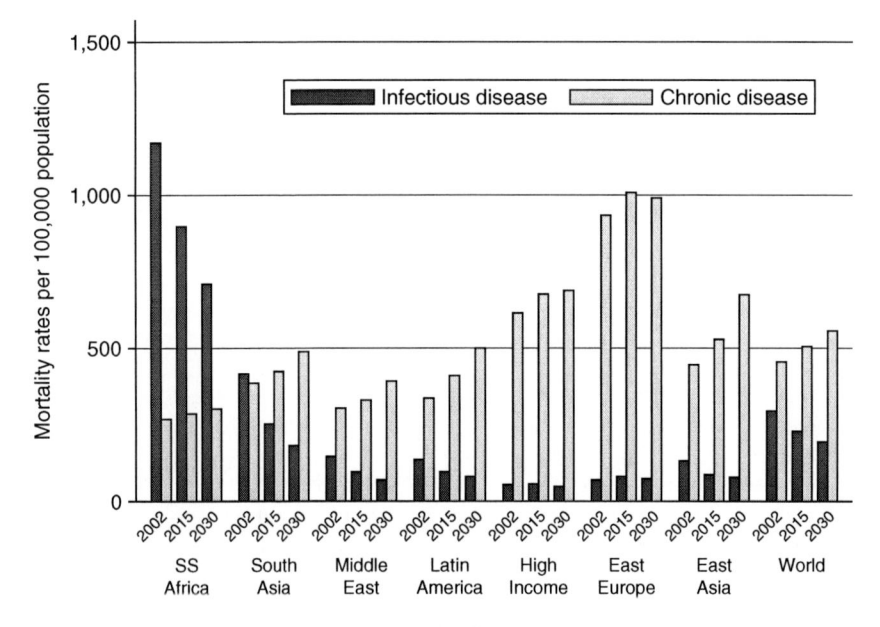

Figure 13.1 Evolution of the global burden of disease, 2002–30

Notes: Infectious disease classification is based on WHO's type 1 infectious disease cluster. Chronic disease classification is based on cardiovascular disease, cancers, respiratory disease and diabetes mellitus, subcategories of WHO's type 2 burden of disease cluster.

Source: Stuckler (2008).

rises in global health financing (Garrett, 2007). Yet, a string of recent publications have suggested that this is not the case, instead claiming that global chronic diseases are 'neglected', 'silent', 'a hidden epidemic', and that their epidemiologic and economic impacts have not translated into a proportionate global response (Yach et al., 2004; Horton, 2005 and the *Lancet* special issue on 'the neglected epidemic of chronic disease').

Are chronic diseases actually being neglected in low- and middle-income countries? If so, does this mean that global chronic disease governance is failing? As an initial step in addressing these questions, this chapter evaluates the governance of chronic disease by first analysing the ways in which diseases are prioritized and then mapping the actions of key players in chronic disease prevention and control.

How do we define and evaluate governance?

Before proceeding, a brief discussion of the term 'governance' and its application to health is needed. Governance is frequently described as comprising the actions that steer decision-making procedures, rules and authority (Buse

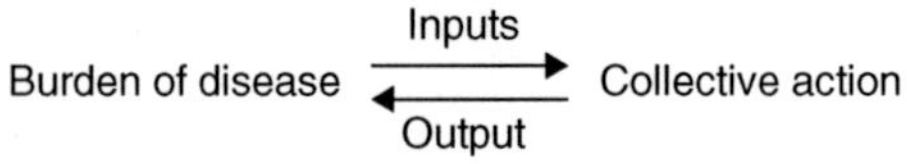

```
                        Inputs
    Burden of disease  ⇄  Collective action
                        Output
```

Figure 13.2 Input-output model of health governance

and Walt, 2000; Mayntz 2005). For example, Rosenau writes that 'Governance can be defined as the process whereby an organization or society steers itself' (1995 in Buse and Walt, 2000), and Fidler claims '[health] governance refers to how societies structure responses to the [health] challenges they face' (2004: 799). One strength of these definitions for contemporary policy analysis is that they separate the content of *governance* from the actions of *government*; however, a limitation is that they do not give rise to objective criteria for identifying governance success or failure as has been done for market and state failure (Jessop, 1998).

Our analysis starts from a more generalized and integrative view of health governance: we consider health governance, in a quantitative sense, as a function that maps burden of disease parameters into a set of collective societal responses and further maps those reactions back upon the burden of disease. Governance then becomes, in a social sense, equivalent to the dynamic relationship between the burden of disease and the complete set of civil society, private sector, non-governmental organization, nation-state, and other national and transnational institutional responses.[3]

Figure 13.2 models this input-output governance dynamic. The forward arrow in the model represents the 'inputs to governance', or the political economy. This involves considerations such as which diseases are prioritized and why? The reverse arrow in the model can be thought of as the 'outputs of governance'.[4] This involves considerations such as whether actors' policy actions are coherent and coordinated.

Governance failure occurs when the level of 'inputs', or the priority assigned to the disease burden, conflicts with the level of 'outputs', or the action on the disease.[5] This definition of governance offers criteria for what governance is supposed to maximize, while avoiding the normative aspects of what ought to be the appropriate level of action. To evaluate chronic disease governance as a system, therefore, we must first consider the 'inputs', or what determines whether chronic diseases are prioritized, against the 'outputs', or the current actions of relevant chronic disease actors. The rest of this chapter evaluates each of these elements of the governance system in turn.

Political economy of chronic diseases: the 'inputs'

A number of scholars have suggested that the epidemiological and economic consequences of chronic diseases in developing and developed countries have not translated into a global response proportionate to the magnitude of their impacts (Table 13.1). Below we present a brief list of reasons why chronic diseases are receiving less attention than would be proportional to their contribution to the global burden of disease (see Stuckler, 2008 for greater detail):

- *Orientation of health systems.* Historically, acute conditions have been the principal concerns for health-care systems. When health problems are chronic in nature, however, the acute care practice model breaks down. Yet the acute care paradigm is pervasive and now permeates the thinking of decision-makers, health-care workers, administrators and patients.
- *Risk accumulation and distribution.* (i) Long and variable lag times between accumulation of risk and the onset of illness make chronic diseases easier to ignore and less likely to fit shorter-term political cycles; (ii) Conditions which afflict middle-aged and older persons or are more dispersed in the population are less politically salient than those which afflict younger populations or greater concentrations (see Reich, 1995). The higher prevalence of chronic diseases among older age groups has promoted the ageing of the population as the leading population explanation of chronic disease growth. This has given rise to the notion that chronic diseases are 'inevitable consequences of ageing', implying that public policy cannot make a difference (World Bank, 2007; see Stuckler, 2008 for a critique); (iii) Chronic diseases have also tended to impact higher socio-economic groups first, and as a result chronic diseases were branded as 'diseases of affluence'.[6] But over time the within-population distribution of chronic diseases and their risks undergoes a 'social transition' to disproportionately afflict lower socio-economic groups – as witnessed for both tobacco/lung cancer and obesity/diabetes (Monteiro et al., 2004; Yach, 2005; Suhrcke et al., 2006).
- *Social and economic determinants.* Chronic diseases are often seen as problems of individual behavioural choices – choosing to smoke, drink alcohol, eat an unhealthy diet and not to be physically active. This assumption neglects the fact that macroeconomic drivers – and the industries that power them – shape the markets and the regulations within which people make choices (see Box 13.1). Figures 13.3a and 13.3b show that macroeconomic forces such as trade liberalization, foreign direct investment and economic growth are connected with rising chronic diseases in poor countries. Capacity in the health sector for addressing these socio-economic drivers is low.

More generally, policymakers often 'reason by metaphors' as a way to simplify complex policy trade-offs into a few consistent strategies when prioritizing health resources (Lau and Schlesinger, 2005). Of five leading global health metaphors that have been identified, namely global health as *foreign policy, security, charity, investment* and *public health* (Stuckler and McKee, 2008, see Table 13.2 for a description), chronic diseases tend to be

Table 13.1 Effect of expected changes in chronic disease mortality rates on economic growth, 2002–30

Region	Projected chronic disease increase (% change from 2002 to 2030)	Estimated effect on growth rates in 2030 (% per year)
World	21.90	−1.02
High income	12.06	−0.56
Eastern Europe and Central Asia	5.73	−0.27
East Asia and Pacific	52.23	−2.43
South Asia	27.89	−1.30
Latin America	48.01	−2.24
Middle East and North Africa	28.28	−1.32
Sub-Saharan Africa	12.13	−0.57

Source: Stuckler (2008).

Box 13.1   Role of economic globalization in chronic disease risks

Flow of goods

Facing saturated markets at home, TNCs in developed countries have sought new markets for tobacco, alcohol and food products in developing economies. Trade liberalization has facilitated this process. In the case of tobacco, the 1994 Uruguay Round of the General Agreement on Tariffs and Trade (GATT) liberalized trade in unmanufactured tobacco. World Trade Organization (WTO) agreements have since significantly reduced tariff and non-tariff barriers to tobacco trade. The result has been an increasing flow of tobacco between countries, leading to increased supply, lower prices, more extensive marketing of all forms – and increased risk of chronic diseases. Trade liberalization has had similar effects for food and dietary patterns (Rayner et al., 2006; Hawkes, 2005, 2006).

Flow of money and resources

Like trade, investing across borders plays a fundamental role in integrating the global marketplace. One of the most important types of investment is foreign direct investment (FDI). FDI has played an unprecedented role as a source of funding and economic development in developing nations. FDI has risen dramatically over the past 25 years – US$162.1 billion flowed into developing countries in 2002, mainly from TNCs in developed countries. Developing country governments have liberalized investment rules and introduced incentives in order to benefit from the much needed capital, skills, technology and goods and services promised (though not always realized) by FDI. TNCs, meanwhile, benefit from the potential of new, emerging markets and low-cost resources.

FDI has important implications for chronic diseases because investment in tobacco, food and alcohol products is high. TNCs have specific incentives to invest in tobacco, food and alcohol because they favour investments in concentrated markets where there is high brand recognition, of which cigarettes, alcohol, soft drinks and other processed food products are prime examples. FDI has also been crucial in transforming chronic disease risks as countries grow: (i) by directly changing the way tobacco, alcohol and food products are produced and distributed and (ii) by indirectly shaping physical activity patterns.

The more liberal investment regime put into place by governments to attract FDI can preclude the introduction of regulations or the raising of standards concerning the good or service in which the investment has been made in line with what has been shown to be effective in developed countries for protecting health. For example, globalization may bring with it pressures for tax competition, creating disincentives for a tobacco tax in countries wishing to attract FDI, illustrating the tensions faced by countries between the market opportunities and potential risks inherent in FDI. See Stuckler (2008) for empirical evidence.

Flow of information

The trade of and investment in tobacco, alcohol and food products around the world, along with technologies that affect physical activity patterns, is accompanied by a flow of information and images designed to encourage their use or consumption. These images, such as brands, logos and promotional initiatives, influence behaviour and consumption patterns through their emotional appeal and have the ability to shift cultural and social norms to encourage regular and frequent use and consumption of tobacco and alcohol, energy-dense, nutrient-poor foods, cars, personal computers and so on.

TNCs invest significantly in advertising and other forms of promotion, spreading brands all over the world while tailoring their campaigns to local conditions. Children and young people are targeted directly via advertising, sponsorship and other strategies such as sports and music events. This process has been greatly facilitated by the transnationalization and consolidation of advertising and communications agencies (Hawkes, 2005, 2006).

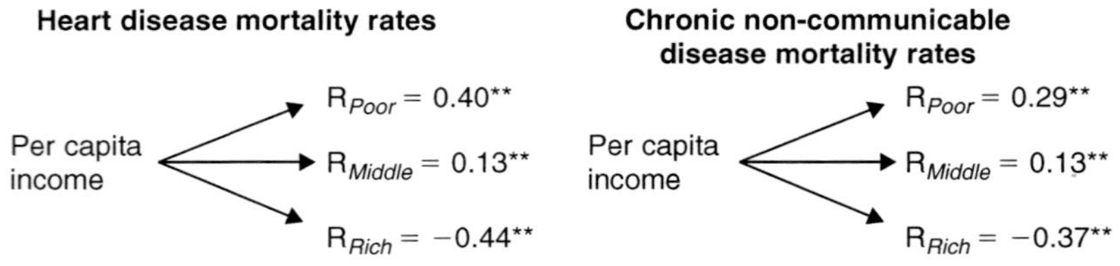

Heart disease mortality rates

Per capita income

$R_{Poor} = 0.40^{**}$
$R_{Middle} = 0.13^{**}$
$R_{Rich} = -0.44^{**}$

Chronic non-communicable disease mortality rates

Per capita income

$R_{Poor} = 0.29^{**}$
$R_{Middle} = 0.13^{**}$
$R_{Rich} = -0.37^{**}$

Figure 13.3a Associations between country-income levels per capita and log heart disease and chronic non-communicable disease mortality rates

Notes: Poor countries <US$3000 per capita income, middle countries >$3000 and <$7000, and rich countries >$7000 on average from 1960 to 2002. Male mortality rate data are from the WHO Global Mortality Database and are in logs. Chronic non-communicable disease is WHO's type 2 burden of disease category. Economic data are from the World Bank's World Development Indicators, 2005 edition, and the International Monetary Fund's International Financial Statistics, 2007 series. Per capita income is based on gross domestic product per capita (GDP). Cross-country data are de-trended for effects of changing ICD classifications.
Significance at * $p < 0.05$, ** $p < 0.01$.
Source: Stuckler (2008).

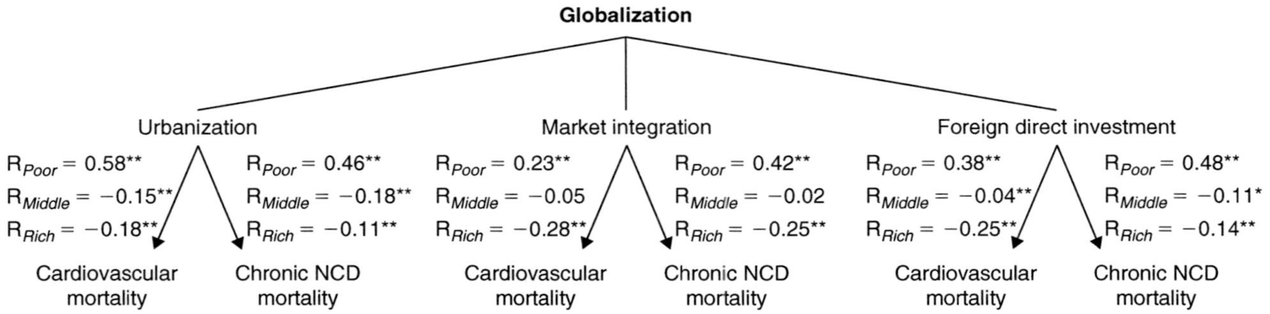

```
                              Globalization
          ┌───────────────────────┼───────────────────────┐
      Urbanization           Market integration    Foreign direct investment
```

$R_{Poor} = 0.58^{**}$ $R_{Poor} = 0.46^{**}$ $R_{Poor} = 0.23^{**}$ $R_{Poor} = 0.42^{**}$ $R_{Poor} = 0.38^{**}$ $R_{Poor} = 0.48^{**}$
$R_{Middle} = -0.15^{**}$ $R_{Middle} = -0.18^{**}$ $R_{Middle} = -0.05$ $R_{Middle} = -0.02$ $R_{Middle} = -0.04^{**}$ $R_{Middle} = -0.11^{*}$
$R_{Rich} = -0.18^{**}$ $R_{Rich} = -0.11^{**}$ $R_{Rich} = -0.28^{**}$ $R_{Rich} = -0.25^{**}$ $R_{Rich} = -0.25^{**}$ $R_{Rich} = -0.14^{**}$

Cardiovascular mortality | Chronic NCD mortality | Cardiovascular mortality | Chronic NCD mortality | Cardiovascular mortality | Chronic NCD mortality

Figure 13.3b Associations between globalization and log heart disease and chronic non-communicable disease mortality rates

Notes: Poor countries < US$3000 per capita income, middle countries > $3000 and <$7000, and rich countries > $7000 on average from 1960 to 2002. Male mortality rate data are from the WHO Global Mortality Database and are in logs. Chronic NCD is chronic non-communicable disease mortality based on WHO's type-2 burden of disease category. Economic data are from the World Bank's World Development Indicators, 2005 edition, and the International Monetary Fund International Financial Statistics 2007 series. Urbanization is the percentage of population living in urban settings. Market integration is total capital flows as a percentage of GDP. Foreign direct investment is the log level of foreign direct investment inflows. Cross-country data are de-trended for effects of changing ICD classifications.
Significance at * $p < 0.05$, ** $p < 0.01$
Source: Stuckler (2008).

Table 13.2 Five leading global health metaphors

Principle	Selected goals	Priority diseases	Key institutions
Global health as foreign policy	Trade, alliances, democracy, economic growth, reputation, stabilize or destabilize countries	Infectious diseases, HIV/AIDS	US State Department, USAID, President's Emergency Plan for AIDS Relief
Global health as security	Combat bioterror, infectious diseases, and drug resistance	Avian influenza, severe acute respiratory syndrome, multidrug-resistant tuberculosis, AIDS	US Centers for Disease Control and Prevention
Global health as charity	Fight absolute poverty	Famine or malnutrition, HIV/AIDS, tuberculosis, malaria, rare diseases	Bill and Melinda Gates Foundation, other philanthropic bodies
Global health as investment	Maximize economic development	HIV/AIDS, malaria	World Bank and International Monetary Fund, International Labour Organization, private sector
Global health as public health	Maximize health effect	Worldwide burden of disease	WHO, vertical disease-specific non-governmental organizations

Source: Stuckler and McKee (2008).

given more emphasis by actors who view global health as public health, which aims to maximize health impact, and, increasingly, by actors who view global health as investment, which aims to maximize economic development (Suhrcke et al., 2006; World Bank, 2007).

Mapping the actions of key chronic disease actors: the 'outputs'

We have identified eight actors who are currently or potentially, directly or indirectly active in chronic disease prevention and control: the WHO, international financial institutions, United Nations organizations, nation-states/national health ministries, NGOs, the private sector, donors and academic institutions.

Before we map out the actions of these players on chronic diseases, we need some criteria for understanding ways in which these actions might be inefficient, independent of the level of prioritization. Table 13.3 provides examples of four types of policy inefficiencies that can arise for the possible cases of action on the burden of disease: (i) one actor on one disease (lack of consonance); (ii) one actor on multiple diseases (inconsistence); (iii) multiple actors on one disease (incoherence); and (iv) multiple actors on multiple diseases (lack of coordination). Because each of these cases refers to a different policy issue, it is helpful to differentiate them in order to diagnose more accurately the problems that may arise in chronic disease policymaking. This is important for the policy analysis, even if the first three criteria appear to be similar, because many terms and phrases, such as lack of coordination, fragmentation, disengagement and incoherence, are frequently applied in the governance literature in ways that appear synonymous but actually involve, and potentially derive from, different policy problems. For example, a lack of consonance for one actor on heart disease, when aggregated with multiple actors, may look like incoherence on heart disease according to the commonly applied usage, even though the actual problem stemmed from the level of one actor's policies on heart disease. Similar logic applies to, say, inconsistence on chronic diseases by the IMF and a lack of coordination on chronic diseases for all actors. Thus, these four criteria – consonance, consistency, coherence and coordination – are applied throughout the discussion below.

World Health Organization: few resources but many resolutions

The WHO has historically focused on infectious diseases and operations have not kept pace with changes in the global burden of disease (so-called institutional inertia). There are, however, some signs of policy responsiveness to chronic diseases, particularly in resolutions from WHO member states at the World Health Assembly. In 1998, the WHO established a cluster dedicated to chronic non-communicable diseases at its headquarters. In 2000, a Global Strategy on the Prevention and Control of Chronic Non-communicable

Table 13.3 Four types of policy failures: consonance, consistence, coherence and coordination

Dimension	One actor/one disease	One actor/multiple diseases	Multiple actors/one disease	Multiple actors/multiple diseases
Description of failure	Actors' direct responses to one disease are not consonant with other actions which have effects on, but are not directly in relation to, the disease	Actors efforts in one disease domain have spillover consequences on other disease domains	Actors' efforts counteract each other or are not synchronized	Antagonistic as opposed to neutral or synergistic interactions between actors and diseases
Hypothetical negative example(s)	IMF programmes provide financial support for HIV/AIDS bundled with financial packages, yet the IMF does not evaluate potential consequences of their financial packages on HIV/AIDS	Vertical TB intervention programmes divert public health capacity horizontally away from other disease control efforts like malaria – yielding success in TB control but risking losses in malaria control	WHO seeks to introduce taxes for tobacco control, but FAO seeks to subsidize farmers tobacco crops	WHO, World Bank, and NGOs launch campaigns on malaria, tuberculosis and HIV/AIDS. Some duplicate programmes and functions are in place that act antagonistically rather than synergistically
Governance indicator	Lack of consonance	Inconsistence	Incoherence	Lack of coordination

Diseases requested that the director general prioritize chronic diseases in developing countries. A resolution on diet, physical activity and health passed in 2002, followed by a global strategy on diet, physical activity and health approved at the 2004 World Health Assembly. A 2005 WHO report, 'Preventing Chronic Diseases: a Vital Iinvestment' has the potential to stimulate global action. Significant capacity for tobacco control has built around the development and passage of the Framework Convention on Tobacco Control.

Most WHO chronic disease activities are not well coordinated. Research and policy work for chronic diseases has focused on developing more extensive surveillance in conjunction with the WHO Evidence for Information and Policy cluster. All regional offices have departments with a specific mandate to address chronic disease prevention and control. Capacity is currently inadequate, but is being addressed through the development of regional networks. Most country offices have extremely limited capacity in the majority of core areas of chronic disease prevention and control. Virtually no WHO country offices have expertise in chronic diseases, and when they do, such expertise is usually underutilized. WHO collaborating centres have considerable capacity for chronic disease research and training, but are insufficiently engaged in global and country work.

WHO resources allocated to chronic diseases represent a disproportionately small part of their overall contribution to the global burden of disease. In 2002, WHO spent 3.5 per cent of its total budget (US$43.6 million) on chronic non-communicable diseases. In 2000/01, only $1 was spent for every chronic disease death compared with $15 spent for every communicable disease death (Yach et al., 2004b). The inverse relationship between the burden of disease and resources allocated appears to be the greatest for so-called extra-budgetary funds (that is, voluntary contributions), which have risen over the past several decades from composing just one-quarter of the WHO budget in 1971–72 to more than two-thirds in 2004–05.

United Nations: excluding chronic diseases but emerging possibilities

Outside the WHO, several UN organizations with non-health mandates play a major role in setting out principles, goals and actions that affect global health. The focus of these organizations has been on the WHO's own historic focal areas: infant and maternal mortality, malnutrition and HIV/AIDS. The prominent health and development risks posed by chronic diseases have not been directly recognized by any of the major initiatives intended to have sustained impact.

The Millennium Development Goals (MDGs), the United Nations' social development agenda for 'reducing poverty and improving lives', do not include chronic diseases (Fuster and Voute, 2005). The main global health MDG, number 6, aims 'to halt and begin to reverse the spread of infectious diseases (HIV/AIDS, malaria, and other diseases)'. Although 'other diseases' theoretically include chronic diseases, in practice they are ignored because they do not serve as a measurable indicator of MDG progress.

Exclusion of chronic diseases is further evident in the agendas of multiple UN actors and initiatives. The International Labour Organization's (ILO) report to the World Commission on the Social Dimension of Globalization and the Multinational Enterprises (MNE) Declaration (2002) do not refer to chronic diseases. The UN Children's Fund's (UNICEF) goal-setting programme, *A World Fit for Children* (2003) fails to include risk factors for chronic diseases among the 25 action points proposed to 'promote healthy lives' despite evidence of the widespread risks of tobacco, obesity and diabetes in children. The UN Population Fund (UNFPA) does not incorporate chronic diseases in its strategy on population and development.[7] The FAO has expressed its concern about the rise of obesity and chronic diseases and jointly published the report on diet, nutrition and the prevention of chronic disease (WHO/FAO2003), although the Committee on Agriculture of the FAO actively expressed disapproval of the resulting WHO strategy on diet, physical activity and health because of its perceived threat to the sugar industry.

In December 2006 the UN adopted the first resolution on diabetes (61/225), designating 14 November as World Diabetes Day, which may serve as an entry point for broader action on chronic diseases.

International financial institutions: low priority, but policy development under way

International financial institutions, primarily the World Bank and the International Monetary Fund, are leading players in global health. The World Bank in particular is one of the top three financiers of global health, committing over US$1 billion per year, while the IMF plays a lesser role though it has begun to support HIV/AIDS control for countries that comply with its economic programmes (see Stuckler et al., 2009).

Historically, the primary objective of these institutions has been to boost economic growth. Because the World Bank and IMF have no policy specific to chronic diseases, activities thus far have been limited in scope. Though the World Bank has conducted important work on the economics of tobacco control, the Poverty Strategy Reduction Papers, which are intended to dictate the bank's investment priorities to fight poverty, to our knowledge do not contain strategies for chronic diseases prevention and control. All World Bank health sector loans used for chronic diseases were provided to Eastern European countries and were primarily a response to two factors: first, the epidemic rise of chronic diseases in the Central and Eastern European and former Soviet region connected with the economic policies advised by the bank (Stuckler et al., 2008); and second a recent bank report that found that feasible action on chronic non-communicable diseases would achieve five times the health gains of the region's MDGs targets (World Bank, 2004).

A recent World Bank report, 'Public Policy and the Response to the Challenge of Non-Communicable Chronic Diseases', which summarizes market failure and avoidable economic costs associated with chronic diseases, has the potential to stimulate greater action.[8]

National health ministries: weak capacity but high awareness

Direct actions by nation-states on chronic diseases are mainly taken through health ministries. Most non-health state institutions do not consider chronic disease a priority and are, as a result, disengaged – similarly to the incoherence observed between the WHO and the rest of the UN. Partly because many of the drivers of chronic diseases are transnational (Hawkes, 2006; Stuckler, 2008), national health ministries have been particularly vocal about seeking support from global institutions such as the WHO. Among health ministries, a 2001 survey of 167 countries revealed nearly universal recognition of chronic diseases as a health priority. This awareness, however, had not resulted in the development of significant fiscal or human resources for chronic diseases. Nearly two-thirds of the health ministries surveyed did not even have a budget line for chronic disease.

Non-governmental organizations: no integrated effort for all chronic diseases, but past successes show potential

A limited number of international NGOs participate in chronic disease control efforts at the global level, ranging from advocacy groups to NGOs focused on programme management. Most global efforts have been buttressed by domestic NGOs. For example, GLOBALink is an initiative supported by the American Cancer Society and the International Union Against Cancer that links over 4000 tobacco control advocates and policymakers around the world. During the development of the WHO Framework Convention on Tobacco Control, GLOBALink played a vital and low-cost role in responding to the need for advocacy and action on tobacco control in its member countries. More recently, the Framework Convention Alliance (FCA) has formed as a loose international alliance to support the continued development and ratification of an effective FCTC. Originally composed of developed country and international NGOs, the FCA systematically reached out to new and small NGOs in developing countries. Today the FCA encompasses more than 180 NGOs from over 70 countries and has established itself as an important lobbying alliance.

Despite important progress on tobacco, major gaps in NGOs' responses to the threat posed by chronic disease persist. There is little unity between the different categories of NGOs with overlapping health interests, weakening the potential for both grassroots and high-level advocacy. Part of this disaggregation results from NGOs focusing on specific chronic diseases and risks. For example, obesity NGOs, such as the International Obesity Task Force, do not collaborate with diabetes NGOs, such as the International

Diabetes Federation. Similarly, obesity NGOs for specific groups, such as children, often do not coordinate efforts with obesity NGOs focused on the general population.

Initiatives such as those made to advance the agenda on issues related to drug access for HIV/AIDS, malaria and other infectious diseases by global NGOs such as Oxfam and Médecins Sans Frontières have not materialized for chronic diseases.

Private sector: historic tensions but emerging possibilities for engagement

There are two main categories of private sector action on chronic diseases: private action and private-public interaction.[9] Action by the private sector only occurs when doing so maximizes shareholder wealth (see Buse and Naylor, Chapter 9 above). Traditionally, in the private sector, action on health has come through corporate social responsibility initiatives (CSR), which often involve voluntary private regulation as a means to avoid more stringent compulsory public regulation. However, CSR initiatives have also been used as strategies for improving brand image, and in recent years a growing number of companies have voluntarily pledged support to HIV/AIDS, malaria and tuberculosis campaigns incorporated into the UN Global Compact and OECD World Economic Forum. Because chronic diseases do not square easily with the 'global health as charity' paradigm (Table 13.2), similar action is not likely to be forthcoming in the area of chronic disease.

Over the years tobacco companies Philip Morris and BAT have implemented elaborate own-product CSR campaigns to persuade the public that their products are less dangerous than the epidemiologic evidence suggests they are. When evidence appeared that tobacco could be harmful to health, the response by producers and manufacturers was similar: consistent denial of the evidence, creation of front groups to oppose public health action, and decades of intense and sustained lobbying of policymakers in an attempt to thwart regulatory progress at national and international levels. The same strategy emerged from the sugar industry to frustrate the development of the WHO strategy on diet, physical activity and health. Many chronic disease prevention aims are at odds with the profit maximization goals of private food and beverage companies. Table 13.4 further summarizes the pathways and performance of the private sector's influence on chronic disease control.

Some direct private sector action on chronic diseases has also come through corporate wellness programmes, although this has mostly been observed in developed countries in settings where companies bear the costs of insuring employees, such as the USA. There is a clear business case for investing in employee health to reduce costly turnover, limit absenteeism and improve on-the-job productivity – on average US$3 for every $1 invested in developed countries (Suhrcke et al., 2005; Goetzel et al., 2005).

Table 13.4 Pathways of private sector influences on chronic disease

Type of influence	Description	Summary of effects
Self regulation: independent or voluntary	*Social standards* Corporate social responsibility (CSR), centring on voluntary codes of conduct and self-imposed business standards	*Poor performance* Has been used to mislead public and manipulate policymaking Co-opt health messages as public relations strategy without changing behaviour Hedge social image by performing on health dimensions unrelated to products
	Market standards Investment community pressure to manage risk and maximize profits Socially responsible investment (SRI) in companies with good governance Wellness programmes	*Mixed performance* Favourable effects when driven by investment community pressure or by prospects of return-on-investment Diversifying product lines and changing business models, facilitated by support of trade bodies SRI has not focused on health performance Proliferation of employee health promotion programmes in western countries
Shared/co-regulation: public–private partnerships	*Reciprocal benefits* Systems/issues partnership based on social concerns and priorities Product-based partnership to increase demand for health good or service Product-development partnership to create markets, expand product lines and distribute health information	*Positive performance* Beneficial effects, but limited issue-based partnerships Emerging systems/issues partnerships for chronic diseases as awareness grows Initiation from pharmaceutical sector has helped expand access to treatment and promoted earlier detection of chronic diseases Initiation from public sector has stimulated product-development partnerships
Public regulation	*Agenda and priority setting* Non-profit scientific research organizations International monitoring and standardizing bodies	*Poor performance* Influence public regulation through industry funded non-profit organizations and monitoring bodies Create industry front groups supporting industry-friendly science, sometimes commissioning and publishing fraudulent research Divert public health agenda by influencing key actor priorities Attempt to generate self-regulation to reduce pressure or substitute for public regulation Public recognition of issue by private actors can increase potential for public regulation

Although close to 25 public-private partnerships have formed to address diseases of poverty, to our knowledge none focus on chronic disease at the present time. Part of the failure of public-private partnerships to tackle this problem derives from the prevailing anti-corporate culture in public health fostered by a better understanding of the activities of tobacco companies (Wiist, 2006).

Academic and research institutions: historically low engagement but emerging consensus on research priorities

Increased funding for international research has not been proportionally allocated to the growing burden of chronic disease. Most major international research funding portfolios, including the Wellcome Trust in the UK and the Medical Research Council, focus their global research programmes almost exclusively on infectious disease. One noteworthy exception is the Fogarty International Center at the US National Institutes of Health, which has allocated one-third of its resources for the next several years to chronic disease research and training programmes in developing countries. There remains a need for a '90/10'-style report on chronic diseases (Global Forum, 2004).

Much of the international public health training occurs in the United States, where thousands of future health professionals from developing countries seek graduate instruction in schools of public health. Surveys of the core requirements of members of the Association of Schools of Public Health indicate that global health coursework does not contain instruction for the global challenges facing chronic disease control. Although selected leading institutions, such as Johns Hopkins, Yale and the University of North Carolina at Chapel Hill have expanded their curricula to address obesity in nutrition courses and Yale has launched an international tobacco seminar, the emphasis remains on primary health-care and infectious disease.

Research institutions also play a vital role in shaping the research agenda and diffusing academic knowledge. In November 2007 *Nature* published 'Grand Challenges in Chronic Non-Communicable Diseases' outlining the top twenty policy and research priorities for leading chronic diseases and marking the founding of a global partnership comprising the Oxford Health Alliance, the UK Medical Research Council, the Canadian Institutes of Health Research, the US National Institutes of Health, and the Indian Council of Medical Research. However, unlike the grand (infectious disease) challenges in global health, the chronic disease challenges were not linked to up-front funding commitments (Daar et al., 2007).[10]

Donors: critical lack of funds

Most non-profit, philanthropic organizations, such as the Bill and Melinda Gates Foundation, have yet to incorporate chronic diseases into their health portfolios. There has been modest support for tobacco control from the UN Foundation, the Open Society Institute and the Rockefeller Foundation, but in recent years this has been declining. Until the public in developed countries perceives chronic disease as a priority in developing countries, or until the WHO prioritizes chronic diseases in proportion to their global health burdens, donor resources will probably remain insufficient.

Policy recommendations

Emerging from this analysis is a long-term picture of the proliferation of chronic diseases and an inadequate response to the need for control by individuals, states, markets and global players. What strategies can be used to strengthen the governance weaknesses observed in chronic disease control? What do governance interventions even look like?

A starting point is to look at governance interventions currently promoted by the WHO. Consider the WHO's strategy to promote 'inter-sectorality', which has now been pushed for decades. We argue that this approach, implicitly, is a governance intervention. One of the problems facing the WHO in implementing inter-sectorality is that it has not clearly detailed what this implies in practice or how such a framework should be operationalized. From our perspective, the pursuit of inter-sectorality is nothing more than a plea for establishing coherence; inter-sectoral action is coherent action. Inter-sectoral approaches aim to move away from multi-sectoral approaches, which risk incoherence, and towards direct action by relevant, but indirectly engaged, actors. Thus, improving coherence will mean directing what is currently indirect action on chronic diseases taking place in non-health bodies at the global level (UN development agencies) and the nation-state level (non-health ministries), and as a result redirecting the NGOs that are reproducing the incoherent platforms of these global bodies.

A recent example of governance intervention by the WHO is the Framework Convention on Tobacco Control (FCTC). Beyond flexing its treaty-making muscle for the first time, the WHO implemented three major and significant governance interventions in building the FCTC: (i) it established an internal advisory board leading to internal coherence and coordination; (ii) it established an external or inter-UN board which dislodged existing tobacco company influence and ensured that for the first time UN organizations spoke with one voice on tobacco; and (iii) it established a platform for NGOs to scale-up efforts and connect WHO/UN strategies to the public and nation-states. In a similar way, the exemplary FCTC approach could be replicated or scaled-up for the four leading chronic diseases singled out in this chapter.

Until the WHO establishes consistence in its own chronic disease operations, as it did with tobacco, the organization will have difficulty implementing a more general FCTC-style platform for chronic diseases. Another complication is that tobacco is known to be a global vice, whereas other chronic disease factors, such as diet, can be either healthy or unhealthy, making them more difficult to mobilize around. Many of the chronic disease risks which are being driven at a population level by macroeconomic forces are at present being engaged at an individual and biomedical level by the public health field – a counterproductive strategy when a major limiting political economy factor is the perception that chronic diseases are 'lifestyle-related' or the result of 'individual choices'.

The WHO's efforts to engage the World Bank, FAO, ILO and other players mirror the action that should be taken by health ministries for players at similar levels: finance ministries, agricultural ministries and so on. Of these, interactions with ministers of finance in particular are crucial in order to align economic growth strategies with public health policy. Economic development need not lead to chronic disease. More generally, to achieve such coherence there is a need for public health to look at how chronic disease relates to a range of social and economic dependent variables. This would be relatively easy to do and may in the long run result in greater population health gains than the plethora of studies within the field which further characterize the relationships between individual risk factors and chronic diseases.

For the WHO the *priorities of populations*, not just the *priorities of donors*, should be emphasized, irrespective of the source of budgetary funding. In the past several decades, national health ministries have raised more than forty resolutions at WHO World Health Assemblies to develop stronger systems for combating chronic diseases. Heeding these national calls for global change would bring the world's health closer to what it aspires to be: an equitable practice, committed to the egalitarian principles espoused by the WHO's 'Health for All' population health approach, originally outlined in the Alma Ata Declaration (WHO, 1978; see also recent calls by the WHO Commission on the Social Determinants of Health to return to the Alma Ata principles, WHO, 2007). Instead, when the WHO devotes budgetary resources to disease that are disproportionate to the actual global burden of disease, it sends a powerful signal to the rest of the world – irrespective of whether the organization does so intentionally – about what global health priorities *should* be.

A general governance strategy for the WHO is to shape more proactively more accurate perceptions of the global burden of disease. Social marketing campaigns from the WHO might be better directed at establishing more accurate public perceptions of the burden of chronic diseases than in direct intervention. Perhaps targeting World Bank and UNICEF officials rather than sick persons in poor countries would yield greater long-term health gains as the WHO tries to establish intergovernmental coherence on chronic diseases and to correct the political economy failures which underlie it.

While the WHO is arguably the best positioned to take rational action towards setting the stage for the global health system to work properly, the organization is losing its place at the centre of global health. Non-profit philanthropic foundations are increasingly undermining WHO legitimacy, and more such foundations are coming on line as extensions of private companies, with consequent dangers to chronic disease coherence. Greater competition in global health is leading to a closer correspondence between global health actions and the public's perception of what global health means. Foundations will continue be driven by, rather than driving, the public's view of global health. For chronic disease, this means, at least in the short run, continued governance weaknesses.

NGOs appear to be well positioned to make advances in this field. They can find organizational niches in responding to the global burden of disease which exploit the neglect of chronic disease governance. The Oxford Health Alliance provides an example. This has built multi-sectoral partnerships and gathered momentum by integrating disparate chronic disease efforts, effectively strengthening coherence in research. Evidence redressing pervasive chronic disease myths, such as that they are 'inevitable consequences of ageing' or 'diseases of affluence', must be more widely disseminated (WHO, 2005).

For health ministries, one option is a coordinated approach to combating infectious and chronic diseases, that is, to build the capacity of health systems while transforming the systems from acute to chronic care. As recent studies have shown, AIDS treatment in resource-poor settings is failing owing to poor adherence (Rosen et al., 2007). What the studies do not mention is that *AIDS is a chronic disease*. That AIDS is one of the few infectious diseases that are on the rise reflects the same limitations fuelling the unchecked growth of chronic diseases in poor countries today. Yet learning and sharing regarding the control of AIDS, cardiovascular disease and diabetes is not taking place, and a tremendous opportunity for enabling health systems to address long-term population health-care problems is lost as billions of dollars are spent controlling AIDS and TB.[11]

Public health's anti-corporate culture is leading to missed opportunities for engaging the private sector in synergistic ways: public health distrusts CSR yet is not using its scientific authority to set standards or to engage in partnerships. This can be seen in the poor performance of public health in the battle to set food labelling standards in the UK in 2008. Public health has an important role to play in convincing corporations to expand healthy product lines and as 'health investment advisers' to show the economic benefits of doing so. Likewise, public health can learn from the private sector, and collaboration could yield significant gains in the effectiveness of public health.

Within public health, the rhetoric of 'disease neglect' has gone a long way to perpetuating the rift between infectious and chronic diseases. Overall, both types of diseases are receiving too little support in developing countries. Yet, infectious disease advocates have garnered much greater resources, and held onto them tightly, relative to the burden of such diseases. As part of those campaigns, chronic diseases have been branded as 'diseases of affluence' and 'diseases of ageing'. Other arguments have suggested that, because so much research and development goes into chronic diseases in rich countries, they cannot possibly be neglected – ignoring the fact that the highly specialized and medicalized research into western treatments offers little help for developing countries. Just as rolling out antiretrovirals in poor countries is a challenge, so is roll-out out of insulin. Such infighting in public health is perverse. Overall it weakens a fundamental goal of global health: to raise resources for reducing the global burden of disease as much as possible.

While numerous cost-effective interventions for chronic diseases have been tested and are available (Suhrcke et al., 2006; World Bank, 2007), we still need a road map of appropriate interventions based on the causes of chronic diseases at population and individual level, from which a coherent prevention plan can be constructed. Such a road map could begin with broad economic, political and social factors, and narrow down to the psychological and biological factors that affect eating and activity. In the case of eating, these would be taste, accessibility, convenience, cost and the amount of promotion. The factors between the broad and narrow approaches must be defined so that prevention can be based on estimates of the most effective point at which to intervene in the causal chain of chronic disease progression (Yach et al., 2006; Stuckler, 2008).

The academy can be of great help in all these processes, but currently it is not doing enough. The evidence that upstream forces are playing a role in driving chronic diseases is clear and robust. Genetics or biomedical factors alone cannot of themselves explain any of the rises in chronic diseases within populations. Yet almost all the scant academic resources today are being devoted to genetic research, mainly driven by the pharmaceutical sector, with the hope of creating ways to cure obesity and other afflictions. As a result, this individual biomedical paradigm is being reproduced in public health and medical classrooms worldwide.

What is desperately needed – and long overdue in the academic world – is cross-disciplinary collaboration between public health and social sciences to identify the key social transformations at population levels that are driving chronic diseases and to develop feasible and effective strategies to reverse them. Until then, the chronic disease prevention road map will implicitly remain fixated on the narrow set of biomedical factors.

Conclusions

Our analysis suggests that a number of political economy factors are weakening the global response to chronic disease. These include, among others, the historic orientation of health systems toward acute infectious diseases, the slow and steady rise of chronic diseases compared to the rapid and variable outbreak of infectious diseases, low levels of public awareness about the significance of chronic diseases in developing countries, individualization/medicalization of chronic disease risks, and the socio-economic nature of chronic disease risk factors. We have provided evidence of significant incoherence on chronic diseases between health and non-health actors at local, national and global levels. We propose that the WHO is the best positioned to correct the observed failures in chronic disease governance, but to do so it must first address the political economy problems that are driving the inadequate prioritization of chronic diseases as well as resolving its own lack of coordination on chronic disease control. Building upon the strategies used in the WHO Framework Convention on Tobacco Control – an example of a successful global chronic disease governance intervention – would be a good place to start.

Notes

1. Parts of this chapter have been drawn from a previous unpublished report by the authors, 'Towards a WHO Long-Term Strategy for Prevention and Control of Leading Chronic Diseases' and from Stuckler (2008).
2. For brevity, in this article the term *chronic disease* refers to these four chronic, non-communicable diseases, based on the usage by the Oxford Health Alliance (www.oxha.org) and the recent identification of 'Grand Challenges' in chronic disease control (Daar et al., 2007). This simple taxonomic division between infectious and chronic diseases, originally institutionalized by the World Health Organization (WHO) as types 1 and 2 burden of disease categories has become increasingly problematic for epidemiologists and policymakers. Diseases can be acute or chronic and infectious (communicable) or non-infectious (non-communicable), with considerable overlap between these categories (for a comprehensive discussion on medical problems associated with developing a disease taxonomy, see Nolte and McKee, 2008). An epidemiological justification for focusing on the four leading chronic diseases is that more than four-fifths of all deaths and two-fifths of all disabilities due to chronic non-communicable diseases are derived from them. Although other important chronic non-communicable diseases such as neuropsychiatric disorders and sensory organ diseases have high morbidity rates, they have comparably lower mortality rates. Another pragmatic policy motivation for concentrating on this subset of chronic non-communicable diseases pertains to their similar set of determinants: of the many chronic non-communicable diseases, these four in particular are related to three modifiable risks: (i) tobacco use, (ii) alcohol consumption and (iii) unhealthy diet and physical inactivity. Although this does not mean that the other chronic non-communicable diseases are not important, if the risks of contracting the leading chronic diseases were lowered, the outcome of many of the high-burden, low-probability chronic non-communicable diseases would be improved as well.
3. Several definitions in the literature reflect partial aspects of the model introduced here. For a definition closer to ours, global health governance can be considered 'the totality of collective regulations to deal with international and transnational interdependence problems in health' (Bartsch and Kohlmorgen, 2005, in Hein, 2005). According to the World Bank and the IMF, 'Governance encompasses the state's institutional arrangements, the processes for formulating policy,

decision-making and implementation; information flows within government; and the overall relationship between citizens and government' (World Bank, 1997; Woods, 2000). Promoting 'good governance' has typically involved superimposing a set of values on this system: accountability, efficiency, fairness, transparency, participation and ownership (see IMF and WB definitions of 'good governance': Woods, 1999; World Bank, 1997). However, we argue that these values typically refer to the relationship between the forward and reverse arrows (see Figure 13.2) and often for how these relationships vary across actors. For example, lack of transparency leads to a lack of observability in inputs and outputs, and possibly inefficient exchange; lack of participation leads to a smaller forward arrow than might be socially optimal; lack of ownership can lead to smaller reverse arrows and so on. While these value-based criteria suggest a way of evaluating the process or *means of governance*, governance failures might exist even in the presence of success on these factors. They also face similar normative evaluation problems: what is the optimal level of transparency? What is fair? To whom should actors' be held accountable? Thus, we stress a focus on the *ends of governance*.
4. Although health policy analysis sometimes considers political feasibility, the emphasis is overwhelmingly on the 'outputs' rather than 'inputs', or the policy content rather than what determines whether a certain disease is prioritized. A possible explanation is that policy inputs (access/selection) are much harder to observe than policy outputs (content/action).
5. Two distinct issues must be disentangled here: governance 'effectiveness and ineffectiveness', or properties of the inputs and outputs themselves, and governance 'success and failure' which is a property of the exchange between inputs and outputs. For example, let us suppose all actors have an unrealistic perception of the burden of disease, so the aggregate priority level p assigned to the disease is lower in magnitude than p^*, or the level that would be socially optimal. Such a case relates solely to the inputs and could constructed as a 'political economy failure'. But let us similarly pose a level of output o that perfectly matches the socially desired level p. In this case, the governance system is behaving properly (like a market clearing supply and demand). Alternatively, let us suppose there is a lack of coordination in response to the disease burden, so the effect output is $o - c$, or the output minus a loss due to coordination failure. This can be conceived of as a 'policy failure'. These two issues, political economy and policy problems, are distinct from the problems associated with the exchange between priority and action, inputs and outputs.
6. This has led some advocates to argue that 'any shift in attention from communicable diseases toward [chronic disease] ailments...would work to the detriment of the poor...[and] the shift's primary beneficiaries would be the rich, who would therefore gain at the expense of the poor' (Gwatkin, 2000).
7. See http://www.unfpa.org/public/ (accessed 4 February 2009), for example, 'Population, Reproductive Health and the Millennium Development Goals' (2007).
8. Social epidemiologists have also provided empirical evidence that macroeconomic policies promoted by IFIs, such as market integration, foreign direct investment and economic growth, are linked to increasing CDs (Hawkes, 2006, 2007; Stuckler, 2008).
9. A third, driven by public regulation, is not considered here.
10. See http://www.grandchallenges.org/Pages/default.aspx (accessed 4 February 2009).
11. Recent studies have also identified significant interactions between the control of infectious diseases and of chronic diseases and their associated risk factors, for

example, TB, MDR-TB, and diabetes (Bashar et al., 2001; Stevenson et al., 2007), AIDS and TB incidence and tobacco (Bates et al., 2007; Furber et al., 2007), and stunting and obesity (Popkin et al., 1996), which further emphasize the need for a more coordinated approach to infectious and chronic disease interventions.

References

Bartsch, S. and L. Kohlmorgen, 'Nichtregierungsorganisationen als Akteure der Global Health Governance – Interaktion zwischen Kooperation und Konflikt', in Joachim Betz and Wolfgang Hein (eds), *Neues Jahrbuch Dritte Welt*, Zivilgesellschaft (Opladen: VS-Verlag, 2005).

Bashar, M., P. Alcabes, W.N. Rom and R. Condos, 'Increased Incidence of Multi-Drug Resistant Tuberculosis in Diabetic Patients on the Bellevue Chest Service, 1987 to 1997', *Chest*, 120(2001): 1514–19.

Bates, M.N., A. Khalakdina, M. Pai, L. Change, F. Lessa and K.R. Smith, 'Risk of Tuberculosis from Exposure to Tobacco Smoke: a Systematic Review and Meta-Analysis', *Archives of Internal Medicine*, 167 (2007): 335–42.

Beaglehole, R. and D. Yach, 'Globalisation and the Prevention and Control of Non-Communicable Disease: the Neglected Chronic Diseases of Adults', *Lancet*, 362 (2003): 903–8.

Buse, K. and G. Walt, 'The World Health Organization and Global Public-Private Health Partnerships: in Search of "Good" Global Governance', in M. Reich (ed.), *Public-Private Partnerships for Public Health*, Harvard Center for Population and Development Studies (Cambridge, MA: Harvard University Press, 2000), chapter 7.

Daar, A.S., P.A. Singer, D.L. Persad et al., 'Grand Challenges in Chronic Non-Communicable Diseases', *Nature*, 450 (2007): 494–6.

Fidler, D., 'Germs, Governance and Global Public Health in the Wake of SARS', *J Clin Invest*. 113 (2004): 799–804.

Fuster, V. and J. Voute, 'MDGs: Chronic Diseases are not on the Agenda', *Lancet*, 366 (2005): 1512–14.

Garrett, L., 'Challenge of Global Health', *Foreign Affairs*, 86 (2007): 14–38.

Global Forum for Health Research, '10/90 Report on Health Research 2003–2004', http://www.globalforumhealth.org/Site/002__What%20we%20do/005__Publications/ 001__10%2090%20reports.php (accessed 11 July 2008).

Goetzel, R., R.J. Ozminkowski, C.M. Baase and G.M. Billotti, 'Estimating the Return-on-Investment from Changes in Employee Health Risks on the Dow Chemical Company's Health Care Costs', *Journal of Occupational and Environmental Medicine*, 47(8) (2005): 759–68.

Gwatkin, D. and M. Guillot, 'The Burden of Disease among the Global Poor: Current Situation, Future Trends and Implications for Strategy', World Bank and Global Forum for Health Research, World Bank, 2000, http://siteresources.worldbank.org/ INTPAH/Resources/Publications/Seminars/burden.pdf (accessed 31 March 2008).

Hawkes, C., 'The Role of Foreign Direct Investment in the Nutrition Transition', *Public Health Nutrition*, 8 (2005): 357–65.

Hawkes, C., 'Uneven Dietary Development: Linking the Policies and Processes of Globalization with the Nutrition Transition, Obesity and Diet-Related Chronic Diseases', *Globalization and Health*, 2 (2006):1–18.

Horton, R., 'The Neglected Epidemic of Chronic Diseases', *Lancet*, 366 (2005): 1514.

Jessop, B., 'The Rise of Governance and the Risks of Failure: the Case of Economic Development', *International Social Science Journal*, 50 (1998): 29–45.

Lau, R.R. and M. Schlesinger, 'Policy Frames, Metaphorical Reasoning, and Support for Public Policies', *Political Psychology*, 26 (2005): 77–114.

Mathers, C.D. and D. Loncar, 'Projections of Global Mortality and Burden of Disease from 2002 to 2030', *Public Library of Science Medicine*, 3 (2006): e442.

Mayntz, R., 'Governance Theory als fortentwickelte Steuerungstheorie?' in Gunnar Folker Schuppert (ed.), *Governance-Forschung. Vergewisserung über Stand und Entwicklungslinien* (Baden-Baden: Nomos, 2005), pp. 11–20.

Monteiro, C.A., E.C. Moura, W.L. Conde and B.M. Popkin, 'Socioeconomic Status and Obesity in Adult Populations of Developing Countries: a Review', *Bulletin of WHO*, 82 (2004): 940–6.

Murray, C.J. and A.D. Lopez, *The Global Burden of Disease: a Comprehensive Assessment of Mortality and Disability from Disease, Injuries and Risk Factors in 1990 and Projected to 2020*, Harvard School of Public Health, World Health Organization, and the World Bank (Geneva: World Health Organization, 1996).

Nolte, E. and M. McKee, *Caring for People with Chronic Conditions: a Health System Perspective* (Buckingham: McGraw-Hill, 2008).

Popkin, B.M., M.K. Richards and C.A. Montiero, 'Stunting is Associated with Overweight in Children of Four Nations that are Undergoing the Nutrition Transition', *American Journal of Nutrition*, 126 (1996): 3009–16.

Rayner, G., C. Hawkes, T. Lang and W. Bello, 'Trade Liberalization and the Diet Transition: a Public Health Response', *Health Promotion International*, 21(S1) (2006): 67–74.

Reich, M., 'The Politics of Agenda Setting in International Health: Child Health versus Adult Health in Developing Countries', *Journal of International Development*, 7 (1995): 489–502.

Rosen, S., M. Fox and C. Gill, 'Patient Retention in Antiretroviral Therapy Programs in Sub-Saharan Africa: a Systematic Review', *Public Library of Science Medicine*, 2007, http://medicine.plosjournals.org/perlserv/requestgetdocumentdoi10.1371/journal.pmed.0040298 (accessed 15 December 2008).

Rosenau, J.N., 'Governance in the Twenty-First Century', *Global Governance*, 1 (1995): 13–43.

Stevenson, C.R., N.F. Forouhi, G. Roglic, B.G. Williams, J.A. Lauer, C. Dye and N. Unwin, 'Diabetes and Tuberculosis: the Impact of the Diabetes Epidemic on Tuberculosis Incidence', *BioMed Central Public Health*, 7 (2007): 234.

Strong, K., C. Mathers, J. Epping-Jordan and R. Beaglehole, 'Preventing Chronic Disease: a Priority for Global Health', *International Journal of Epidemiology*, 35 (2006): 492–4.

Stuckler, D., 'Population Causes and Consequences of Leading Chronic Diseases: a Comparative Analysis of Prevailing Explanations', *Milbank Quarterly*, 86 (2008): 273–326.

Stuckler, D. and M. McKee, 'Five Metaphors about Global-Health Policy', *Lancet*, 372 (2008): 95–7.

Stuckler, D., L. King and M. McKee, 'Mass Privatization and the Post-Communist Mortality Crisis: a Cross-national Analysis', *Lancet* (2009, in press).

Suhrcke, M., D. Stuckler, S. Leeder et al., 'Economic Consequences of Chronic Diseases and the Economic Rationale for Public and Private Intervention', London, Oxford Health Alliance, 2005.

Suhrcke, M., R. Nugent, D. Stuckler et al., 'Chronic Diseases: an Economic Perspective', Oxford Health Alliance, London, 2006, http://www.oxha.org/knowledge/publications/oxha-chronic-disease-an-economic-perspective.pdf (accessed 15 December 2008).
Wiist, W.H., 'Public Health and the Anticorporate Movement: Rationale and Recommendations', *American Journal of Public Health*, 96(2006): 1370–5.
Woods, N., 'Good Governance in International Organizations', *Global Governance*, 5 (1999): 39–61.
Woods, N., 'The Challenge of Good Governance for the IMF and World Bank Themselves', *World Development*, 28 (2000): 823–41.
World Bank, *World Development Report: Investing in Health* (New York: Oxford University Press, 1993).
World Bank, 'Millennium Development Goals for Health in Europe and Central Asia: Relevance and Policy Implications', World Bank, Washington, DC, 2004.
World Bank, *Public Policy and the Challenge of Chronic Noncommunicable Diseases* (Washington, DC: World Bank, 2007).
World Health Organization, 'Declaration of Alma-Ata' (Geneva: World Health Organization, 1978), http://www.who.int/social_determinants/links/events/alma_ata/en/index.html (accessed 31 March 2008).
World Health Organization, *Financial Management Report: Expenditure on Implementation of Objectives in Programme Budget 2002–2003* (Geneva: World Health Organization, 2003).
World Health Organization, *Preventing Chronic Diseases: a Vital Investment* (Geneva: World Health Organization, 2005).
World Health Organization, 'Achieving Health Equity: from Root Causes to Fair Outcomes', Commission on the Social Determinants of Health, Interim Statement, World Health Organization, Geneva, 2007, http://whqlibdoc.who.int/publications/2007/interim_statement_eng.pdf (accessed 31 March 2008).
World Health Organization and Food and Agriculture Organization, *Report of the Joint WHO/FAO Expert Consultation on Diet, Nutrition, and the Prevention of Chronic Diseases* (Geneva: World Health Organization, 2003).
Yach, D., 'Chronic Disease', in B. Levy and V.W. Sidel (eds), *Social Injustice* (Oxford: Oxford University Press, 2005)
Yach, D. and C. Hawkes, 'Towards a WHO Long-Term Strategy for Prevention and Control of Leading Chronic Diseases', unpublished report, World Health Organization, Geneva, 2004.
Yach, D., C. Hawkes, C.L. Gould and K.J. Hofman, 'The Global Burden of Chronic Diseases: Overcoming Impediments to Prevention and Control', *Journal of the American Medical Association*, 291 (2004): 2616–22.
Yach, D., D. Stuckler and K. Brownell, 'Epidemiologic and Economic Burden of the Global Epidemics of Obesity and Diabetes', *Nature Medicine*, 12 (2006): 62–6.

14
Fighting HIV/AIDS and the Future of Health Systems

Nina Veenstra and Alan Whiteside

This chapter looks at the ways in which HIV/AIDS and the renewed focus on infectious diseases are impacting on health systems in Africa. It considers the role of global health governance (GHG) on influencing outcomes. The focus is on Africa, since this is where HIV/AIDS is worst and health systems are weakest. The epidemic arrived in Africa when health systems were already struggling and lacked the reserves to accommodate the extra demands. As morbidity and mortality increased, resources started flowing in to assist. This global mobilization of resources, and the associated need for a rapid scale-up of services, has resulted in the favouring of certain approaches to expanding care at a national level. These approaches, while addressing an immediate priority, will not assist in the long-term reconstruction and development of health systems in Africa.

Since there are many ways to understand GHG, we have chosen a simple working definition for the purposes of this analysis, drawn from a conceptual review of the topic (Dodgson et al., 2002). In this chapter we think about GHG as 'actions and means' by which collective action can be brought to fruition around global health issues. We acknowledge that globalization is creating a new set of challenges for health, in turn fuelling greater interest in the governance of global health. We also consider issues of power, in the belief that GHG should ideally have a positive influence on the governance of health at a national level. Ultimately this is where the chapter focuses: on the interface between the global and the national, using HIV/AIDS as a case study to understand how global involvement can guide, facilitate or undermine local efforts to make health systems work.

The first section of this chapter sets the scene by looking at the reasons for weakened health systems and the current crisis of strategies for expanding care. This is followed by an analysis of changing disease patterns: the re-emergence of infectious diseases, the resulting mortality trends, and the motivations for resource mobilization. Attention is given to trying to understand the current and future implications of HIV/AIDS for health systems, since these should logically inform any choice of approach. The second part of the chapter looks at different approaches to utilizing resources and expanding care, and the evidence that we have to suggest whether these might be working or not. Finally we look at opportunities for reconstructing health systems and the role that GHG might play.

Health systems in context

Health systems in Africa have undergone many reforms, but these have not enabled the vast majority of populations to access appropriate care. Here we look briefly at what the reforms have entailed and at factors that might explain the current crisis of strategies to expand national health systems. The World Health Organization has described reforms in terms of 'three generations': first the establishment of national health systems, then the move to an emphasis on primary health care (PHC) and finally reforms based on the economic value of services (WHO, 2000). We focus on the second and third-generation reforms, following on from the International Conference on Primary Health Care in 1978 in Alma Ata and the commitment to 'Health for All by the Year 2000' (Declaration of Alma Ata, 1978).

At its inception, PHC was seen as a comprehensive approach to health that would address the underlying social, economic and political causes of poor health and would be broader than simply the provision of primary healthcare services. In so doing, it opposed disease-specific technology and the culture of curative hospital care. Yet it was soon criticized for being idealistic, too costly and having an unrealistic timeframe. Subsequently the concept of selective primary health care (SPHC) emerged, encompassing an interim strategy in developing countries of concentrating resources on those medical interventions that would ultimately be most cost-effective in improving the health of the majority of people (Walsh and Warren, 1979).

In the years subsequent to Alma Ata SPHC triumphed, with many PHC-labelled programmes simply an extension of existing top-down medical systems to underserved areas. Some people described PHC as a failed experiment, while others felt it had never really been tried (Werner et al., 1997). Reasons for the demise of PHC included both local difficulties and environmental constraints: conservative bureaucracies in developing countries, lack of political commitment, political instability and a lack of clarity around how PHC should be financed (Rifkin and Walt, 1986; Macfarlane et al., 2000; Chatora and Tumusime, 2004; Cueto, 2004). Yet other reasons derived from a broader involvement in health issues. For example, donor agencies latched on to SPHC because of the appeal of 'cost-effectiveness' and easily measurable outputs. It became apparent that goals, techniques and financing had to be aligned to achieve such a holistic response to health issues (Cueto, 2004). Furthermore, there needed to be widespread support at both national and global levels for a reform agenda to be translated into sustained action.

During the 1980s, the global recession and structural adjustment programmes provided greater motivation for the support of SPHC – this was the start of neo-liberal thinking and the first steps towards the third-generation of reforms. Broadly speaking, these followed the proposals in the World Development Report of 1993 'Investing in Health' and focused heavily on the economic value of services (World Bank, 1993; Sen and Koivusalo, 1998). They aimed at increasing the role of market mechanisms in healthcare provision and financing by expanding the role of the private sector, increasing cost-sharing and focusing on efficiency and cost-effectiveness. The cost-recovery mechanisms, user fees and community financing were most damaging because of their effects on health-care utilization. Uganda abolished user fees in 2001 because of concerns over their detrimental effects and subsequently witnessed a marked increase in the utilization of health services (Nabyonga et al., 2005).

Most importantly perhaps, 'health-care reform', in the sense of the World Bank, did not take cognisance of earlier commitments made to expand health-care to all. It also had other fundamental oversights. First, it did not acknowledge the links between macroeconomic policies (such as structural adjustment) and their effects on public sector reform and health-care provision. Second, the validity of the economic assumptions and the whole ideology on which the reforms were based was not sufficiently questioned

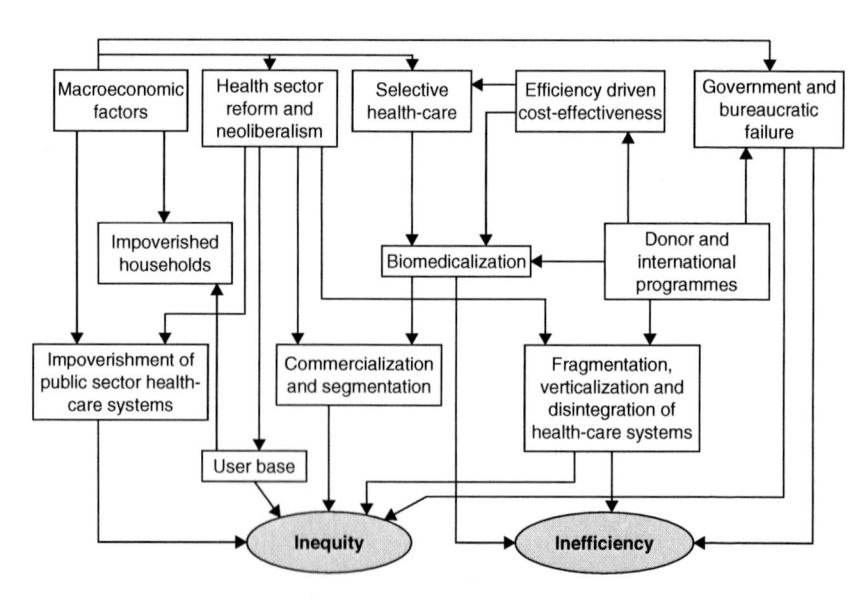

Figure 14.1 Factors undermining the PHC approach
Source: Global Health Watch (2005).

(Sen and Koivusalo, 1998). What resulted were health systems that contradicted principles of redistribution and development at a time when HIV/AIDS was impairing development and demanding a rapid expansion of care. Figure 14.1 illustrates how some of the key processes undermining PHC approach have worked to hinder equity and efficiency in health systems (Global Health Watch, 2005). There are many reasons why health-care reforms have failed to achieve their objectives, but perhaps most can be learnt from the tensions between national priorities and global influences.

The disease burden is changing with serious consequences: HIV/AIDS and other infectious diseases

The HIV/AIDS pandemic superimposed itself on weakened health systems, creating new demands and resulting in a greater mobilization of resources for global health, with significant implications for health system governance. The epidemic is, however, not simply an add-on to an existing disease burden; it is part of a dynamic disease burden that is seeing a renewed focus on infectious diseases.

The resurgence of infectious diseases and the mobilization of resources for global health

Increasing rates of infectious diseases since the late 1980s have resulted in diverging mortality trends across the world. These trends have gone against earlier predictions, which foresaw a global convergence towards lower mortality. Scientists did not predict the latest or 'third' epidemiological transition of emerging infectious diseases, characterized by a large number of new pathogens (including HIV) and a rebound in pre-existing diseases such as malaria and tuberculosis (Barrett et al., 1998; McMichael et al., 2004; Moser et al., 2005). The high rates of infectious diseases being witnessed this century in African countries are illustrated by WHO burden of diseases estimates for 2002 (see Figure 14.2).

There are two salient points to make about the resurgence of infectious diseases. First, this has affected a certain group of countries, mainly in Africa (see Figure 14.3). Second, globalization has not prevented the divergence in health status and the world has failed in its collective responsibility for universal human health. Changing combinations of socio-economic and political circumstances, overlaid by a breakdown in public health, have resulted in avoidable deaths. With HIV/AIDS in particular, these deaths have occurred in a section of the population that does not normally die – young adults.

The global mobilization of resources has not been driven only by disease trends. Equity and human rights have become important, with increased pressure applied by advocacy movements. This is demonstrated by the Millennium Development Goals (MDGs) agreed by world leaders at the United Nations Millennium Summit in September 2000. The MDGs are an

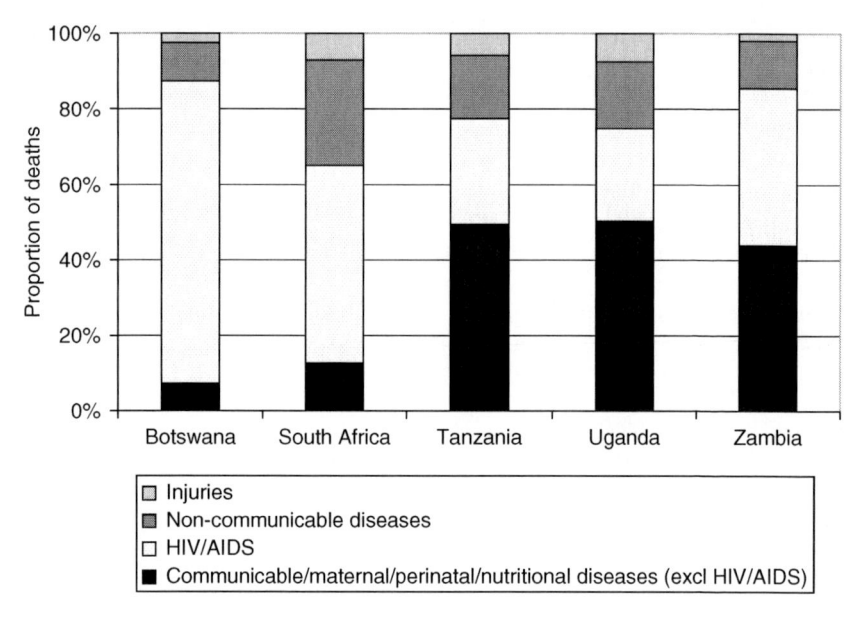

Figure 14.2 World Health Organization mortality estimates for selected countries in Africa
Source: Global burden of disease estimates (WHO, 2002).

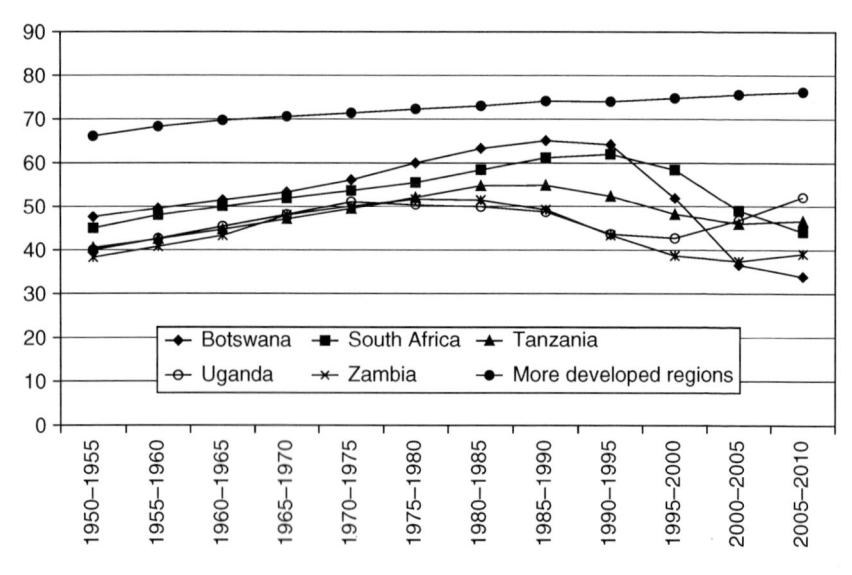

Figure 14.3 Life expectancy at birth in selected countries
Source: UN World Population Prospects (UN Population Division, 2004).

important mechanism for mobilizing global support for targets to reverse the spread of diseases (especially HIV/AIDS and malaria). However, the summit's declaration also outlines a wide range of commitments to human rights, good governance and democracy, as a necessary basis for putting shared values into action (UN General Assembly, 2000).

In addition, good health is an important contributor to economic growth. The Commission on Macroeconomics and Health (CMH), established by then WHO Director-General Gro Harlem Brundtland in 2000, provided convincing arguments for viewing health not only as a priority in its own right, but also as an investment in economic development and poverty reduction (Commission on Macroeconomics and Health, 2001). The CMH went further, highlighting the way in which a few health conditions (for which there are effective interventions) remained responsible for a high proportion of the burden of poor health, meaning that relatively limited investments could result in huge gains. The dilemma here is that some investments will have better returns than others. For example, recent research has demonstrated that chemotherapy for a whole batch of debilitating parasitic and infectious diseases (lymphatic filariasis, schistosomiasis, intestinal helminths, onchocerciasis and trachoma) can cost as little as US$0.40 per person annually, while treatment for HIV/AIDS exceeds US$200 per person annually and has to continue for a lifetime (Molyneaux et al., 2005). From a purely economic perspective some interventions may not immediately make sense, relying instead on concerns for human rights, governance and long-term socio-economic development. Often it becomes more meaningful to compare the costs of 'treatment' to 'no treatment'.

Finally, HIV/AIDS and other health issues have also been seen as threats to human security, and this has urged global involvement. In 2000, the UN Security Council held its first ever meeting on a health issue, 'AIDS in Africa'. Then US Vice President Al Gore suggested that the meeting set an example as to how 'security' could be understood according to a new, more expansive definition for the twenty-first century (Aita, 2000).

The focus on global health and the urgency of mobilizing resources for this purpose has resulted from epidemiological, ideological and political shifts. The re-emergence of infectious diseases, coupled with a focus on the right to health, the ways in which improving health status can potentially catalyze socio-economic development, and concerns over human security, have all been fundamental. Yet, while overtly positive, the fresh resources also raise concerns, including potential difficulties in coordinating many actors and the use of resource-based power. The proliferation of disease-specific initiatives has implications for prioritization within health systems. Simply mobilizing resources will not revitalize and sustain health systems in the future – this will depend on a number of factors, including the type of approach adopted in scaling-up care.

The advent of AIDS

In order for health systems adequately to manage the re-emergence of infectious diseases, and in particular the burden of HIV/AIDS, it is necessary to understand current and future demands. Here we look at considerations which should inform the discussion on various approaches to scaling-up care and, ultimately, an analysis of health governance with respect to HIV/AIDS.

Questions around the demand for HIV/AIDS care and the associated impact on health systems relate predominantly to issues of timing and magnitude. The HIV/AIDS epidemic can be seen to comprise three waves, in each case capturing the time lags that occur between infection, illness, death and impact (Barnett and Whiteside, 2002). Initially, countries experienced rising prevalence rates. But it is the second wave, that of illness, that has struck health systems in many African countries, in many instances resulting in more than 50 per cent of medical hospital beds occupied by HIV-infected individuals (Hassig et al., 1990; Tembo et al., 1994; Arthur et al., 2000; Hansen et al., 2000; Colvin et al., 2001; Fabiani et al., 2003). The age profile of patients has changed in accordance with HIV/AIDS morbidity and mortality patterns, with many young adults now being admitted for care (see Figure 14.4).

Unfortunately, the demand for care in communities is very difficult to measure and is not reflected in health service utilization data. This is because of the many barriers that people face in accessing health services; even then, the care that is provided may be limited. Studies in Kenya, Lesotho and

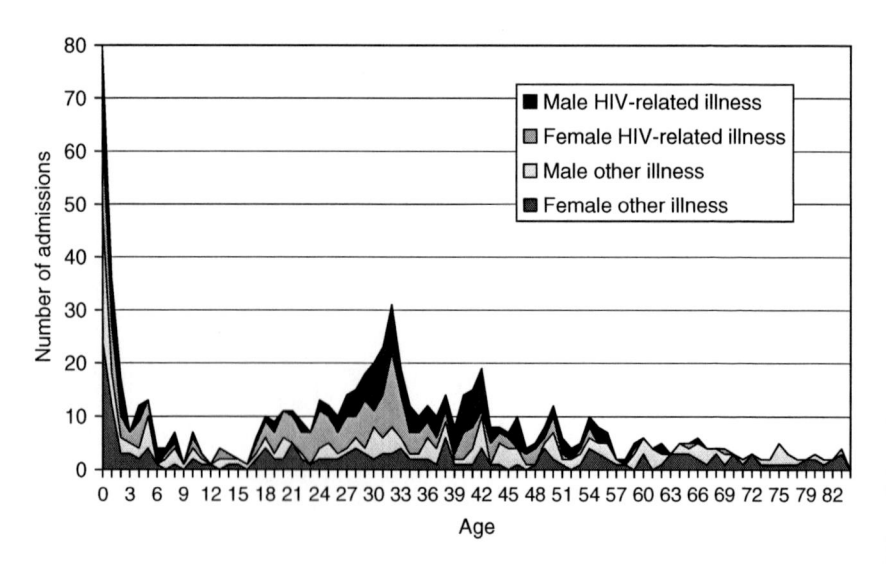

Figure 14.4 Age profile of hospital inpatients in the medical wards of five hospitals in KwaZulu-Natal, South Africa
Source: HEARD database, 2005.

Swaziland, as well as our own work in South Africa, have suggested that as the epidemic progresses, proportionately fewer people with HIV/AIDS are accessing care (Arthur et al., 2000; Mburu and Naidoo, 2004; HDA 2005). While the epidemic has created a major new burden on health systems, there is also a hidden dimension of care shifted onto households and communities.

In terms of the future demand for health-care, we can consider the 'AIDS transition' as an analogous concept to the demographic transition (see Figure 14.5); here births are replaced by HIV infections and overall mortality replaced by AIDS mortality (Over, 2004). This allows us to consider various future scenarios. For example, the scenario which presumes victory over the HIV/AIDS epidemic will see AIDS deaths declining due to ART scale-up, with infection rates remaining high. The health sector will be temporarily burdened by an explosion of patients demanding care, until such time as infection rates drop and the demand for care settles at more manageable levels.

Given the weakened state of health systems, the observation that the AIDS epidemic has not yet peaked in many countries, and the potential 'explosion' of patients, we are left with the question as to whether health systems will ever be able to respond appropriately to the epidemic. The need for rapid scale-up of HIV/AIDS programmes, with tremendous resource implications, must be balanced against a longer-term objective of rebuilding health systems. Resources are flowing in from the global community to assist with financing health programmes (in particular HIV/AIDS), but will these resources be directed and sustained in a way that will strengthen health systems? This is where scenarios and projections are currently underutilized,

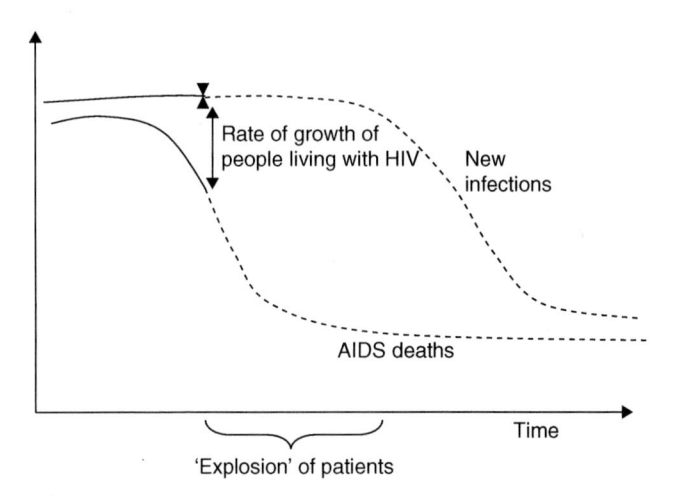

Figure 14.5 The 'AIDS transition'
Source: Over (2004).

since they would allow some consideration as to how various actions might modify outcomes.

How should the burden of HIV/AIDS be managed by health systems? Vertical versus horizontal approaches to expanding care

The need for national health systems to scale-up programmes to manage the burden of HIV/AIDS and the mobilization of global resources explicitly for this purpose have brought renewed attention to the appropriateness of 'vertical' programmes, or 'mass campaigns'. Is this the only way to achieve the rapid scale-up that the epidemic demands? What effects will this approach have on the long-term development of health systems in Africa? This section takes a closer look at what is meant by the different types of approaches, and attempts to answer some of these questions.

Definition, pros and cons

A number of different terms are used to refer to vertical and horizontal approaches to care and the dichotomy between these approaches is not as rigid as it is often made out to be. Here we consider a 'vertical' approach as one in which programmes for specific health conditions are largely freestanding and executed through dedicated health workers, and a 'horizontal' approach as a delivery mode in which all health interventions are implemented through the regular health service infrastructure. In practice there is a continuum between vertical and horizontal approaches to care and the continuum can be more easily understood by dissecting out different programme components, some of which are inherently more vertical in nature. For example, managerial structures (dealing with strategy, monitoring and evaluation) are often vertically oriented, yet there is integration at the service delivery level (Oliveira-Cruz et al., 2003; Elzinga, 2005; Mills, 2005). Where programme components differ in their orientation, a vertical-horizontal interface develops, with opportunities for synergy and collaboration.

The tension between vertical and horizontal approaches, exposed as a resource allocation dilemma, was identified in the 1960s (Gonzalez, 1965). Gonzalez considered the long-term need for organized health services against specific interventions for certain diseases that could rapidly improve health in the shorter-term. This dilemma is no less relevant today (Mills, 2005). The push to implement vertical programmes is indeed stronger where epidemics, poverty and weakened health systems coincide. The burden created by a specific disease, such as HIV/AIDS, can become so large that priority interventions will result in huge health status gains. Yet implementing vertical programmes usually also comes at a cost. Table 14.1 summarizes some of the pros and cons of the different approaches, extracted from a

Table 14.1 Pros and cons of vertical and horizontal approaches to expanding care

Vertical approaches	Horizontal approaches
Community and household level	
• May not promote community reliance • May not account for variations between and within countries	• May be more centred on the health needs of individuals and communities • Are more frequently planned according to local circumstances and with more widespread involvement • May allow for the delivery of a range of services selected to suit national health policies and local demands • May allow for a more holistic response
Health services delivery level	
• May result in efficiency gains (if objectives are specific, work schedules clear, techniques defined, staff motivated and supervision adequate) • May be more appropriate when technology is sophisticated and tasks require specific skills • May provide greater capacity for a focused effort to reduce morbidity or mortality	• May not be effective under certain circumstances (drug shortages, inadequate staff training and supervision, low staff morale, poor support) • Have the potential for delivering technically efficient services due to economies of scale and scope • May be more flexible in adjusting to changing disease patterns
Health sector policy and strategic management level	
• May circumvent the general health system with a parallel structure and hence not contribute to strengthening the system • May duplicate or undermine existing efforts, e.g. by diverting time and attention of health workers and managers • May be used to avoid addressing absorptive capacity issues • Are often more attractive to donors (easier to measure, less chance of corruption, overcomes the weak capacity of national health systems) • Are often short-term, raising concerns about sustainability	• Allow for opportunities to strengthen health systems • Often rely on regular budgetary resources (as opposed to aid) and so may be under funded • Are more sustainable

Source: Adapted from Oliveira-Cruz et al. (2003).

synthesis of the available evidence (Oliveira-Cruz et al., 2003). These are simply arguments – the synthesis itself found supporting evidence to be limited and sometimes contradictory, depending on the context and the design of specific programmes.

HIV has created additional concerns for the potentially adverse effects of vertically-oriented programmes because of its co-morbidity with other infectious diseases such as tuberculosis. It is no longer simply a matter of inefficiencies and system effects, since clinical care may also be compromised. This was brought out in a study of TB and HIV care in a primary care setting in South Africa even before the government implemented its programme of ART (Coetzee et al., 2004). The study found that while the TB and HIV services had a good relationship and referral system, lessons learned were not transferred, there were inefficiencies in service delivery and patient care was not optimal. Patient folders were kept separately, clinicians weren't aware of other treatments, and dually infected patients had to be seen by different health-care workers at different times and places. In acknowledgement of such issues resulting from high levels of HIV-related TB, the ProTEST initiative was established by WHO in 1997 to develop collaboration between TB and HIV/AIDS programmes. The initiative conducted a series of pilot projects in Malawi, South Africa and Zambia and demonstrated that collaborative efforts are necessary and feasible (WHO, 2004).

If collaboration between two vertically-oriented programmes can be developed, is there potential for creating synergies across entire health systems, between all programmes? Or, alternatively, should the goal be to avoid vertical approaches altogether? Before trying to answer some of these questions, we first consider the validity of concerns for the deflection of resources when HIV/AIDS programmes are vertically structured.

Current evidence on the deflection of resources and other system effects

The assumption that HIV/AIDS deflects resources and so contributes towards weakening health systems more generally needs to be critically examined, since HIV/AIDS has also contributed to an increased inflow of external resources to heavily affected countries. While financial resources often receive the most attention, they are not necessarily the greatest concern. This section analyses some of the evidence for the deflection of resources within the health sector for three major resource categories which are potential constraints/barriers for implementing programmes of all kinds – financial resources, infrastructure resources and human resources. In looking at financial resources, the focus is on the role of donor aid, since this has many implications for health sector governance and relates closely to any discussions around vertical and horizontal approaches to expanding care.

Financial resources

As a number of funding streams finance HIV/AIDS programmes in developing countries, it is not necessarily domestic public spending that carries the burden of ever-increasing resource requirements in the health sector. Funding

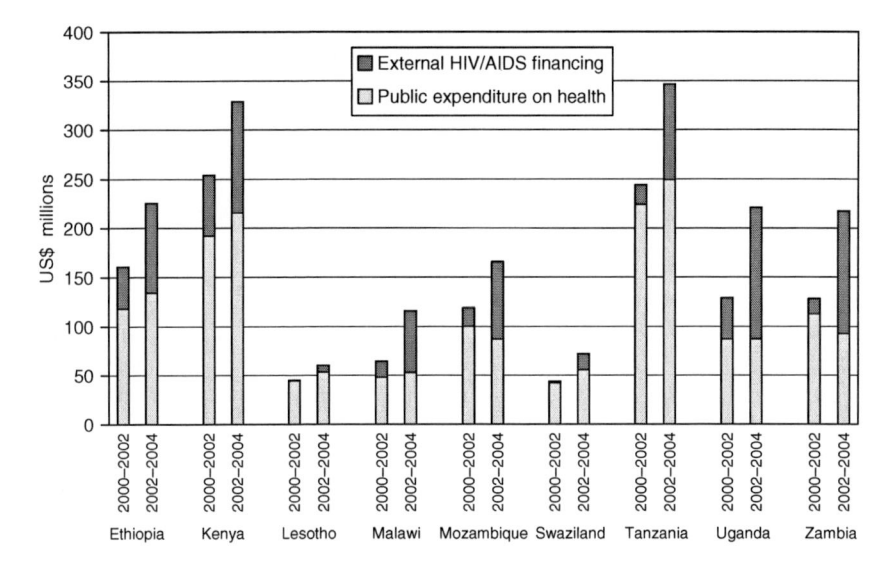

Figure 14.6 Trends in domestic public health funding and external financing for HIV/AIDS, 2000–04
Source: Lewis and Stout (2006).

from bilateral agencies, multilateral agencies, mechanisms such as the Global Fund to Fight AIDS, TB and Malaria and philanthropic foundations has all been increasing, particularly for the provision of ART. In theory then, aid money could mitigate the need to divert domestic funds towards HIV/AIDS programmes. Figure 14.6 looks at trends in domestic public health-care funding and external financing for HIV/AIDS in a selection of African countries, to gauge to what extent this might be happening (Lewis and Stout, 2006). What these data show is that, despite massive increases in HIV/AIDS funding, public health funding has only increased modestly or in some instances even declined. External financing for HIV/AIDS during the period 2002 to 2004 in fact exceeded the public health budget in some African countries.

> What is puzzling is how countries can accommodate and wisely allocate new resources for HIV/AIDS while their overall health spending declines or only modestly rises. (Lewis, 2005: 11)

The mobilization of aid for HIV/AIDS programmes has clearly not facilitated parallel increases in domestic public health expenditure and this has implications for health system strengthening, health system governance and the sustainability of all programmes. As Lewis (2005) points out, effectively scaling-up programmes with donor monies generally requires some 'collateral' domestic resources, such as human resources and infrastructure. Absorptive capacity constraints are also not the only side of the story; other concerns with such large amounts of aid relative to domestic spending are that it will increase corruption and induce aid dependency by weakening governments' abilities to generate resources locally (Bevan, 2005).

There are other system effects associated with utilizing large amounts of donor aid. The tendency for donor funds to be disease-specific and to sway countries' responses towards vertical approaches has already been discussed. What has not been mentioned is the volatile and unpredictable nature of donor aid, which impacts negatively on the sustainability and effectiveness of programmes and limits countries' abilities to plan. Aid volatility has been demonstrated empirically and extends to the discrepancy between commitments and disbursements (Bulir and Hamann, 2003). Unfortunately the discrepancy is becoming larger, as needs continue to rise (see Figure 14.7).

Another problem with the number of donors is that of coordination. Where a proliferation of donors results in increasing demands on already scarce human and financial resources simply in order to manage the aid, then the benefits of aid become questionable. The issue of donor coordination has received attention in discussions around 'aid effectiveness' and constituted much of the rationale behind the 'Paris Declaration of Aid Effectiveness' (2005). Over 100 countries and organizations committed themselves to this declaration, which focuses on 'ownership, harmonization, alignment, results and mutual accountability' as means to improve aid effectiveness.

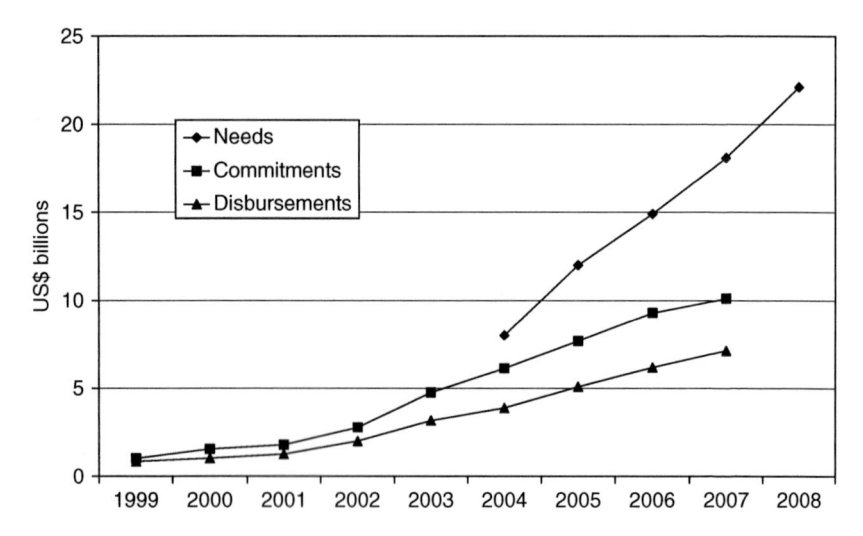

Figure 14.7 The widening gap between needs, commitments and disbursements for HIV/AIDS
Source: CHGA (2005b).

Lastly, an important observation that is often neglected when trying to gauge the additional resources required to finance the health system response to HIV/AIDS is that much of the burden of HIV/AIDS on heath systems is currently being absorbed by the general health services and not by HIV/AIDS-specific programmes. Given the rate of scale-up of ART programmes in many African countries, this is likely to remain the case for the foreseeable future. A significant proportion of beds in medical wards are occupied by patients being treated for opportunistic illnesses and a large number of outpatients are seeking HIV-related care. This can have major effects on resource requirements. The complicated nature of HIV means that under optimal conditions, or where there is good availability of drugs and other investigations, care for HIV can be significantly more costly than care for other types of illnesses (Decosas and Whiteside, 1996). Such costs were already evident in the mid-1990s in Zimbabwean hospitals (Hansen et al., 2000). Fifty per cent of patients in medical wards were thought to be HIV positive and their treatment costs were on average US$174.83, compared to US$110.03 for patients presenting with other diseases. More recently in South Africa we found that HIV-related care is often not only significantly more costly for inpatients, but that this observation extends to outpatient care as well (see Figure 14.8). It is in such instances that the deflection of resources acquires greater meaning.

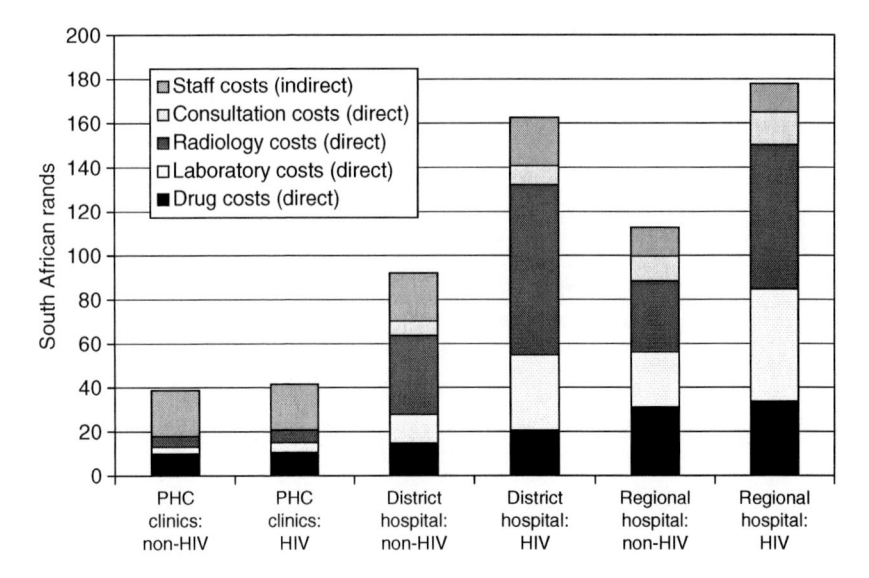

Figure 14.8 Costs of HIV-related care and non-HIV-related care at clinics, a district hospital and a regional hospital in KwaZulu-Natal, South Africa
Source: Veenstra and Oyier (2006).

Infrastructure resources

Even where financial resources are available, the physical infrastructure required to provide health-care cannot be created without a long lead-in time; meanwhile hospital beds may increasingly be allocated for HIV-related care, to the exclusion or detriment of other patients. Certainly, a quick review of a number of the studies focusing on HIV-related care in health facilities in Africa (see Table 14.2) demonstrates the large proportion of beds, particularly in medical and paediatric wards, that have been taken up with HIV patients. In Kenyatta National Hospital in Nairobi, between 1988/89 and 1992, bed occupancy rates remained at around 100 per cent, but a steep rise in the number of HIV-positive patients admitted was accompanied by a significant fall in the number of HIV-negative patients admitted (Arthur et al., 2000). The HIV burden on the hospital seemed to stabilize between 1992 and 1997, with more HIV-negative patients being admitted, but with bed occupancy rates rising to a staggering 190 per cent. This demonstrates the deflection of beds towards HIV-related care; either other patients are excluded or the infrastructure is stretched beyond its limits.

Table 14.2 The impact of HIV on health facilities in Africa

Location	HIV prevalence
Mama Yemo Hospital, Kinshasa, DRC (Hassig et al., 1990)	50% (1988, adult medical inpatients)
Rubaga Hospital, Kampala, Uganda (Tembo et al., 1994)	55.6% (1992, adult medical inpatients)
Various hospitals, Zimbabwe (Hansen et al., 2000)	50% (1995, adult medical inpatients)
Chris Hani Baragwanath Hospital, Soweto, South Africa (Meyers et al. 2000)	29.2% (1996, paediatric inpatients)
Kenyatta National Hospital, Nairobi, Kenya (Arthur et al., 2000)	18.7% (1988/89, adult medical inpatients) 38.5% (1992, adult medical inpatients) 40% (1997, adult medical inpatients)
Tertiary level hospital, Durban, South Africa (Colvin et al., 2001)	54% (1998, adult medical inpatients)
King Edward VIII hospital, Durban, South Africa (Pillay et al., 2001)	62.5% (1998, paediatric inpatients)
St Mary's Hospital, Lacor, Uganda (Fabiani et al., 2003)	42% (1999, adult medical inpatients)
Various hospitals and clinics, South Africa (Shisana et al., 2003)	46.2% (2002, medical and paediatric inpatients) 25.7% (2002, ambulatory PHC facility patients)

Even though health system infrastructure is being stretched by HIV/AIDS, as demonstrated at Kenyatta Hospital, earlier concerns that hospitals would be completely overrun by people dying of AIDS have been tempered. Access to health-care facilities has always been mediated by geographical barriers, by the direct and indirect costs of seeking care, and by health-care providers. The increasing burden of AIDS is evident and growing in communities. In recognition of this, different care models have emerged, addressing the lack of physical infrastructure and other barriers to accessing care. Some of these new care models, such as 'step-down care' (referring to palliative care in facilities with fewer highly trained medical personnel and lower operating costs) still require the development of physical infrastructure. Community Home-Based Care (CHBC) however often leads to physical, emotional and psychological, as well as social and economic stresses on the caregivers, who are usually female (Akintola, 2004). If clinical care is to be shifted to communities, partly as a way to alleviate infrastructure constraints, then there needs to be more recognition of the 'care economy' and support for the work that caregivers are doing (Ogden et al., 2004).

Human resources

Closely related to the issue of infrastructure resources, but most pressing of all, is the concern for human resources. Here not only does HIV/AIDS create additional demands, but it also impacts on supply, so compounding existing difficulties in managing an increasing HIV/AIDS burden. On the supply side, the impact of HIV/AIDS on health-care workers has been described as a 'triple threat': an increasing burden of disease affecting health workers' workloads and skill demands, serious reduction of the workforce through infection and the psychological stress of providing palliative care (Joint Learning Initiative, 2004). The loss of health-care workers due to illness has been substantiated by research; for example, a study of doctors in Uganda revealed that 30 per cent died within 20 years of graduation, with HIV/AIDS largely to blame (Dambisya, 2004). In Malawi, 48 per cent of health-care worker loss was found to be due to deaths and 80 per cent of these deaths were due to HIV-related illness (Mukati et al., 2004). The loss of health-care workers due to increasing workloads and psychological stress is somewhat more difficult to measure, but nevertheless remains a huge concern.

There are massive human resource implications in the need to scale-up care. The Commission on HIV/AIDS and Governance in Africa (CHGA) has estimated that if all eligible Zambians were to be provided with ART, the programme would by its fifth year require that the health service employ one and a half times the current number of physicians and twice the number of laboratory technicians (CHGA, 2005c). In Malawi, 90 per cent of public health facilities did not even have the capacity to provide a minimum package of care, due to high vacancy rates. As a result, the introduction of new services for HIV/AIDS was at the expense of other service areas, creating concerns for equity (Aitken and Kemp, 2003; EQUINET, 2003).

Given an environment of reduced supply and increasing demands, the deflection of human resources towards HIV/AIDS care is inevitable. A recent multi-country pilot study of health systems in South Africa, Tanzania and Zambia and their operation in the context of HIV/AIDS documented perhaps two of the most important ways in which this happens, at both management and facility level (Cheelo et al., 2005). First, within health facilities the creation of new posts becomes inadequate to contend with the disproportionate burden of HIV/AIDS on the health system. Care for HIV/AIDS patients is more time consuming than care for other types of patients because of the complexity of the disease. Second, managers tasked with overseeing HIV/AIDS and other communicable disease programmes find themselves under pressure to spend a disproportionate amount of time on HIV/AIDS issues, to the detriment of other programmes.

The deflection of human resources also relates closely to the debate around vertical and horizontal approaches to expanding care. Where HIV/AIDS programmes are more horizontally structured, ambitious scaling-up may surpass worker capacity and so force trade-offs between a range of important tasks (Joint Learning Initiative, 2004). Yet, where HIV/AIDS programmes are vertically structured and there is a general shortage of managers and health-care workers, these programmes may have to draw their human resources from other priority programmes. If HIV/AIDS programmes are run by Non-Governmental Organizations (NGOs) or donors with different working conditions to government employees, then the draw might be even stronger (USAID, 2003).

The movement of health-care workers is ultimately the result of combinations of 'push' and 'pull' factors and is far more widespread than health-care workers migrating between programmes or from public to private facilities. There is also extensive migration from rural to urban areas, from the underdeveloped south to the more developed north, and between neighbouring countries, so creating a complex web of migration streams (Joint Learning Initiative, 2004). In such situations, HIV/AIDS is most commonly a push factor, because it increases the workload, causes stress, and may diminish job satisfaction. However it can also be a pull factor, where pay in HIV/AIDS programmes is higher, management of these programmes is better, or more career opportunities present themselves. The movement of health-care workers will never be entirely dependent on the impact of HIV/AIDS, but rather will be the result of a whole host of factors influencing working conditions.

Interfaces and synergies

Although there may not be a significant body of evidence to substantiate the effects of vertical and horizontal approaches on health systems, arguments for and against suggest that there is no one right approach to expanding care. Observations that the two approaches should not be mutually exclusive, but rather combined in various ways to achieve longer-term goals, remain relevant (Mills, 2005). With HIV/AIDS, high levels of donor involvement, constrained settings and the pressure for rapid scale-up favour vertical approaches. These may indeed be appropriate in the shorter term to bring down the disease burden, but if sustainability and the strengthening of health systems remain our goal, in time HIV/AIDS programmes will have to be assimilated into the general health services. Furthermore, a large share of the burden of care is likely to remain with the general health services. Management of HIV/AIDS will remain dependent on functioning horizontal health systems, regardless of whether programmes such as ART are integrated or not.

If HIV/AIDS-specific programmes are initially vertical in nature, but the intention is later to assimilate them into the general health services, the question of optimal timing arises. A typical vertical programme designed to control acute infectious diseases can have different phases: an attack phase to control transmission and reduce new infections; a more limited consolidation phase to prevent a resurgence of cases; and a maintenance phase for surveillance (Mills, 1983). With HIV/AIDS the phases are not so distinct and there is uncertainty as to the future course of the epidemic, but it is still possible to use concepts like the 'AIDS transition' to determine the demands that will be placed on health systems. The attack phase can be compared to the rapid scale-up of ART now being undertaken in many countries to address a backlog of patients, while the consolidation phase may refer to stabilizing infection rates and high coverage of ART for those that require it. As the HIV/AIDS programmes consolidate there should be fewer demands on the capacity of health systems and so this would be a logical time for them to become more embedded into the general health services. However, unless new infections are tackled, the consolidation phase will never transpire and the treatment of ever-increasing numbers of AIDS patients will become too expensive. An integrated approach comprising prevention, treatment and care and impact mitigation remains crucial.

Given the current reality of vertical and horizontal approaches, the ideal would be for these to complement each other in synergistic ways, with the interfaces between the approaches highlighting important areas for collaboration. Vertical programmes make use of important elements of the general health service infrastructure (laboratory facilities, drug supply chains, information systems and so on), creating possibly the most obvious opportunities for health system strengthening. Indeed, some of these opportunities have been recognized in country plans and through external programme assistance. The Centers for Disease Control and Prevention (CDC) Global AIDS Program (GAP) for example has included laboratory capacity and laboratory infrastructure development in 25 countries (Martin et al., 2005). The programme has developed a systematic process for strengthening the capability and capacity of the laboratory infrastructure in resource-constrained countries, with such activities being designed to benefit all health programmes.

Another approach to looking at system-wide interfaces between vertical and horizontal approaches involves identifying common constraining barriers to improving service delivery for a range of different programmes. Where programmes – whether more horizontal in nature (such as maternal and child health) or those commonly more vertical in nature (TB, Malaria, HIV/AIDS) – share common concerns opportunities arise for collaboration and system strengthening. A summary of some important constraints identified from reviews of major global health initiatives has illustrated how system barriers encountered by specific programmes are rarely unique to that disease programme (Travis et al., 2004). Yet the responses are frequently disease-specific, and these responses have the potential to crowd out ongoing health sector activities. More health system focused responses will ensure that programmes are more sustainable in the longer term. For example, a disease-specific response to the physical inaccessibility of health services might involve focal outreach for the disease in question. Alternatively, and perhaps more appropriately, attention could be paid to capital investment and the siting of facilities.

Health system responses require funding, but the increased mobilization of resources for HIV/AIDS and other infectious diseases has been very disease-specific. Even though the Global Fund to Fight AIDS, TB and Malaria was created in 2002, only in Round 5 (September 2005) were proposals accepted for programmes to strengthen national health systems (Friends of the Global Fight, 2005). Just 1 per cent of fund financing has been for health system strengthening. Similarly, the American Administration's PEPFAR funding has been very treatment-focused, with Congress requiring that 55 per cent of funds go towards treatment, 15 per cent for palliative care, 20 per cent for HIV/AIDS prevention and 10 per cent for helping orphans and vulnerable children (Office of the United States Global AIDS Coordinator, 2004). These funding mechanisms have therefore not supported a health system response to overcoming barriers to scaling-up treatment. Given the limitations in public health-care financing in most countries heavily impacted by the epidemic, it is too much to expect that these countries complement aid money with their own resources to develop the necessary support geared towards health system development.

More broadly speaking, the proliferation of disease-specific funding coming from global sources and the growth in the number of institutions required by recipient countries to sustain this funding create problems of coordination and provoke tensions between different approaches and between existing country-level bodies. These tensions have been described in a review of early implementation processes of the GFATM in four African countries (Brugha et al., 2004). Most obviously perhaps, disease-specific funding appears to be at odds with country-level sector-wide approaches (SWAp), promoted since the mid-1990s as a mechanism to reduce fragmentation and develop national leadership of policymaking and planning (Cassels and Janovsky, 1998). Separate funding might protect spending on priority programmes and fulfil donor interests, but it is questionable whether an appropriate balance in sector spending can be achieved at a national level without pooling resources. The GFATM for example, might have 'country-led processes' in the sense that individual countries can decide on which interventions to pursue, but these interventions can only relate to a specific disease and will ultimately be prioritized through the acceptance or rejection of proposals. Such influences capture the governance concerns that arise with resource-based power.

Lastly, the idea of 'interfaces and synergies' should be extended to include all sectors whose policies could potentially benefit health. Staff in ministries of health need new skills to engage in a globalized world (see for example Fidler and Drager, 2006). They need to understand the links between foreign policy and health, be aware of how they can shape the external policy environment, and develop strategic alliances with their own ministries. By advising and working through such alliances, countries can ensure that any new policy directions have favourable outcomes for health. In some instances it might even make sense to have a specific unit or cell in the ministry to focus on, say, trade issues.

Building the synergies between health and foreign policy should not just be a responsibility of developing countries. In fact, it is middle-income countries that are most likely to have success in addressing foreign policy issues. The potential also exists for developed countries to find new, more appropriate ways of working in today's context of globalization. In particular, their role in development cooperation could be enhanced by, for example, having budgeted funds for global public health functions.

Opportunities for (re)-constructing health systems

Now, perhaps more than ever, we have opportunities to (re)-construct health systems in Africa. Our starting point might be weak, but we have a greater understanding of what led to the weakened state of these systems in the first place, we are slowly recognizing and adapting to the demands of HIV/AIDS and other infectious diseases, scaling-up care is becoming a global concern, and perhaps most importantly, resources are being mobilized to assist heavily affected countries. So why are we not capitalizing on these opportunities?

The answer lies in our approach, and here we don't specifically refer to horizontal versus vertical approaches, but rather a need for system-focused responses in preference to disease-specific responses. While vertical programmes are often blamed for contributing to weakened health systems, we have demonstrated that it is not always so much the orientation of these programmes that is the problem, but rather the disease-specific focus that they adopt. Countries are strongly pushed to adopt this focus because of the global proliferation of disease-specific initiatives for HIV/AIDS and other infectious illnesses. While countries are logically in the best position to see HIV/AIDS in the context of other health priorities, they are not being supported to do so. Global health governance bodies, such as the WHO, might advocate for the most relevant form that global involvement in health should take, but are largely powerless to ensure compliance. This governance issue needs to be considered.

Governance of issue- or disease-specific initiatives can happen through global or national level action, but ideally should involve both, since there is a need to build capacity at lower levels. One suggestion most amenable to rapid implementation is for all national programmes and global initiatives to be held accountable for health system strengthening through the inclusion of system indicators in their monitoring and evaluation frameworks (Atun et al., 2004; Global Health Watch, 2005). This would be facilitated by the development of relevant health system indicators. New programmes and initiatives should, in addition, be required to conduct systems impact assessments, to ensure that from the outset they are thinking in terms of the system.

It may be all very well to suggest activities or strategies to improve GHG, but the question often returns to the institutional arrangements that are required to facilitate these. Given the proliferation of actors that countries already have to engage with, creating new structures would simply complicate an already chaotic environment. The WHO already has a comparative advantage for sound governance in the health sector because of its strategic position, broad health focus, ability to place health in the context of development, and its humanitarian approach. Its mandate needs strengthening, so that it can develop into a governance structure that can hold its own against global health actors (particularly those with resources) and ensure accountability (Global Health Watch, 2005). Perhaps then we would see a return to the 'health for all' agenda.

Most importantly, the type of response chosen by countries in scaling up HIV/AIDS care should drive the mobilization and allocation of resources for global health, and not the other way around. In other words, financing should not only be predictable and sustainable, but also flexible enough to respect local priorities and preferences. Indeed, the CHGA suggests that absorptive capacity will not be an issue if countries have more flexibility in financing their health systems (CHGA, 2005a). SWAps were created with this goal in mind, but seem to have fallen out of favour. Will the 'Paris Declaration on Aid Effectiveness' (2005) make the difference we need? Similarly, International Monetary Fund loan conditions need to be more flexible to allow increases in HIV/AIDS funding and associated health system strengthening, particularly since there is somewhat conflicting evidence and a lack of consensus on what constitutes 'macroeconomic stability'. If countries are given a range of scenarios illustrating the trade-offs between increasing health sector spending and controlling inflation, then they will be in the best position to decide on a path to follow (Rowden et al., 2004).

While financial resources are certainly needed, the human resource crisis and the deflection of human resources as a result of HIV/AIDS are probably the greatest challenge currently faced by health systems in Africa. Here again, if programmes or initiatives are disease-specific, then they should consider what effect they are having on the human resource capacity of the system as a whole. They should be held accountable for contributing towards human resource development. Since individual countries themselves will never be able to address their 'brain drain', this is also a relevant issue for GHG. While perhaps difficult to address given an environment of free trade governed by the General Agreement on Trade in Services (GATS), we still propose that those countries benefiting from the global migration of health-care workers should have to pay some type of 'tax' for this benefit. This will potentially not only discourage active poaching, but also give some reimbursement to countries for their loss, and in so doing contribute to the development of human resource capacity where it is needed.

The HIV/AIDS epidemic has increased tensions between ideological standpoints and in so doing has created greater confusion in countries whose health sectors are most seriously affected. The concept of 'global policy networks', introduced in relation to health-care financing reform (Lee and Goodman, 2002), could be useful in understanding this predicament. Briefly described, a policy network develops out of a proliferation of initiatives, which in turn creates interlinkages through projects, individuals and policy ideas. The concern with such networks is that the resulting influential global 'policy elite' might not be representative, in particular of those affected by policy changes, thus putting question marks against the legitimacy and appropriateness of reforms. The idea that there are different global policy networks clustering around focus areas such as HIV/AIDS, SWAps, PHC and so on, might help us to understand the current situation and to develop the architecture for GHG in the twenty-first century.

This chapter focuses on HIV/AIDS, the impact it is having on health systems in Africa, and the role of global involvement in shaping this impact. In many countries HIV infection rates are still rising. The majority of AIDS cases, and hence also the long-term costs of ART, are in the future. There may be lessons in looking at those countries that have seen the AIDS cases peak, but they are few in number (Uganda and Thailand). There are more resources being made available because of HIV/AIDS (although we note that in January 2006 in Beijing the global community asked for US$1.2 billion to respond to SARS and received $1.9 billion – some diseases are more fundable than others). However, these resources are for specific diseases and the opportunity to build the health system is being lost. We do not believe a pandemic like HIV/AIDS can be treated by specifically focused health interventions in the long term. If it is, then consequences for the rest of the health sector will be damaging. This is an important and challenging issue.

References

Aita, J., 'U.N. Security Council Holds Historic Session on AIDS in Africa. U.S. Announces New Contribution for Fighting AIDS', USIS Washington File, USIS, Washington, DC, 2000.

Aitken, J. and J. Kemp, 'HIV/AIDS, Equity and Health Sector Personnel in Southern Africa', Regional Network for Equity in Health in Southern Africa (EQUINET), Harare, 2003.

Akintola, G., 'A Gendered Analysis of the Burden of Care on Family and Volunteer Caregivers in Uganda and South Africa', Health Economics and HIV/AIDS Research Division, Durban, 2004.

Arthur, G., S. Bhatt, D. Muhindi, G. Achiya, S. Kariuki and C. Gilks, 'The Changing Impact of HIV/AIDS on Kenyatta National Hospital, Nairobi from 1988/89 through 1992 to 1997', *AIDS*, 14(11) (2000): 1625–31.

Atun, R., F. Lennox-Chhugani, F. Drobniewski, Y. Samyshkin and R. Coker, 'A Framework and Toolkit for Capturing the Communicable Disease Programmes within Health Systems: Tuberculosis Control as an Illustrative Example', *European Journal of Public Health*, 14 (2004): 267–73.

Barnett. T. and A. Whiteside, *AIDS in the Twenty-First Century: Disease and Globalization* (Basingstoke: Palgrave Macmillan, 2002).

Barrett, R., C. Kuzawa, T. McDade and G. Armelagos, 'Emerging and Re-emerging Infectious Diseases: the Third Epidemiologic Transition', *Annual Review of Anthropology*, 27 (1998): 247–71.

Bevan, D., 'An Analytical Overview of Aid Absorption: Recognising and Avoiding Macroeconomic Hazards', International Monetary Fund Seminar on Foreign Aid and Macroeconomic Management, Maputo, Mozambique, 2005.

Brugha, R., M. Donoghue, M. Starling, P. Ndubani, F. Ssengooba, B. Fernandes and G. Walt, 'The Global Fund: Managing Great Expectations', *Lancet*, 364 (2004): 95–100.

Bulir, A. and J. Hamann, *Aid Volatility: an Empirical Assessment* (Washington: International Monetary Fund, 2003).

Cassels, A. and K. Janovsky, 'Better Health in Developing Countries: are Sector-Wide Approaches the Way of the Future?' *Lancet*, 352 (1998): 1777–9.

Chatora, F. and P. Tumusime, 'Primary Health Care: a Review of its Implementation in Sub-Saharan Africa', *Primary Health Care Research and Development*, 5 (2004): 296–360.

Cheelo, C., S. Dawad, G. Frumence, F. Masiye, C. Mpukha, M. Mwangu, T. Quinlan, M. Sengwana, M. Sherrif, D. Simba, J. Sundewall and N. Veenstra, 'Synthesis Report of the Healthy Systems Project Pilot Study in South Africa, Tanzania and Zambia', Health Economics and HIV/AIDS Research Division (HEARD), Durban, Dar es Salaam, Lusaka; The Muhimbili University College of Health Sciences (MUCHS), and the School of Economics, University of Zambia, 2005.

CHGA, 'Financing the AIDS Response. Securing Africa's Future', Commission of HIV/AIDS and Governance in Africa, Addis Ababa, 2005a.

CHGA, 'Funding Africa's AIDS Crisis', Commission of HIV/AIDS and Governance in Africa, Addis Ababa, 2005b.

CHGA, 'Impact of HIV/AIDS on Health Workers: Kenya and Zambia', Commission of HIV/AIDS and Governance in Africa, Addis Ababa, 2005c.

Coetzee, D., H. Hilderbrand, E. Goemaere, F. Matthys and M. Beolart, 'Integrating Tuberculosis and HIV Care in the Primary Care Setting in South Africa', *Tropical Medicine and International Health*, 9(6) (2004): A11–A15.

Colvin, M., S. Dawood, I.Kleinschmidt, S. Mullick and U. Lallo, 'Prevalence of HIV and HIV-Related Diseases on the Adult Medical Wards of a Tertiary Hospital in Durban, South Africa', *International Journal of STD and AIDS*, 12(6) (2001): 386–9.

Commission on Macroeconomics and Health, *Macroeconomics and Health: Investing in Health for Economic Development* (Geneva: World Health Organization, 2001).

Cueto, M., 'The Origins of Primary Health Care and Selective Primary Health Care', *American Journal of Public Health*, 94(11) (2004): 1864–74.

Dambisya, Y., 'The Fate and Career Destinations of Doctors who Qualified at Uganda's Makerere Medical School in 1984: Retrospective Cohort Study', *British Medical Journal*, 329(7466) (2004): 600–1.

'Declaration of Alma-Ata', International Conference on Primary Health Care, Alma-Ata, USSR, 1978.

Decosas, J. and A. Whiteside, 'The Effect of HIV on Health Care in Sub-Saharan Africa', *Development Southern Africa*, 13(1) (1996): 89–100.

Dodgson, R., K. Lee and N. Drager, 'Global Health Governance: a Conceptual Review', Discussion Paper No. 1, London School of Hygiene and Tropical Medicine and World Health Organization, Geneva, 2002.

Elzinga, G., 'Vertical-Horizontal Synergy of the Health Workforce', *Bulletin of the World Health Organization*, 83(4) (2005): 242.

EQUINET, 'ART Treatment Access and Effective Responses to HIV and AIDS – Providing Momentum for Accessible, Effective and Sustainable Health Systems', Harare Regional Network for Equity in Health in Southern Africa (EQUINET), 2003.

Fabiani, M., S. Accorsi, R. Aleni, G. Rizzardini, B. Nattabi, A. Gabrielli, C. Opira and S. Declich, 'Estimating HIV Prevalence and the Impact of HIV/AIDS on a Ugandan Hospital by Combining Serosurvey Data and Hospital Discharge Records', *Journal of Acquired Immune Deficiency Syndromes and Human Retrovirology*, 34(1) (2003): 62–6.

Fidler, D. and N. Drager, 'Health and Foreign Policy', *Bulletin of the World Health Organization*, 84(9) (2006): 687.

Friends of the Global Fight, 'New Funds Committed in Round 5 to the Global Fight Against AIDS, Tuberculosis and Malaria', Friends of the Global Fight Against AIDS Tuberculosis and Malaria, Washington, DC, 2005.

Global Health Watch, *Global Health Watch 2005–2006: an Alternative World Health Report* (London: Zed Books, People's Health Movement, Medact and Global Equity Gauge Alliance, 2005).

Gonzalez, C., *Mass Campaigns and General Health Services* (Geneva: World Health Organization, 1965).

Hansen, K., G. Chapman, I. Chitsike, O. Kasilo and G. Mwaluko, 'The Costs of HIV/AIDS Care at Government Hospitals in Zimbabwe', *Health Policy and Planning*, 15(4) (2000): 432–40.

Hassig, S., J. Perriens, E. Baende, M. Kahotwa, K. Bishagara, N. Kinkela and B. Kapita, 'An Analysis of the Economic Impact of HIV Infection among Patients at Mama Yemo Hospital, Kinshasa, Zaire', *AIDS*, 4(9) (1990): 883–7.

HDA, 'Study of the Health Service Burden of HIV and AIDS and Impact of HIV and AIDS on the Health Sector in Swaziland', Health and Development Africa (Pty) Ltd/JTK Associates, Parktown, South Africa, 2005.

Joint Learning Initiative, *Human Resources for Health: Overcoming the Crisis* (Cambridge, MA: Harvard, Global Equity Initiative 2004).

Lee, K. and H. Goodman, 'Global Policy Networks: the Propagation of Health Care Financing Reform since the 1980s' in K. Lee, K. Buse and S. Fustukian (eds), *Health Policy in a Globalising World* (Cambridge: Cambridge University Press: 2002), pp. 97–119.

Lewis, M., *Addressing the Challenge of HIV/AIDS: Macroeconomic, Fiscal and Institutional Issues* (Washington DC: Centre for Global Development, 2005).
Lewis, M. and S. Stout, 'Financing HIV: the Roles of International Financial Institutions', in E. Beck, N. Mays, A. Whiteside and J. Zuniga (eds), *The HIV Pandemic: Local and Global Implications* (Oxford: Oxford University Press, 2006), pp. 625–41.
Macfarlane, S., M. Racelis and F. Muli-Musiime, 'Public Health in Developing Countries', *Lancet*, 356 (2000): 841–6.
Martin, R., T. Hearn, J. Ridderhof and A. Demby, 'Implementation of a Quality Systems Approach for Laboratory Practice in Resource-Constrained Countries', *AIDS*, 19, May, suppl 2 (2005): S59–S65.
Mburu, F. and S. Naidoo, 'Impact of HIV/AIDS on Mortality among the Inpatients at Motebang Hospital, Lesotho', *Southern African Journal of HIV Medicine*, 16 (2004): 33–7.
McMichael, A., M. McKee, V. Shkolnikov and T. Valkonen, 'Mortality Trends and Setbacks: Global Convergence or Divergence?' *Lancet*, 363 (2004): 1155–9.
Meyers, T., J. Pettifor, G. Gray, H. Crewe-Brown and J. Galpin, 'Pediatric Admissions with Human Immunodeficiency Virus Infection at a Regional Hospital in Soweto, South Africa', *Journal of Tropical Pediatrics*, 46(4) (2000): 224–30.
Mills, A., 'Vertical vs Horizontal Health Programmes in Africa: Idealism, Pragmatism, Resources and Efficiency', *Social Science and Medicine*, 17(24) (1983): 1971–81.
Mills, A., 'Mass Campaigns versus General Health Services: What Have We Learnt in 40 Years about Vertical versus Horizontal Approaches?' *Bulletin of the World Health Organization*, 83(4) (2005): 315–16.
Molyneaux, D., P. Hotez and A. Fenwick, 'Rapid-Impact Interventions: How a Policy of Integrated Control for Africa's Neglected Tropical Diseases Could Benefit the Poor', *Public Library of Science Medicine*, 2(11) (2005): e336.
Moser, K., V. Shkolnikov and D. Leon, 'World Mortality 1950–2000: Divergence Replaces Convergence from the Late 1980s', *Bulletin of the World Health Organization*, 83(3) (2005): 202–9.
Mukati, M., A. Gonani, A. Macheso, B. Simwaka, S. Kinoti and B. Ndyanabangi, 'Challenges Facing the Malawian Health Workforce in the era of HIV/AIDS', Commonwealth Regional Health Community Secretariat (CRHCS), Washington, DC, United States Agency for International Development (USAID), and Support for Analysis and Reseach in Africa (SARA), 2004.
Nabyonga, J., M. Desmet, H. Karamagi, P. Kadama, F. Omaswa and O. Walker, 'Abolition of Cost-Sharing is Pro-Poor: Evidence from Uganda', *Health Policy and Planning*, 20(2) (2005): 100–8.
Office of the United States Global AIDS Coordinator, *The President's Emergency Plan for AIDS Relief: U.S. Five-Year Global HIV/AIDS Strategy* (Washington, DC: United States Department of State, 2004).
Ogden, J., S. Esim and C. Grown, *Expanding the Care Continuum for HIV/AIDS: Bringing Carers into Focus* (Washington, DC: Population Council and International Centre for Research on Women, 2004).
Oliveira-Cruz, V., C. Kurowski and A. Mills, 'Delivery of Priority Health Services: Searching for Synergies within the Vertical versus Horizontal Debate', *Journal of International Development*, 15 (2003): 67–86.
Over, M., 'Impact of the HIV/AIDS Epidemic on the Health Sectors of Developing Countries', in M. Haacker (ed.), *The Macroeconomics of HIV/AIDS* (Washington, DC: International Monetary Fund, 2004).

'Paris Declaration on Aid Effectiveness: Ownerships, Harmonisation, Alignment, Results and Mutual Accountability', 2005, http://www.adb.org/media/articles/2005/7033_international_community_aid/paris_declaration.pdf#search=%22paris%20declaration%20on%20aid%20effectiveness%22 (accessed 26 September 2006).

Pillay, K., M. Colvin, R. Williams and H. Coovadia, 'Impact of HIV-1 Infection in South Africa', *Archives of Disease in Childhood*, 85 (2001): 50–1.

Rifkin, S. and G. Walt, 'Why Health Improves: Defining the Issues Concerning "Comprehensive Primary Health Care" and "Selective Primary Health Care"', *Social Science and Medicine*, 23(6) (1986): 559–66.

Rowden, R., P. Zeitz, A. Taylor and J. Carter, *Blocking Progress: How the Fight against HIV/AIDS is Being Undermined by the World Bank and International Monetary Fund* (Washington DC: ActionAid International USA, 2004).

Sen, K. and M. Koivusalo, 'Health Care Reforms and Developing Countries – a Critical Overview', *International Journal of Health Planning and Management*, 13 (1998): 199–215.

Shisana, O., E. Hall, K. Maluleke, D. Stoker, C. Schwage, M. Colvin, J. Chauveau, C. Botha, T. Gumede, H. Fomundam, N. Shaikh, T. Rehle, E. Udjo and D. Gisselquist, 'The impact of HIV/AIDS on the Health Sector: National Survey of Health Personnel, Ambulatory and Hospitalised Patients and Health Facilities, 2002', Report prepared for South African Department of Health, Pretoria, 2003.

Tembo, G., H. Friesan, G. Asiimwe-Okiror, R. Moser, W. Naamara, N. Bakyaita and J. Musinguzi, 'Bed Occupancy due to HIV/AIDS in an Urban Hospital Medical Ward in Uganda', *AIDS*, 8(8) (1994): 1169–71.

Travis, P., S. Bennet, A. Haines, T. Pang, Z. Bhutta, A. Hyder, N. Pielemeier, A. Mills and T. Evans, 'Overcoming Health-Systems Constraints to Achieve the Millennium Development Goals', *Lancet*, 364 (2004): 900–6.

UN General Assembly, *United Nations Millennium Declaration* (New York: UN, 2000).

UN Population Division, 'World Population Prospects: the 2004 Revision. Population Database', 2004, http://esa.un.org/unpp (accessed 9 January 2006).

USAID, 'The Health Sector Human Resource Crisis in Africa: an Issues Paper', United States Agency for International Development (USAID), Washington DC, Support for Analysis and Reseach in Africa (SARA) and Academy for Educational Development (EAD), 2003.

Veenstra, N. and A. Oyier, 'The Burden of HIV-Related Illness on Outpatient Health Services in KwaZulu-Natal, South Africa', *AIDS Care*, 18(3) (2006): 262–8.

Walsh, J. and K. Warren, 'Selective Primary Health Care: an Interim Strategy for Disease Control in Developing Countries', *New England Journal of Medicine*, 301(18) (1979): 967–74.

Werner, D., D. Sanders, J. Weston, S. Babb and B. Rodriguez, *Questioning the Solution: the Politics of Primary Health Care and Child Survival* (Palo Alto: Healthwrights, 1997).

WHO, 'The World Health Report 2000. Health Systems: Improving Performance', World Health Organization, Geneva, 2000.

WHO, 'Revised Global Burden of Diseases Estimates 2002 by Country', World Health Organization, Geneva, 2002.

WHO, 'Report of a "Lessons Learnt" Workshop on the Six ProTEST Pilot Projects in Malawi, South Africa and Zambia', World Health Organization, Geneva, 2004.

World Bank, *World Development Report 1993: Investing in Health* (Washington, DC: World Bank, 1993).

15
Moving Global Health Governance Forward

Ilona Kickbusch

Introduction

This chapter maps some of the key recent developments of global health governance and focuses in particular on two dimensions of the global health action sphere: development and interdependence. It argues that a new geography of power has emerged that is very different from that of the short unilateral period following the collapse of the Soviet Union. Global health governance today is being conducted in a non-polar world, a context that provides a new dynamic for multilateral institutions, which can strengthen their role as platforms and brokers between the myriad of actors in the health field as well as gaining acceptance for strengthening international law for health. The emerging economies and new power centres are also increasingly using the existing institutions – such as the World Health Organization – to increase their own influence on global decision-making for health. The chapter provides examples of this power shift and introduces some of the emerging trends in global health governance.

The global nature of health governance

Global governance has become a widely-used term, expressing the relationships that have emerged between the multitude of players in the global arena. It covers a wide range of instruments and mechanisms – from informal to formal and from soft to hard law. It goes far beyond the multilateral and bilateral relationships between sovereign nation-states and the wide variety of structured ways in which they interact in the international system. Today global governance not only includes the many new types of organized efforts and partnerships that have been put in place to solve common problems, but it also mirrors the power asymmetry in an interdependent and interconnected world (Rosenau, 2003). The same holds for global health governance, which can be understood as a mechanism for collective problem-solving for improved health through the interplay of different institutional forms and actors at different levels. Like other forms of governance, global health governance is subject to reconfigurations of power – it is therefore always also a political undertaking.

The governance of health and health systems is a core area of national policymaking and many countries still have not understood the extent to which health has become a transnational issue. But increasingly the protection of the health of the population within a national boundary is situated between domestic and foreign affairs; it is as dependent on the decisions made in international and regional bodies and in other countries as it is on decisions made 'at home'. For example, the access to and the price of medicines, the mobility of health-care professionals or the economic impacts of public health measures are now also negotiated at the global level. It is becoming more important for countries to be able to conduct negotiations for health in the global arena and many of them are not well prepared to do so.

The global nature of health governance was established through two symbolic 'cosmopolitan moments' which lie about twenty years apart: the emergence of HIV/AIDS in the 1980s and the emergence of SARS in 2003. Both are deeply connected to the impact of globalization on health. A 'cosmopolitan moment' (Beck, 2007: 109) is a prism which brings into focus the need to address a problem at the global level through collective action. It can include both a normative dimension – 'We have a global responsibility' – and a dimension of realpolitik – 'The national interest can only be resolved through joint global action.' Indeed moral obligation (as well as indignation!) and 'enlightened self interest' have become two strong driving forces of global health governance. Cosmopolitan moments usually open up new political spaces and allow – and sometimes oblige – new actors to join the global governance effort.

All the elements that we can characterize as defining features of global health governance were first played out in the HIV/AIDS arena (Kickbusch, 2007):

- Public health can no longer be pursued just at the national level – it needs strong global institutions, mechanisms and funding for development and global public goods.
- The health sector can no longer deal with the emerging challenges on its own – it needs multi-sectoral action and broad public and private partnerships at national and international levels.
- Health can no longer be seen as a purely professional and technical endeavour – it needs the strong voice and the support of civil society and of political leaders to address the equity and human rights issues at stake.

The response to the HIV/AIDS epidemic was initially driven in particular by civil society voices and strong non-governmental organizations with a special focus on human rights, and it was not fully accepted as a global security issue when taken to the UN Security Council in 2000. This response can be compared with that to the SARS threat, which was taken forward rapidly by political leaders at the highest level in Asia as a result of concerns about the potentially high economic impact of the disease on the region. This is exemplified by the emergency SARS summit called by the prime ministers of Singapore and Thailand at the end of April 2003 when the Chinese Premier came to Bangkok to brief leaders from the 10-member Association of Southeast Asian Nations about the Chinese efforts to combat the disease. While both outbreaks have come to represent a 'cosmopolitan moment' and both illustrate the blend between a health crisis, a governance crisis and a crisis in confidence, they also exemplify two worlds of global health action based on different rationales that are still too far apart.

The action sphere of global health governance

Any debate on global health governance must acknowledge the many different discourses on global health that are under way. While there is a general broad agreement that there is a need for 'good' global health governance, the concerns raised by a multiplicity of actors reflect very different interests: a better management of interdependence; more financing for development; a greater concern for equity, social justice and human rights; an increase in aid efficiency; reliable agreements on managing health risks and ensuring health security; a more level playing field for the poorest countries; a greater market share for the emerging economies; and mechanisms to strengthen the commitment to global public goods and rule of law. These are just some that deserve mention.

In the global north, different health interests frequently compete for influence and resources within the complex policy triangle of development agencies, foreign affairs and ministries of health. In the south they require the management of the multitude of donors and programmes at national and global levels. Global health governance is defined by *unstructured pluralism* – that is, a wide range of very diverse approaches and solutions to global health challenges are being implemented by a continuously growing set of actors (Beck and Lau, 2004).

Yet as a result of the asymmetry of power, this 'shopping mall' of global health is not set up to allow the recipient 'customers' a real choice. For a decade or so this unstructured growth filled a void in a world without clear health leadership and a global health gold rush was able to generate increasing financial resources for global health activities. This now seems to have reached its limit as a result of two important developments: first, there are increasing calls for a 'new global health architecture' that would address the power imbalances and the lack of coordination at all levels of governance; and second, there is a considerable rediscovery of integrated approaches such as primary health care. Both reflect doubts as to the sustainability of the multitude of disease-specific programmes at global and at country levels. The debate even includes proposals to shut down agencies, as was recently suggested in relation to UNAIDS (England, 2008) – an organization established in 1994 by a resolution of the UN Economic and Social Council and launched in January 1996.

In part, the difficulty of the discourse lies in the fact that two key governance challenges need to be resolved at the same time. The first challenge is related to development: the increasing health inequities between the winners and losers of globalization, the chasm between what we know and what we do in relation to development aid, the unwillingness of the rich countries to meet their commitments and the unwillingness of some poor countries to consider the health of their people as a priority. HIV/AIDS, access to treatment and the tragedy of Sub-Saharan Africa are the central symbolic themes of this narrative. It comes to the fore in particular over the lack of support for the implementation of the UN Millennium Development Goals which are to be achieved by 2015 (United Nations, 2007). The response to criticism with regard to the overall impact of aid has led to a flurry of governance activities for better coordination of development aid, such as the Paris Declaration on Aid Effectiveness (2005). In health it has also resulted in the creation of a number of new organizational and financing structures that aim to address priority health problems more effectively at country level, such as UNAIDS, UNITAID, and the Global Fund to Fight AIDS, TB and Malaria (GFATM). In particular these structures include a wide range of societal actors both in their governance structure and in the implementation of programmes.

These organizations were founded not only because trust in the effectiveness of the World Health Organization (WHO) had eroded in some of the major donor countries but also because a group of nation-states had a strong interest in moving decision-making away from the multilateral venue of the United Nations towards a more restricted 'coalition of the willing' model composed of a limited and like-minded number of actors. Most of the new alliances and organizations were supported through venture philanthropy, in particular through the significant start-up financial input of the Bill and Melinda Gates Foundation. It is this rise of new public-private partnerships and non-state actors that has been the focus of much recent writing on global health governance as well as the catalyst for calls for a 'new global health architecture' (see Walt et al., Chapter 3 above).

The second challenge is related to interdependence: it builds on the realization that most health risks in the twenty-first century are transnational and that all attempts to control them lead us into the global arena (Jamison et al., 1998). This interdependence in health blurs the dividing line between domestic and foreign policy, between health and security and between health and other policies such as trade (see Helble et al., Chapter 8). In particular the concept of health security has opened up a new political space between foreign policy and health and security and health – precisely because it is not achieved through a balance of great powers and grand strategies, but in the containment of risk with the weakest link. Governance under conditions of interdependence requires trust, a level playing field for decision-making, and willingness to negotiate the collective provision of global public goods, as well as transparency and accountability. SARS, polio and avian flu are at the centre of this narrative. In health it has led to what Beck (2007: 368) terms 'cosmopolitan realpolitik', that is an increasing recognition by nation-states of the utility of multilateralism, hard law and pooling of sovereignty as an instrument of global governance: examples include the International Health Regulations, the Framework Convention on Tobacco Control and World Trade Organization agreements on intellectual property in relation to pharmaceuticals. In a significant turn-around it has brought nation-states to a renewed acknowledgement of the value of 'their' World Health Organization as both a broker and a rule-maker, in particular driven by the emerging economies that can now use the UN system to flex their muscles and express their interests. This renewed willingness of states to cooperate with one another as well as with other players in the global governance system has become a critical dimension of global health governance.

The differences in perspective are also reflected in the very use of the term 'global health'. Some definitions focus on containing transnational risks which lie beyond the reach of national governments, others aim to stress the determinants of health and the global commitment and responsibility to support health for its own sake. The TIME Global Health Summit 2005 saw global heath as focused on 'saving one life at a time' (Hilts, 2005) and more or less excluded the hard law dimensions of 'governing interdependence'. Yet in the global governance debate in general as well as with regard to health it is critical to be clear whether one is addressing redistributive issues of global equity and access or issues related to governing interdependence and providing global public goods. This is not in order to juxtapose them but to ensure that they become more transparent, coherent and mutually supportive at all levels of governance and in consequence are also better understood not only by politicians but also the general public. Figure 15.1 illustrates the action sphere of global health governance – in principle one could show for every single issue and challenge in global health how the two circles of action overlap to varying degrees and where they need to work separately through different instruments and mechanisms and engage different actors.

The new multilateralism

For this chapter, global health is concerned with 'those health issues which transcend national boundaries and governments and call for actions to influence the global forces that determine the health of people. It requires new forms of governance at national and international level which seek to include

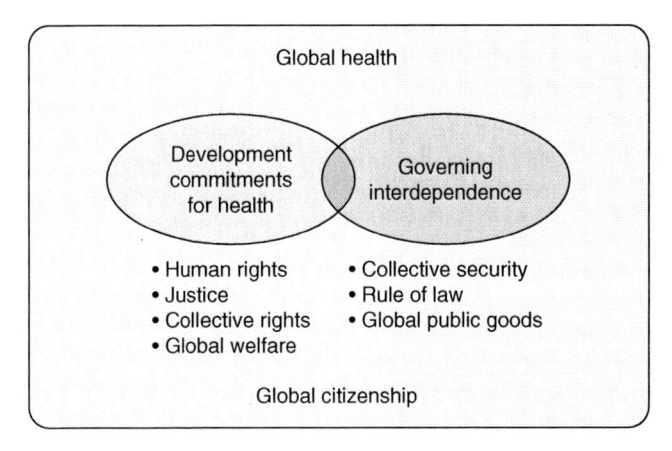

Figure 15.1 The action sphere of global health

[Diagram content: Global health / Development commitments for health / Governing interdependence / • Human rights • Justice • Collective rights • Global welfare / • Collective security • Rule of law • Global public goods / Global citizenship]

a wide range of actors' (Kickbusch and Lister, 2006: 482). Global health governance as a mechanism of collective problem-solving presently has no defined centre of action or accountability (Kickbusch, 2003). A new multilateralism has emerged, which moves out of the realms of traditional diplomacy and is characterized as multi-actor, multi-issue, multi-role and multi-valued.

Within this system, both the roles of national governments and international organizations are being redefined. 'Nation states have become enmeshed in and are functionally part of a larger pattern of global transformations and global flows' (Held et al., 1999: 45). Much has been written about the many hybrid forms of global organizations and financing mechanisms that have emerged within the last decade. Their key characteristic is probably that of the 'interface' (Bartsch et al., 2007), meaning the recurrent interactions and new forms of influence – discursive, organizational, legal and resource transfers – that take place in the many transnational arenas. New types of coalitions based either on risk and its distribution or on the economic impact of global public health measures emerge – often overcoming other value-based or political differences. At the same time strong value-based alliances and initiatives come forward that concentrate on the urgency to address the failures of globalization, often in coalition with high-profile actors: Bono, Mandela, Clinton, Gates, to name but a few. Global health governance today allows for innovation, creativity, entrepreneurship, rapid action and flexible alliances, and new types of partnerships abound. This opens new political space and increases the importance of a wide range of platforms – including the international organizations – as brokers and convenors.

The 'interface' led in the 1990s to the emergence of a new form of multilateralism that changed the generalized principles according to which global governance is conducted. It brings the norms of multilateralism and the interest of market actors together; Bull and NcNeill (2006) call this new form *market multilateralism*. The most obvious example of this approach was the announcement of the UN Global Compact to embrace, support and enact a set of core values in the areas of human rights, labour standards, and environmental practices by Kofi Annan, then Secretary General of the United Nations, at the meeting of the World Economic Forum (sic!) in Davos in 1999. 'We have shown' – he says in his speech – 'through cooperative ventures – both at the policy level and on the ground – that the goals of the United Nations and those of business can, indeed, be mutually supportive' (Annan, 1999).

Bull and McNeill (2006) propose that a double dynamic is under way: transnational companies are behaving more like states while the multinational organizations take on the characteristics of companies – this has made each side more able and willing to work with the other. After about ten years of experience it is possible to show how the dynamic process of engagement leads to a change in all partners: it redefines the role of international organizations, the political strategies of transnational corporations and the rules of engagement of non-governmental organizations. Health is the global policy arena in which this form of collaboration is found to be most advanced: because it is of high interest to the private sector players as a growing global market, because health outcomes lend themselves to measurable results and because health is a high visibility issue of life and death that can gain high media attention.

The significant growth and visibility of actors and activities in global health can in the first instance overshadow the problems inherent in this new polycentric system (Kohlmorgen, 2005). Early warnings of the flip-side of this pluralism of actors and approaches (Buse and Walt, 2000) were given little attention amid the euphoria over the rapid expansion of global health initiatives, but are now coming back into focus (Garrett, 2007). Indeed the main argument for new types of governance mechanisms (such as public-private partnerships, global funds, alliances) was to:

- provide better results (in particular more efficiency and effectiveness) than the international state-based system (that is, the UN organizations);
- be driven by technical agendas not the political contingencies of state-based decision-making processes; and
- be more inclusive by involving a wide range of stakeholders, in particular the private sector.

But many of the 'seven deadly sins' (Birdsall, 2004) of donor behaviour are replicated in the new attempts at governance, not least because in many cases the key players have changed hats rather than their perspective or 'the game' itself. As these new organizations have grown both in size and number, one of their key advantages has often been lost: speed of action in implementation. They have also begun to develop their own institutional identities and interests, simply adding to the many already competing in the global health arena. And they have had to recognize that they cannot bypass governments and international organizations if they aim for sustainability. As Levine (2004) notes in her analysis of global health success stories, where greater efficiency (defined as reduced transaction costs) and even significant success was achieved for individual diseases, projects and separate parts of the system, the key factor for success at country level remained the political will and leadership of the government. Or as Kirton (2008) has shown for the G8 commitments on health, their pledges have been most successful when made in partnership with the World Health Organization.

It is therefore worth considering for a moment the various sources of legitimacy from which different actors in global health governance draw their support and rationale for action and how they change over time or gain new relevance. While the multilateral health system of the World Health Organization gains much of its legitimacy from its universalistic structure (one country – one vote) and its moral standing ('Health for All'), it is also judged in relationship to less traditional forms of legitimacy: on the quality of its technical expertise, its ability to achieve commonly set goals and its ability to act in the face of crisis. Bull and McNeill (2006) argue that results-based legitimacy – a characteristic of market multilateralism – is becoming more important for all actors. Indeed much of the repeated criticism of the WHO was and is that it does not get things done. Yet Bull and McNeill have also remained too narrowly focused on arguing within the development circle of the global health action sphere (see Figure 15.1) and have neglected the interdependence dimensions of the work of the WHO.

I would argue instead that the WHO's ability to react speedily following the SARS crisis, to respond well to the avian influenza outbreaks, to produce within a very short period of time two legally binding agreements – the Framework Convention on Tobacco Control (FCTC) adopted in 2003 and the revised International Health Regulations (IHR) adopted in 2005 – have increased its attraction to member states and other global actors in a new way in the new context of a non-polar world. It also recently showed its capacity to provide the political space to negotiate another major public health breakthrough: the strategy on public health, innovation and intellectual property adopted at the 2008 World Health Assembly. One could argue that the problems for the WHO in the early 1990s were related in part to a basic misunderstanding of its function; a multilateral agency was expected to act as an implementation body for development aid in health, rather than being acknowledged and strengthened in its constitutional ability to develop hard and soft law. One must also not forget that this misguided expectation was reinforced by those who wanted to reduce the legitimacy of the organization and weaken its rule-setting authority and power, in particular as expressed by the hegemonic unilateral position taken by the United States. Direct and indirect attacks were also mounted by the tobacco companies, pushing the view that the WHO should concentrate on diseases of poverty and not deal with chronic disease.

The WHO – like the UN – by its very nature does not work well under conditions of unipolarity; it works best as a unifying force among a divergence of centres of power and influence which it seeks to bring together so that they cooperate for health. Today nearly all actors and networks that set out to work in parallel or even against the WHO have been obliged to recognize its convening power as well as its traditional legitimacy in lawmaking and rule-setting. In the new global governance arena, the opening of new discursive spaces for quite different players creates 'added value' and provides a gain in legitimacy through utility, which in turn comes from brokering the cooperation with and between countries. Here we frequently find the 'cosmopolitan realpolitik' at work, pragmatically combining divergent views – including those of the lobbyists – through the myriad of committees and coffee breaks into a formula that enables global public health action, as the negotiators of the IHR, the FCTC or the Intergovernmental Working Group on Public Health, Innovation and Intellectual Property (IGWG) can illustrate in great detail. But the value of the WHO continues to be reflected in the area of soft law, the changing of standards, the setting of norms and expectations as well as the promotion of ethical principles and human rights.

The new geographies of power: two power shifts and back

The governance issues intrinsic to health were brought into focus by the tectonic shift to a globalized non-polar world which began at about the same time as the appearance of the HIV/AIDS epidemic and was consolidated in the decades following the collapse of the Soviet Union. For a brief period, the United States seemed to dictate the rules and there was much analysis of empire and hegemony – in relation to global health as well as to other issues (Kickbusch, 2003). But what was actually rapidly being fashioned below the radar screen was 'a world dominated by dozens of actors, possessing and exercising various kinds of power' (Haas, 2008: 44). There has not yet been enough analysis to help understand and differentiate the different types of power and influence at work in global health governance at different points in time. Hein et al. (2007) in their excellent analysis of global health governance in relation to HIV/AIDS differentiate at least four types of power that need to be considered: discursive, decision-making, legal and resource-based power (see also Hein et al., Chapter 4).

The first seminal power shift has been described above. The increasing influence of non-state actors in many spheres of global policymaking was aided by the rise of efficient and low-cost communication, as well as by the increasing inability of states and international organizations, as the traditional actors in international relations, to fully control or address the threats imposed by the global era. Strong non-governmental organizations had the ability and means to shape the agendas and the issues at stake and benefited from the historically unique availability of significant new funds through foundations, private sector contributions and new commitments by nation-states and regional organizations such as the European Union. This combination of discursive and resource-based power shaped the new environment for global health action. However, while all actors would adamantly maintain that their key objective is to improve global health, care must be taken not to equate their shared interest in global health governance with any shared interest in a common agenda. This is clearly illustrated and reiterated in the debate on sexual and reproductive health and rights (Buse et al., 2006).

Countries increasingly recognize the need to cooperate in global health, but they are now doing this in the context of a second seminal power shift. It is not only the types and number of actors that have brought about a change, increasingly nation-states are forming new constellations through which to establish their spheres of influence on a global scale in what Khanna (2008) has recently described as a geopolitical marketplace. As Held et al. (1999: 45) note, 'Nation states have become enmeshed in and are functionally part of a larger pattern of global transformations and global flows'; despite the rise of market multilateralism they remain at the core of global governance. States are still primarily responsible for delivering health-care in most countries and can be held accountable for doing so, both as part of the social welfare agenda and as part of people-centered security. In recognition of this, many states have actively moved health higher on their political agendas; understanding better its role in many different spheres of policy, in overall economic development, foreign policy, security and trade (Ministers of Foreign Affairs, 2007). Indeed this expansion of health considerations and the global dimensions of many spheres of policymaking are defining features of the growth of global health governance that also make for tougher negotiations than in the past because the stakes are higher. In consequence, many global health issues become highly politicized and move out of the purely technical arena of global public health.

The new global health arena is marked not only by the growing influence of emerging economies, such as China, India, Brazil, South Africa and Russia, but also that of regional organizations such as the European Union. Khanna (2008) analyses a group of countries which have a tipping point of power in relation to global agendas; he calls them 'the second world countries'. These countries are increasingly discovering and actively using both the decision-making power and the legal power provided to them in the global arena through the universalistic and legal structures of multilateral organizations, and many of them practise sophisticated forms of multi-alignment and diplomacy. This 'second world' encompasses a large group of countries – including all the emerging economies – that are undergoing simultaneous domestic, regional and global transitions. This means they have much to lose from global decisions that counteract their national policies or their geopolitical and global interests.

The HIV/AIDS arena provides some classic examples of this new importance of multilateral influence. The capacity to produce generic antiretroviral treatments in China and India and the leadership of Brazil in negotiating favourable access to licences and reduced prices for antiretrovirals for the treatment of HIV infections has significantly challenged western-based pharmaceutical companies and the first world governments that support them. Indonesia's refusal in early 2007 to share H5N1 influenza virus samples with the WHO out of concern that the developing countries would not have access to any vaccines that the wealthy-country drug companies might subsequently produce provides another example. The government of Indonesia pushed for new, more transparent virus-sharing policies that would be fairer to it and other developing nations.

The virus sharing case illustrates how health is brought into political alignments and – at the same time – how representatives of non-health groups are brought into the health arena. On the occasion of the sixty-first World Health Assembly, Indonesia's idea for a new mechanism of virus sharing and benefit sharing of avian influenza virus samples was discussed and supported at a meeting of 112 Non-Aligned Movement (NAM) countries at the very first meeting of the NAM health ministers on 21 May 2008. Furthermore, NAM representatives met to prepare a position leading to the Inter-Governmental Meeting on Pandemic Influenza Preparedness in November 2008.

Emerging trends in global health governance

The key trend in global health governance is the expansion of health into different areas of policy and politics; it is clearly gaining a strategic place in the international agenda in both circles of the global health action sphere (Figure 15.1). There is implicit agreement among major actors on the nature of global health challenges, although they might prioritize them very differently. At a minimum, these priorities include pandemics, bioterrorism, development, human rights, trade and humanitarian activities. Below, some additional emerging trends are identified and briefly described.

Relevance of global commitments: prioritizing the Millennium Development Goals

Looking at the two circles of the global health action sphere (Figure 15.1), the development circle is clearly dominated by the commitment to reach the health-related Millennium Development Goals. A growing number of initiatives are being put in place to move this agenda forward. It is in this action sphere of development commitments that top politicians have helped push the agenda forward, either from their national pulpits or using club models such as the G8 Gleneagles meeting or meetings of the World Economic Forum. It is here that one finds the major public-private partnerships and innovative financing mechanisms, such as the GAVI Alliance or the use of capital markets to raise funds for specific problems as illustrated by the launch of a 'vaccine bond' in Japan in early 2008 in order to accelerate efforts to immunize children in the world's poorest countries. The European Union has also asked the WHO to monitor progress towards the health MDGs and to contribute more forcefully to their achievement.

Gostin (2007) goes one step further and proposes a legal treaty, a 'Framework Convention on Global Health', which would focus on such 'basic survival needs'. It would commit states to a set of targets, both economic and logistic, and dismantle barriers to constructive engagement by the private and charitable sectors. It would stimulate creative public-private partnerships and actively engage civil society stakeholders. It would also set achievable goals for global health spending, define areas of cost-effective investment to meet basic survival needs, build sustainable health systems, and create incentives for scientific innovation for affordable vaccines and essential medicines.

New relevance of inter-governmental processes: concerted non-polarity

The area of the global health action sphere related to governing interdependence is dominated by new frameworks for cooperation which reflect the renewed importance assigned in a non-polar world to intergovernmental processes. In order to fulfil their national obligations, states must be able to act globally; this applies for practically all fields of state action, including health. A 'cosmopolitan realpolitik' is slowly beginning to emerge where national interests are secured through transnational agreements negotiated with shifting alliances in a new geopolitical marketplace. Held et al. (1999: 56) speaks of the need for 'concerted non polarity' which is much the same thing. The global risk society provides nation-states with a new logic for intervention and regulation which implies a certain amount of pooling of sovereignty. This also includes the increasing importance of health in regional and bilateral accords, for example in relation to trade, and increasing cooperative multilateralism in club model organizations such as the OECD.

For example, the FCTC has so far been signed by 168 nations and ratified by 157: among the signatories is the European Commission, a historical novelty. Since the FCTC entered into force, its new governance mechanism the Conference of the Parties to the WHO Framework Convention on Tobacco Control (COP) has met formally on two occasions, in February 2006 in Geneva and June-July 2007 in Bangkok. The COP in its deliberations continues to balance the unique health interest – such as the adoption of guidelines for establishing 100 per cent smoke-free public and work spaces – with expanding health into other policy arenas such as smuggling, and has agreed to begin negotiations on a protocol on the illicit tobacco trade.

A new role for international organizations such as the WHO

International organizations no longer represent the extension of national policies; they change them, bundle them and sometimes provide the groundwork for national legislation – both the FCTC and the IHR are typical examples. Alvarez (2006) has shown in great detail how international organizations as law-makers affect the behaviour of states and of individuals – one of his case studies is concerned with the creation of the FCTC at the WHO. He describes the deep impact that international organizations can have through hard and soft law and how their role in relation to nation-states has, therefore, changed significantly during the past years.

Today international organizations open up new avenues to maximize and extend national interests and link them to transnational interests. Brazil's very active involvement in the WTO and the IGWG activities in relation to intellectual property and access to medicines are typical cases in point. States will need to address the 'unstructured plurality' and its weakness in ensuring the production of global public goods and long-term sustained interventions for development objectives (see Smith, Chapter 6). Not only because of the dark side of the 'unstructured plurality', which includes the potential for fragmentation, competition and duplication, but also because of the lack of legitimacy and accountability of many of the major actors. The danger is, as Haas (2008: 52) writes, that 'left to its own devices, a non polar world will become messier over time. Entropy dictates that systems consisting of a large number of actors tend towards greater randomness and disorder in the absence of external intervention.' One proposal to address the issue of fragmentation head-on has recently been put forward by Silberschmidt et al. (2008). This suggests creating a 'Committee C' of the World Health Assembly (WHA), a transparent, accountable and democratic mechanism through which major non-state global health players are enabled to engage in dialogue with all nation-states. The WHA is the only place where all health ministers meet and debate on equal footing. The legitimacy and coordinating role of the WHO ensues from the fact that it is an organization of all the world's nation-states, and that even the poorest and smallest states can attend the WHA because their attendance is enabled through the WHO budget. Such a proposal would both reinforce the role assigned to the WHO by its constitution and ensure that it strengthens its discursive and brokering power. By bringing the actors together within the WHA another step towards concerted non-polarity could be undertaken. This could also provide a first step towards binding a wide range of actors to joint provision of clearly defined global public goods for health. Some authors have other recommendations to further develop the tripartite governance of global public goods for global health governance. Kempa et al. (2005), for example, suggest that efforts be made to strengthen the normative and 'steering' role of the representatives of the international organizations and national governments and create separate service-providing agencies and quasi-independent oversight bodies. In this way they suggest that all three components of 'good governance' could be significantly strengthened: delivering results (efficient and effective), ensuring that results delivered are deemed good (fairness, reducing poverty, increasing equity), and addressing the distribution of power through increased participation and spaces of interaction.

Application of a health lens to foreign policy

Much excellent analysis has been made of the nexus of foreign policy and health (Fidler, 2006). Of great interest to a discussion of the trends in global health governance in this context is the Global Health and Foreign Policy Initiative launched by the ministers of foreign affairs of Brazil, France, Indonesia, Norway, Senegal, South Africa and Thailand in 2006. They issued a joint statement in Oslo on 20 March 2007 which underlines the urgent need to broaden the scope of foreign policy in an era of globalization and interdependence:

> We believe that health is one of the most important, yet still broadly neglected, long-term foreign policy issues of our time ...We believe that health as a foreign policy issue needs a stronger strategic focus on the international agenda. We have therefore agreed to make 'impact on health' a point of departure and a defining lens that each of our countries will use to examine key elements of foreign policy and development strategies, and to engage in a dialogue on how to deal with policy options from this perspective.
>
> (Ministers of Foreign Affairs, 2007)

Since then the group has held meetings with foreign ministers around the globe as well as with senior UN officials and the UN secretary general in order to move this agenda forward and gain the support of other countries and key multilateral players. The group has also hosted a meeting on Foreign Policy and Global Health together with the WHO, which it considers to be the mandated organization for global health governance.

Five analytical issues are particularly important in relation to this initiative:

- It takes the power of taking initiatives in global health back into the hands of nation-states and places it firmly in relationship to a commitment to multilateral action;
- It engages health from a launch pad of 'hard politics' but states that a health lens is essential to foreign policy in an age of interdependence;

- It brings together the two circles of the global health action sphere: commitments to development and governing interdependence;
- It creates a 'coalition of the willing' comprised of the seven initiator countries and seeks to widen the group along the lines of an open and loose coalition; and
- It aims for action as much as it aims at changing the mindsets of key policymakers within foreign policy and within health.

Foreign policy, according to the key message of the initiators, needs to be conducted differently. Such policy needs to be as much concerned with human security as it is with state security – and it needs to understand that state security has a fundamentally different meaning today. The initiative is an excellent example of what the diplomat Robert Cooper (2004: 85) described as the postmodern perspective of foreign policy: 'The objective of foreign policy is taken to be peace and prosperity rather than power and prestige.'

Providing global public goods for health

The challenge increases to improve the capability of the international system and all global players to ensure the production paths of global and transnational public goods. This insight is best expressed by Inge Kaul et al. (1999: xxi), who stress that 'the pervasiveness of today's crises suggests that they might all suffer from a common cause, such as a common flaw in policy making, rather than from issue specific problems. If so, issue specific responses, typical to date, would be insufficient – allowing global crisis to persist and even multiply.' Laurie Garrett's (2007) analysis of global health also illustrates this failure clearly. Kaul has written extensively on how the production and financing of global public goods could be organized. An additional proposal comes in the form of the suggestion of a Global Health Treaty at the sixth Global Conference on Health Promotion which was then included in the Bangkok Charter for Health Promotion in a Globalized World (2005). Such a treaty should aim to ensure a common high level of health protection and health rights for all citizens of the world with reference to those risks and threats to their health, safety and well-being that are beyond the control of individuals and communities and cannot be effectively tackled by nation-states alone. They need to be multi-actor so as to address the diversity of challenges such as direct health threats, unsafe products or unfair commercial practices.

Such a treaty would set the ten or so most important global health parameters, and agree on the key global goods for health that should be jointly produced and maintained and on their means of financing. Kaul and Le Goulven (2003) have proposed that the financing of global public goods be based on the 'beneficiary pays' principle: this means that rich nations and their citizens, as well as major transnational companies, will in the short term have to introduce new sustainable financing mechanisms as they are the prime beneficiaries of global action. A global health treaty would then be supplemented by a set of regimes or multi-actor commissions created by self-interested actors with the aim of solving or at least ameliorating collective-action problems (Young, 1999) with specific mandates for each of the domains (global, local, network). For example this could be undertaken to

- Control unsafe goods and products and ensure corporate accountability
- Address health dimensions of transboundary/collective human security issues
- Ensure access for all to essential medicines, vaccines and health knowledge
- Fight major diseases and defined global health emergencies including rapid response
- Create surveillance and information systems
- Harmonize aid to give priority support to primary health care (PHC) and public health (PH) health infrastructures
- Strengthen professional capacity and ensure human resources at a global level, and address the brain drain

Any such treaty would of course need to have mechanisms to ensure compliance, transparency, accountability and dispute settlement, all of which are still lacking in the present fragmented global health system. Most importantly it would create the mechanisms to move beyond voluntary development aid to the agreed financing of global public goods to which all actors contribute, particularly those that benefit most from global restructuring. The financing mechanism created by UNITAID provides an innovative model for such a development: it is financed primarily from the proceeds of a 'solidarity tax' on airline tickets which ensures a steady flow of contributions.

The need for policy coherence 'at home'

Countries are now also seeking policy mechanisms to address the point of intersection between national and global health policy. Anne Marie Slaughter (2004) notes in her influential book on global policy networks that understanding domestic issues in a regional or global context will have to become part of doing a good job. The optimal solution to domestic issues will depend increasingly on what is happening abroad, and foreign issues will be affected in turn by what is happening on the domestic front. Switzerland has been at the forefront of developing a national global health strategy – the Swiss Health Foreign Policy (Federal Department of Home Affairs, 2007) – which is unique in documenting the interface between the protection of the health interests of the Swiss population and the improvement of the global health situation. It forms the basis for a new type of policy coherence between national interests and global responsibilities. It was developed by the Departments of the Interior (represented by the Swiss Federal Office of Public Health) and the Department of Foreign Affairs. The document brings together three major strands of global health action that generally run in parallel with little coordination or even in competition. These strands are: (i) the activities within the health sector that address normative health issues, international agreements and cooperation, global outbreaks of disease and pandemics; (ii) the commitment to health in the context of assistance towards development; and (iii) the policy initiatives in other sectors – such as foreign policy and trade. It underlines the commitment of Switzerland to human rights and defines five priorities in foreign health policy: (i) the health of the Swiss population; (ii) the coherence between national and international health policy; (iii) the strengthening of international health cooperation; (iv) the improvement of the global health situation; and (v) the strengthening of the Swiss commitment as host country to the WHO and to major health industries, in particular the pharmaceutical and food industries.

In September 2008, the UK government launched a national global health strategy which aims at greater coherence between government departments in matters of global health, and a number of other European countries are working on similar agreements between sectors in order to advance global health. It is vital that the many actors in the national health arena better understand these important interrelations and contribute in their own way to taking this joint agenda forward.

Creating capacity for global health diplomacy

Consultation, negotiation and coalition-building are increasingly important in a non-polar world. As diplomacy is frequently referred to as the art and practice of conducting negotiations, the term 'global health diplomacy' aims to capture the multilevel and multi-actor negotiation processes that shape and manage the global policy environment for health (Kickbusch et al., 2007). In view of the significant power imbalance in the global system, mechanisms need to be put in place that allow the participants in this complex world to engage with each other on a more level footing if not of state power then of negotiating competence. This is all the more important if one keeps in mind Khanna's (2008) analysis of the tipping point capacity of the states comprising the 'second world'. All these factors underline the need to build capacity for global health diplomacy by providing appropriate training for public health professionals and diplomats and bringing them into contact with other global health players.

Ideally global health diplomacy results in three key outcomes: (i) it helps to ensure better health security and population health outcomes for each of the countries involved (thus serving the national and the global interest), (ii) it helps to improve the relations between states and strengthens the commitment of a wide range of actors to work to improve health and (iii) it provides an understanding of health as a common endeavour, a human right and a global public good with the goals to deliver results that are deemed fair. A small number of initiatives have been developed to improve skills in global health diplomacy and a network of training institutes is in preparation (Kickbusch et al., 2007).

Health in its own right

Health is a right of global citizenship – this is the view of many of the non-state actors involved in global health (Berlinger, 1999; Dower, 2003; Singer, 2002; Sen, 1999) and it is the premise of the work of the World Health Organization and enshrined in its constitution. It is particularly the dimensions of equity and rights that have been a strong driving force in the debates on globalization and health and these are likely to gain in influence. Buzan (2004) speaks of a global 'inter-human' ethics that is taking shape and finds its expression in initiatives such as the 'Make Poverty History' campaign and the Millennium Development Goals. These movements argue for global public goods that address the social, economic and cultural rights of people in a global world. In consequence, their priorities lie with addressing global inequality and poverty as social justice and health as a human right. In this they are joined by many governments from the poorest countries as well as from the second world. As Dahrendorf (2002) has observed, in an enlightened and civilized society privilege must be replaced by generalized entitlements and if the aim falls short of world citizenship the goal should be citizens' rights for all human beings. Global health governance should be geared towards helping reach such a goal.

References

Alvarez, J.E., *International Organizations as Law-Makers* (Oxford: Oxford University Press, 2006).

Annan, K., 'Secretary-General Proposes Global Compact on Human Rights, Labour, Environment, in Address to World Economic Forum in Davos', United Nations Press Release SG/SM/6881, United Nations, 1999, http://www.un.org/News/Press/docs/1999/19990201.sgsm6881.html (accessed 16 June 2008).

'The Bangkok Charter for Health Promotion in a Globalized World' (2005), http://www.who.int/healthpromotion/conferences/6gchp/en (accessed 17 June 2008).

Bartsch, S., W. Hein and L. Kohlmorgen, 'Interfaces: a Concept for the Analysis of Global Health Governance', in W. Hein, S. Bartsch and L. Kohlmorgen (eds), *Global Health Governance and the Fight against HIV/AIDS* (Basingstoke: Palgrave Macmillan, 2007).

Beck, U., *Weltrisikogesellschaft* (Frankfurt a.M.: Suhrkamp, 2007).

Beck, U. and C. Lau, *Entgrenzung und Entscheidung. Was ist neu an der Theorie reflexiver Modernisierung?* (Frankfurt a.M.: Suhrkamp, 2004) (Edition Zweite Moderne).

Berlinger, G., 'Health and Equity as a Primary Global Goal', *Development*, 42 (4) (1999): 17–21.

Birdsall, N., 'Seven Deadly Sins: Reflections on Donor Failings', Center for Global Development Working Paper Number 50, December 2004, http://ssrn.com/abstract=997404 (accessed 14 June 2008).

Bull, B. and D. McNeill, *Development Issues in Global Governance: Public-Private Partnerships and Market Multilateralism* (Oxford: Routledge, 2006).

Buse, K. and G. Walt, 'Role Conflict? The World Bank and the World's Health', *Social Science and Medicine*, 50 (2) (2000): 177–80.

Buse, K., A. Martin-Hilber, N. Widyantoro and S. J. Hawkes, 'Management of the Politics of Evidence-Based Sexual and Reproductive Health Policy', *Lancet*, 368 (9552) (2006): 2101–3.

Buzan, B., *From International to World Society* (Cambridge: Cambridge University Press, 2004).

Cooper, R., *The Breaking of Nations: Order and Chaos in the Twenty-First Century*, revised and updated edition (London: Atlantic Books, 2004).

Dahrendorf, R., *Die Krisen der Demokratie* (München: Beck Verlag, 2002).

Dower, N., *An Introduction to Global Citizenship* (Edinburgh: Edinburgh University Press, 2003).

England, R., 'The Writing is on the Wall for UNAIDS', *British Medical Journal*, 336 (10 May 2008): 1072.

Federal Department of Home Affairs (FDHA) and Federal Department of Foreign Affairs (FDFA), 'Swiss Health Foreign Policy: Agreement on Health Foreign Policy Objectives' (Bern, 2007).

Fidler, D.P., 'Health as Foreign Policy: Harnessing Globalization for Health', *Health Promotion International*, 21 (1) (2006): 51–8.

Garrett, L., 'The Challenge of Global Health', *Foreign Affairs*, 86 (1) (2007): 1–17.

Gostin, L.O., 'A Proposal for a Framework Convention on Global Health', *Journal of International Economic Law*, 10 (4) (2007): 989–1008.

Haas, R.N., 'The Age of Nonpolarity: What Will Follow US Dominance', *Foreign Affairs*, 87 (3) (2008): 44–56.

Hein, W., S. Bartsch and L. Kohlmorgen (eds), *Global Health Governance and the Fight against HIV/AIDS* (Basingstoke: Palgrave Macmillan, 2007).

Held, D., A. McGrew, D. Goldblatt and J. Perraton (1999), *Global Transformations* (Oxford: Polity, 1999).

Hilts, P., *Rx for Survival: Why We Must Rise to the Global Health Challenge* (New York: The Penguin Press, 2005).

Jamison, D.T., J. Frenk and F. Knaul. 'International Collective Action in Health: Objectives, Functions, and Rationale', *Lancet*, 351 (9101) (1998): 514–17.

Kaul, I., I. Grunberg and M.A. Stern (eds), *Global Public Goods: International Cooperation in the 21st Century* (New York: Oxford University Press, 1999).

Kaul, I. and K. Le Goulven, 'Financing Global Public Goods: a New Frontier of Public Finance', in I. Kaul, P. Conceição, K. Le Goulven and R.U. Mendoza (eds), *Providing Global Public Goods: Managing Globalization* (New York: Oxford University Press, 2003).

Kempa, M., C. Shearing and S. Burris, 'Changes in Governance: a Background Review', working paper presented at the Salzburg Seminar on the Governance of Health, 12 May 2005–12 August 2005, http://www.temple.edu/lawschool/phrhcs/salzburg/Global_Health_Governance_Review.pdf (accessed 2 May 2008).

Khanna, P., *The Second World: Empires and Influence in the New Global Order* (Harmondsworth: Penguin, 2008).

Kickbusch, I., 'Global Health Governance: some Theoretical Considerations on the New Political Space', in K. Lee (ed.), *Health Impacts of Globalization* (Basingstoke: Palgrave Macmillan, 2003).

Kickbusch, I., 'Governing Interdependence (Foreword)', in W. Hein, S. Bartsch and L. Kohlmorgen (eds), *Global Health Governance and the Fight against HIV/AIDS*, (Basingstoke: Palgrave Macmillan, 2007).

Kickbusch, I. and G. Lister, *European Perspectives on Global Health: a Policy Glossary* (Brussels: European Foundation Centre, 2006).

Kickbusch, I., G. Silberschmidt and P. Buss, 'Global Health Diplomacy: the Need for New Perspectives, Strategic Approaches and Skills in Global Health', *Bulletin of the World Health Organization*, 85 (3) (2007): 161–244.

Kirton, J., Personal communication, 2008.

Kohlmorgen, L., 'The International Organizations and Global Health Governance: the Role of the World Health Organization, World Bank and UNAIDS', working paper presented at the Salzburg Seminar on the Governance of Health, 12 May 2005–12 August 2005.

Levine, R., *Millions Saved: Proven Successes in Global Health* (Washington, DC: Center for Global Development, 2004).

Ministers of Foreign Affairs of Brazil, France, Indonesia, Norway, Senegal, South Africa, and Thailand, 'Oslo Ministerial Declaration. Global Health: a Pressing Foreign Policy Issue of our Time', *Lancet*, 369 (9570) (21 April 2007): 1373–8.

'Paris Declaration on Aid Effectiveness. Ownership, Harmonisation, Alignment, Results and Mutual Accountability', Paris: High Level Forum, 28 February–2 March 2005, http://www.oecd.org/dataoecd/11/41/34428351.pdf (accessed 16 June 2008).

Rosenau, J., *Distant Proximities. Dynamics beyond Globalization* (Princeton and Oxford: Princeton University Press, 2003).

Sen, A., *Development as Freedom* (New York: Knopf, 1999).

Silberschmidt, G., D. Matheson and I. Kickbusch, 'Creating a Committee C of the World Health Assembly', *Lancet*, 371 (2008): 1483–6.

Singer, P., *One World: the Ethics of Globalization* (New Haven, CT: Yale University Press, 2002).

Slaughter, A.M., *A New World Order* (Princeton, NJ: Princeton University Press, 2004).

United Nations, *The Millennium Development Goals Report 2007* (New York: United Nations, 2007).

Young, O., *Governance in World Affairs* (Ithaca and London: Cornell University Press, 1999).

Glossary

This glossary provides concise definitions of key terms used in various chapters in the book which may not be fully explained.

Accountability: Concerns answerability and the duty to explain. Relationship in which an individual, group or other entity can make demands on an agent to report on his or her activities, and has the ability to impose costs on the agent.

Agency: Capacity for individual or collective actors to make choices and to pursue strategies to impose those choices on others and the environment they inhabit (as opposed to structure determining the behaviour of actors).

Alignment: Aid reflects partner countries' priorities as reflected in its development strategies and is delivered through recipients' institutions and procedures.

Authority: The right to set rules, control resources and influence others; legitimate power (see also: power – which is about the ability to set rules, control resources and so on).

Collective action problem: A situation in which all participants (individuals, groups, governments) pursue their own individually rational choices and thereby make all participants worse off than if they pursued individually sub-optimal choices (also known as prisoner's dilemma). The theory of collective action is concerned with the provision of public goods (and collective consumption) through the collaboration of two or more individuals. A collective action problem may, for example, involve 'free-riding' by an individual who enjoys the benefits of a public good without paying for it.

Constructivism: An approach to political analysis which posits that shared *ideas*, rather than material forces, structure people's lives and that their interests and identities are also constructed by these shared ideas. For constructivists, power is quite diffuse, has its basis in beliefs and is reproduced through social practice rather than residing in particular persons, positions, institutions or relationships. Constructivism helps to explain the emergence of specific paradigms in global health governance – such as the human rights approach.

Corporate social responsibility: A concept whereby businesses consider the interests of society by taking responsibility for the impact of their activities on various stakeholders, local communities and society at large. The responsibility extends beyond company obligations to comply with legislation (also called corporate citizenship).

Discourse: In the social sciences (following Foucault), a discourse is considered to be an institutionalized way of thinking; a socially determined field defining what can be said about a specific topic. Discursive processes can change the content of policy issues and thus open up new options (or exclude others), as has been demonstrated in the critical discourse on intellectual property rights and access to medicines.

Epistemic community: A network of knowledge-based experts with an authoritative claim to policy-relevant knowledge within the area of their expertise. Members hold a common set of causal beliefs and shared normative commitments. Powerful epistemic communities in global health include those concerned with health-care financing, tobacco control and access to ARV therapies.

Essential medicines: Medicines that satisfy the priority health-care needs of a population. The WHO has published a Model List of Essential Medicines every two years since 1977. This includes the most needed medicines to provide health-care for the majority of the population.

Generic medicines: A generic drug is a pharmaceutical product which is usually intended to be interchangeable with an innovator product. Generic medicines are manufactured without a licence from the innovator company and marketed after the expiry date of the patent or other exclusive rights.

Global civil society: Extends the concept of civil society (as a social sphere separate from both the state and the market) to the global arena. Civil society organizations are non-state, not-for-profit, voluntary organizations formed by people in that social sphere, including networks, associations, groups and movements, but excluding political parties and firms. Global civil society refers to citizens in one country acting in support of citizens in another (for example, to improve health-care) or to transnational groups promoting global goals (such as access to essential medicines) facilitated by the globalization of communications.

Global health diplomacy: The multi-level and multi-actor negotiation processes that shape and manage the global policy environment for health. The relationship between health, foreign policy and trade is at the cutting edge of global health diplomacy. Issues of international trade impinge on health, often in significant ways. The main aim is to forge consensus between the various actors of global health governance (states, intergovernmental organizations, the private sector and civil society) and agreements on rules and norms, guidelines and funding.

Global health partnership: Typically including both public and private representation in formal decision-making bodies, such partnerships involve groups from more than one country pursuing common aims related to health. These aims might include undertaking research and development on diagnostics and medicines for neglected diseases, improving access to medicines or mobilizing action or additional finance for health-related concerns.

Global governance: In the widest sense, this concerns the manner in which global society organizes itself. Encompasses the totality of collective regulations and norms to deal with international and transnational interdependence problems in the absence of overarching political authority. Problem-solving arrangements normally include a variety of actors including state authorities, intergovernmental organizations, non-governmental organizations, private sector entities, other civil society actors, and individuals.

Global public goods for health: Public goods which improve health and which are strongly universal in terms of countries (covering more than one group of countries), people and generations (extending to the needs of current generations without foreclosing options for future generations). Public goods are defined as goods and services that are 'non-rival' (*no one can be excluded from their benefits*) and 'non-excludable' (*consumption by one person does not reduce the availability for others, for example, peace*). Public goods become global in nature when the benefits flow to more than one country and no country can effectively be denied access to those benefits. Global public goods for health include fighting globally spread infectious diseases, eradicating diseases, global health regimes and producing knowledge to improve health outcomes.

Globalization: Understood to include two interrelated elements: (1) increasing transborder flows of goods, services, finance, people and ideas; and (2) changes in institutional and policy regimes at the international and national levels that facilitate or promote such flows. Globalization extends beyond economic activities to political, cultural, environmental and security issues and implies an increasing transnational interconnectivity of people and communities and the creation of common identities based on characteristics other than nationality.

Governance: Concerned with 'how a society or organization steers itself' (Rosenau, 1995). Can also be defined as the 'management of the course of events in a social system'. Modern governance is seen as polycentric, with multiple agencies and sites of steering.

Harmonization: Prescription that different actors and different levels within a system should adopt the same rules and procedures. In relation to aid effectiveness, concerns the implementation by donors of common arrangements at country level for planning, funding, disbursement, monitoring, evaluating and reporting on donor activities and aid flows.

Health: The constitution of the WHO (1946) defines good health as a state of complete physical, social and mental well-being, and not merely the absence of disease or infirmity.

Health system: The sum total of all the organizations, institutions and resources whose primary purpose is to improve health. The health system can be categorized according to core functions (financing, provision of inputs and services, monitoring and evaluation), main actors (government, public and private providers, and consumers/households) and outcomes (health, fairness in financing and responsiveness). A variety of health system models operate in different countries despite globalization.

Human rights approach to health: Human rights are those rights to which humans are entitled by virtue of being human and are universal in that they pertain to all irrespective of specific characteristics – such as sex or ethnicity. Human rights are codified in a number of international treaties. The right to the highest attainable standard of health is seen as the guiding norm for a human rights approach to health. This right has been enshrined in numerous treaties, such as the International Covenant on Economic, Social and Cultural Rights.

Institutions: A collective pattern of action (or systems of rules guiding social behaviour) that is socially enforced and enjoys a measure of stability. From an economic perspective, institutions reduce transaction costs between actors. These collective patterns of action can be formalized in organizations, such as global health partnerships, or remain informal rules governing social interaction, such as the desirability to reach agreement by consensus rather than by voting in some partnership governing bodies.

Integration: The condition of being formed into a whole by the addition or combination of constituent parts or elements. Political integration refers to the centralization of power within a polity; regional integration is the joining of individual states within a region into a larger whole. The degree of integration depends upon the willingness and commitment of independent sovereign states to share their sovereignty. Global health governance reflects new mechanisms for the integration of state and non-state actors through networked and more formal interaction.

Interdependence: Mutual dependence between actors. In international relations it refers to the constraints on national autonomy through mutual economic, political or environmental dependence (including the spread of diseases). Interdependence is the central argument of (neo-)institutionalist analysts who recognize it as the primary interest compelling nation-states to cooperate in problem-solving through international regimes and institutions. Interdependence between actors working through networks is reflected in many global health governance mechanisms.

Interface: The communication boundary between two entities. In political science, an interface can be seen as an important point of interaction or linkage between different political actors, policy fields or levels where structural discontinuities based upon differences of normative value and social interest are most likely to be found (modifying Long's (1989) definition of 'social interface'). The quest for coordination through global health governance confronts the interfaces between different systems of actors.

Intergovernmental organization: International public organizations that are established by the formal agreement of, and ultimately are governed by, states. Examples include the United Nations and its specialized agencies, such as the WHO and the World Bank. They are important actors in global governance, spreading information, serving as forums for deliberation, negotiation and norm-setting.

Legitimacy: Broadly means rightfulness and transforms power into authority. Can be conferred on individuals, organizations, norms and standards.

Liberalization: Refers to the relaxation of governmental restrictions. In relation to global governance, the economic aspect of liberalization is the most prominent and is most often associated with the easing of rules on cross-border trade and investment within a system of non-discrimination, reciprocity, transparency and fairness (GATT/WTO principles). Liberalization tends to increase the cross-border movement of pathogens and other health risks as well as health products and services.

Low- and middle-income countries: Classification of countries by the World Bank based on gross national income (GNI) per capita. In 2007, low-income pertained to a GNI below US$935 while upper-middle pertained to US$3706–$11,455.

Neglected tropical diseases: Although medically diverse, these diseases share features that allow them to persist in conditions of poverty, where they cluster and frequently overlap. Over one billion people suffer from such diseases, the most common of which are malaria, tuberculosis and lymphatic filiariasis. The diseases are considered neglected because proportionately little investment has been made in the research and development of medicines to prevent and treat them.

Neo-liberalism: A set of principles, beliefs and economic policies concerned with promoting global trade and investment as the most efficient, equitable and fair way for all nations to develop and prosper based on their comparative advantages. Mechanisms to encourage global trade include liberalization through eliminating barriers to trade including tariffs and restrictions on capital flows and investments.

Networks (social): A social structure consisting of nodes (which are generally individuals or organizations) that are connected by one or more specific types of interdependency, such as friendship, kinship, values, visions, ideas, political or economic interests, trade and conflict (resolution). Networks are, for a number of reasons, increasingly numerous and dense in global health governance.

Nodal governance: Analytic framework which builds on network theories to describe distributed governance and the way in which institutions project power across networks to govern the systems they inhabit. Nodal governance does not view the state as the central point of reference, but places equal emphasis on the activities of non-state and hybrid actors.

Non-governmental organizations: Any not-for-profit organization outside government, but frequently refers in a narrower sense to organizations delivering social services or advocating particular norms, standards or action. May be national or international and increasingly involved in global health governance.

Norms: A rule or mode of conduct that is enforced by members of a community – from the local to global level. These rules may be explicit or implicit, formal or informal. A legal norm is backed by the state's monopoly on the legitimate use of force.

Paris Declaration on Aid Effectiveness: Endorsed in 2005 by over 100 countries and international organizations. It lays down a roadmap to improve the quality of aid and its impact on development based on five key principles: ownership, alignment, harmonization, managing for results and mutual accountability.

Policy coherence: The systematic promotion of mutually reinforcing policy across government departments and agencies (in the national and international field) creating synergies towards achieving agreed objectives.

Post-Westphalian politics: Emerging system of global politics after the demise of the 'Westphalian' system of international relations between sovereign nation-states. Treaty regimes, and the international institutions that managed them, mirrored the rule of law enjoyed by successful states. Globalization increased direct interaction between non-state actors beyond state borders, thus establishing new transnational spaces of interests and power that increasingly limit the political options of nation-states. Post-Westphalian politics increases possibilities for cooperation and conflict between nation-states, intergovernmental organizations, NGOs, and transnational corporations.

Power: Concerns the ability to influence. May be based on means of coercion, legally conferred rights, position in decision-making processes, control of material resources, expertise, or persuasion.

Regime: Implicit or explicit principles, rules, social or cultural norms and decision-making procedures around which stakeholders' expectations converge in any given area (Krasner, 1983). Regimes provide a framework for ongoing interaction on many global health issues. Some important ones include those governing trade (for the example the GATT/WTO treaty framework), human rights protections, harmonization of drug testing or tobacco control.

Regulation: Mostly referring to government intervention enforcing rules and standards to promote stability or desired developments (for example, food safety) in a particular policy field. Self-regulation is increasingly prevalent in global health governance.

Representation: Principle of delegating political power (usually for a defined period) to a smaller subset of the members of a population who act on their behalf.

Sovereignty: Absolute and unlimited power over a territory. Representative democracies permit a transfer of the exercise of sovereignty from the people to the parliament or the government. National sovereignty forms the basis of the Westphalian system of international relations, but is increasingly challenged through globalization and post-Westphalian politics, which includes the dynamics of transborder health threats and global health governance.

Standards: An established norm or requirement that includes specific and concrete measures (which can therefore be assessed). A technical standard establishes uniform engineering or technical criteria, methods, processes and practices. It may be developed unilaterally, for example by a corporation, regulatory body, or health ministry, or by a standards organization (such as the International Organization for Standardization).

Transparency: Metaphorical extension of the physical property of 'transparency – the ability of light to pass through a material' to social and political processes and organizations. Implies openness, communication and disclosure. Supports participation and is a precondition to accountability.

References

Krasner, S.D., *International Regimes* (Ithaca: Cornell University Press, 1983).
Long, N., 'Encounters at the Interface: a Perspective on Social Discontinuities in Rural Development', Wageningen, Agricultural University, 1989.
Rosenau, J., 'Global Governance in the Twenty-First Century', *Global Governance*, 1(1) (1995): 13–43.

Index

Note: Figures in bold refer to tables/figures

Abbott Laboratories, 198
academic institutions, and neglect of chronic diseases, 284
Accelerating Access Initiative, 87
access, 20–1
  antiretroviral medicines, 20; Brazil-USA legal battle, 150; compulsory licensing, 140–1; human rights, 149; nodal governance/interfaces analysis, 85–9; South African legal battles, 150–1; transnational pharmaceutical corporations, 141–2, 153
  Campaign for Access to Essential Medicines, 53, 87, 137
  cost of medication, 86
  to essential medicines, 123, 137
  global health governance structure, 99
  improving, 117
  to resources, 103
accountability, 3, 16, 19–20, 99, 109–10
  definition of, 109
  external accountability, 111–12; improving, 118; mechanisms of, 111
  of global health partnerships, 250, 254
  good governance, 29
  importance of, 109
  internal accountability, 110–11; mechanisms of, 110
  and nodal governance, 93
  sanctions, 111
  transparency, 110–11
Act Up, 54
ActionAid, 202
advance purchase commitments, 131–2
Advanced Market Commitment (AMC), 6, 253
advocacy, 9, 52, 56, 85, 89, 205, 212, 234, 235, 257, 281

Aeras Global TB Vaccine Foundation, 110
Afghanistan, 39
Africa
  HIV/AIDS, 294; deflection of resources, 304–10; demands for health-care, 300–1; financing, **305**; impact on health facilities, **308**
  and infectious diseases, 297; estimates of burden of, **298**
  (re)-constructing health systems, 313–15
African Comprehensive HIV/AIDS Partnership, 261
African Development Bank, 60
African National Congress (ANC), 147, 148
African Programme for Onchocerciasis Control, 241
African Union, 233
ageing population, and chronic diseases, 271
agency, 63–5, 67
  incentives, 65
  neglect of, 47, 48
agenda setting, 48, 103, 169, 255
Agreement on Sanitary and Phytosanitary Measures (SPS), **11–12**, 139, 166–7
Agreement on Technical Barriers to Trade (TBT), 166, 167
Agreement on Trade-Related Aspects of Intellectual Property Rights, *see* Trade-Related Aspects of Intellectual Property Rights
aid
  absorptive capacity, 314
  accountability, 23, 41, 60, 66, 93, 109–12, 118, 236, 245, 250, 259, 315

Index 347

alignment, 23, 59, 60, 62, 66, 104, 254, 256
bilateral agencies, 66
capacity building in trade, 170
coordination, 306
effectiveness, 306
general budget support, 58, 256
good governance, 3
and HIV/AIDS, 305–6
predictability of, 253, 257, 314
volatility of, 306
see also Paris Declaration on Aid Effectiveness
AIDS, *see* HIV/AIDS
Aidspan, 216
alcohol
 abuse of, 15, 33, 38, 42, 127
 and chronic diseases, 271, 289
 trade and investment in, 272, 273
Alliance for a Corporate-Free UN, 202
Alma Ata, Declaration of (1978), 39, 40, 41, 49, 50, 218, 219, 295
 and People's Health Movement, 227
American Cancer Society, 281
American Public Health Association, 223
Amnesty International, 202
anarchy, and international relations, 47, 66, 263
Annan, Kofi, 10, 212, 326
Anti-Slavery Society, 209
antibiotics, resistance to, 4
antiretroviral medicines/therapy, 14
 access to, 20, 137; Brazil-USA legal battle, 150; compulsory licensing, 140–1; as human right, 149; South African legal battles, 150–1; transnational pharmaceutical corporations, 141–2, 153; use of different interfaces, 153–6
 nodal governance of HIV/AIDS, 84; interfaces with intellectual property rights' governance, 85–9
 Treatment Action Campaign, 54
architecture of global health governance, 18–19
 agency, 63–5, 67; neglect of, 47, 48, 63
 calls for new, 47, 322
 era of partnerships (1990s–2007), 56–7

 health reforms (mid-1980s–late 1990s), 51–6; growing role of non-state actors, 52–6
 limitations of analogy, 47
 local implementation, neglect of, 48
 over-emphasis on global strategy, 48
 and primary health-care (1970s–mid-1980s), 48–9; contested discourses of, 49–51
 proliferation of actors, 57–8; different approaches of, 58; potential for conflict, 58; potential problems, 60–1; working towards consensus, 58–60
 putting global agreements into practice, 61–3
 suggestions for improvement, 67
Argentina, 25, 143
ARISE (Associates for Research into the Science of Enjoyment), 189
ASAQ, 261
ASEAN, *see* Association of South East Asian Nations
Association of Academics, 33
Association of Schools of Public Health (USA), 284
Association of South East Asian Nations (ASEAN), 125, 171–2, 179, 322
 Framework Agreement on Services, 171, 172
 Mutual Recognition Arrangements, 171
 Sectoral Integration Protocol for Health Care, 171–2
Aventis, 202
avian influenza, 122, 123

balance of power, *see* power
Bangkok Charter for Health Promotion in a Globalized World (2005), 334
Bangladesh, 227
Bank for International Settlements (BIS), 211
Belgium, 234
Bhagwati, Jagdish, 140
bilateral trade agreements, 178–9
 and intellectual property rights, 140, 143, 156
 see also international trade

Bill and Melinda Gates Foundation, 6, **11–12**, 22, 23, 41, 42, 56, 60, 92, 128, 190, 232, 242, 284
  effectiveness, 103
  and HIV/AIDS, 85
  influence of, 64, 213, 323
  public-private partnerships, 56
  resource-based power, 116
  see also foundations
Bolivia, 25
Brazil, 8, 14, 25, 332
  access to health, 149
  HIV/AIDS in, 86–7, 138, 143–5; civil society organizations, 145–7, 152; cooperation with international organizations, 151–2; response to, 145–7, 149–50, 151–2, **154–5**
  and intellectual property rights, 143; legal battle with USA, 150
Brazilian Interdisciplinary AIDS Association (ABIA), 146, 152
breast-milk substitutes, 39, 50, 222
Bretton Woods agreement (1944), 233
Bretton Woods Project, 216
Bristol-Meyers Squibb, 197
British American Tobacco, 200, 282
Brot für die Welt, 147
Brundtland, Gro Harlem, 299
Buchanan, Sir George, 37
Buffet, Warren, 56, 232
Bush, George W, 61
business, *see* private sector
Business Software Alliance, 78

Canada, 181–2
Canadian Institutes of Health, 284
Canadian Public Health Association, 223
capacity-building, 15
capital markets, 331
cardiovascular disease, 180, 269, 287
  see also chronic/non-communicable diseases
Care International, 213
Caribbean Forum of African, Caribbean and Pacific States (CARIFORUM), 179
Carter, Jimmy, 10
Centers for Disease Control and Prevention (CDC), 84–5, 311–12

Central America-Dominican Republic (CAFTA-DR) Free Trade Agreement, 179
Central Office of International Associations, 34
chemotherapy, 299
children, and marketing aimed at, 2
Children's Vaccine Initiative, 41
Chile, 25
China, 14, 40, 66
cholera, 30, 31
Christian Medical Association, 218
chronic/non-communicable diseases, 23–4, 288–9
  academic and research institutions, 284, 288
  country-income levels, **274**
  definition, 289 n. 2
  and donors, 284–5
  and economic growth, **273**
  foundations, 286–7
  global burden of, 268–9
  and globalization, 272–3, **275**
  health system orientation, 271
  input-output model of health governance, 270
  and international financial institutions, 280–1
  lack of attention to, 13, 127, 262, 271
  national health ministries, 281, 286, 287
  non-governmental organizations, 281–2, 287
  policy failures, 277, **278**
  policy recommendations, 285–8; academic institutions, 288; national health ministries, 286, 287; non-governmental organizations, 287; private sector, 287; public health sector, 287–8; road map of interventions, 288; socio-economic variables, 286; World Bank report, 280; World Health Organization, 285–6
  political economy of, 270–7
  private sector, **283**, 287; private action, 282; public-private partnerships, 284
  risk accumulation/distribution, 271

socio-economic determinants, 271–3, 286
and United Nations, 279–80
and World Health Organization, 277–9, 285–6
cigarettes, *see* smoking
civil society, as loose concept, 210
see also global civil society
civil society organizations (CSOs), 14, 22, 99
  accountability, 112
  characteristics of, 91
  definition of, 175, 210
  and discursive power, 115
  diversity of, 213, 217, **218**
  funding of, 214
  and global health governance, 210–17; economic/ideological orientation, 214–15; foundations, 213; global health partnerships, 211–12; intergovernmental organizations, 211; United Nations, 210–11, 212; ways of engaging with, 215–17
  and government: dependence on, 214; established by, 214
  growth of, 209
  and HIV/AIDS: Brazil, 145–7, 152; South Africa, 148, 149
  increasing influence of, 56
  legitimacy, 214
  and private sector: distinguished from, 210; established by, 214
  and superstructural nodes, 78
  and trade and health, 175–6
  and World Health Organization, 176, 210, 218; breast-milk substitutes, 222; challenging and monitoring of, 225–6; essential medicines, 219–21; relations between, 221–2, 224–5, 226; representativeness, 226; support for, 226; tobacco consumption, 223–4
  and World Trade Organization, 175–6
  see also non-governmental organizations; non-state actors
climate change, 1, 29
Clinton Foundation, 62, 85, 153, 241
co-regulation, 21, 22, 197–201
  conditions for, 205 n2
  public health involvement in, 204–5

see also regulation
Code of Pharmaceutical Marketing Practices, 194
codes of conduct, 194–6
Codex Alimentarius (FAO/WHO), 167
CODEX/SPS, **11–12**
coercion, 40, 106, 114, 255
cognitive function, 252
coherence, *see* policy coherence
collaboration, 2, 51, 53, 62, 65, 67, 130, 145, 165, 167, 169, 170, 180, 182, 234, 236, 243, 246, 253, 287, 302, 304, 311, 326
  see also coordination
collective action problems, 20
  and global public goods, 124, 126, 127–9
commercial sector, *see* private sector
Commission on HIV/AIDS and Governance in Africa (CHGA), 309
Commission on Intellectual Property Rights, Innovation and Public Health (CIPIH), 8, **11–12**, 88
Commission on Macroeconomics and Health (CMH), 299
Commission on the Social Determinants of Health (CSDH), 8, **11–12**, 91, 92, 227–8
Commonwealth Fund, 35, 36
Community Home-Based Care, 309
complex multilateralism, 211–12
compliance
  foundations, 237
  rules, 106
comprehensive primary health-care, 49, 50
  see also primary health-care
compulsory licensing, 140–1, 150, 157 n3, 158 n8, 165, 174
consensus, 14
  and global health governance, 57, 58, 59, 60, 63
  and global health partnerships, 253
Consortium for Research on Equitable Health Systems, **11–12**
Consumer Project on Technology (CpTech), 88, 151, 220
coordination
  aid, 306
  expanding care, 312–13

coordination – *continued*
  global health initiatives, 62–3
  HIV/AIDS programmes, 62
  improving, 67, 118
  incentives, 65
  a need for, 58
  non-governmental organizations, 281–2
  and 'Three Ones' initiative, 62, 92, 95 n9, 104
  and World Health Organization, 42, 48, 49
  see also collaboration
Corp-Watch, 202
Corporate Champions Programme, 253
corporate citizenship, 194
  see also corporate social responsibility
corporate social responsibility, 112, 193–4, 282
cost-effectiveness, 85, 99, 219, 254, 288, 295, 296, 299, 331
Costa Rica, 25
Council on Foundations (USA), 233, 239
country coordinating mechanism (CCM), 255
CpTech, *see* Consumer Project on Technology
crime, transborder, 1
Cuba, 25, 40

Declaration of Commitment on HIV/AIDS (UN, 2001), 8
democratic deficit, 75, 93
Department for International Development (UK), 58
developing countries
  chronic diseases, 268–9
  civil society organizations, 216
  intellectual property rights, 137, 143
  negotiations on trade and health, 177–8
  see also low-and-middle income countries
development, 24
  global health governance, 323; Millennium Development Goals, 330–1
DFID, *see* Department for International Development

diabetes, 2, 280
  see also chronic/non-communicable diseases
diagnostic tools, and trade and health, 170
diagonal financing, 64
diet, and trade and health, 180–2
diplomacy, *see* global health diplomacy
disability adjusted life years (DALY), 127
discourse, and global health partnerships, 252
distributive governance, *see* co-regulation
Doha Declaration on the TRIPS Agreement and Public Health, 7, 87, 88, 140–1, 166
Doha Development Round, 155, 177, 220
domino effect, and free trade agreements, 179
donors
  advance purchase commitments, 131–2
  aid alignment, 256
  chronic diseases, 284–5
  coordination, 65, 306
  criticism of recipient states, 41
  different policy approaches, 58
  failure to institutionalize incentives, 60–1
  financing mechanisms, 131
  health sector reforms, 51
  non-state actors, 55
  sector-wide approaches, 58–9
  selective primary health-care, 295
  see also individual organizations
drug resistance, 4
Drugs for Neglected Diseases initiative (DNDi), **11–12**, 25, 240, 248, 261

Ebola, 4
economic factors
  in chronic diseases, 271
  affecting health, 227–8
economic growth
  in chronic diseases, **273**
  health, 299
Ecuador, 25
effectiveness, 19–20, 99, 100–1
  aid, 306

assessment of, 101–2, 104–5, 118
  dimensions of, 101, **102**
  global health partnerships, 250
  health sector reforms, 51
  influences on, 102–5; access to resources, 103; institutional interplay, 103; non-state actors, 103–4
efficiency, and health sector reforms, 51
El Salvador, 25
Elizabeth Glaser Pediatric AIDS Foundation, 85
environment, and health, 8
epidemic diseases, 30
  Global Outbreak Alert and Response Network, 53
equity, 8, 39, 58, 63, 117, 221, 252, 262, 297, 310, 322, 324, 333, 337
essential medicines, 50
  access to, 123, 137; transnational pharmaceutical corporations, 141–2
  Campaign for Access to Essential Medicines, 53, 87, 137
  and primary health-care, 219
  and Trade-Related Aspects of Intellectual Property Rights, 219–20
  and World Health Organization, 219–21
  see also antiretroviral medicines/therapy
ethical dilemmas, 5
Ethiopia, 62
Europe in the World Initiative, 234, 236–7
European Commission, 331
European Foundation Centre (EFC), 243
  good practice for foundations, 237–8
  legal framework for foundations, 238–9
European Foundation Statute, 238–9
European Malaria Vaccine Initiative, 260
European Partnership for Global Health (EPGH), 237
European Union, 125, 179
  co-regulation, 199
  development aid, 58
  and foundations, 233, 236
  Millennium Development Goals, 331
evaluation, 61
  by civil society organizations, 216
  improving, 67, 118
  oversight, 259–60
  performance monitoring, 259–60, 263–4
exclusion, and nodal governance, 93

Family Health International, 152
FCTC, *see* Framework Convention on Tobacco Control
Federation of International Institutions, 37
financing and funding, 3
  civil society organizations, 214
  deflection of resources, 304–7
  developed country governments, 129–30
  global health partnerships, 253, 260–1
  global public goods, 334–5
  health sector reforms, 51
  health systems, 60
  innovations in, 6, 15
  mechanisms of, 130–3
  and neo-liberalism, 51
  new public finance, 130–1
  non-governmental organizations, 130
  private sector, 130
  public-private partnerships, 133
  results-oriented, 132
  sources of, 127–30, 133
  see also new public finance
Fogarty International Center, 284
Food and Agriculture Organization of the United Nations (FAO), 280
food, and trade and health, 180–2
food labelling, 181–2, 287
Ford Foundation, 147
foreign direct investment (FDI), and chronic diseases, 272
foreign policy, and health concerns, 15, 24, 313, 333–4
  see also global health diplomacy; international relations
forum shifting, 78, 85
  and intellectual property rights, 140, 143
Foundation for Improved Diagnostics, 6
foundations, 22–3, 190, 213, 242–3
  advantages of, 235
  categories of, 234
  and chronic diseases, 286–7

foundations – *continued*
  cooperation between, 237
  definition of, 234–5
  diversity of, 234
  effectiveness, 103
  future development of, 243
  and global governance, 233–4, 242–3
  and global health partnerships, 41, 239–42
  good practice in internal governance, 237–8
  and HIV/AIDS, 85
  increasing importance of, 232, 233
  innovation, 237
  leadership role, 237
  legal framework for operation of, 238–9
  limitations of, 236
  priorities of, 237
  and research, 237
  resource-based power, 116
  role of, 235–7
  role of American foundations in interwar period, 35–6
  strengthening contribution of, 237
  tax treatment of, 236
  see also individual foundations
Framework Convention Alliance, **11–12**, 223, 281
Framework Convention on Global Health, 331
Framework Convention on Tobacco Control (FCTC), 7, **11–12**, 24, 92, 126, 167, 168, 174, 223–4, 279, 281, 285, 327, 331
  Conference of the Parties to, 331–2
  historical context of, 42–3
framing, and discursive power, 115
France, 14
Free Trade Agreement of the Americas (FTAA), 179
free trade agreements, 89
  regionally-based, 171
  trade and health, 178–9
  see also international trade
funding, *see* financing and funding

G7, 5, 58
G8, 5, 211, 327, 331
  and HIV/AIDS, 84

G20, 58, 177
G33, 177
G90, 177
Gates, Bill, *see* Bill and Melinda Gates Foundation
Gates Foundation, *see* Bill and Melinda Gates Foundation
GATS, *see* General Agreement on Trade in Services
GATT, *see* General Agreement on Tariffs and Trade
GAVI Alliance, 6, **11–12**, 14, 41, 56, 60, 211, 240–1, 242, 248, 253, 254, 257, 260, 331
General Agreement on Tariffs and Trade (GATT), 55, 139, 164–5, 272
General Agreement on Trade in Services (GATS), 139, 166, 183 n1, 315
  and health-care workers, 180
General Comment No 14, 8, 88
generic drugs, 86, 87, 94 n4
  barriers to production of, 137
  Brazil-USA legal battle, 150
  compulsory licensing, 140–1
  and intellectual property rights, 139–40
Geneva Convention (1925), 37
Geneva Group, 39
GFATM, *see* Global Fund to Fight AIDS, Tuberculosis and Malaria
Ghana, 141
Global AIDS Program (GAP) (of CDC), 311–12
Global Alliance for Improved Nutrition, 56
Global Alliance for TB Drug Development, 6
Global Alliance of Mental Illness Advocacy, 189, 197
Global Alliance to Improve Nutrition, 264 n2
Global Business Coalition on HIV/AIDS, 119 n1, 189
global citizenship, 325, 337
global civil society, 21, 209–10
Global Conference on Health Promotion, 334
Global Framework on Essential Health Research (WHO), 88, 220–1
Global Fund for Health, 262

Global Fund to Fight AIDS, Tuberculosis
  and Malaria (GFATM), 6, **11–12**, 14,
  41, 60, 61, 62, 81, 84, 86, 92, 211,
  212, 242, 248, 305, 312, 323
  and aid alignment, 256
  assessing effectiveness, 101
  contributions to, 131
  Corporate Champions Programme,
    253
  Country Coordinating Mechanism,
    255
  harmonization, 256
  legitimacy, **107**, 108–9
  local fund agents, 254, 259
  performance monitoring, 259, 264
  and South Africa, 147
  transparency, 93
global governance, 8, 17, 19–22, 25, 100,
  125–6
  actors in, 233
  concept of, 233, 245
  nature of, 320
  and United Nations, 210
Global Health and Foreign Policy
  Initiative, 333–4
Global Health Council, **11–12**, 237
global health diplomacy, 5, 24
  creating capacity for, 336
  outcomes of, 336–7
global health governance (GHG)
  action sphere of, 322–4, **325**
  characteristics of, 72–3
  common principles and values, 13–14
  complexity of, 13
  definition of, 3, 138, 210, 294, 320–1;
    features of, 321
  establishment of, 321; HIV/AIDS,
    321–2; SARS threat, 321, 322
  and foreign policy, 333–4
  foundations to build on, 14–15
  functions of, 9–10, **11–12**
  and health challenges, 330
  innovations in, 6–8
  input-output model of, 270
  literature on, 16
  multiple actors, 99
  and nation-state, 321
  need for proactive approach, 10–13
  and new geographies of power,
    328–30; nation-states, 329;

non-governmental organizations,
  328–9; second world countries,
  329–30
and new multilateralism, 324–8;
  market multilateralism, 326;
  problems with, 326–7
norms of, 8–9
opportunities for, 10
policy goals, 9
as political undertaking, 321
as 'slippery' concept, 29
transition from international health
  governance, 29
unstructured pluralism, 322, 332
weaknesses of past initiatives, 13
see also architecture of global health
  governance; historical dimensions
  of global health governance;
  international health governance
global health initiatives, 248
  coordination, 62–3
  and World Health Organization, 41
  see also global health partnerships;
    individual initiatives
global health partnerships (GHPs), 6–7,
  23
  accountability, 250, 254
  aid alignment, 256, 257
  board membership, 247–8, **249**, 257–8
  and civil society organizations, 211–12
  consensus, 253
  cooperation in health sector, 253
  definition of, 247
  discourse functions in, 252
  diversity of, 247
  and effectiveness, 250
  examples of, 240–2
  financing, 253; corporate support for,
    261; ensuring adequacy of, 260–1
  and foundations, 240–2
  future development of, 263–4
  and global governance, 250–1;
    contributions to, 263
  and global health governance,
    contributions to, 251–5
  governance structure, 250
  growth of, 56–7, 245
  harmonization, 256–7
  historical development of, **246–7**
  and HIV/AIDS financing, 254

global health partnerships (GHPs) – *continued*
  and human resource concerns, 260
  impact of, 245
  improving oversight, 259–60
  innovation, 251, 253
  legitimacy, 250
  limitations of research on, 248–50
  number of, 247–8; the 'big 5', 248
  objective setting, 258–9
  and Paris Declaration principles, 255–7
  performance monitoring, 263–4
  and private sector, 212
  and public relations, 251
  reassessing prevailing paradigm of, 261–2
  reform of, 255–62
  representativeness, 250
  roles and responsibilities, 259
  stakeholder involvement, 253, 257–9
  transparency, 250
  see also public-private partnerships
Global Health Watch, **11–12**, 22, 78, 205, 216
Global Health Workforce Alliance, 6, **11–12**, 241, 262
Global Information Infrastructure Commission (GIIC), 192–3
Global Outbreak Alert and Response Network (GOARN), **11–12**, 53
global policy networks, 315, 335
Global Polio Eradication Initiative, 248
global politics, 72
Global Programme on AIDS (WHO), 38, 83
global public goods (GPGs), 20, 75
  collective action problem, 124, 126, 127–9
  definition of, 123–4
  financing, 15, 133, 334–5; developed country governments, 129–30; mechanisms of, 130–3; non-governmental organizations, 130; private sector, 130; sources of, 127–30, 133
  national self-interest, 129–30, 133
  promotion of, 9, **11–12**
  provision of, 334–5
Global Strategy on Diet, Physical Activity and Health, 181, 279

Global Strategy on the Prevention and Control of Chronic Non-communicable Diseases (WHO), 277–9
Global Task Team, 25, 60, 62
GLOBALink, 281
globalization
  and chronic diseases, 272–3, **275**
  definition of, 2, 28
  governance structures, 125
  health impacts of, 1–2, 3, 4–5, 28–9, 122
  integration of global markets, 139
  interdependence, 122, 133
  managing risks and opportunities, 2–3
  nature of, 28, 122
  and private sector, 187
  responses to, 3
glocal, 73
good GHG, 76
good governance, 3, 29, 75
  promotion of, 75
Gore, Al, 299
governance
  and collective action, 124
  and complex multilateralism, 211–12
  definition of, 3, 73, 269–70
  and global politics, 72
  and globalization, 125
  good governance, 3, 29, 75; promotion of, 75
  hybrid structures, 74, 93
  incentives to change, 65
  networked governance, 74
  as polycentric, 73
  and private (non-state) structures, 74
  and public (state) structures, 73–4
  standards of, 99–100
  and supra-state structures, 125
  and Westphalian system, 73, 74, 92
Greater Involvement of People Living with HIV (GIPA), 117
Green Light Committee, 6
Greenpeace, 202, 203
Group of 77, 39
GTZ, 152

H8 (Health 8), 23, 60, 66, 242
  composition of, 57, 247
  harmonization, 66, 256

Health Action International (HAI), 87, 219
Health and Development Network, 118
health-care workers
  expanding care, foreign policy implications, 313
  and HIV/AIDS, 309–10
  migration of, 180
'Health for All by the Year 2000', 39–40, 41, 49, 295
  see also Alma Ata, Declaration of (1978)
Health for All movement, 8
health governance, and definition of, 29
Health Metrics Network, 6, **11–12**, 61, 241
Health, Nutrition and Population (HNP) (World Bank), **11–12**
health promotion, and primary health-care, 49
health sector reform, 295–7
  mid-1980s–late 1990s, 51–6
health systems
  and Alma Ata Declaration, 49
  confusion and competition in, 61
  expanding care: combined approaches, 310–11; coordination problems, 312–13; deflection of resources, 304–10; financing, 312–13, 314–15; horizontal approaches, 302, **303**, 310; human resources, 315; identifying barriers, 312; interfaces between approaches, 311–12; synergies between approaches, 311; systems-focused approaches, 313–14; vertical approaches, 302, **303**, 304, 310
  health sector reforms, 51–6, 295–7
  and HIV/AIDS: deflection of resources, 304–10; demands for health-care, 300–1; horizontal approaches, 302, **303**, 310; impact on health facilities, **308**; vertical approaches, 302, **303**, 304, 310
  migration of health-care workers, 180
  national basis of, 17
  opportunities for (re)-constructing, 313–15
  orientation of, 271
  reform of, 295

  resource allocation problems, 302
  strengthening, 9, **11–12**, 60, 64
Health Systems Action Network (HSAN), **11–12**
Health Systems and Financing (HSFG) (World Bank), **11–12**
hegemony, 114
highly active antiretroviral therapy (HAART), 84
historical dimensions of global health governance, 18, 28, 42–3
  1970s onwards, 39–42
  growth of international cooperation (1915–1914), 31–4
  and international sanitary conferences (1851–1903), 30–1
  interwar period, 34–5; League of Nations Health Organization, 36–7; role of American foundations, 35–6
  and World Health Organization, 38–9
HIV/AIDS, 5, 24, 62
  access to medicines: Brazil-USA legal battle, 150; compulsory licensing, 140–1; South African legal battles, 150–1; transnational pharmaceutical corporations, 141–2; use of different interfaces, 153–6
  and Africa, 294
  AIDS transition, **301**
  attempts to coordinate efforts, 62
  and Brazil, 86–7, 138, 143–5; cooperation with international organizations, 151–2; response of, 145–7, 149–50, 151–2, **154–5**
  co-morbidity with other diseases, 304
  cost of treatment, 299, 307
  deflection of resources, 304; financial resources, 304–7; human resources, 309–10; infrastructure resources, 308–9
  demands for health-care, 300–1
  expanding care: combined approaches, 310–11; coordination problems, 312–13; deflection of resources, 304–10; financing, 312–13, 314–15; foreign policy, 313; horizontal approaches, 302, **303**, 310; human resources, 315; identifying barriers, 312; interfaces between approaches, 311–12;

HIV/AIDS – *continued*
  (re)-constructing health systems, 313–15; synergies between approaches, 311; systems-focused approaches, 313–14; vertical approaches, 302, **303**, 304, 310
  financing, 61, 62, **305**; deflection of resources, 304–7
  and global health governance, 321–2
  and global health partnerships, 254
  impact on health facilities, **308**
  improving coordination in approach, 60
  large number of actors involved with, 61–2
  and Malaysia, 173–4
  and the media, 2
  and nodal governance, 89–91; forum shifting, 85; interfaces with intellectual property rights' governance, 85–9; multiple actors, 83–5
  nodal governance of, 83–5
  and non-governmental organizations, 52
  and South Africa, 21, 24, 53, 143–5; age profile of patients, **300**; co-morbidity, 304; cooperation with international organizations, 152–3; demands for health-care, 300–1; legal battle over intellectual property rights, 220; response of, 147–9, 150–1, 152–3, **154–5**; Treatment Action Campaign, 52–3, 54, 94, 148, 149, 220
  and 'Three Ones' initiative, 62, 92, 95 n9, 104
  and UN Declaration of Commitment on HIV/AIDS, 8
  see also antiretroviral medicines/therapy; Global Fund to Fight AIDS, Tuberculosis and Malaria
Honduras, 25
Hong Kong, 177, 178
horizontal programmes, 302, **303**, 310
Human Development Report (2002), 209–10
human resources
  deflection of, 309–10
  expanding care, 315
  and global health partnerships, 260
human rights
  access to medicines, 87, 149
  global health norms, 8
  and health, 337
  and mobilization of resources, 297–9
  and nodal governance, 89–90
humanitarian movements, nineteenth-century development of, 33
hybrid governance structures, 74, 93
hypertension, 180

IAVI, *see* International AIDS Vaccine Initiative
IFPMA, *see* International Federation of Pharmaceutical Manufacturers and Associations
IKEA Group, 238–9
implementation, 13, 19, 48, 51, 58, 62, 91, 103, 168, 183, 198, 219, 222, 241, 312, 327
incentives
  agency, 65
  coordination, 65
  failure to institutionalize, 60–1
  financing mechanisms, 131
  international cooperation, 133
  neglect of, 47
India, 8, 14, 39
Indian Council of Medical Research, 284
Indonesia, 14, 171, 178
  and co-regulation, 199
inequality, 5, 18, 72, 218, 239, 337
Infant Formula Action Coalition (INFACT), 39
infectious diseases, 4
  control of, 124
  economic cost of, 5
  resurgence of, 297
innovation
  and foundations, 236, 237
  and global health partnerships, 251, 253
Institute for Health Metrics and Evaluation, **11–12**, 61
Institute for One World Health, 248
institutional interplay, 79, 80, 103, 104, 105, 220, 320

institutions, 3, 6
  concepts of power, 114
  definition of, 168
  interplay between, 103
  and nodal governance, 78–9
Intellectual Property Committee (IPC), 175, 198
intellectual property rights (IPRs)
  Brazil-USA legal battle, 150
  and developing countries, 143
  and HIV/AIDS governance, 85–9
  internationalization of, 139–41, 142–3
  see also Trade-Related Aspects of Intellectual Property Rights
interdependence, 24, 52, 122, 133
  and global health governance, 323–4
  and intergovernmental processes, 331–2
  new role for international organizations, 332–3
Interface, 262
interfaces, 19, 79–81
  definition of, 73, 138, 325
  discursive, 81, 138
  and HIV/AIDS, 89–91, 139, 153–6; Brazil's response to, 145–7, 149–50, 151–2, **154–5**; expanding care, 311–12; intellectual property rights' governance, 85–9; South Africa's response to, 147–9, 150–1, 152–3, **154–5**
  horizontal, 81
  legal, 81, 138
  and nodal governance, 82
  organizational, 81, 138
  and power relations, 79, 81
  resource-transfer, 81, 138
  social interfaces, 80–1
  and transnational pharmaceutical corporations, 141–2
  vertical, 81
intergovernmental organizations, 211 and *passim*
intergovernmental processes, 331–2
  re-engineering of, 134
  see also individual organizations
Intergovernmental Working Group on Public Health, Innovation and Intellectual Property (IGWG), 8, **11–12**, 14, 88, 156, 178

International Agreement on the Unification of Pharmacopoeial Formulas for Potent Drugs, 33
international agreements, and global health, 7–8
International AIDS Vaccine Initiative (IAVI), 6, 240, 248
International Alliance of Patients' Organizations, 189
International Anti-Slavery Conference, 33
International Baby Food Action Network (IBFAN), **11–12**, 222
International Bureau for the Suppression of Traffic in Women and Children, 34
International Central Bureau for the Campaign against Tuberculosis, 33
International Chamber of Commerce (ICC), 192
  ICC-UN Global Compact, 202–3
International Code for the Marketing of Breast-Milk Substitutes, 39, 50, 222
International Committee of the Red Cross, **11–12**, 18, 33
International Conference on Finance for Development, 58
International Conference on Primary Health Care, 39–40, 295
International Congresses of Charities, Correction and Philanthropy, 33
International Council of AIDS Service Organizations (ICASO), 152
International Covenant on Economic, Social and Cultural Rights, 88
International Diabetes Federation, 281–2
International Federation of Pharmaceutical Manufacturers and Associations (IFPMA), 25, 88, 141, 175, 194, 261
International Finance Facility (IFF), 253
International Finance Facility – Immunization (IFFIm), 6, **11–12**, 253
international financial institutions, and chronic diseases, 280–1
  see also International Monetary Fund; World Bank
International Geodetic Association, 33

International Health Commission
   (1913), 35
international health governance (IHG),
   29
International Health Partnership (IHP),
   7, **11–12**, 23, 58, 95 n10, 242
   goal of, 60
International Health Regulations (IHR),
   7, 9, **11–12**, 90, 92, 167–8, 327
International Labour Office (ILO), 36
International Labour Organization, 195,
   202, 280, 286
   governance structure, 211
international law, 7, 81, 90
   integration of global markets, 139
   state sovereignty, 9
International Life Sciences Institute,
   189, 197
International Monetary Fund (IMF), 41,
   58, 125, 131, 314
International Obesity Task Force, 281
International Office of Public Health, 31
International Organization for
   Standardization (ISO), 189
international organizations
   accountability, 112
   changing role of, 325
   corporate-like behaviour, 326
   development and growth of, 32–4
   new role for, 332–3
International Planned Parenthood
   Federation, 213
International Private Practitioners
   Association, 189
international relations
   changing character of, 137
   concepts of power, 113–15
   post-Westphalian, 17
   Westphalian, 17, 25, 73
   see also foreign policy; global health
   diplomacy
international sanitary conferences
   (1851–1903), 18, 30–1
International Statistical Institute, 33
International Temperance Bureau, 33
International Trachoma Initiative, 241,
   261
international trade, 1, 15, 21, 182
   bilateral trade agreements, 140, 143,
   156, 178–9

development of governance
   arrangements, 164–5
diagnostic tool and workbook, 170
and dietary patterns, 180–2
institutions spanning health/trade
   sectors, 169, 182; civil society
   organizations, 175–6; Malaysia,
   173–5; policy coherence, 174–5;
   regional agreements, 171–2;
   Thailand, 172–3; World Health
   Organization, 169–70
links with health sector, 164, 165
migration of health-care workers, 180
policy recommendations for health
   and trade, 183
power shift in negotiations on trade
   and health, 177–8
regional free trade agreements, 178–9
and SARS outbreak, 164
trade agreements, 7
and World Health Organization
   agreements, 167–8
and World Trade Organization
   agreements related to health, 165–7
   see also trade liberalization; World
   Trade Organization
International Union Against Cancer, 281

Jong-wook, Lee, 227
junk food, 2

Kaiser Family Foundation, **11–12**, 152
Kassar, Adnan, 203
Kenya, 143, 300–1
Khayelitsha HIV/AIDS project, 148
Knowledge Ecology Institute, 25
Kochi, Arata, 64
KPMG, 190
KwaZulu-Natal Enhancing Care
   Initiative, 147–8

Lancet, 216, 269
Latin American and Caribbean Council
   of AIDS Service Organizations, 152
League of Nations, 34
   Committee on Social Questions, 37
   International Labour Office, 36
League of Nations Health
   Organization, 18, 34, 36–7, 233
League of Red Cross Societies (LRCS), 37

legitimacy, 19–20, 99, 105
  civil society organizations, 214
  dimensions of, **107**; input legitimacy, 108; output legitimacy, 108; throughput legitimacy, 108
  empirical/strategic approach, 107
  global health governance, 93, 327
  global health partnerships, 250
  normative-assessment approach to, 106
  participation, 117–18
  results-based, 327
  significance of, 105–6
Lesotho, 300–1, 305
local implementation, 48
LoveLife, 152
low- and middle-income countries (LMIC), 5, 21, 50, 147, 181, 194, 199, 223, 257, 268, 269
  see also developing countries

Mahler, Halfdan, 227
Make Poverty History campaign, 337
malaria, 2, 4
Malaria Eradication Programme, 40
Malaria Vaccine Initiative, 247–8
Malawi, 257, 304, 309
Malaysia, 171
  and HIV/AIDS, 173–4
  trade and health, 173–4
Mandela, Nelson, 10, 150
Mann, Jonathan, 83
MAP, *see* multi-country AIDS programme
market-based norms, 8
market failure, 10, 56, 180, 214, 215, 226, 240, 281
market fundamentalism, 214, 215, 226
market multilateralism, 326
marketing
  attacks on policies of transnational corporations, 39
  and children, 2
  and chronic diseases, 273
Mbeki, Thabo, 53
McKinsey and Company, 190
Médecins Sans Frontières (MSF), 7, 25, 54, 62
  Campaign for Access to Essential Medicines, 53, 87, 137
  and HIV/AIDS, 84, 87, 148

media, 2
Medical Research Council, 284
medical travel, 166, 171
Medicines for Malaria Venture, 6, **11–12**, 110, 133, 240
Merck, 261
Microbicide Development Programme, 247
migration, and health-care workers, 180
Milbank Memorial Fund, 35
Millennium Challenge Corporation, 65
Millennium Development Goals (MDGs), 6, **11–12**, 14, 42, 60, 87, 123, 132, 239, 242, 255, 297–9, 323, 330–1, 337
  exclusion of chronic diseases, 279–80
Monterrey Consensus, 58
Misereor, 147
Mittler, Daniel, 203
Monterrey Consensus, **11–12**, 58
Mozambique, 257
MSF, *see* Médecins Sans Frontières
multi-country AIDS programme (MAP), 61, 83
Multi-Country HIV/AIDS Programme (World Bank), 61
multilateralism, 14, 24
  and global health governance, 324–8; problems with, 326–7
  market multilateralism, 326
Multinational Enterprises Declaration (2002), 280
multiplier effect, and free trade agreements, 179

nation-states, 17
  accountability, 111
  changing role of, 325
  and chronic diseases, 281, 287
  concepts of power, 113–14
  decision-making power, 115
  and good governance, 29
  and health governance, 321
  intergovernmental processes, 331–2
  and international governance, 72
  and international health governance, 29
  legal power, 116
  new geographies of power, 329
  and nodal governance, 79

nation-states – *continued*
  reduced role of, 47
  resource-based power, 116
  role of, 134
  weakening of, 55
National Institutes of Health (USA), 284
neo-liberalism, 50–1, 214
  and health sector reforms, 52, 296
  hegemonic power, 114
Nestlé, 39, 222
Netherlands, 234
network theory, 19
networks
  international campaigns, 52–3
  networked governance, 74
  see also nodal governance
New International Economic Order, 40
New Partnership for Africa's Development, 233
new public finance, 20, 130–1
new public health, 40
new public management, 74
Newell, Ken, 50
nodal governance, 19, 73, 76–9
  forum shifting, 78
  and HIV/AIDS, 85, 89–91; forum shifting, 85; interfaces with intellectual property rights' governance, 85–9; multiple actors, 83–5
  implications of, 89–92
  institutional focus of, 78–9
  integration of networks, 77
  and interfaces, 82
  legitimacy, 93
  missing nodes, 93
  nature of nodes, 77
  and the state, 79
  superstructural nodes, 77–8
  types of power, 78
Non-Aligned Movement (NAM), 330
non-communicable diseases, *see* chronic/non-communicable diseases
non-governmental organizations (NGOs), 8
  activities of, 55–6
  campaigns by, 52–3
  and chronic diseases, 281–2, 287

corporatization of, 213
development of role of, 41, 51–6
dominance of large northern-based, 213, 225
and global public goods, 130
growth of, 209
historical role of, 18
and HIV/AIDS, 52; Brazil, 145–7
international, 32
new geographies of power, 328–9
professionalization of, 213
see also civil society organizations; non-state actors
non-intervention, and erosion of norm of, 9
non-state actors, 7, 17
  decision-making power, 115–16
  effectiveness, 103–4
  governance structures, 126
  growing role of, 52–4, 55, 156–7
  growth of, 29
  and nineteenth-century international cooperation, 32
  see also civil society organizations; non-governmental organizations; private sector
nondiscrimination, 8
norms, and global health governance, 8–9, 13–14
  see also accountability; balance of power; effectiveness; legitimacy
North American Free Trade Agreement (NAFTA), 125, 140
Norway, 14

obesity, 180, 181
  children, 2
OECD, *see* Organization for Economic Cooperation and Development
Office International d'Hygiène Publique (OIHP), 31
Onchocerciasis Control Programme, 241
Open Society Institute, 188, 284
Organization for Economic Cooperation and Development (OECD), 5, 58, 211
Oslo Declaration, 333
Oslo Initiative on Global Health and Foreign Policy, 14
Ottawa Charter, 40

oversight, and global health
  partnerships, 259–60
Oxfam, 213
Oxford Health Alliance, 284, 287

Pakistan, 39
Pan American Health Organization
  (PAHO), 151
Pan American Sanitary Bureau (PASB), 31
Pan American Sanitary Organization, 38
Paris Declaration on Aid Effectiveness
  (2005), **11–12**, 15, 25, 58, 92, 256,
  306, 323
participation
  improving, 117–18
  pro-democracy movements, 212
Partnership for Maternal, Newborn and
  Child Health, 248
partnerships, *see* global health
  partnerships; public-private
  partnerships
patented medicines, 87, 140, 141, 150
People's Health Assembly, **11–12**, 227
People's Health Charter, 227
People's Health Movement, 22, 226,
  227
PEPFAR, *see* President's Emergency Plan
  for AIDS Relief
performance monitoring, 259–60
  global health partnerships, 263–4
  see also evaluation
Peru, 25
Pfizer, 189, 198, 261
pharmaceutical industry
  donations to global health
    partnerships, 261
  essential medicines, 219–21
  industry concentration, 55
  resource-based power, 116
  and Trade-Related Aspects of
    Intellectual Property Rights, 86
  see also transnational pharmaceutical
    corporations
Pharmaceutical Manufacturer's
  Association of South Africa, 140,
  150–1
Pharmaceutical Research and
  Manufacturers of America (PhRMA),
  141, 150
PharmaMarketing Network, 189

PHC, *see* primary health-care
philanthropy, 6, 18
  inter-war corporate philanthropy, 34
  philanthropic venture
    capitalists, 235
  see also Bill and Melinda Gates
    Foundation; Clinton Foundation;
    foundations
Philip Morris International, 200, 282
Philippines, 171
PMTCT, *see* prevention of
  mother-to-child transmission
  programmes
policy coherence, 9, **11–12**, 14
  inter-sectorality, 285
  multiple actors, 58–9, 66
  national/global interface, 335–6
  regional institutions, 171
  trade and health, 174–5, 183
policymaking, 15
  different policy approaches, 58
  and global health metaphors, 271–5,
    276, 277
  policy failures, **278**
  research, 134
policy triangle, 48
polio eradication, 129, 130
political-economy, and chronic diseases,
  24, 270–7
poverty, 5, 91, 337
  poverty reduction, 132, 256
power
  balance of power, 99, 113; changes in,
    116–17
  coercive power, 78, 114
  concepts of, 113–15
  Country Coordinating Mechanism,
    255
  decision-making power, 115–16
  definition of, 113
  discursive power, 78, 80, 115
  economic power, 78
  hard power, 114
  and interfaces, 81
  legal power, 78, 81, 116
  and negotiations on trade and health,
    177–8
  new geographies of, 328–30;
    nation-states, 329;

power – *continued*
  non-governmental organizations, 328–9; second world countries, 329–30
  organizational power, 78, 81
  regulatory power, 116
  resource-based power, 116
  soft power, 114–15
  types of, 78, 81
President's Emergency Plan for AIDS Relief (PEPFAR), 61, 62, 65, 83–5, 86, 312
  and South Africa, 148
prevention of mother-to-child transmission (PMTCT) programmes, 54, 147
primary health-care (PHC), 40, 295
  1970s–mid-1980s, 48–9; contested discourses, 49–51
  comprehensive, 49, 50
  demise of, 295
  and essential medicines, 219
  selective, 50
  selective primary health-care, 295–6
private sector
  and chronic diseases, **283**, 287; private action, 282; public-private partnerships, 284
  and civil society, 188
  and civil society organizations, 214
  co-regulation, 197–201; conditions for, 205 n2; ICC-UN Global Compact, 55, 202–3; public health involvement in, 204–5
  corporate wellness programmes, 282
  definition of, 188, **189**
  and global health governance, 21–2, 189–91
  and global health partnerships, 212
  and global public goods, 130
  and globalization, 187
  and health sector reforms, 52, 296
  impact of, 187
  market-orientation, 188
  and not-for-profit organizations, 188
  public-private partnerships, 188
  and public regulation: curbing influence on, 205; influence on, 196–7
  role of, 21

self-regulation, 192–3; codes of conduct, 194–6; corporate social responsibility, 193–4, 282; public health involvement in, 203–4
and Trade-Related Aspects of Intellectual Property Rights, 198–9
and World Health Organization, 225
see also public-private partnerships; transnational corporations; transnational pharmaceutical corporations
pro-democracy movements, 212
ProductRed initiative, 253
ProTEST initiative (WHO), 304
protest movements, 216–17
public goods, 123–4
see also global public goods
public health expenditure, 144, 145, 305
public-private partnerships, 20, 99, 188
  accountability, 112
  aims of, 57
  caution about, 57
  and chronic diseases, 284
  co-regulation, 199–201
  drug access, 87
  and foundations, 240
  global, 41, 127
  growth of, 56–7, 239–40
  hybrid governance structures, 74
  impact of, 127
  and Millennium Development Goals, 331
  partnership interaction, 57
  see also global health partnerships

quarantine, 30, 31

Reagan, Ronald, 51
realpolitik, 321
  cosmopolitan realpolitik, 324, 328, 331
reciprocity, and social interfaces, 80
redistribution, and foundations, 236
reform movements, and nineteenth-century development of, 33–4
regime shifting, and intellectual property rights, 142–3
regional free trade agreements, 178–9
see also international trade

regional institutions, and trade and health, 171–2
regulation
  co-regulation, 21, 22, 197–201; conditions for, 205 n2; public health involvement in, 204–5
  private sector influence, 196–7; curbing, 205
  regulatory power, 116
  self-regulation, 192–3; codes of conduct, 194–6; corporate social responsibility, 193–4, 282; public health involvement in, 203–4
  and trust, 201–3
representativeness
  civil society organizations, 226
  global health partnerships, 250
  good governance, 29
research and development, 6, 8
  Global Framework on Essential Health Research, 88
  neglect of chronic diseases, 284
  policymaking, 134
resource mobilization, 91, 102, 248, 264, 294, 297–9, 302, 305, 312, 314
resource-transfer, 81
responsiveness, 13, 79, 92, 99, 108, 154, 201, 277
Rio Group, 14, 25
risk, and chronic diseases, 271
Robinson, Mary, 10
Rockefeller Foundation, 18, 34, 35–6, 37, 40, 48, 233, 284
  see also foundations
Roll Back Malaria Partnership, 6, 56, 211, 248
Rosenau, James, 3, 233, 240, 242, 270
Rotary International, 130
rules
  compliance with, 106
  legitimacy, 106; empirical/strategic approach, 107; input legitimacy, 108; normative-assessment approach, 106; output legitimacy, 108; throughput legitimacy, 108
Russia, 14
Rwanda, 62, 254

Sage Foundation, 35
San Francisco agreement (1944), 233
sanctions, and accountability, 111

Save the Children, 213
science, and growth of international cooperation (1915–1914), 32–3
second world countries, 329–30
sector-wide approaches (SWAps), 58–9, 256, 257, 313, 314
security, 114, 323–4
  health threats, 5, 299
selective primary health-care, 50, 295–6
  see also primary health-care
self-regulation in private sector, 192–3
  codes of conduct, 194–6
  corporate social responsibility, 193–4
  public health involvement in, 203–4
  see also regulation
Senegal, 14
Serra, José, 158 n15
Severe Acute Respiratory Syndrome (SARS), 4, 7, 164
  economic cost of, 5
  and global health governance, 321, 322
sexually transmitted diseases, 146, 147
  interwar period, 37
Singapore, 171
Smallpox Eradication Programme, 40
smoking, 4, 174, 187, 200, 223, 272
  see also chronic non-communicable diseases; Framework Convention on Tobacco Control; tobacco industry
social factors
  and chronic diseases, 271
  and health, 8, 49, 227–8
social justice, 8, 39, 216, 218, 221, 322, 337
social standards, 192, 193, 194, 283
  private sector, 203–4
Social Watch, 216
Society for International Development, 214
Soros, George, 188
South Africa, and HIV/AIDS, 21, 24, 53, 138, 143–4
  age profile of patients, **300**
  co-morbidity, 304
  cooperation with international organizations, 152–3
  deflection of resources, 304; financial resources, 304–7; human resources, 309–10; infrastructure resources, 308–9

demands for health-care, 300–1
legal battle over intellectual property rights, 150–1, 220
response to, 147–9, 150–1, 152–3, **154–5**
Treatment Action Campaign, 52–3, 54, 94, 148, 149, 220
South African National AIDS Council, 147
South Centre, 87, 90
sovereignty, 8–9, 13, 122, 134, 324, 331
Soviet Union, 40
Spanish influenza, 164
SPS, *see* Agreement on Sanitary and Phytosanitary Measures
standards
  Codex Alimentarius (FAO/WHO), 167
  League of Nations Health Organization, 36, 37
  self-regulation, 192–3; codes of conduct, 194–6; corporate social responsibility, 193–4
  setting, 48
  social standards, 203–4
Stichting Ingka, 238–9
Stop TB Partnership, 6, 248, 259
Strategic Advisory Group of Experts (SAGE), **11–12**
strokes, 180
structural adjustment programmes, 114, 296
Suriname, 25
Sustained Patent Treaty (SPT), 142
SWAps, *see* sector-wide approaches
Swaziland, 301, 305
Swiss Society of Preventive Medicine, 223
Switzerland, 335–6
systems-building, 15

TAC, *see* Treatment Action Campaign
Tanzania, 298, 305, 310
taxation
  charitable giving, 236
  global public goods, 131, 133–4
TBT, *see* Agreement on Technical Barriers to Trade
technical review panels, 254
Teixeira, Paulo, 152
telemedicine, 2

Thailand, 7, 8, 14, 171
  trade and health, 172–3
Thatcher, Margaret, 51
Third World Network, 25, 216
'Three Ones' initiative, 62, 92, 95 n9, 104
TIME Global Health Summit (2005), 324
tobacco industry, 200–1, 203, 223–4, 282
  trade liberalization, 272
  see also Framework Convention on Tobacco Control
trade agreements, 7
trade liberalization, 1, 171, 272
  food, 181
  service sector, 166
  see also international trade; World Trade Organization
Trade-Related Aspects of Intellectual Property Rights (TRIPS), 7, 78, 86, 139
  amendment of, 141
  compulsory licensing, 140–1, 157 n3, 165
  developing countries, 137
  Doha Declaration, 87, 88, 140–1, 166
  essential medicines, 219–20
  health implications of, 165–6
  and private sector, 198–9
traditional medicine, 40
transnational corporations (TNCs), 20, 21, 29
  accountability, 112
  and global health policymaking, 55
  and state-like behaviour, 326
transnational pharmaceutical corporations (TNPCs), 83, 84, 85, 88–9
  and access to medicines, 141–2, 219–21; Brazil-USA legal battle, 150; South African legal battles, 150–1; successful negotiations, 153
  interfaces, 141–2
  internationalizing of intellectual property rights, 142–3
  and Trade-Related Aspects of Intellectual Property Rights, 86, 137
transparency, 3, 75
  and accountability, 110–11
  and civil society organizations, 22
  and global health partnerships, 250
  and nodal governance, 79, 93

Transparency International, **11–12**
travel and trade measures, 167, 168
Treatment Action Campaign (TAC), 52–3, 54, 94, 148, 149, 220
tripartite governance, 202, 210, 211, 332–3
TRIPS, *see* Trade-Related Aspects of Intellectual Property Rights
trust, and regulation, 201–3
tuberculosis (TB), 4
 and HIV/AIDS, 304

Uganda, 296, 298, 305, 308, 309, 315
UNAIDS, *see* United Nations Programme on HIV/AIDS
UNICEF, *see* United Nations Children's Fund
Unilever, 202
Union of International Associations (UIA), 34, 37
UNITAID, 241, 253, 323, 335
United Nations, 48, 58, 125
 and chronic diseases, 279–80
 and civil society organizations, 212
 criticism of, 54
 diversity of governance structures, 211
 and global governance, 210
United Nations Children's Fund (UNICEF), **11–12**, 40, 48, 49, 280
 and global health partnerships, 262
 and HIV/AIDS, 83–4
 and selective primary health-care, 50
United Nations Commission on Global Governance, 210
United Nations Commission on Human Rights, 149
United Nations Committee on Economic, Social and Cultural Rights, 8, 88
United Nations Conference on Trade and Development, 125
United Nations Development Group, 60
United Nations Development Programme, 41, 125
United Nations Environment Programme, 125
United Nations Foundation, 284
United Nations General Assembly Declaration of Commitment on HIV/AIDS, 8
 and HIV/AIDS, 5
United Nations Global Compact, 55, 202–3, 210–11, 326
United Nations High Commissioner for Human Rights, 83
United Nations High-Level Panel on UN Systemwide Coherence (2006), 64
United Nations Millennium Summit, 297
United Nations Population Fund (UNFPA), 280
United Nations Programme on HIV/AIDS (UNAIDS), **11–12**, 52, 62, 83, 84, 85, 210, 323
 Coordinating Board, 152
 and governance structure, 211
 Theme Group on HIV/AIDS, 151–2
United Nations Security Council, 299, 322
 and HIV/AIDS, 5
United States, 40
 development aid, 58
 free trade agreements, 179
 and HIV/AIDS, 84
 and World Health Organization, 50, 327–8
United States Agency for International Development (USAID), 48, 84–5, 147
United States Federal Drug Administration (FDA), 118
Uruguay, 25
USAID, *see* United States Agency for International Development

Venezuela, 25
vertical programmes, 302, **303**, 304, 310
Vietnam, 260

Weber, Max, 113
Wellcome Trust, 241, 284
Westphalian system, 73, 74, 92
WHO, *see* World Health Organization
WIPO, *see* World Intellectual Property Organization
World Bank, 3, **11–12**, 41, 50, 58, 125, 131
 assessing effectiveness, 101
 and chronic diseases, 280–1
 governance structure, 211

World Bank – *continued*
  and health sector reforms, 51, 52, 53–4, 296
  and non-state actors, 55
  and resource-based power, 116
World Commission on the Social Dimension of Globalization, 280
World Conference on Tobacco and Health, 197
World Congress of International Organizations, 34
World Council of Churches, 218
World Development Report (1993), 296
World Economic Forum, 326, 331
World Federation of Public Health Associations (WFPHA), 223
World Health Assembly, 8, **11–12**, 39, 40, 156, 220–1
  Committee C, 332
  and governance structure, 221
World Health Organization (WHO), 1, **11–12**, 99, 125
  Alma Ata Declaration, 39, 40, 41, 49, 50, 218
  assessing effectiveness, 101, 104–5
  challenges facing, 92
  and chronic diseases, 24, 277–9; policy recommendations for, 285–6
  and civil society organizations, 176, 210, 218; breast-milk substitutes, 222; challenging and monitoring by, 225–6; essential medicines, 219–21; People's Health Movement, 226, 227; relations between, 221–2, 224–5, 226; representativeness, 226; supported by, 226; tobacco consumption, 223–4
  criticism of, 52
  decision-making structure, 49–50
  and developing countries, 178
  and external actors: constrained by, 226; influence of, 225
  financing of, 131
  and global health partnerships, 262
  and governance structure, 211, 221
  historical development of, 38–9: 1970s onwards, 39–41
  influence of, 50
  and inter-sectorality, 285
  and international trade, 169–70: agreements relating to, 167–8
  legitimacy, **107**, 108, 109, 327
  medical R&D treaty, 143
  'Model List of Essential Medicines', **11–12**, 87
  need for strengthening, 314
  and nodal governance, 90, 92
  and primary health-care (1970s–mid-1980s), 48; contested discourses of, 49–50
  principles governing, 218
  and private sector influence, 225
  reforms of health systems, 295
  regulatory power, 116
  resource-based power, 116
  role of, 92, 217–18, 221
  strengthening health systems, 60
  and tobacco industry influence, 200
  and World Trade Organization, 169–70
World Intellectual Property Organization (WIPO), 78, 86, 139
  Development Agenda, 143, 156
World Trade Organization (WTO), 1, 7, 55, 58, 78, 86, 125, 137, 272
  agreements related to health, 165–7
  and civil society organizations, 175–6
  and developing countries, 177
  protests against, 5
  and World Health Organization, 169–70
  see also Trade-Related Aspects of Intellectual Property Rights
World Vision, 213

Zambia, 141, 298, 304, 305, 309, 310
Zimbabwe, 307, 308